introduction

Macromedia's Flash MX is the professional standard for producing high-impact Web experiences. Macromedia Flash MX delivers an intuitive, approachable authoring environment to enable both designers and developers to more easily create next-generation Web sites and applications.

The Macromedia Training from the Source course introduces you to the major features of Flash MX by guiding you step-by-step through the development of a complex Web site. This 12–16 hour curriculum includes these lessons:

Lesson 1: Flash Basics
Lesson 2: Adding Graphics and Text
Lesson 3: Using Symbols and the Library
Lesson 4: Creating Animation
Lesson 5: Adding Basic Interactivity
Lesson 6: Using Sound and Video
Lesson 7: Programming with ActionScript
Lesson 8: Using Components
Lesson 9: Creating Dynamic Content
Lesson 10: Creating Printable Movies
Lesson 11: Optimizing Flash Content
Lesson 12: Publishing a Flash Web Site

Each lesson begins with an overview of the lesson's content and learning objectives and each is divided into short tasks that break the skills into bite-size units.

Each lesson also includes these special features:

Tips: Shortcuts for common tasks and ways you can use the skills you're learning to solve common problems.

Notes: Additional information or extra background about the tools or commands.

Menu commands and keyboard shortcuts: Alternative methods for executing commands. Menu commands are shown like this: Menu › Command › Subcommand. Keyboard shortcuts are shown like this: Control+Z (Windows) or Command+X (Macintosh). The + between the names of the keys means that you should press both keys simultaneously. Both Windows and Macintosh commands will always be included.

Appendixes A and B contain quick lists of Flash's keyboard shortcuts. Appendix C is a guide to some handy Flash resources. Finally, Appendix D is a reference guide to the ActionScript used in the book, as well as additional ActionScript that may interest you.

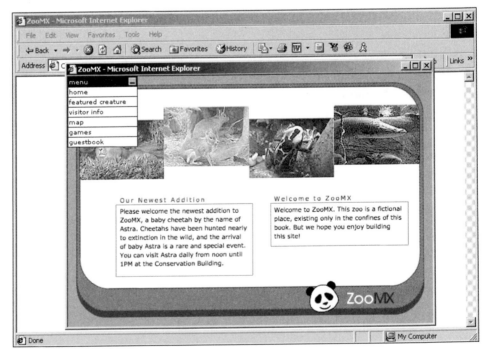

You will create a complete Flash-based Web site during the course of this book, including animations, sound, video, and plenty of interactivity.

macromedia®
FLASH® MX
TRAINING FROM THE SOURCE

macromedia®
FLASH® MX
TRAINING FROM THE SOURCE

Chrissy Rey

macromedia®
PRESS

Macromedia Flash MX: Training from the Source

 Published by Macromedia Press, in association with Peachpit Press, a division of Pearson Education.

Macromedia Press
1249 Eighth Street
Berkeley, CA 94710
510/524-2178
510/524-2221 (fax)
Find us on the World Wide Web at:
http://www.peachpit.com
http://www.macromedia.com

Printed and bound in the United States of America

ISBN 0-201-79482-9

9 8 7 6 5 4 3 2 1

ACKNOWLEDGMENTS

Many thanks to Nancy "Mom" Rey, Al "Dad" Rey, Tommy "Little Baby Bro" Rey, Carol "Editor Extraordinaire" Person, Tom "Studmuffin" Kucan, Jeromy "Guybo" Hill, David "Madpunk" Willis, Eddie "Spageddie" Gonzalez, Tracy "Jam Girl" Kelly, Laura "My Favorite Designer" McCabe, Pablo "AbACUZ" Tailanian, Steve "PedestrianSteve" Waters, Justin "Tdogg" Toncynzyn, Brian "Qball" Kew, Steve "Sliver" Silver, Dan "My Son" McCarthy, and Bill "Pope de Flash" Spencer for all of their help, love, and support while I worked on this project. And thanks to Astra, Aurora, Luna, Gator, and Jinx for keeping me company all day! Thanks also to Matt Renfro of CDNIT for providing space for www.flashtfs.com.

DEDICATION

This book is dedicated to Dad. I think this computer thing just might work out!

table of contents

X

All the files you need for the lessons are included in the Lessons folder on the enclosed CD. Files for each lesson appear in their own folders, titled with the lesson name. You should copy the Lessons folder to your hard drive for quicker access. If you choose to use the files directly from the CD, you may find that you can't test the movies—if that happens, make a copy of the file on your hard drive. The companion Web site for this book, www.flastfs.com, hosts updates, corrections, and additional resources.

Each lesson folder may contain subfolders: Starting, Intermediate, Completed, and Assets. The Starting folder contains the initial file for a lesson, if one exists. The Intermediate folder contains the completed files for each step in the project so that you can compare your work or see where you are headed. The files in this folder will also allow you to jump ahead without having to go through every exercise. The Completed folder contains the final file for a lesson. The Assets folder includes any media files needed for the lesson, such as graphics, sounds, or symbol libraries. The files that you will need are identified at the beginning of each lesson.

MACROMEDIA TRAINING FROM THE SOURCE

The Macromedia Training from the Source and Advanced Training from the Source series are developed in association with Macromedia, and reviewed by the product support teams. Ideal for active learners, the books in the Training from the Source series offer hands-on instruction designed to provide you with a solid grounding in the program's fundamentals.

If you would like more information on ActionScript, check out *Macromedia Flash MX ActionScripting: Advanced Training from the Source* by Derek Franklin and Jobe Makar (Macromedia Press, 2002).

The lessons in this book assume that you are a beginner with Flash but that you are familiar with the basic methods of using commands on a Windows or Macintosh computer, such as choosing items from menus, opening and saving files, and so on. For more information on those tasks, see the documentation provided with your computer.

Finally, the instructions in the book also assume that you have Flash MX installed on a Windows or Macintosh computer, and that your computer meets the system requirements listed on the next page.

WHAT YOU WILL LEARN

By the end of this course, you will be able to:

- Work with Flash's tools, panels, and commands to create Flash movies
- Use symbols, the library, and the Movie Explorer to optimize your files and keep them organized
- Create simple and complex animations, using frame-by-frame animation, motion tweening, and shape tweening
- Add basic interactivity by creating clickable buttons, and using actions to control the timeline
- Add, modify, and customize sounds
- Add video assets to your movies
- Use ActionScript to add drag-and-drop interactivity, dynamic text, and much more
- Use other programs, such as Macromedia ColdFusion, to process information
- Publish, print, and export your Flash movies

MINIMUM SYSTEM REQUIREMENTS

Windows

- 200 MHz Intel Pentium processor or equivalent

- Windows 98 SE, Windows ME, Windows NT 4.0, Windows 2000, or Windows XP

- 64 MB of RAM (128 MB recommended)

- 85 MB of available hard drive space

- 16-bit color monitor capable of 1024 × 768 resolution

Macintosh

- Power Macintosh with Mac OS 9.1 (or later) or Mac OS X version 10.1 (or later)

- 64 MB RAM free application memory (128 MB recommended)

- 85 MB of available hard drive space

- 16-bit (thousands of colors) at 1024 × 768 resolution

learning
Flash basics

LESSON 1

As you read this book, you'll learn how to use Flash MX to create complex movies with animations, sounds, and interactivity. Every long journey starts with a single step—and in this case, the first step involves learning how to set Flash's preferences and how to customize its workspace for your use.

In this lesson, you will first preview the project that you'll build over the course of this book. You'll learn how to find your way around the Flash workspace, and how to get help when and if you need it. You will also learn how to create your panel layouts and custom keyboard sets. Finally, you will modify the properties of your first movie and learn how to test it in the Flash Player.

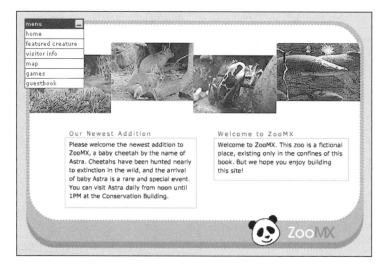

The ZooMX Web site.

Chrissy Rey

WHAT YOU WILL LEARN

In this lesson, you will:

- Preview the finished project
- Learn where to find additional help
- Customize Flash's preferences
- Work with panels to organize the workspace
- Create a custom keyboard shortcut set
- Modify the movie properties
- Save a movie and preview it using Test Movie

APPROXIMATE TIME

This lesson takes approximately 30 minutes to complete.

LESSON FILES

Media Files:

None

Starting Files:

None

Completed Project:

Lesson01/Completed/zoo1.fla

GETTING STARTED

Before you dive into building a movie in Flash, you need to create a folder on your hard drive, where you'll save your files as you work through the lessons. After you've created the folder, it's time to open Flash and take a quick look around. Next, we'll look at the project you're going to create by doing the lessons in this book.

1) Create a folder called FlashTFS on your hard drive.

This course assumes that you're familiar with the conventions of your computer. If you need help creating a folder, please refer to the documentation provided with your system.

After you create the folder, you're ready to open Flash—an important first step!

2) Open Flash.

If you are opening Flash for the first time, you should see something that looks like the screen on the next page. There are very few differences between the Windows and Macintosh versions of Flash. In each version you will see a Welcome panel, which asks how you would like to use Flash. If you have already set up Flash according to the directions in the Welcome panel don't worry! Just choose Window > Panel Sets > Default so that your copy of Flash will look like the one we're using.

Flash has a main menu, which is usually located at the top of the application window on a Windows computer, or at the top of the screen on a Macintosh. The menu on both Windows and Macintosh computers has File, Edit, View, Insert, Modify, Text, Control, Window, and Help options. In Mac OS X, the Flash option is listed in the menu.

When Flash opens, by default the Color Mixer, Color Swatches, Components, and Answers panels are visible along the right side of the screen, and the *toolbox* is visible along the left side. The *timeline* is visible across the top of the screen (you'll learn more about the timeline in Lesson 4). The Property inspector (called Properties in Windows) is visible along (Windows) or near (Macintosh) the bottom; the middle of the screen is a work area known as the *stage*.

MENU   MOVIE NAME   TIMELINE   INFORMATION BAR

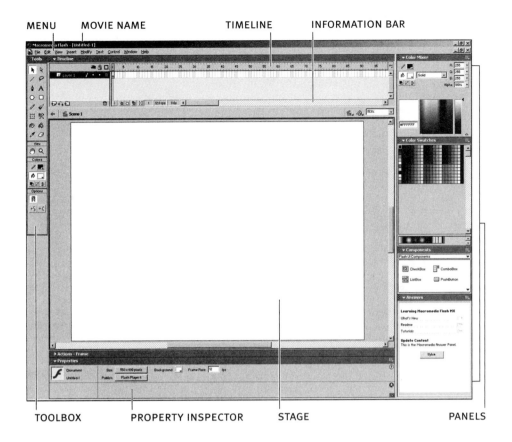

TOOLBOX   PROPERTY INSPECTOR   STAGE   PANELS

The blank document in the stage is a new movie. Every time you open Flash, the program automatically creates a new movie using the default movie settings, which you will learn how to modify later in this lesson. The default name of a new Flash movie, located near the top of the screen should be Untitled-1 or something similar. When you save your movie with a different name, as you'll do later in this lesson, the name on the screen will reflect the change.

NOTE *Flash documents are often referred to as movies because Flash was created originally as an animation program. Of course, Flash can do much more than animation these days, but the movie moniker stuck.*

9

3) Choose File > Close.

The timeline and stage disappear. You also have fewer options in the menu—only File, Edit, Window, and Help remain (plus Flash in Mac OS X). Your screen should now look something like the figure below.

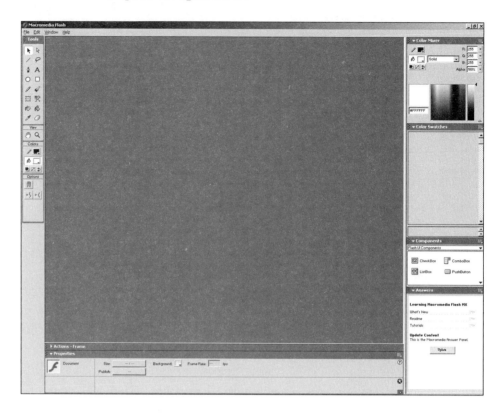

4) Choose File > New.

The timeline and stage reappear. The menu also expands to display all of the options you saw when you first opened Flash. You should also notice that the name of the movie has changed. If your original movie was named Untitled-1, this new movie will be named Untitled-2. Flash automatically updates the name of each new movie and the numbering sequence starts over when you close and then reopen Flash.

5) Open the completed ZooMX Web site in your browser.

N O T E *You need an Internet connection to view the ZooMX Web site. If you do not have an Internet connection, you can open the completed ZooMX Web site from the CD which comes with this book—just open help.html and click the link to view the offline ZooMX Web site. Please be aware that the offline version of the Web site will not have the same functionality as the online version, as some of the files need data only available on the Internet.*

You can find the completed ZooMX Web site, which was created using Flash MX, located at www.flashtfs.com. When you click the ZooMX link, the ZooMX Web site opens in a new browser sized at 600 by 400 pixels. The ZooMX site has functionality that will work only in the latest version of Flash Player. Because Flash Player must be installed on your computer in order to view Flash documents on the Web, you might have been asked to install the latest version. You already have the latest version of Flash Player if you have Flash MX installed. The Flash Player is also distributed with the newest browsers and many operating systems.

If you did download and install the player, you probably noticed that it downloaded quickly. Macromedia is careful about keeping the file size of the Flash Player very small.

Take a few moments to look through the ZooMX Web site. It has graphics, animation, sound, video, dynamic content, and plenty of interactivity. You will learn how to add each of these elements by completing the lessons in this book.

As you create Flash content in the Flash MX authoring tool, you will be working with .fla files. These are editable files that are only used in the authoring tool and are not the files you view over the Web. The files you view over the Web, .swf files, are compressed versions of the content in the .fla file and contain only the information needed to view the file with the Flash Player. You will learn how to view a Flash movie in the .swf format at the end of this lesson. You will also learn how to publish your completed Flash movies as .swf files, along with the HTML required to display them in the browser, at the end of this book.

GETTING HELP

Even after you finish all the lessons in this book, you might still want extra help with Flash. Some resources come with Flash and many others are available on the Internet.

Switch back to Flash if you have the browser window open from the last exercise.

1) Explore the Welcome panel.

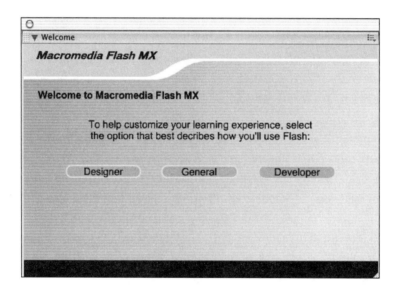

The Welcome panel appears the first time you open Flash. It gives you instructions on setting up the Flash environment depending on what you're going to do. Designers will more likely use the stage, toolbox, and panels related to drawing, while developers will more likely use the Actions panel.

You can also open the Welcome panel from the Help menu (Help > Welcome). Explore the panel by clicking on each of the options, and then follow the instructions for modifying the panel layout. Choose Window > Panel Sets > Default to return to the default panel layout.

12

2) Choose Help > Lessons.

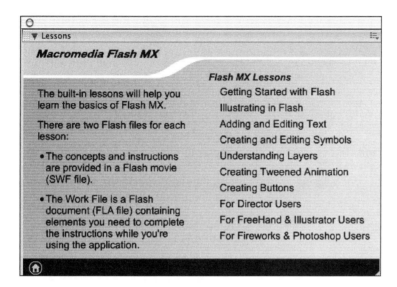

The Lessons panel contains a number of lessons that will help you get started. You may find it useful to go through these lessons whenever you're having trouble with one of the topics listed in the window.

3) Choose Help > Using Flash to open the Flash help files in your browser.

TIP *On a Windows computer, you can also open the help files by pressing F1. This is probably one of the most important shortcut keys to remember!*

The Flash help files contain the information provided in the Flash manual in a searchable, hyperlink format. The files are sorted by topic when they appear in your browser. You can also view an alphabetical list of all help topics by clicking the Index button or you can use the search feature by clicking the Search button.

4) Return to Flash and choose Help > Flash Support Center.

If you're connected to the Internet, choosing this option takes you to Macromedia's Flash Support Center. The Flash Support Center is a clearinghouse for information about Flash, including tutorials, TechNotes, training information, and more.

5) Return to Flash and explore the Answers panel.

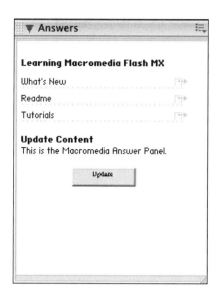

The Answers panel is located at the bottom of the set of panels on the right side of the screen. If you don't see it, choose Window > Answers. This panel is very useful, as Macromedia can provide the latest resources and help right inside of the Flash interface. The contents of the panel can be updated if you are connected to the Internet.

6) Visit some of the resources listed in Appendix C if you need additional help.
Many of the resources, such as FlashLite (www.flashlite.net) and Flash TFS (www.flashtfs.com) have bulletin boards, source files, and tutorials that make learning Flash a bit easier. You don't have to visit all of them right now, but as you go through this book, or as you work with Flash, you might want the additional assistance these resources provide.

7) Subscribe to a Flash mailing list.
The Flash community is a great place to learn more about Flash. By subscribing to a mailing list, you'll be able to communicate with other members of the Flash community. Several mailing lists are described in Appendix C—find one that you think would be suitable for you, and sign up.

SETTING PREFERENCES
Flash has a wide range of preference settings that let you control everything from the number of Undos you can perform to the way objects are selected. In this lesson, you'll check to make sure that most of your preferences are set to Flash's defaults and learn what many of the preferences actually do.

1) Choose Edit > Preferences (Flash > Preferences in Mac OS X) to display the Preferences window. Click the General tab, set the Undo Levels to 50, and make sure the other preferences are set as shown in the figure below.

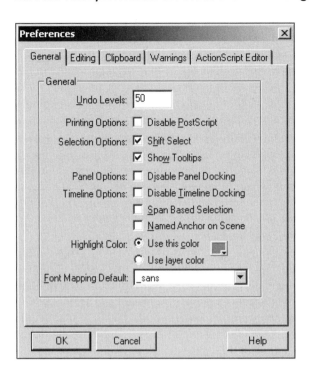

Undo Levels controls the number of steps that Flash remembers. If you need to make corrections to your work, Flash will be able to revert by the number of steps set in the Undo Levels field. With the setting at 50 steps, you should be able to undo almost any mistake. But you should also be aware that each step is saved in memory. With a high Undo Levels setting, your computer might start slowing after you complete several tasks. If you notice your computer slowing and it starts causing problems, return to the Preferences window and lower the Undo Levels setting.

The options checked in the General tab of the Preferences window are Shift Select and Show Tooltips. Selecting Shift Select lets you add to a selection by holding down the Shift key when you click additional objects. Clicking an additional object without holding down Shift simply selects that object. If Shift Select is off, objects are added to a selection as you click them—you don't have to hold down Shift. (If this doesn't make sense to you, don't worry about it; we'll cover it later in the book. Right now, you only need to make sure that your preferences are set correctly.) Show Tooltips is a quick help system, handy for novices. When Show Tooltips is checked, a Tooltip or label, appears whenever you pause the pointer over a control.

The options that are not checked in the General tab of the Preferences window are Disable PostScript (Windows only), Disable Panel Docking (Windows only), Disable Timeline Docking, Span Based Selection, and Named Anchor on Scene. On a Windows computer, you can select the Disable PostScript option if you have trouble printing to a PostScript printer, but you'll find that it slows down printing. When the Disable Panel Docking option is selected on a Windows computer, panels will not attach, or dock, to each other. You'll learn more about panels and docking later in this lesson. Selecting the Disable Timeline Docking option keeps the timeline from attaching to the application window after it has been separated into its own window. The Span Based Selection option determines whether you're able to use span-based or frame-based selection in the timeline—you'll learn more about what that means in Lesson 4. You can select the Named Anchor on Scene option to have Flash add a named anchor to the first frame of each scene, which will allow you to use the Forward and Back buttons in the browser to move from scene to scene.

TIP *You may find that opening a Flash file created on another computer can sometimes result in a Missing Font Warning. This warning indicates that a font in the file you opened is not installed on your computer. You can choose to use the default substitute, or you can indicate a specific font to replace the missing font.*

2) Click the Editing tab, and select the Show Pen Preview option. Make sure that the rest of the Pen Tool and Vertical Text options are deselected, and that all of the Drawing Settings are set to Normal.

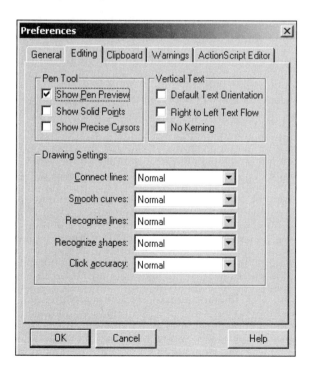

Since you haven't started working with the drawing tools yet, some of the settings under the Editing tab may not look familiar. After you start working with the drawing tools, you might find it useful to return to the Preferences window to modify these settings.

The options in the Pen Tool category modify the way the pen tool, one of the drawing tools found in the toolbox, works. When the Show Pen Preview option is checked, Flash shows the line segment before it's drawn with the pen tool. The Show Solid Points option, which is not checked by default, specifies the way the points of lines are displayed when using the pen or subselection tool. If this option is checked, selected points will appear hollow, while unselected points will appear solid. The opposite is true if this option is not checked. When the Show Precise Cursors option is selected, the pen tool appears as a crosshair instead of as the default pen tool icon.

All of the Vertical Text options are deselected by default, which is just fine for the project we're creating. You might want to use them in the future, so it's good to know what they do. Selecting the Default Text Orientation option will make vertical text the default orientation for any text added to the movie. This is particularly useful if you're working with Asian-language fonts. The Right to Left Text Flow option, when checked, will force text to flow from right to left, instead of the default left to right. Again, you might want this option if you're working with some Asian-language fonts. Finally, selecting the No Kerning option will turn off kerning for all vertical text in the movie. This option might be useful for improving the spacing for some fonts.

The Drawing Settings specify the tolerances for some of the drawing behaviors in Flash. These settings are relative—they depend on the resolution of your computer screen and your current magnification level. So when you zoom in and out as you draw, the drawing behaviors become more or less tolerant. The Connect lines setting determines how close a line being drawn can come to an existing line before its end point automatically connects to the closest point on the preexisting line. The options for this setting are Must be close, Normal, and Can be distant. The Smooth curves setting can be set to Off, Rough, Normal, or Smooth and specifies the amount of smoothing applied to a curved line drawn with the pencil tool. The Recognize lines setting specifies how close to a straight line a segment drawn with the pencil tool must be before it's actually considered a straight line. When Flash recognizes a segment as a straight line, it will make that segment perfectly straight. The Recognize shapes option is similar, except it's used to specify how close to a circle, oval, rectangle, square, 90-degree arc, or 180-degree arc a shape must be before it's recognized and redrawn as one of those geometric shapes. Both the Recognize lines and Recognize shapes settings can be set to Off, Strict, Normal, or Tolerant. Finally, the Click accuracy setting determines how close the pointer has to be to a shape to recognize that shape. As you'll see when you start working with the drawing tools in the next lesson, moving the pointer near a shape causes the cursor to change, depending on the shape and the currently selected drawing tool. The Click accuracy option, which can be set to Strict, Normal, or Tolerant, specifies how close to a shape the pointer must be before the cursor changes appearance.

3) Click the Warnings tab and make sure that all of the options are selected.

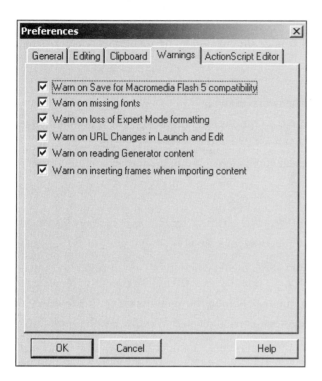

You're just getting started, so it's probably best to let Flash warn you whenever something happens that could potentially mess things up. All of the options under the Warnings tab are checked by default, but as you become more comfortable with Flash, you probably won't need as many warnings. For example, if you have Warn on missing fonts selected, Flash will warn you every time you open a Flash movie that contains a font that is not installed on your computer. If you often work with files that contain fonts not installed on your computer, and you no longer want to see this setting, open the Preferences window and deselect that option.

4) Click OK to close the Preferences window.

When you click OK, any changes you made in the Preferences window take effect. Now that you've taken a look at your preferences, it's time to explore the Flash environment a little more.

WORKING WITH PANELS

Flash MX organizes many of its tools and commands in panels, similar to the palettes in other programs. Panels contain tools that allow you to view, organize, and modify elements in a movie. You can show, hide, and resize panels as you work. You can even combine or dock panels to make it easier to work in Flash. Unlike dialog boxes and windows, panels can remain on the screen while you work so you can easily use them to modify elements in your movie.

In the following exercise, you will arrange the panels and then save your custom panel layout to use later.

1) Close the Color Swatches and Answers panels.

You can close a panel by clicking on the Options menu control in the top right corner of the panel's title bar and choosing Close Panel. If any panel is collapsed, and the Options menu control doesn't appear, click once in the title bar to expand the panel and reveal the control.

TIP *You can also close a panel by Right-clicking (Windows) or Control-clicking (Macintosh) on the title of the panel and choosing Close Panel from the menu.*

You don't need to use these panels right now, so it's safe to close them. If you need to use any of the panels later, you can find them in the Window menu. Just choose Window > Answers to open the Answers panel, or choose Window > Color Swatches to open the Color Swatches panel.

2) Choose Window > Align to open the Align panel.

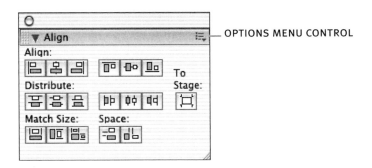

OPTIONS MENU CONTROL

TIP *You can also open the Align panel by pressing Ctrl+K (Windows) or Command+K (Macintosh).*

When you open the Align panel from the Window menu, notice that there are quite a few options in this section of the menu—most of them are for other panels. You will use many of the panels in this menu in later lessons.

3) Click the left side of the Align panel's title bar, and drag the panel over the Components panel on the right side of the screen. Drop the Align panel on the Components panel.

The left side of every panel's title bar contains a control that allows you to drag the panel around. If you move the pointer over the title bar in Windows, it changes, indicating that it's possible to drag the panel. As you move the Align panel, Flash displays an outline of the panel (see the figure below). As you move the Align panel, you'll see an outline, that indicates the location and size of the panel if you were to drop it in that area. Notice that when you drag the Align panel over the Components panel, the outline appears around the panel set on the right side of the screen, indicating that dropping the panel there will place it in that panel set. There should be an outline representing the panel when you start dragging it. There should also be an outline around all of the panels in the panel set when you move it over the Components panel.

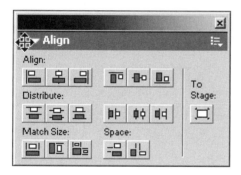

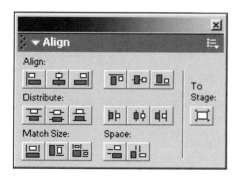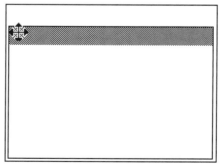

Once you drop the panel, it should appear docked with the Color Mixer and Components panels. The Align panel should appear at the bottom of this set of panels—if it does not, just drag the panels up or down until the Color Mixer appears at the top, the Components panel appears in the middle, and the Align panel appears at the bottom.

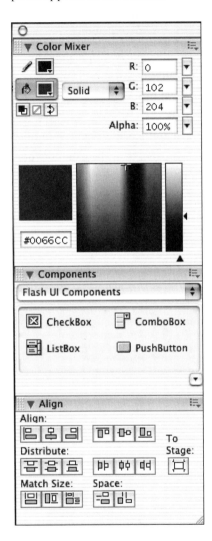

4) Collapse the Components panel by clicking on its title or on the arrow to the left of its title.

One of the nice things about panels in Flash MX is that they're collapsible. You can collapse panels you're not currently using to gain a bit more screen space for the panels you're using. You can open a collapsed panel by clicking on its title (or the arrow). When you collapse a panel, the Options menu control on the right side of the title bar disappears.

5) Choose Window › Save Panel Layout. When the Save Panel Layout window opens, type *Flash TFS* in the Name text box, and click OK.

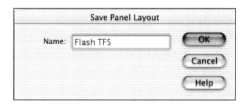

When you choose Window > Save Panel Layout, the Save Panel Layout dialog box appears. Now you need to type in a name for your panel set. If you try to save a panel set with a name that's already being used, Flash will let you know. You will have the option of overwriting the existing panel set, but make sure that's what you want to do before you type in the new name.

When you click OK, Flash saves your panel layout. Pretty painless, wasn't it? Now you can open this panel layout any time by choosing Window > Panel Sets > Flash TFS. If you prefer to use the default panel layout, you can switch back by choosing Window > Panel Sets > Default Layout. As you work more with Flash, you may find that you use certain panels more than others. You can create new panel sets to provide easy access to the panel sets you use frequently.

TIP *If you ever need to delete a panel set, just delete the file with the name of the panel set you want to remove from the Panel Sets folder, which is inside the Flash MX Configuration folder. The location of the Flash MX Configuration folder varies by operating system. In Windows 98 and ME, the folder is C:\[Windows Directory]\Application Data\Macromedia\ Flash MX. For Windows NT it's C:\[Windows directory]\profiles\<user name>\ Application Data\Macromedia\Flash MX. In Windows 2000 and XP, the folder is C:\Documents and Settings\<user name>\Application Data\Macromedia\Flash MX. In Max OS 8.x and above, single-user, it's Hard Drive:System Folder:Application Support:Macromedia:Flash MX, while multi-user puts it in Hard Drive:Users:<user name>:Documents:Macromedia:Flash MX. In Mac OS X, it's Hard Drive/Users/<user name>/Library/Application Support/Macromedia/Flash MX*

USING KEYBOARD SHORTCUTS

You might have noticed that many commands in Flash MX can be executed using keyboard shortcuts instead of selecting menu options. The default keyboard shortcuts are easy to use, but what if you want to customize them to work better with your habits? Or what if you want to use the keyboard shortcuts you're already familiar with from another program? You'll learn how to modify the keyboard shortcuts in this next exercise.

1) Choose Edit > Keyboard Shortcuts (Flash > Keyboard Shortcuts in Mac OS X) to open the Keyboard Shortcuts window.

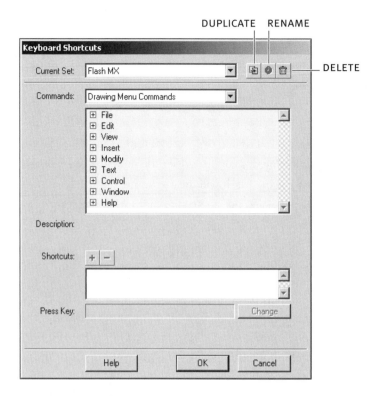

The Keyboard Shortcuts window has a number of options. At the top of the window is the Current Set option, which determines the keyboard-shortcut set being used. Flash MX comes with several sets of keyboard shortcuts, including those for Macromedia Fireworks and FreeHand, but is set to Flash MX by default.

2) Make sure the Current Set is Flash MX, and click the Duplicate Set button. When the Duplicate window opens, set the Duplicate Name to Flash TFS and click OK.

When you click OK, the Duplicate window closes and the Current Set is changed to Flash TFS.

It's nice to have a default set of keyboard shortcuts to go back to if you accidentally mess up; so to do this you need to duplicate the default Flash MX set and modify the duplicate set instead of the original. Flash is foolproof, though—it won't let you make any changes to the Flash MX keyboard shortcut set.

After you know how to modify a keyboard-shortcut set, if you're brave enough, try changing the Flash MX set to see what happens. You should get a warning telling you that you cannot modify that set.

Not only can you duplicate existing sets, but you can also rename and delete keyboard-shortcut sets. Select the set you want to rename or delete from the Current Set, and click either the Rename or Delete button. You cannot rename or delete the Flash MX set.

3) Set the Commands setting to Drawing Tools, and select Dropper from the list.

The Commands setting has four options: Drawing Menu commands, Drawing Tools, Test Movie Menu commands, and Actions Panel commands. Look at the options listed to see what's available for a particular set of commands. The Drawing Tools commands include the shortcut keys for each of the drawing tools in the toolbox. Notice that by default, the shortcut key for the eyedropper tool, which corresponds to the Dropper, is I. If you'd like to be adventurous, go ahead and select some of the other Commands options and poke around in the list of commands for each of them.

When you select the eyedropper tool from the list of commands, the shortcut for that tool appears in the Shortcuts box near the bottom of the Keyboard Shortcuts window. You can add another shortcut, delete the existing shortcut, or modify the existing shortcut. Let's start out by adding a keyboard shortcut that's already in use.

4) Click the Add Shortcut (+) button to add a new shortcut. When ‹empty› appears in the Shortcuts box, press the E key on the keyboard.

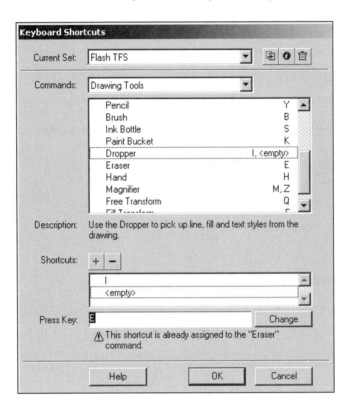

When ‹empty› appears in the Shortcuts box, it indicates that you've added a keyboard shortcut, but haven't yet assigned a key. This line should be selected automatically, and the same text (‹empty›) should appear in the Press Key box. If it doesn't, select the ‹empty› line in the Shortcuts box and click in the Press Key box.

The E keyboard shortcut is already in use by the eraser tool. So when you type the keyboard shortcut E in the Press Key box, a message appears to let you know that E is already being used. If you were to click the Change button at this point, a Reassign window would open asking if you want to reassign the keyboard shortcut to the eyedropper tool. You don't really want to make that change, so if you did click the Change button, just click the Cancel button in the Reassign window to close the window.

NOTE *When you click the Press Key box, Flash will capture one letter plus the Control (Windows), Command (Macintosh), Alt (Windows), Option (Macintosh), and Shift keys. If you want to add a capital E to the keyboard shortcuts, you don't need to press Shift+E—just press E and it will appear as a capital E.*

5) Select the contents of the Press Key box and press D. Click the Change button.

The D key is not being used by another command, so Flash should not give an error message when you press that key. When you click Change, D will be added as a keyboard shortcut for the eyedropper tool.

TIP *If you click the Help button in the Keyboard Shortcuts window, the Flash help files open directly to the help section for working with keyboard shortcuts.*

6) Click OK.

When you click OK, Flash saves the new Flash TFS keyboard shortcut, and the Keyboard Shortcuts window closes. Move your pointer over the eyedropper tool in the toolbox (the one that looks like an eyedropper). A Tooltip should appear if you hold the pointer over the tool for a moment, and the new keyboard shortcut should appear in that Tooltip. If the keyboard shortcut doesn't appear in the Tooltip, choose Edit > Keyboard Shortcuts and make sure that Flash TFS is selected as the Current Set. If it's not, select it from the Current Set and click OK.

MODIFYING THE DOCUMENT PROPERTIES

Before you start making a movie in Flash, you should think about its properties, such as the size and the background color. It's a good idea to decide what the movie's dimensions should be, because it can be difficult to make changes after you've added artwork to the movie.

You can set the dimensions of your movie—as well as the background color, the frame rate, and the units of measure of the stage's ruler—using the Property inspector and the Document Properties dialog box. In the following exercise, you'll modify the dimensions and background color of a movie.

1) Make sure you have a new movie open. Click the Background color box in the Property inspector. When the color palette opens, type #FFC055 (orange) in the space provided and press Enter or Return.

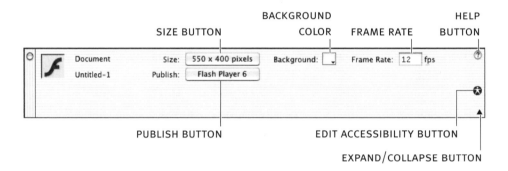

BACKGROUND COLOR

SIZE BUTTON

FRAME RATE

HELP BUTTON

PUBLISH BUTTON

EDIT ACCESSIBILITY BUTTON

EXPAND/COLLAPSE BUTTON

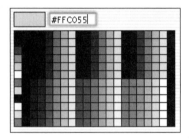

You started a new movie in the first exercise of this lesson. If for some reason you closed your movie, or played around with the drawing tools and added anything to the stage, create a new movie by choosing File > New.

You will use the Property inspector quite a bit, so now is a good time to explore it. The Property inspector, the large panel at the bottom of the screen, is useful for modifying all sorts of things. It is context-sensitive, meaning it displays the settings for only whatever you have selected at the time. If you don't have anything selected, and you haven't clicked on anything in the toolbox or timeline, the Property inspector displays the settings for the document. You should see a Flash icon at the left side of the Property inspector. The word Document should appear to the right of the icon, indicating that the document properties are currently being displayed. The name of the Flash movie, which is currently set to Untitled-2 or something similar, also appears to the right of the icon. If your Property inspector does not look like the one on the previous page, click the arrow tool in the toolbox (the black arrow, not the white arrow), and then click on the stage.

You can only use a solid color as the background color of your movie, so the color palette contains only solid colors. It contains 216 Web-safe default colors, but the background color for the project we're working on is not in that palette. So you have to type its hexadecimal value in the space provided. Notice that when the palette opens, the pointer changes to an eyedropper—you can use the eyedropper to select any color from within Flash. Just move the pointer over the color you want to use and click. That color will become your movie's background color. If you click the eyedropper outside of Flash, the color will be set to #FFFFFF (white).

TIP *You can also modify the background color from the Document Properties window, as you'll see in the next step, but you don't have the option of typing a hexadecimal color value in the Document Properties window.*

2) Click the Size button in the Property inspector to open the Document Properties window.

When you click the Size button in the Property inspector, the Document Properties window opens. In the Document Properties window, you can set the frame rate, dimensions (width and height), background color, and ruler units of your movie. You can also use the Match buttons (Printer and Contents) to set the dimensions of the movie to match the current print size or the current contents of the movie (whatever you have drawn on the stage). The Default button sets the dimensions and background color to Flash's defaults.

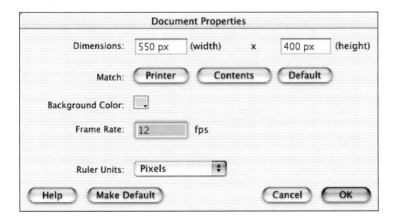

3) Set the Width to 600 and leave the Height at 400.

By default, the dimensions are set in the pixels ruler unit (px), so you can type *600* in the width field and the px ruler unit is added when you apply the settings. If you would like to use a different ruler unit for your movie, you can select one from the Ruler Unit drop-down menu near the bottom of the Document Properties window. Don't use a different ruler unit for this file, because it may cause confusion in later tasks if the ruler unit is different from the one in the instructions.

The default movie size is 550 by 400 pixels. The smallest movie size possible is 1 by 1 pixels, and the largest is 2880 by 2880. You need to set the movie size to 600 by 400 because the designer who created the original layout for the movie you're going to make used this dimension.

4) Click the Make Default button and then click OK.

Another useful feature of the Document Properties window is the Make Default button. If you often use the same settings for your new movies, you can keep those settings as the default by clicking the Make Default button. In later lessons, you will make several movies using the same dimensions and background color as this one, so it might be easier to make these properties the default.

When you click OK, the Document Properties window closes and the movie resizes to the dimensions that you specified.

5) Choose File > Save. When the Save As dialog box opens, browse to the FlashTFS folder on your hard drive, type zoo1.fla in the File Name (Windows) or Save document as (Macintosh) text box, and click Save.

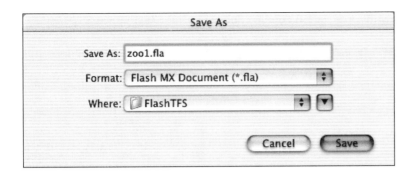

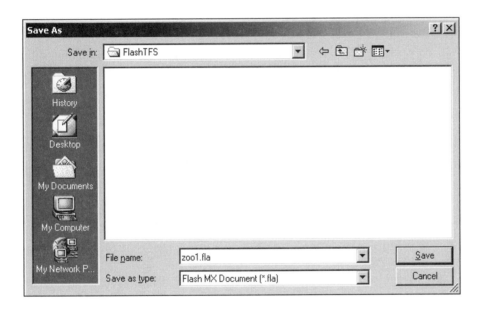

You just saved your first Flash file to the FlashTFS folder. Congratulations! You will use this file again, so leave it open for now.

TESTING A MOVIE

Flash can play movies in the authoring environment, but this playback doesn't always show you exactly how the Flash movie will look when it's finally published for the Web. As you learned at the beginning of this lesson, the files you work with in Flash are .fla files, while the files you will eventually create for the Web, which will be viewed by the Flash Player, are .swf files. The Flash authoring tool's Test Movie command allows you to preview your movies as .swf files.

31

1) Make sure you still have zoo1.fla open. Choose Control > Test Movie.

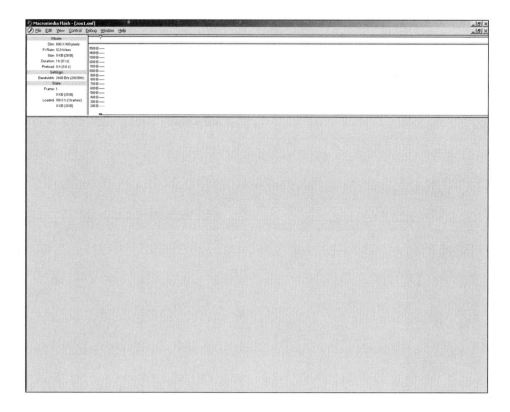

When you choose Control > Test Movie, Flash creates an .swf file in the same folder where you saved your .fla file. Flash opens that .swf file in a separate window and displays it in the Flash Player. We will refer to the Flash preview window as the Test Movie window. You will learn much more about the Test Movie window in Lesson 12.

The .swf version of zoo1.fla is pretty boring right now. It should appear as an empty orange area. Don't worry, you'll add much more to this file in the next 11 lessons, and that empty orange area will soon have lots of content.

2) Close the Test Movie window.

You didn't actually make any changes to zoo1.fla when you tested it, so you don't have to save the file again. Just keep it open for now, as you're going to add some content to it in the next lesson.

WHAT YOU HAVE LEARNED

In this lesson, you have:

- Viewed the completed ZooMX Web site (pages 8–12)

- Learned where to look for additional help (pages 12–15)

- Explored and modified the Flash preferences (pages 15–19)

- Rearranged the panels and created a custom panel layout (pages 20–23)

- Created a custom keyboard shortcut set (pages 23–27)

- Modified the background color and dimensions of a Flash movie (pages 28–31)

- Previewed a Flash movie in the Flash Player (pages 31–32)

adding graphics and text

To make your movie more interesting, you need to add graphics and text. In this lesson, you'll learn how to use Flash MX's drawing tools to add shapes and text to your movie. You'll look at some of the tools Flash offers for controlling and modifying elements. Flash provides multiple tools to let you precisely control the placement of elements, including rulers, guides, panels, and the Property inspector. In this lesson, you'll learn to use all of these.

In addition, Flash uses layers and guides to let you control the way your elements interact. You'll add and modify layers, and you'll work with the layer display to show, hide, lock, and unlock different layers.

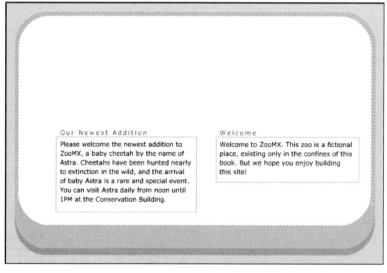

The main page of the ZooMX Web site.

Chrissy Rey

Throughout the lesson, your exercises build to create a graphic that will eventually become the main page of the ZooMX Web site. You'll start simply, but by the time you complete this lesson, you'll have a page with graphics and text. You will add more in later lessons, but this lesson will give you a solid foundation upon which you can build graphically appealing Flash movies.

WHAT YOU WILL LEARN

In this lesson, you will:

- Explore the drawing tools

- Draw some simple shapes

- Modify strokes and fills

- Work with a group

- Add and modify layers

- Add and modify text

APPROXIMATE TIME

This lesson takes approximately one hour to complete.

LESSON FILES

Media Files:

None

Starting Files:

Lesson02/Starting/zoo1.fla

Completed Project:

Lesson02/Completed/zoo6.fla

EXPLORING THE DRAWING TOOLS

Flash has a wide range of tools and commands you can use to create your movies. The easiest way to learn is to actually use them. But first, you need to know what they are and where they are. You will explore the drawing tools and some of their options in this exercise.

1) Open zoo1.fla.

You can find zoo1.fla in the Lesson02/Starting folder on the CD-ROM that comes with this book or use the zoo1.fla file you saved on your hard drive if you closed the file after Lesson 1. If you left the file open, you're ready to go.

Right now there's nothing in this file—just an orange background. So, first let's look at the drawing tools. You have to open a movie to explore all the drawing tools because some of the options for these tools are only available when you have a movie open.

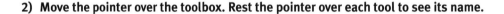 **NOTE** *Just for fun, close any movie you might have open in Flash and start clicking on the tools in the toolbox—some options should appear in the Options area in the toolbox, but the Property inspector will not change. Make sure you reopen zoo1.fla before you continue.*

2) Move the pointer over the toolbox. Rest the pointer over each tool to see its name.

Remember when you turned on Tooltips in the last lesson? That setting will now pay off. You can quickly and easily find the name of any tool by pausing the pointer over its icon. After a second or two, a label with the name of the tool will appear.

As you move the pointer over the icons, you should notice that each tool has a Tooltip. The Tooltip lists not only the name of the tool, but also the key (or keys) you press to select the tool. Shortcut keys can make switching between tools very easy. Notice that the eyedropper tool has two shortcut keys—you set one of them in the last lesson when you created the custom Flash TFS keyboard shortcut set.

TIP *As you become more experienced using Flash, you might find it useful to use keyboard shortcuts to switch between the drawing tools. For example, after you've drawn a rectangle, you can press the O key to draw and oval. You don't need to have the toolbox open to use these keyboard shortcuts. So if you want a little extra screen space, you can close the toolbox and use the shortcut keys to switch between tools.*

3) Click on each tool to see which options appear in the toolbox and the Property inspector.

The toolbox contains Flash's drawing and transformation tools. It also contains additional settings for some of the tools. When you click the arrow, lasso, rectangle, pencil, brush, free transform, paint bucket, eraser, or zoom tool, icons appear in the Options area of the toolbox. You should also notice that many of these tools have additional settings in the Property inspector.

TIP *Not sure which tool you have selected? The button that corresponds to the selected tool should be depressed in the toolbox. What if the toolbox is closed? Simply move the pointer over the stage to see which icon appears. Most of the pointer icons for the drawing tools correspond to the icons in the toolbox.*

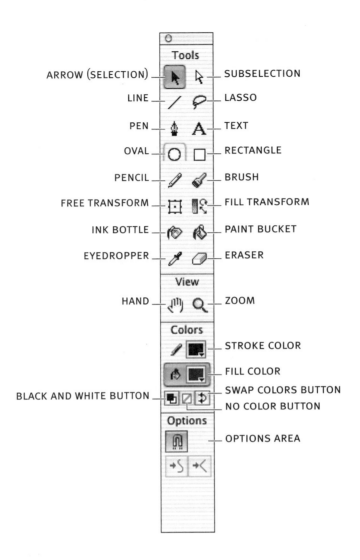

ARROW (SELECTION) — SUBSELECTION
LINE — LASSO
PEN — TEXT
OVAL — RECTANGLE
PENCIL — BRUSH
FREE TRANSFORM — FILL TRANSFORM
INK BOTTLE — PAINT BUCKET
EYEDROPPER — ERASER

View

HAND — ZOOM

Colors

STROKE COLOR
FILL COLOR
BLACK AND WHITE BUTTON — SWAP COLORS BUTTON
NO COLOR BUTTON

Options

OPTIONS AREA

TIP *If the toolbox does not appear on your screen, you can open it by choosing Window > Tools. You will see a check next to the toolbox menu item if it's open.*

Some of the drawing tools create only *strokes*. You can use the pencil tool to draw freehand lines and shapes—it's a lot like drawing with a real pencil. The pen tool is useful for drawing precise paths as straight or curved lines, and the line tool is great for drawing basic shapes that are composed of straight lines.

Other tools create *fills*. The oval and rectangle tools are useful for drawing basic geometric shapes with both a stroke and a fill. The stroke is the outline, and the fill is the solid area of color that appears inside the stroke. You can use these tools to draw basic geometric shapes with both a stroke and a fill, a stroke without a fill, or a fill without a stroke. The brush tool can create freehand shapes that are composed of fills.

The text tool is perfect for adding text to your movie. This tool can create static, dynamic, and input text boxes, each of which can have text with a solid color. You'll learn more about adding static text later in this lesson, and you'll add dynamic and input text later in your project.

The two tools in the View area (hand and zoom) let you control the view of the stage. You can use the hand tool to move the stage around. The zoom tool lets you change the magnification of the stage.

The rest of the drawing tools allow you to select and modify objects on the stage. The arrow, subselection, and lasso tools let you select all or part of an object. You can also use the arrow and subselection tools to modify the shape of strokes and fills on the stage. The ink bottle and paint bucket tools can be used to add and modify strokes and fills, respectively, while the eyedropper tool can copy the properties of a stroke or fill, and then immediately apply them to another shape. The free transform tool is useful for rotating, skewing, scaling, distorting, and moving shapes, and the fill transform tool lets you modify an existing gradient or bitmap fill. Finally, you can use the eraser tool to erase all or part of an object on the stage.

Spend some time exploring the tools—there's a lot more to them than the brief explanations above. If you've used any other drawing, photo-editing, illustration, or paint program, you're probably familiar with most of these tools. If not, the best way to become familiar with them is by using them. Click each of the tools to see which options appear in the Options area of the toolbox and the Property inspector. You can also test drive the tools by using them to draw some shapes on the stage. Just make sure you choose Edit > Select All and then Edit > Clear to clean up the stage before you move on to the next step.

4) Click the rectangle tool to select it. Click the Round Rectangle Radius icon in the Options area of the toolbox to open the Rectangle Settings dialog box. Set the Corner Radius to 50 and click OK.

Rectangle Settings		
Corner Radius:	50	points	OK
		Cancel
		Help

You can create rectangles with rounded corners by modifying the Corner Radius. A Corner Radius of 0 will create a rectangle with square edges. The maximum corner radius is 999.

Don't forget, you can use shortcut keys to select tools. So instead of clicking the rectangle tool in the toolbox, you can press the R key on the keyboard.

5) Click the Stroke Color box in the Property inspector. When the color palette opens, type #FF6600 (orange) in the space provided and press Enter or Return. Set the Fill Color to #FFFFFF (white) in the same way.

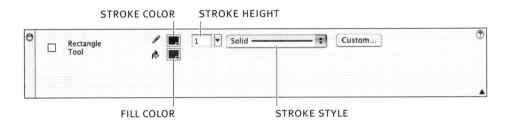

The Stroke Color box has a pencil icon next to it, while the Fill Color box has a paint bucket icon. You can use both a stroke and a fill on a rectangle, and you can control the color of each one separately in the Property inspector. You can also modify the stroke and fill colors in the Colors area of the toolbox or in the Color Mixer panel. Use the method that's easiest for you in this and future exercises. When you click the Stroke Color box, the color pop-up contains only solid color swatches, because strokes can only be solid colors. The Fill Color box pop-up has both solid color and gradient swatches because fills can be solid colors or gradients. You can also apply a bitmap to a fill. Remember, you can set a color in the color palette by either typing the hexadecimal value in the box or by using the eyedropper to select a color.

When you open the color palettes for both the stroke and fill from the Property inspector, a single button, called the No Color button, will appear in the top-right corner. You can use the stroke and fill colors with the oval and rectangle tools, but not for any other tool.

The No Color button allows you to set the color to none (no color). It is only available for the oval and rectangle tools because these are the only tools with the option of using a stroke alone, a fill alone, or both a stroke and fill together. If you open the stroke or fill color palettes from the Colors area of the toolbox, you should see the No Color button and a second button in the top-right corner of the pop-up. The second button opens the Color Picker window where you can choose a color that is not in the color palette window.

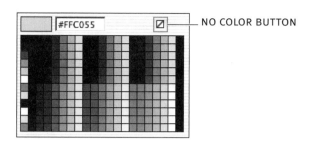

NO COLOR BUTTON

NO COLOR BUTTON

COLOR PICKER BUTTON

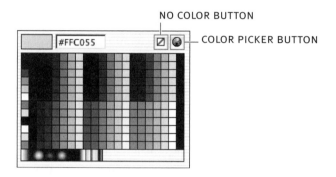

When you use the Color Mixer panel to set the stroke and fill colors, you have more flexibility. First, click on the Stroke Color or Fill Color icon to make sure you set the color for the right property. Then you can use the corresponding color box to set the color, type the hexadecimal value of the color in the Hex Edit box, enter values in the Color Values boxes, or click in the Color Space. You can also set the Fill Type (for fills) to None, Solid, Linear, Radial, or Bitmap using the Fill Type pop-up menu. Play around with the various settings in the Color Mixer panel.

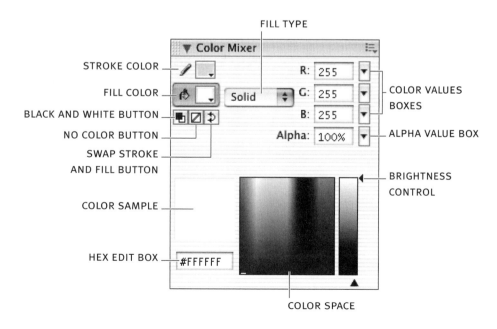

FILL TYPE

STROKE COLOR

FILL COLOR

BLACK AND WHITE BUTTON

NO COLOR BUTTON

SWAP STROKE
AND FILL BUTTON

COLOR SAMPLE

HEX EDIT BOX

COLOR VALUES
BOXES

ALPHA VALUE BOX

BRIGHTNESS
CONTROL

COLOR SPACE

6) Set the Stroke height in the Property inspector to 2 and select Solid from the Stroke Style drop-down menu.

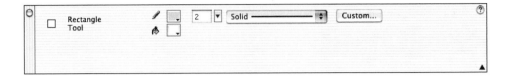

You can set the height of the stroke by typing a number in the Stroke Height box or by dragging the slider to the right of the text box up or down until you get the right height. The stroke height can be set to a number between 0.1 and 10, but you have to actually type in anything smaller than 0.25. The number refers to the line's pixel width.

Flash has several built-in stroke styles. As you'll learn in Lesson 12, you will usually use styles like Hairline or Solid in order to make your files smaller. File size doesn't mean you should not use the other stroke styles; just be aware that they can make the file larger.

In the next exercise you'll actually draw something with the settings you just modified. So don't make any changes yet!

DRAWING BASIC SHAPES

Now it's time to draw something. You can use rulers and draggable guides to position elements precisely on the stage in Flash. You're going to add several guides to aid you in drawing a background for your movie. You'll then use the rectangle tool to add several rectangles.

1) Choose View > Rulers to turn on the rulers. Choose View > Guides > Snap to Guides, and select Snap to Guides.

When you choose View > Rulers, the rulers appear along the top and left sides of the stage. Like real-world rulers, the rulers show units of measure and are useful for positioning elements on the stage.

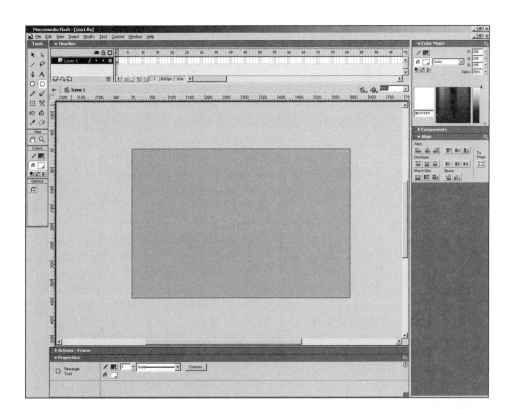

TIP *By default, Flash MX's rulers measure in pixels. If you'd rather see measurements in inches, decimal inches, points, centimeters, or millimeters, choose Modify > Document, and in the Document Properties window, choose a different unit of measure from the Ruler Units setting. For now it's probably best to leave the default pixel setting, so your measurements will match the measurements in this book.*

If there is already a check next to Snap to Guides, it is selected. Selecting Snap to Guides forces anything drawn near a guide line to snap to it. This option makes it much easier to position your elements at exactly the right spot.

2) Select the arrow tool. Click the ruler at the top of the stage and, holding down the mouse button, drag to the stage. A green line, or *guide*, will appear—position the guide at the 15-pixel mark.

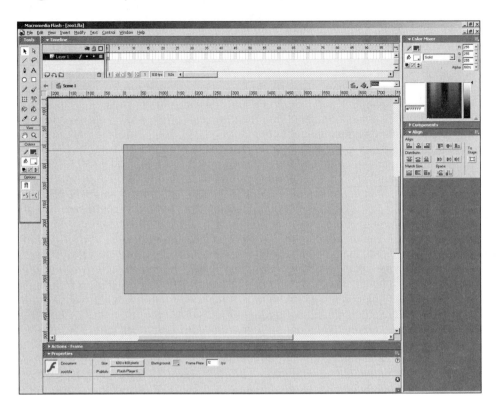

Before you start clicking and dragging, it's best to make sure you have the arrow tool selected. Just click the arrow tool in the toolbox. When you click and drag the ruler, a green line appears on the stage. This is your guide. Use the rulers to help you place your guide properly. Each of the unnumbered hash marks on the rulers represents 10 pixels, while the smaller hash marks represent 5 pixels.

Guides are useful for drawing and positioning items on the stage. They appear only when you're authoring the movie, not in the finished product. If you test the movie (Control > Test Movie), you'll see that the guides do not appear.

3) Position three more guides 15 pixels from the bottom, the right side, and the left side of the movie. Choose View > Guides > Lock Guides.

You should end up with four guides on the stage. They'll create a rectangle, which you'll use to draw a background for your movie. Since you already turned on the Snap to Guides command, anything you draw close to a guide will automatically snap to the guide.

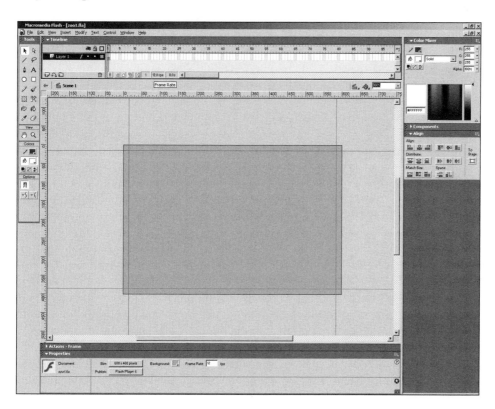

Once you have positioned each of your guides, 15 pixels from each side of the movie, you can lock them. This will prevent them from being moved accidentally. After the guides have been locked, try dragging them—you will find that they won't budge.

TIP *To reposition a guide, select the arrow tool; then click and drag the guide. To remove a guide, use the arrow tool to drag the guide to the horizontal or vertical ruler. You have to unlock the guides (View > Guides > Lock Guides) before you can reposition or remove a guide— if you try to move a guide and it won't budge, make sure the Lock Guides option is not checked.*

4) Select the rectangle tool in the toolbox. Click the top left-corner of the rectangle created by the guides on the stage and drag to the bottom-right corner.

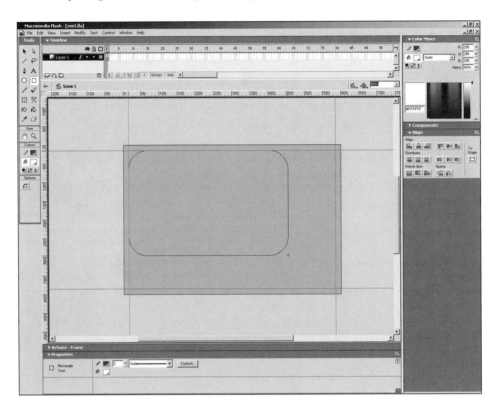

Before you draw the rectangle, make sure you still have the same settings we used in the previous exercise. If you don't know how to check, go back and complete the last exercise, then come back to this step. The Corner Radius should be 50, Stroke Color #FF6600, Stroke Style Solid, Stroke Height 2, and Fill Color #FFFFFF.

As you drag the rectangle tool across the stage, Flash creates the outline of a rectangle with rounded corners. The rectangle should snap right to the guides, which is exactly what you want. It's OK if you don't click directly on the corner made by the guides—if you get close enough the tool will snap to the guides. When you release, a white rectangle with an orange outline and rounded corners appears.

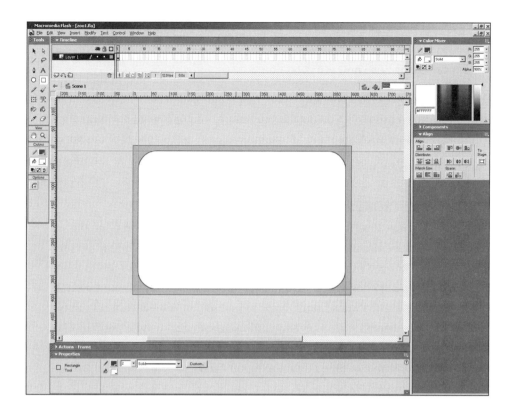

When you draw a rectangle with the rectangle tool, you can hold down the Shift key to constrain it to a perfect square. You can also control the corner radius (roundness) by pressing the up and down arrow keys on the keyboard as you draw the rectangle.

Because the stroke outlines the shape, the rectangle can appear to be larger than the guides. The stroke is 2 pixels wide, and the edges of a shape are based on the edges of the fill and not the stroke. It's easy to test—switch to the arrow tool and then double-click on the stroke (not the fill) and press the Delete or Backspace key to remove the stroke. The edges of the fill, which should be all that's left, line up with the guides. Before you move on to the next step, press Ctrl+Z (Windows) or Command+Z (Macintosh) until the outline comes back.

When you double-click on the stroke, it selects the entire stroke. If you single click on the stroke, it only selects a segment of the stroke, not the whole thing.

Now that you know how to use the rectangle tool, you might find it useful to create a new Flash movie and play with some of the other drawing tools. The best way to learn how to use these tools is to try them. Go ahead—play around with the tools and get creative.

5) Save your movie as zoo2.fla in the FlashTFS folder on your hard drive.

It's a good idea to save your file whenever you make a major change. You've made some major changes, so now is a good time to save.

When you save files with a new name (i.e., zoo2.fla instead of zoo1.fla), you will always have a copy to go back to if you decide you want to add or discard any changes. If you save your work with the same file-name, you can't go back to previous versions.

You're going to continue working with this movie, so just keep it open.

MODIFYING STROKES AND FILLS

Now that you know how to draw basic shapes, it's time to start modifying those shapes. You can use the paint bucket, ink bottle, eyedropper, and eraser tools to modify the strokes and fills that you draw. The paint bucket applies fills to shapes, and the ink bottle applies stroke attributes to lines and outlines. You can use the eyedropper to grab attributes from a shape or line so that those attributes can be applied to other shapes or lines, and you can use the eraser to erase portions of a drawing. You can also make changes to existing strokes and fills by using the arrow tool to select the stroke or fill you want to modify and then changing the settings in the Property inspector.

You should still be working in zoo2.fla, which you saved in the preceding exercise.

1) Choose View > Guides > Show Guides to hide the guides. Select the arrow tool, and click the stroke outline of the rectangle on the stage to select only a segment. Then double-click on the stroke to select the whole outline.

Unlike many programs, Flash treats strokes and fills as separate entities. When you click the stroke, it only selects a segment, not the entire stroke. When you double-click the stroke, you select the entire stroke. You should also notice that when you select the stroke, the fill is not selected.

TIP *You can select a fill and its outline by double-clicking the fill with the arrow tool. To test it out, choose Edit > Undo to bring the rectangle's fill back, then double-click the fill.*

Notice when you select the stroke, the Property inspector changes. It indicates that you have a shape selected. The properties of that shape, namely the stroke color, stroke height, stroke style, and fill color, appear. The Fill Color box should have a red line through it indicating that the shape has no fill color. This may seem odd, since there is in fact a fill on the stage. We're not going to select it right now, so the fill color won't appear in the Property inspector. If you choose Edit > Select All, the fill color appears in the Property inspector.

2) Change the Stroke Style to the dotted line in the Property inspector, and then deselect the stroke.

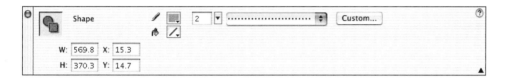

When you change the stroke style, it might not look as if anything happened, but it did! Deselect the stroke by clicking outside of it—you should see that the stroke has the new style applied to it.

TIP *When you want to deselect a shape, or shapes, just click any empty area of the stage. If you click another shape, you'll deselect the first one, and select the new one.*

3) Select the paint bucket tool and change the Fill Color to #FF6600. Click inside the rectangle on the stage.
When you click inside the rectangle with the paint bucket tool selected, the current fill color is applied to the rectangle.

You can select the paint bucket tool, and any other tool in the toolbox, by either clicking the icon in the toolbox or using its shortcut key. The shortcut key for the paint bucket tool is K—remember you can always check to see what a tool's shortcut key is by moving the pointer over the icon until the Tooltip appears.

The fill color can be changed in the Property inspector, the Colors section of the toolbox, or the Color Mixer panel. If you have a fill selected when you change the fill color, its color should change without your having to click inside of the fill. The same is true when you select a stroke and change the stroke color.

When you select the paint bucket tool, if there are no shapes selected on the stage, you should see that only the Fill Color setting appears in the Property inspector. A couple of icons should also appear in the Options area of the toolbox. One of those options, the Gap Size, specifies the relative size of gaps that the paint bucket tool can tolerate. If you set this option to Don't Close Gaps, Flash will not fill the outline if there are any gaps. You can set the Gap Size to Close Small Gaps, Close Medium Gaps, or Close Large Gaps to let Flash fill an outline that has gaps. In the case of our rectangle outline, the spaces between the dots don't actually count as gaps, even though they might look like gaps on the screen. The outline is actually a completely closed shape, so you can set the Gap Size to Don't Close Gaps and still be able to apply a fill.

NOTE *You must select a fill color to use the paint bucket tool. Notice that the No Color button is not available when the paint bucket tool is selected.*

TIP *Sometimes you click inside an object with the paint bucket tool and nothing seems to happen. Your problem might be a gap in the outline of your object. You can change the gap size for the paint bucket tool in the Options section of the toolbar; just click the Gap Size button and then choose the Close Large Gaps option from the pop-up menu. Be aware, however, that what might be a large gap to you could be an enormous gap to Flash! So you might need to close some of the gaps in your outline on your own.*

4) Make sure nothing on the stage is selected. Turn the guides back on, and place a new guide 25 pixels from the bottom of the stage.

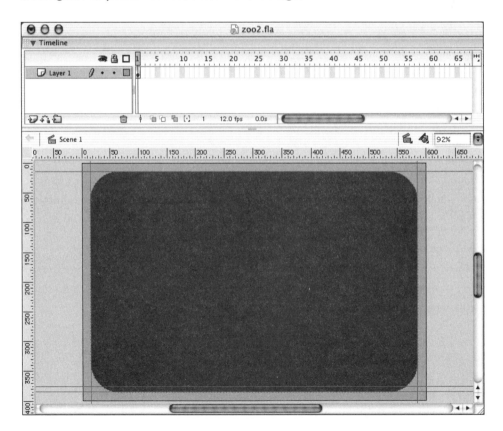

You can turn the guides back on by choosing View > Guides > Show Guides. You may need to unlock the guides by choosing View > Guides > Lock Guides; otherwise it might be difficult to position the new guide—if you drop a guide in the wrong place, you won't be able to drag it to the correct place if the guides are locked.

Once the guide is placed 25 pixels from the bottom of the stage, you can choose View > Guides > Lock Guides to once again lock the guides to prevent you from moving them around as you try to draw and select shapes on the stage. You might find it useful to leave the guides locked so you don't accidentally move any of the guides already on the stage.

5) Select the rectangle tool from the toolbox. Set the Fill Color to #FF9933. Use the guides to draw a rectangle that is 10 pixels shorter than the one already on the stage.

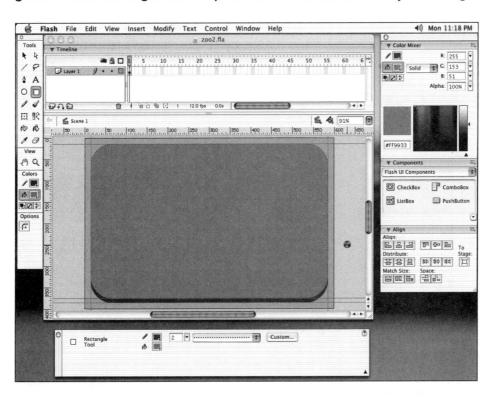

Before you draw this rectangle, make sure the rest of the properties are the same as the ones for the last rectangle. The Stroke Color should be #FF6600, the Stroke Height should be 2, and the Stroke Style should be a dotted line. The Corner Radius, which can be found by clicking the Round Rectangle Radius icon in the Options area of the toolbox, should be set to 50. When you're ready to draw the rectangle, just click in the top left-corner of the rectangle created by the guides, and drag to the bottom right-corner created by the new guide 25 pixels from the bottom of the stage.

If you somehow changed the stroke settings before you drew this new rectangle, all is not lost! You can use the eyedropper tool to grab the settings from the first rectangle you drew, and then apply them to the new rectangle. Just select the eyedropper tool and move it over the bottom stroke outlining the first rectangle that you drew (the rest of the stroke is covered by the new rectangle). As you move over the stroke, a pencil appears next to the eyedropper icon in the pointer—this indicates that you currently have the tool over a stroke. If a paintbrush appears next to the eyedropper icon in the pointer, you are over a fill. When you are sure you are over the stroke you want to copy, click and the pointer changes to the ink bottle tool. Now you just need to click the stroke to which you want to apply these stroke settings.

NOTE *You can also click on the fill that is surrounded by the stroke to apply stroke settings with the ink bottle tool.*

6) Add three guides 20 pixels from the top, right, and left sides of the stage. Add another guide 60 pixels from the bottom of the stage.

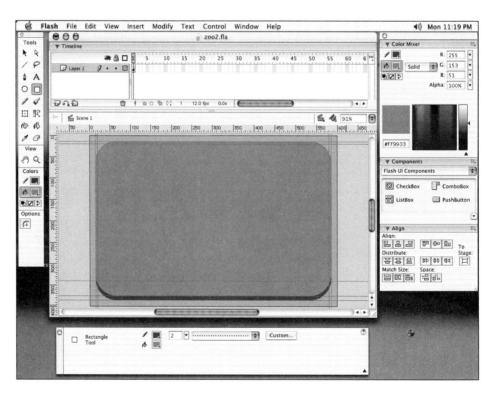

You're going to draw one more rectangle inside of the smaller rectangle created by these new guides. Remember that you can lock or unlock the guides as needed, to make things easier for you. You might find it best to use the arrow tool when you work with guides, as it difficult to select guides with any other tool.

TIP *You can press the shortcut key for the arrow tool (V) to quickly switch to the arrow tool.*

7) Select the rectangle tool and change the Fill Color to #FFFFFF. Draw a third rectangle using the guides that you just added.

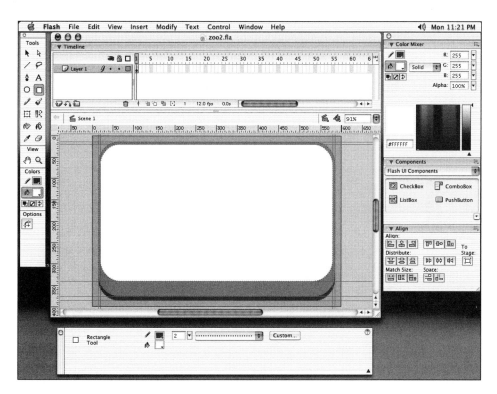

Once again you should use the same stroke settings (height, color, and style) and still have a Corner Radius of 50. Before you change the fill color, make sure nothing on the stage is selected, otherwise you may end up changing the fill color for whatever is selected. Click in the top-left corner of the inner rectangle created by the guides. There are now three corners at the bottom right side of the stage—just drag to the innermost of these corners to make your rectangle. You should end up with a nice background for the movie, made up of three rectangles of varying sizes.

8) Hide the guides and save your movie as zoo3.fla in FlashTFS folder on your hard drive.

You can, and probably should, hide the guides by choosing View > Guides > Show Guides. You're going to keep working on this file in the next exercise, so keep it open for now.

CREATING A GROUP

You can manipulate elements on the stage as a single object by grouping them. This capability can be useful when you're working with a complex graphic because, as you will see in this exercise, Flash treats each piece of a vector graphic as a separate object. If you have a graphic that contains several pieces, manipulating all the pieces consistently can be difficult.

In this exercise, you will group all the rectangles that make up the background graphic. You should be working in your zoo3.fla file.

1) Select the arrow tool and click in the white fill of the innermost rectangle on the stage. Press Delete or Backspace.

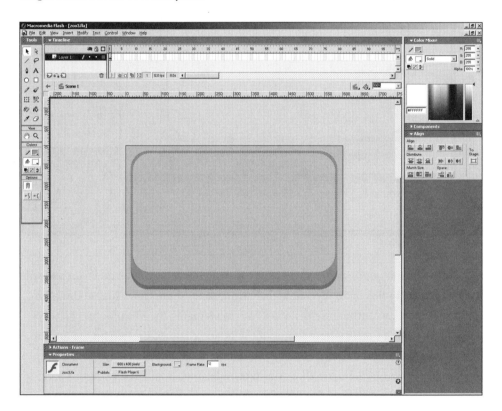

What happened to the other rectangles? You should now have a drawing that looks something like the figure above. If you're familiar with other drawing tools, you're probably somewhat surprised by the results.

Unlike many programs, Flash treats strokes and fills as separate entities. When you selected the rectangle's fill by clicking it with the arrow tool, you selected the interior (the fill), but not the exterior (the stroke). If you use the arrow tool to select a fill and move it, the outline stays behind.

Another interesting behavior is that every time one shape overlaps another, the shapes are divided into segments wherever they intersect. So you might have noticed that when you deleted the rectangle's fill, the fill that was behind it is no longer there. That's because drawing the rectangle on top of it removed the other fill from your drawing. The same would be true if you drew a fill over a line—removing the fill would also remove the line behind it.

2) Press Ctrl+Z (Windows) or Command+Z (Macintosh).

This is probably one of the most useful shortcuts in Flash—by pressing Ctrl+Z or Command+Z on the keyboard, you can undo the previous action. It's the same as selecting Edit > Undo from the menu. The number of undo levels is set in the preferences (Edit > Preferences), as you learned in Lesson 1.

When you undo the previous action, the fill you deleted should reappear. Now it's time to select all the shapes you've drawn and put them into a single group so they're a little easier to handle.

TIP *Flash also has a sort of "mega-undo" command. If you really messed up, and just want to go back to the previously saved version of a file, choose File > Revert.*

3) Choose Edit > Select All.

Everything on the stage is selected.

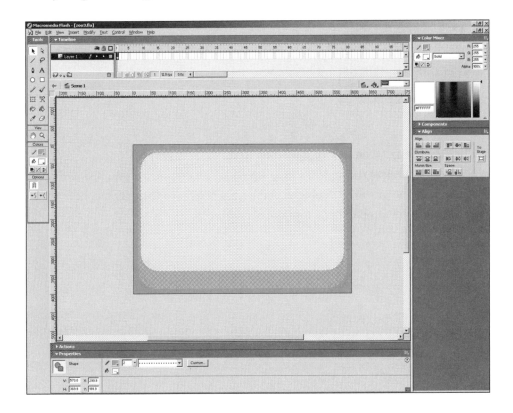

Instead of choosing Edit > Select All, you can press Ctrl+A (Windows) or Command+A (Macintosh). Many of the commands in the menus have shortcuts. You can customize the keyboard shortcuts by choosing Edit > Keyboard Shortcuts, as you learned in Lesson 1.

4) Choose Modify > Group.

Everything you selected—the entire background drawing—is now part of a group. A blue bounding box appears around the group, indicating that it is a single selected element.

As with many commands in Flash, the Group command has a shortcut key. Just press Ctrl+G (Windows) or Command+G (Macintosh) to create a group.

TIP *You can change the color of the bounding box in the preferences window. Choose Edit > Preferences and modify the Highlight Color setting. By default the Highlight Color is blue—change this color by clicking the color box and selecting a new color with the pointer.*

5) Double-click the group.

In the top-left corner of the screen, just below the timeline, an icon labeled Group appears, indicating that you are editing a group. You can now edit any part of the group without disturbing the rest of the movie.

6) Click the Scene 1 icon next to the Group icon.

This takes you back to the movie, so you are no longer editing the group. You can also go back to the movie by double-clicking anywhere outside the group, or by clicking the Back button to the left of the Scene 1 icon.

NOTE *The Scene 1 and Group icons are found in an area of the screen known as the information bar. There are several other icons and settings here—move your pointer over each one to see a Tooltip indicating its name. The drop-down menu on the far-right side of the information bar is the zoom control, which allows you to choose different magnification settings for the stage. You can choose 25%, 50%, 100%, 200%, 400%, or 800% to zoom in or out from the current magnification. The Show Frame option lets you view the entire stage, while the Show All option lets you view the contents of the stage. If you choose Show All, and the stage is empty, the entire stage is displayed. You can also type a number into the zoom control, and when you press Enter, Flash will set the current magnification to that level. Flash can zoom in as much as 2000% and out as little as 8%.*

7) Save your movie as zoo4.fla in the FlashTFS folder on your hard drive.

Now it's time to add a little content to the movie. That's what you'll do over the course of the next several lessons in this book.

USING LAYERS

Layers act like a stack of transparent sheets. Layers are "stacked" on top of one another, and you can see their stacking order in the timeline. The layer on top is the highest in the stacking order, and the layer at the bottom is the lowest in the stacking order. Objects in the higher layer can obscure objects in the lower layer.

Layers are great for organizing content in your movie. You can name layers, hide their contents, and lock them so that they cannot be edited. Layers are also great for keeping shapes from segmenting each other.

You should still have zoo4.fla from the last exercise open.

1) Choose Modify › Layer. In the Layer Properties dialog box, type *Background* in the Name field, select the Lock option, and click OK.

When you choose Modify > Layer, the Layer Properties dialog box opens.

You have only one layer in your movie right now; it's called Layer 1. Because you have only one layer, the Layer Properties dialog box displays the properties of that layer.

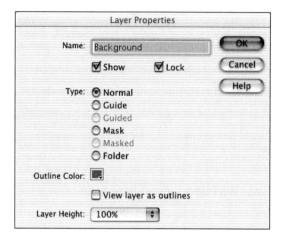

After you type *Background* in the Name field, select the Lock option, and click OK. The Layer Properties dialog box should close. The name of the layer changes from Layer 1 to Background and a lock icon appears to the right of the layer name. This indicates that the layer is now locked. The Lock option lets you lock a layer, which is useful when you don't want to move items in a layer accidentally. When you lock a layer, you can no longer select anything in that layer, but you can still see its contents. You are also prevented from adding anything to the layer.

When the Show option in the Layer Properties dialog box is selected, as it is by default, the layer is visible. If you deselect this option and click OK, you'll see that the layer becomes invisible. Be aware that the layer is only invisible in authoring mode. If you test the movie you will see that the layer is still there.

The more complex your movie, the more layers it might contain, and the harder it is to keep track of each layer. It's a good idea to name each layer. Try to give each layer a meaningful name to make it easier to find the layer you need.

2) Choose Insert > Layer to add another layer to the movie.

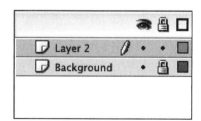

A new layer is added above the Background layer, which means that it sits at the top of the layer stacking order. Whenever you add a layer to your movie, it's added above the currently selected layer. In this case, you have only one layer, so it's selected by default and the new layer is added above it. Objects in a higher layer can obscure objects in the layers below it, so if you add anything to this new layer, it may obscure the contents of the Background layer.

There is no keyboard shortcut for the Insert Layer command, but as you learned in Lesson 1, you can add one. In addition to the menu command for inserting a layer, you can also right-click (Windows) or Control-click (Macintosh) the name of a layer and choose Insert Layer. There is a button associated with the Insert Layer command—it's at the bottom left of the timeline, just above the information bar.

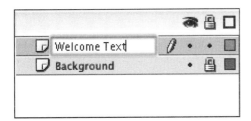

INSERT LAYER BUTTON   DELETE LAYER BUTTON

If you ever need to remove a layer, just click its name, and then click the Delete Layer button. You can also right-click (Windows) or Control-click (Macintosh) the layer's name and choose Delete Layer.

3) Double-click the name of Layer 2. When the name is highlighted, type *Welcome Text* to change the layer name.

The layer is now named Welcome Text. You could have renamed it using the Layer Properties dialog box, as you did in step 1, but this method is a little faster. If you double-click the icon to the left of the name, the Layer Properties dialog box opens. You can use either method to rename a layer.

You now have two layers in your movie. Take a look at the timeline—do you see a pencil icon to the right of the Welcome Text layer's name? That icon indicates that the Welcome Text layer is the active layer, which means that the layer is currently selected, and anything you add to the stage will be added to that layer. You should see a lock icon at the far right of the name of the Background layer. If you select the Background layer, you will notice that the pencil icon appears to the right of the

Background layer's name with a red line through it. The red line indicates that even though you have the Background layer selected, you can't add to it.

In addition to the lock and pencil icons, you should notice a few dots to the right of your layer names. Click each of the dots to see what happens. If you click a dot below the Show/Hide All layers control, you toggle the visibility of that layer. This is the same as selecting or de-selecting the Show option in the Layer Properties dialog box. If you click on a dot below the Lock/Unlock All layers control you will lock or unlock that layer.

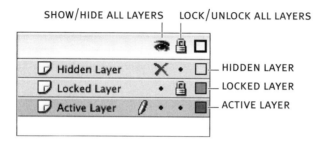

4) Select the Welcome Text layer.

You can select the Welcome Text layer by clicking on its name. Don't double-click, as that will highlight the name so you can change it. Remember that the pencil icon indicates that a layer is active.

5) Select the rectangle tool and in the Property inspector set the Fill Color to no color, the Stroke Color to #FF9933, and the Stroke Style to Hairline. Set the Corner Radius to 0 and draw a small rectangle on the stage.

The dimensions for this rectangle don't really matter right now—you're going to change them soon. Just make sure that when you draw the rectangle, it appears with a thin orange outline, and no fill. The corners of the rectangle should also be sharp, since you set the Corner Radius to 0.

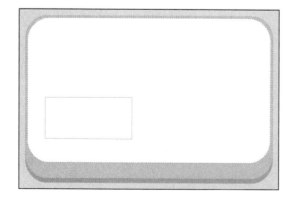

NOTE *Did you forget how to change the Corner Radius? Simply click the Round Rectangle Radius button in the Options area of the toolbox, and change the settings.*

The most important thing is to make sure you drew the rectangle in the correct layer. If you checked to make sure the pencil icon indicated that the Welcome Text layer was active, you should be OK. You should be doubly OK if the lock icon still appears to the right of the Background layer's name—you can't draw anything in a layer if it is locked. Check the timeline and you should see a black dot in the Welcome Text layer if you drew the rectangle in the right place. Otherwise you may see a hollow dot. You'll learn much more about the timeline in Lesson 4, including the name for those dots.

6) Select the arrow tool, and double-click any segment of the stroke you just added to the stage. In the Property inspector set the Width (W) to 225, Height (H) to 115, x-coordinate (X) to 80, and y-coordinate (Y) to 205.

NOTE *It's usually a good idea to press Enter or Return after typing a value in a panel. Otherwise the value will not take effect. You can also press Tab after entering a value—that will apply the value and take you to the next setting.*

The Property inspector can do much more than change colors for you! You can use it to set the dimensions and coordinates of any shape you select. That's often easier than attempting to draw shapes exactly where you want them, at exactly the dimensions you'll need.

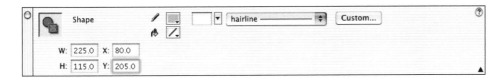

If you would rather draw a shape on the stage and resize it by eye (so it looks right, instead of having exact dimensions) you can use the free transform tool. Just select the shape you want to modify and then select the free transform tool from the toolbox. A set of rectangular handles and a bounding box appear around the selected element. You can drag the handles to scale the selected element horizontally, vertically, or both. Just drag one of the corner handles to scale the selected element proportionally, or drag one of the center handles to scale the element horizontally or vertically. You can also skew and rotate an element selected with the free transform tool. To skew the selected element, move the pointer over the bounding box between the handles and drag. To rotate the selected element, move the pointer just outside a corner handle and drag.

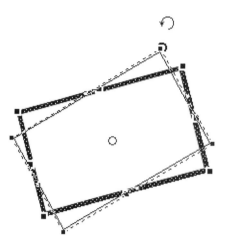

You can also use the free transform tool to distort shapes, but not anything else (for example, you can't distort groups or imported bitmaps). Just press the Ctrl (Windows) or Command (Macintosh) and drag a corner handle or a center handle to distort that corner. You can also Shift+Ctrl-drag (Windows) or Shift+Command-drag (Macintosh) a corner handle to taper a shape, or to move the selected corner and the adjoining corner equal distances from their origins.

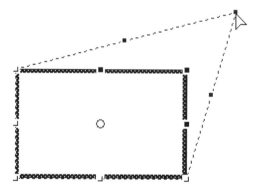

7) Make sure you still have the rectangle in the Welcome Text layer selected. Choose Edit > Duplicate to create a copy of the rectangle.

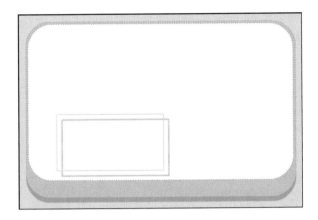

The Duplicate command is a shortcut for Copy and Paste. It creates an exact copy of whatever you had selected and pastes it on the stage. The new copy should still be selected—if it's not, click each of the line segments to select it. If you double-click the new copy, Flash will select not only the new copy, but also the old copy.

8) Choose Window > Transform to open the Transform panel. Deselect the Constrain option and set the height to 60%.

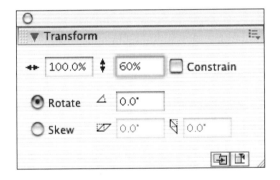

The Transform panel lets you scale, rotate, and skew an element. It's sort of like using the free transform tool, only more precise. If you deselect the Constrain option, you can scale an elements height and width independently, otherwise you will find that as you type a value in one setting, the other setting will change to the same value.

NOTE *If for some reason the height and width percentages are something other than 100% before you make this transformation, delete the duplicated rectangle and click the Reset button in the bottom-right corner of the Transform panel. Then duplicate the original rectangle and attempt this step again.*

9) In the Property inspector set the x-coordinate (X) for the selected rectangle to 335 and the y-coordinate (Y) to 205. Save the file as zoo5.fla in the FlashTFS folder on your hard drive.

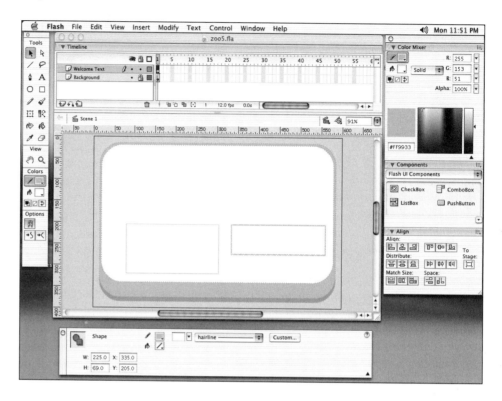

The rectangle should now line up with the top of the other rectangle in the Welcome Text layer. You'll add to this file in just a bit, but you've done so much on the file that now is a great time to save it.

After you save, but before you move on to the next exercise, take a moment to play around with the layers. See what happens if you change the stacking order, which you can do by simply dragging a layer to the desired position. When the Welcome Text layer is beneath the Background layer, you can't see its contents because objects in a higher layer obscure those in a lower layer. You can see the contents of the Welcome Text layer when it's on top because there's nothing above it to obscure that layer. When you're finished playing, make sure you choose File > Revert to return to the previously saved version of the movie, and then continue to the next exercise.

ADDING TEXT

You can use the text tool to add static, dynamic, or input text to your movie. In this exercise you'll add some static text, and you'll use the Property inspector to modify the settings for that text.

You should have zoo5.fla open from the previous exercise.

1) Select the text tool from the toolbox. In the Property inspector set the Font to Verdana, the Font Size to 10, Character Spacing to 2, and Text (fill) Color to #CC0000 (red).

To set the Font Size and Character Spacing, you can either type the desired value in the box, or drag the slider to the right of the text box up or down until you get the desired value.

You should have no trouble setting the Text (fill) Color—it works much like the stroke and fill color settings. Click the Text (fill) Color box and either type the hexadecimal number for the color you want in the space provided, or choose the color from the color pop-up.

Leave all the other settings in the Property inspector in their default positions. Specifically, bold and italic should not be selected, the Character Position should be Normal, the URL link box should be empty. The Text Direction should be horizontal, and the text should be left justified. You should also deselect the Auto Kern option if it's selected.

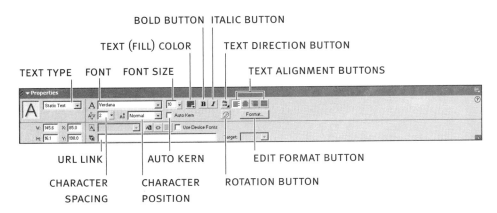

It's important to consider the font when you add text in Flash. When adding static text, if you use a font that is installed on your system, the characters that you add are embedded in the file. This will ensure that the font is displayed exactly as it's displayed on your computer, regardless of whether the person viewing the finished movie has that font installed. Not all fonts can be exported with a movie. A quick

65

test to see if a font can be embedded is to choose View > Antialias Text. If the text becomes jagged, Flash cannot embed the font.

You can also use *device fonts*, namely _sans, _serif, and _typewriter in your movies. Device fonts are not embedded in Flash .swf file; rather the Flash Player uses whatever font most closely resembles the device font. Device fonts are not anti-aliased (edges smoothed out), so they can be sharper and more legible than embedded fonts at small point sizes (below 10 points). Because different computers have different device fonts, the text may appear differently on a different computer.

If you like the sharp look of a smaller device font but want to make sure that your text appears the same on every computer, you should use a pixel font. Pixel fonts are specially designed fonts that appear aliased, making them much more legible at smaller sizes. Appendix C lists several Web sites that have more information about pixel, and other, fonts.

2) Click the stage and type *Our Newest Addition*. Select the arrow tool and click the text box to select it.

When you click the stage, a text box appears. Anything you type appears in that text box, using the properties you set in the Property inspector.

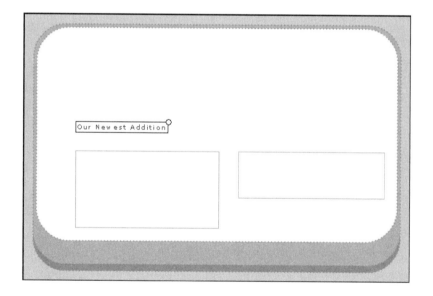

When you add static text to the stage, you can click and type to create a text box with a single line that expands as you type, as you did in this step. Or you can click, drag, and type to create a fixed-width block (for horizontal text) or fixed-height block (for vertical text) that expands and automatically wraps words. When adding or editing text in a text box, Flash displays a handle at the top-right corner of the text box to

66

identify its type. Text boxes that extend have a round handle and text boxes with a defined height have a square handle.

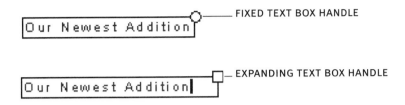

When you use the text tool, you can't just press V to switch to the arrow tool, because the letter *v* will appear in the text box. And if you don't switch to the arrow tool before you click the stage, Flash will create another text box.

If you accidentally double-click the text box you just created, Flash will switch back to the text tool. Make sure that you click the text box just once.

3) Use the Property inspector to set the X and Y of the selected text box to 85 and 190, respectively.
The text box is now just above the rectangle on the left.

4) Deselect the text box and select the text tool again. In the Property inspector, change the Character Spacing to 0 and the Text (fill) Color to black (#000000).
Leave all the other settings as they were for the last text box. If you don't deselect the text box before you make these changes in the Property inspector, the selected text box will have the changes applied to it. You don't want this to happen—it looks nice the way it is! So just click outside it to deselect the text box and then make the changes.

5) Click the stage and drag to the right to create a text box that's just a bit smaller than the rectangle on the left side of the stage in the Welcome Text layer. Add some text to this new text box.

Our Newest Addition

It doesn't matter what you type in this text box, as long as it's enough text to demonstrate that the fixed-width text box will automatically wrap words. The text that was used in the source file on the CD is as follows:

Please welcome the newest addition to ZooMX, a baby cheetah by the name of Astra. Cheetahs have been hunted nearly to extinction in the wild, and the arrival of baby Astra is a rare and special event. You can visit Astra daily from noon until 1PM at the Conservation Building.

6) Select the arrow tool. Position the text box that you just added inside of the rectangle on the left side of the stage.

Our Newest Addition

Please welcome the newest addition to
ZooMX, a baby cheetah by the name of
Astra. Cheetahs have been hunted nearly
to extinction in the wild, and the arrival of
baby Astra is a rare and special event.
You can visit Astra daily from noon until
1PM at the Conservation Building.

You can use the Align panel to position the text box so that it lines up with the text box you added earlier in this exercise. Just select both text boxes and click the Align Left Edge button in the Align panel. This will line up the text boxes on the farthest-left edge. Play around with the settings in the Align panel until you like the way text box looks. If you make a change, and it doesn't look great, just choose Edit > Undo or press Ctrl+Z (Windows) or Command+Z (Macintosh).

N O T E *The Align panel should be on the right side of the screen, where you placed it in Lesson 1. If you can't find it, choose Window > Align to open it again.*

ALIGN LEFT EDGE ——

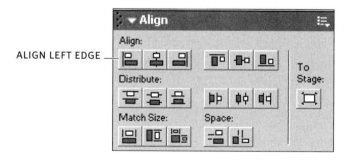

If you don't want to use the Align panel to position the text box, you can use the Property inspector. Or, you can always drag it around with the arrow tool until you find the position you want.

7) Duplicate the text box containing the text *Our Newest Addition* and position it above the rectangle on the right side of the stage. Double-click the text box and change the text to *Welcome*.

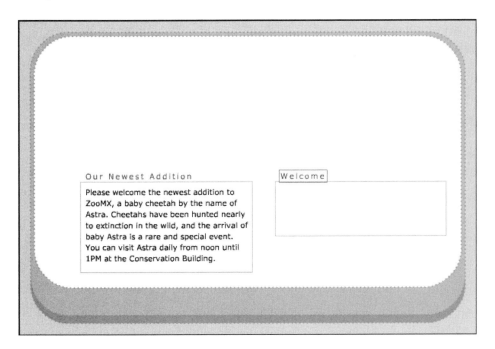

To duplicate the text box, use the arrow tool to select it, and choose Edit > Duplicate to make a copy. You can then use the arrow tool to move the text box above the rectangle on the right side of the stage. If you'd like to make sure the new text box lines up with the rectangle on the bottom, you can use the Align panel—select both text boxes and click the Align Top Edge button.

8) Add a fixed-width text box containing some text inside the rectangle on the right side of the stage. Choose Control > Test Movie.

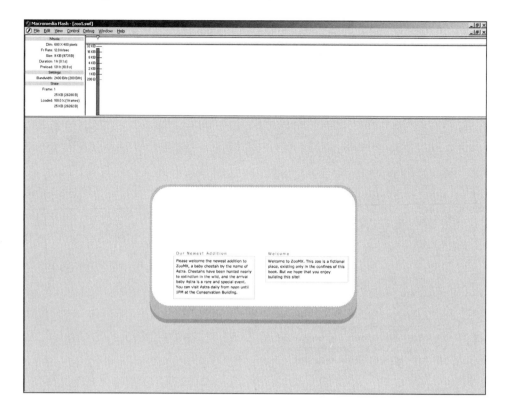

For this text box, you should use the settings you used for the text box inside the rectangle on the left side of the stage. You can quickly grab those settings using the eyedropper tool. Select the eyedropper tool from the toolbox and click the text box that has the properties you want to duplicate. The pointer will switch to the text tool's icon, at which point you can click and drag to create your fixed-width text box.

As before, you can add any text you want. The source file on the CD uses this text:

Welcome to ZooMX. This zoo is a fictional place, existing only in the confines of this book. But we hope that you enjoy building this site!

When you choose Control > Test Movie, Flash creates an .swf file in the same folder where you saved your .fla file. It then opens that .swf file in a separate window and displays it in the Flash Player. This is what your Flash movie would look like if you were to prepare it for the Web right now. It's still pretty boring, but now it contains some graphics and text.

If you don't like the way the text looks, think about how you could modify it. You could easily change the size if it's too small for your taste, or you could change the font, color, or any other setting. Don't limit your experimenting to the settings listed in these exercises—you'll find it's much easier to learn Flash when you play around with the settings as you go through each step.

9) Close the Test Movie window and save the file as zoo6.fla.
You've made some major changes to your movie, so now is a great time to save your work.

WHAT YOU HAVE LEARNED

In this lesson, you have:

- Explored the drawing tools (pages 36–42)

- Used the drawing tools to draw several rectangles (pages 42–48)

- Used the Property inspector to modify the settings for each rectangle (pages 48–53)

- Created a group and learned how to edit that group (pages 54–57)

- Added and modified layers, while exploring many of the settings for layers (pages 57–64)

- Learned how to use the text tool and learned about many of the properties for that tool (pages 65–71)

using symbols and the library

You've learned how to use Flash's tools and panels to create, modify, position, and import basic elements—such as text and graphics—for your Flash movies. Even using simple elements, your movies can quickly become large and complex. In this lesson, you'll learn how to use symbols, libraries, and the Movie Explorer to manage your movies and keep them small, fast, and organized. You will also learn how to use and import bitmaps.

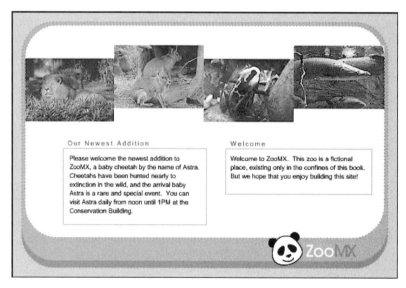

This is what the ZooMX Web site will look like after this lesson.

Chrissy Rey

WHAT YOU WILL LEARN

In this lesson, you will:

- Learn about the file types that can be imported

- Import bitmaps

- Create a symbol

- Explore the Library panel

- Create a folder to organize the contents of the library

- Open an existing movie as a library

- Add instances of symbols to the movie

- Edit symbols and groups

- Use the Movie Explorer

APPROXIMATE TIME

This lesson takes approximately one hour to complete.

LESSON FILES

Media Files:

Lesson03/Assets/assets.fla

Lesson03/Assets/fish.jpg

Lesson03/Assets/frog.jpg

Lesson03/Assets/lion.jpg

Lesson03/Assets/mara.jpg

Lesson03/Assets/sleepy_tiger.jpg

Starting Files:

Lesson03/Starting/zoo6.fla

Completed Project:

Lesson03/Completed/zoo13.fla

IMPORTING BITMAPS

Flash supports two image formats: *vector* and *raster*. Vector graphics are created with lines, curves, and descriptions of their properties. Commands within a vector graphic tell your computer how to display the lines and shapes, what colors to use, how wide to make the lines, and so on. You have already added some vector graphics to your movie—the shapes you drew in Lesson 2. In fact, most strokes and fills you make using Flash's drawing tools are vector graphics. You might have also used a drawing program, such as Macromedia FreeHand, to create such images. Raster images, also called *bitmaps*, are created with pixels. When you create a raster image, you map out the placement and color of each pixel, and the resulting bitmap is what you see on the screen.

You are by no means limited to artwork you can create in Flash. You can use your favorite draw program, or you can import existing artwork. Flash can import the following formats in Windows and on a Macintosh: GIF and Animated GIF, JPEG, PNG, Adobe Illustrator (EPS, AI version 6.0 or earlier), AutoCAD DXF (DXF), FreeHand (FH7, FH8, FH9, FH10), FutureSplash Player (SPL), and Flash Player (.swf) files.

In Windows, you can also import Bitmap (BMP), Enhanced Windows Metafile (EMF), and Windows Metafile (WMF) files. On a Macintosh, you can also import PICT files.

If QuickTime 4 is installed, you can import MacPaint (PNTG), Adobe Photoshop (PSD), QuickTime Image (QTIF), PICT, Silicon Graphics Image (SGI), TGA, and TIFF files. QuickTime also lets you import BMP on a Macintosh and PICT in Windows.

In this exercise, you will import some bitmap graphics to add to your movie.

1) Open zoo6.fla.

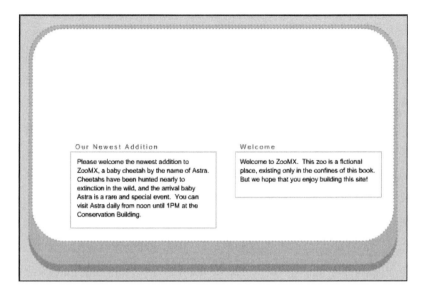

You'll find zoo6.fla in the Lesson03/Starting folder on the CD-ROM that comes with this book. This is the file you completed at the end of Lesson 2, so if you still have it open, you're ready to go.

2) Select the Welcome Text layer, and add a new layer above it. Name the new layer *Main Page Bitmaps*.

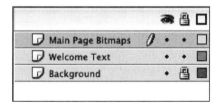

You are going to add your bitmap graphic to this new layer.

You might find it useful to lock all the other layers so you don't accidentally move anything. Right-click (Windows) or Control-click (Macintosh) the name of the newly added Main Page Bitmaps layer and choose Lock Others from the contextual menu.

Remember, you can add a new layer by clicking the Insert Layer button at the bottom of the timeline. You can also choose Insert > Layer or right-click (Windows) or Control-click (Macintosh) the Welcome Text layer and choose Insert Layer from the contextual menu to add a new layer above the selected layer.

75

NOTE *To delete a layer, just select that layer and click the Delete Layer button at the bottom of the timeline.*

3) With the Main Page Bitmaps layer selected, choose File › Import. Browse to lion.jpg in the Lesson03/Assets folder on the CD, and select it. Click Open.

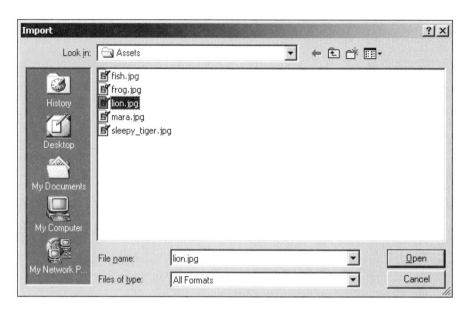

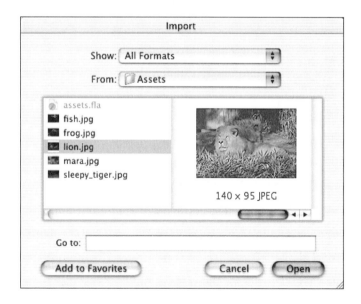

A bitmap graphic, lion.jpg, should appear on the stage. Though Flash is a vector-based authoring tool, you can also use bitmap images in Flash. Bitmap images are not created natively in Flash; you need to use an external application such as Macromedia Fireworks to create the files and then import them into Flash.

Unlike vector graphics, bitmap images are not very scalable. Simple bitmap images are often larger in file size than simple vector graphics, but very complex bitmap images (photographs, for example) are often smaller than comparable vector graphics. Flash can use Bitmap (BMP), GIF Image, JPEG Image, PNG Image, Macintosh PICT Image, MacPaint Image (PNT), and TIFF Image

You can resize imported artwork the same way you resize artwork drawn in Flash, but be careful when you resize bitmap graphics. When you scale a bitmap, you can get *pixelation*, which means that parts of the graphic will not appear smooth. When you resize a vector graphic, such as the graphics you added in Lesson 2, the edges will stay smooth.

4) Select the arrow tool and click the bitmap you just imported. Use the Property inspector to set the X and Y to 20 and 70, respectively.
When you set the X and Y properties, the bitmap appears near the top-right corner of the stage. It overlaps the orange portion of the background a bit, but you'll fix that later in this lesson.

When you select an imported bitmap, the Property inspector indicates that you have selected a bitmap. The usual Height (H), Width (W), X, and Y settings are available. The Property inspector also displays the name of the selected bitmap (lion, jpg, or lion.jpg, depending on your platform). There are also two buttons in the Property inspector: The Swap button lets you swap the selected image with another imported image, and the Edit button opens the imported image in an image editor if you have one installed.

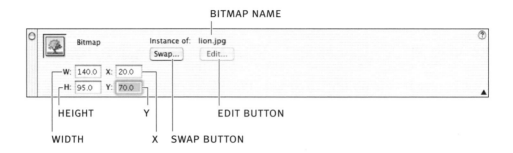

BITMAP NAME

HEIGHT   Y   EDIT BUTTON

WIDTH   X   SWAP BUTTON

5) Choose File > Import to Library. Import fish.jpg, frog.jpg, mara.jpg, and sleepy_tiger.jpg.

When you use the Import to Library command, Flash imports the graphics, but you won't see them on the stage as you did with the lion bitmap. That's because the images are imported directly into the library. Don't worry if you don't know what the library is yet—you'll learn that later in this lesson.

6) Select the lion.jpg bitmap image on the stage, and choose Edit > Duplicate. Select the duplicate copy of the bitmap, and use the Property inspector to set the X and Y to 160 and 50.

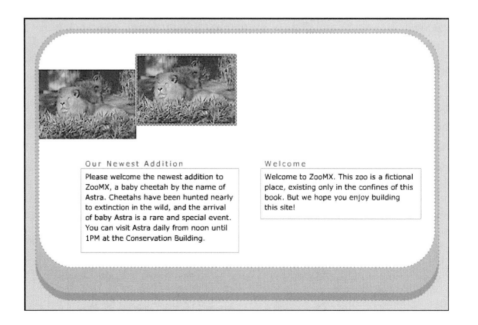

The Duplicate command creates an exact copy of the selected element and pastes the copy on the stage. The duplicated copy should be selected when it's created. If the duplicated copy is not selected when it's copied, use the arrow tool to select the copy. You can then use the Property inspector to move the bitmap to the desired coordinates.

7) Make sure you still have the second copy of the lion.jpg bitmap selected, and click the Swap button in the Property inspector.

When you click the Swap button, the Swap Bitmap dialog box opens. Use this dialog box to swap the selected bitmap for one in the library.

8) Select mara.jpg in the Swap Bitmap dialog box, and click OK.

After you click OK, the second instance of the lion.jpg graphic should be swapped with the mara.jpg graphic.

The Swap Bitmap dialog box displays all the bitmap graphics in the library. You will only see one bitmap on the stage, the lion.jpg graphic, but you should see several bitmaps in the Swap Bitmap dialog box.

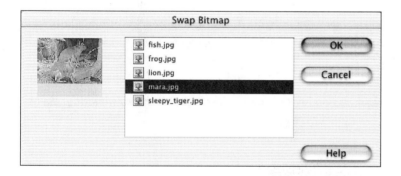

Click each of the filenames. As you do, a thumbnail of the image appears in the dialog box.

9) Save the file as zoo7.fla in the FlashTFS folder on your hard drive.

Now that you have some bitmaps in the movie, let's learn about symbols.

CREATING A SYMBOL

Each object you create increases the size of your final movie. What if you could reuse objects? You can. Any object you intend to use more than once should be turned into a symbol.

Symbols reside in the Flash library. You can drag multiple copies of a symbol from the library to the stage. Each copy of the symbol on the stage is an *instance* of the symbol. Adding multiple instances to your movie does not significantly increase the movie's size. Flash only saves the properties of the new instance; its description already exists in the library. When you change an instance in the library, all instances on the stage are updated.

Instances of symbols can have different colors, sizes, and behaviors.

In this exercise, you'll create a symbol. Later in the lesson, you'll edit this symbol in your Flash movie.

1) Select both of the bitmaps in the Main Page Bitmaps layer, and choose Insert > Convert to Symbol.

To select both bitmaps, Shift-click one bitmap, and then select the second one.

When you choose Insert > Convert to Symbol, the Convert to Symbol dialog box opens. The Convert to Symbol command nests whatever you have selected into a symbol. You can also create a new, empty symbol by choosing Insert > New Symbol, which opens the Create New Symbol dialog box. This dialog box is identical to the Convert to Symbol dialog box.

NOTE *For future reference, both Convert to Symbol and Create New Symbol dialog boxes will be referred to as the Symbol Properties dialog box. The dialog boxes are identical, except for their titles.*

2) In the Symbol Properties dialog box, name the symbol *Bitmap Animation*. Make sure the Behavior is set to Movie Clip.

NAME

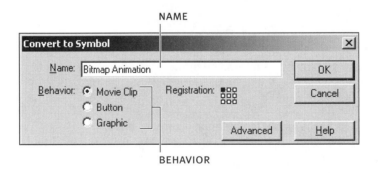

BEHAVIOR

The Symbol Properties dialog box lets you set a name and behavior for a symbol. The name is important because it allows you to keep track of all your symbols; each symbol must have a unique name.

Flash has four symbol behaviors: graphic, button, movie clip, and font. You can create graphic, button, and movie clip symbols using the Symbol Properties dialog box.

Graphic symbols are useful for static images and reusable animations that are tied to the timeline. Graphic is the best behavior for a static graphic that you plan to use more than once in your movie. Graphic symbols can contain bitmaps, graphics, and other graphic symbols but cannot contain interactions or sounds. Graphic symbols can also contain movie clips, but if the movie clip includes interactions or sounds, the clip might not work properly in the graphic symbol.

You can use the button behavior to create interactive buttons with different graphics for each button state—you'll make and use a button in Lesson 5. Buttons can contain sounds, graphic symbols, bitmaps, movie clips, and vector graphics.

Many of the symbols you create through the course of this book will be movie clips. Movie clips are great for reusable pieces of animation, which is exactly what the Bitmap Animation is going to be. Unlike graphic symbols, the animation in a movie clip is not tied to the timeline. You'll learn more about timelines in Lesson 4 when you start creating animations. Movie clips are basically minimovies inside the main movie. Movie clips can contain interactions, sounds, and other movie clips, as well as vector graphics, bitmaps, and graphic symbols.

3) Set the Registration to the top-left corner. Click OK.

REGISTRATION

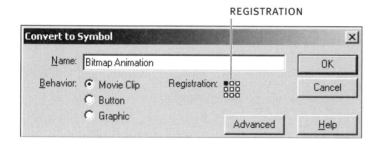

To set the registration, click the top-left square of the diagram in the Symbol Properties dialog box. Selecting the top-left square sets the registration point of the symbol to its top-left corner. The registration point of a symbol is the origin for the symbol, where its X and Y coordinates are both 0. You can set the registration point of a symbol to its top-left corner, top-middle edge, top-right corner, middle-left edge, center, middle-right edge, bottom-left corner, bottom-middle edge, or bottom-right corner. As you move right and down from the registration point of a symbol, the X and Y coordinates increase.

When you click OK, Flash creates an instance of the Bitmap Animation movie clip. You should see a bounding box around both of the bitmaps, which are now nested inside the symbol. You should also notice a crosshair and white dot, the registration point, in the top-left corner of the symbol.

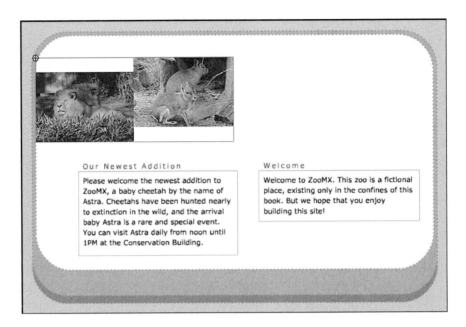

In addition to the Name, Behavior, and Registration properties, the Symbol Properties dialog box has an Advanced button. Clicking the Advanced button expands the dialog box to include Linkage and Source. You'll learn more about these properties later in the book.

NOTE *When you set the Behavior and Registration properties for a symbol, the next symbol you create automatically has the same properties. For example, if you create a symbol and set its Behavior to Movie Clip, the next time you open the Symbol Properties dialog box to create a new symbol, the Behavior will be set to Movie Clip. You can easily change the settings for the behavior and registration.*

4) Save the file as zoo8.fla.

You now have a symbol in your movie. An instance of that symbol sits on the stage in the Main Page Bitmaps layer. Remember, an instance is just a copy of the original symbol.

Keep the file open, as you will use it in the next exercise.

USING THE LIBRARY

All symbols and any bitmaps, sounds, or videos you import are stored in the movie's library. You can take an instance of anything in the library and place it on the stage. The Library panel has many useful features that allow you to organize your movie's assets (symbols, bitmaps, and sounds).

In this exercise you'll explore some of the library's features. Before you begin, make sure that zoo8.fla, the file you saved in the last exercise, is open.

1) Open the Library panel by choosing Window > Library or by pressing Ctrl+L (Windows) or Command+L (Macintosh).

The Library panel appears. The name of the current Flash movie should appear at the top of the panel. Since you can open libraries from other movies, it's important to remember which movie you're currently using.

Symbols, bitmaps, sound files, and video clips are stored in the Library panel. You can use the column headings to sort the assets in the library. When you click the Wide Library View button, you will see additional columns. The Kind column lists the type of asset—for example, Bitmap. The Use Count column lists the number of times an asset is used in the movie—you can update this number by choosing the Update Use Counts command from the Options menu. The Linkage menu lists whether the symbol is to be exported with the movie—you'll learn more about this later in the book. The Date Modified column shows the last date and time an asset was modified. You can reverse the sort order by clicking the Toggle Sorting Order button. Click the Narrow Library View button to return the Library panel to its original size.

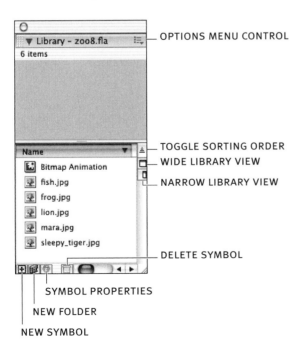

OPTIONS MENU CONTROL

TOGGLE SORTING ORDER
WIDE LIBRARY VIEW
NARROW LIBRARY VIEW

DELETE SYMBOL

SYMBOL PROPERTIES

NEW FOLDER

NEW SYMBOL

2) Click the Options menu control in the top-right corner of the Library panel, and take a look at the available commands.

The Library panel's Options menu has a lot of commands—more than any other panel. Don't be intimidated, though! These commands will be very useful as you work with assets in your Flash movies.

NOTE *If you'd like to practice using these commands as we go along, you might want to make a new movie and experiment on it.*

The New Symbol command opens the Symbol Properties dialog box. When you create a new symbol using the New Symbol command or choose Insert > New Symbol from the main menu, the symbol opens in editing mode. You can also access this command by clicking the New Symbol button in the bottom-left corner of the library. After you add graphics and other assets to the new symbol, choose Edit > Edit Document to return to the main movie. You'll learn more about editing symbols later in this lesson.

The New Folder command lets you create a new folder in the Library panel. You should use folders to help organize the assets in the library. You'll create a folder and move some assets to a folder later in this exercise.

If you created a test movie, go through and select some of the other options in this menu. You will use many of the Option menu commands later in this book, but try using some of the commands such as Expand Folder and Collapse Folder throughout this lesson. If you mess up, you can always choose File > Revert to go back to the previously saved version of your file.

> **NOTE** *One word of caution: Don't delete anything from the Library panel unless you're absolutely sure you don't need it. You can't undo deletions of assets from the Library panel. To get a deleted asset back, you have to revert to the previously saved version of the file.*

3) Select the Bitmap Animation symbol in the Name column.

If you don't see the Bitmap Animation symbol, just scroll through the library using the scroll bar on the right side of the window until you find it.

When you select the symbol, a graphic representation of that symbol will appear in the Library panel. Notice the icon to the left of the symbol's name—this icon indicates that the symbol is a movie clip.

4) Select the frog.jpg bitmap in the Name column.

When you select a bitmap in the Library panel, you will see a thumbnail of the graphic. Notice the icon to the left of the symbol's name is different from the one next to the Bitmap Animation movie clip that you selected in the last step. Each asset type in the Library has a different icon—even different symbol types have different icons. As you use Flash, you'll learn to recognize the different icons.

NOTE *The name of this bitmap might be either frog.jpg or frog, depending on your system.*

5) Click the New Folder button located in the bottom-left corner of the Library panel.
A new folder appears in the Library panel, with an editable name.

Folders are great for organizing assets in the Library panel. When you add a folder to the library, it's initially empty. You can then drag symbols into the folder, as you're going to do in just a moment. Folders can also be nested inside other folders.

6) Type *Bitmaps* in the folder-name space, and press Enter (Windows) or Return (Macintosh).

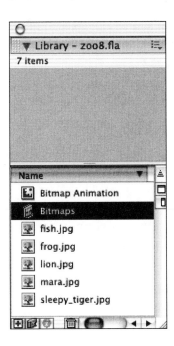

The folder is automatically sorted in alphabetical order with the rest of the contents of the library, unless you clicked one of the other column headers earlier in this exercise.

7) Select each bitmap in the library, and drag them into the Bitmaps folder.

To move a bitmap into the folder, just click the bitmap's name and drag the name over to the folder. Release the mouse button, and the bitmap drops into the folder. If the folder is closed, you won't see the bitmap in the library, but you can double-click on the icon to the left of the folder's name to open the folder. You'll also see the name of each bitmap listed below the folder name.

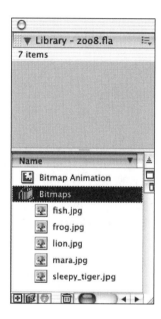

NOTE *When you open the folder, the folder icon changes to indicate that it's open.*

8) Save the file as zoo9.fla.

You now have several assets in this movie's library. You will add more in the next exercise.

OPENING AN EXISTING MOVIE AS A LIBRARY

You are not limited to using the internal library of a Flash movie; you can open other Flash movie libraries by using the Open as Library command (File > Open as Library). You can drag items from one library to another, or drag items onto the stage.

You should have zoo9.fla open when you start this exercise.

1) Choose File > Open as Library. In the Open As Library dialog box, navigate to the Lesson03/Assets folder and select the assets.fla file. Click Open.

The library for assets.fla either opens as a separate Library panel or is nested with the Library panel for zoo9.fla. It's easy to tell which library belongs to assets.fla because the name appears in its title bar. Notice that the newly opened assets.fla library is gray, which indicates that it is not the current library for the file you are editing. You should also see that the buttons along the bottom of the assets.fla library are inactive—you can't edit the library if it's opened as a library, only if it's opened as a movie (File > Open).

NOTE *You cannot open a movie that's opened as a library. For example, if you try to open assets.fla right now, using File > Open, Flash will tell you that the movie is already open. Technically, it is! You have to close the library first, then open the movie.*

2) Select the Logo symbol in the assets.fla library. Drag the symbol to the zoo9.fla library. Then drag the Panda symbol from the assets.fla library to the zoo9.fla library.

When you drag the Logo and Panda symbols into the zoo9.fla library, make sure you don't drop them into the Bitmap folder. You should now have three symbols and a folder full of bitmaps in the zoo9.fla library.

When you add a symbol from another movie's library, you can drag it into the current movie's library, as you just did, or onto the stage. If a symbol in the current movie's library has the same name as a symbol you want to add from another movie's library, Flash will ask you if you want to replace the existing library asset. Make sure you don't replace an asset accidentally, as you can't undo that mistake.

TIP *You can drag individual assets from another movie's library into the current movie's library as well as move entire folders. This capability is a great way to move a large number of assets from one movie to another.*

NOTE *You can only move assets into the current movie's library. In order to add assets to another movie's library, the movie must be open (File > Open).*

3) Click the Options menu control in the top-right corner of the assets.fla library. Choose Close Panel.

The assets.fla library closes. If for some reason you need to, you can now open assets.fla as a movie.

4) Save the file as zoo10.fla.

Now it's time to include some of the assets you added to the library in your movie.

USING INSTANCES

Each instance of a symbol has its own properties. With the options in various panels you can change the appearance of individual instances. The best thing about this capability is that you can change the original symbol (the one that lives in the library) and affect all instances on the stage.

1) Select the Main Page Bitmaps layer, and add a new layer named Logo above it.

You can add a new layer by clicking the Insert Layer button at the bottom-left side of the timeline, or by choosing Insert > Layer.

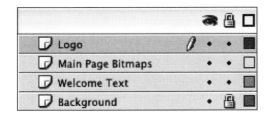

If you don't have the Main Page Bitmaps layer selected when you add this new layer, it will be added above the layer you have selected. You can move the new layer to the top of the layer list, where it needs to be, by clicking its name and dragging it to the top. Drop the Logo layer above all the other layers.

2) Locate the Logo symbol in the zoo10.fla library. Make sure you have the new Logo layer selected, and add an instance of the symbol to the stage by selecting its name and dragging it onto the stage.

You added the Logo symbol in the last exercise—if you don't see it in the zoo10.fla library, all is not lost! Just open assets.fla as a library again, and drag the instance onto the stage from that library.

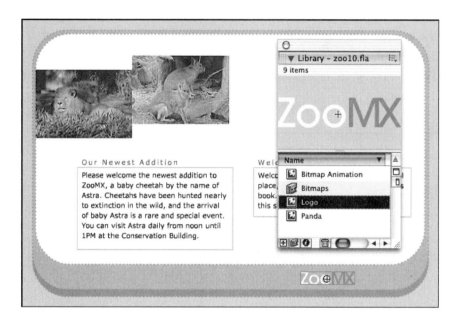

When you are ready to add an asset from the library to the movie, you can drag it by its name, or by the graphic at the top of the Library panel. Make sure you have selected the layer you want before you start dragging the asset. Remember, you will see a pencil icon to the right of the layer's name indicating that it's selected. If there's a line through the pencil icon, the selected layer is either locked or hidden. You can't add assets from the library to locked or hidden layers—you have to unlock or unhide the layer first.

Each copy of the symbol you add to the stage is called an *instance*. Every instance of a symbol has its own properties, such as Width, Height, and Alpha. You can use the Property inspector and several panels to modify the properties of each instance. Although each instance has its own properties, it is linked to the original symbol in the library. Any changes you make in the original symbol affect all instances on the stage and instances inside other symbols.

3) Select the instance of the Logo symbol on the stage. Use the Property inspector to set the X and Y to 460 and 350, respectively.

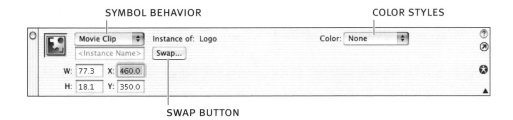

When you select the instance of the Logo symbol, the Property inspector indicates that you currently have a movie clip selected. Use the Symbol Behavior pull-down menu if you need to set an instance to a different behavior (for example, graphic or button).

Below the Symbol Behavior is the Instance Name setting. The instance name for a movie clip is very important when you're working with ActionScript—you'll use this setting later in the book.

The Swap button in the Property inspector lets you swap this instance of the Logo symbol with any other symbol in the library. You can only swap with another movie clip, graphic, or button symbol—not with a font symbol, bitmap, sound, or video. If you do swap the symbol, it will keep all the properties of the original symbol except the dimensions (if the swapped symbol has different dimensions).

The Color Styles property settings are located at the right side of the Property inspector. You can choose None, Brightness, Tint, Alpha, or Advanced from this menu. None removes all color styles from an instance. Brightness modifies the relative lightness or darkness of the image, measured on a scale from black (-100%) to white (100%). Tint colors the instance a percentage of the tint color on a scale from 0% to 100% saturation. Alpha adjusts the transparency of the instance, from completely transparent (0%) to completely opaque (100%). Advanced adjusts the red, green, blue, and transparency values of an instance separately.

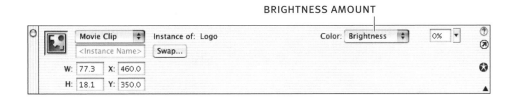

USING SYMBOLS AND THE LIBRARY

As you choose most of the Color Styles options, additional properties are available in the Property inspector. When you select the Brightness and Alpha options, a slider and text box appear on the right side of the panel. You can drag the slider up and down to modify the Brightness and Alpha settings, or you can type a value from –100 to 100 in the text box to modify the Brightness or 0 to 100 to modify the Alpha.

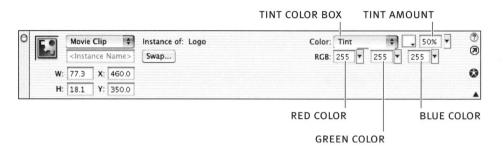

When you select Tint, color options appear where you can set a hue's saturation. When you choose the Tint option, a slider appears. The R (Red), G (Green), and B (Blue) settings determine the hue. You can set the R, G, and B in several ways: by clicking the R, G, and B arrows and dragging the sliders up and down; by typing a number between 0 and 255 in each of the text boxes; or by clicking the Color box in the Property inspector and choosing a color from the color palette.

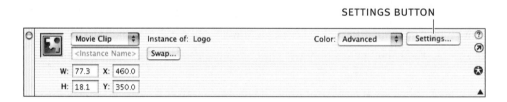

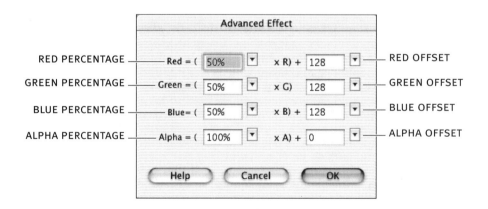

The Advanced option is, to put it mildly, much more advanced. You can use this option to modify the color and the transparency of the instance in relation to the original symbol. When you choose the Advanced option, a Settings button appears. Click that button to open the Advanced Effect dialog box. Typing numbers in the percentage boxes, or dragging the sliders next to them, multiplies the color or transparency value by a percentage of the original. If the instance is pure red, for example, changing the Blue percentage value will not cause a change, but changing the Red percentage will reduce the intensity of the red. Typing a number in the Red offset box (or dragging the slider) adds or subtracts the relevant saturation or transparency from the entire instance. Using the same pure-red instance and typing a positive number in the Blue offset box results in a shade of purple, for example. The equation used to determine the new color is $(a * y + b) = x$ where a is the percentage specified in the percentage boxes, y is the color of the original instance, and b is the value in the offset boxes. Take some time to play with the Advanced option—it's a lot of fun and more obvious in action than in explanation.

4) Insert a new layer named Panda above the Logo layer. Add an instance of the Panda symbol to this layer. Position the instance to the left of the Logo instance.

You are going to animate the instances of the Panda and Logo symbols in the next lesson. As you'll learn when you go through the next lesson, each instance you animate must be on its own layer.

5) Use the Transform panel to set the instance of the Panda symbol to 75% of its original size. Set its rotation to –15.

You can open the Transform panel by choosing Window > Transform. You looked at this panel in Lesson 2, so it should be somewhat familiar. In order to scale both the width and height at the same time, select the Constrain option. Otherwise you have to type 75% in both the Width and Height setting boxes.

TIP *Remember to press Enter or Return after you type a value into a panel to apply any changed setting.*

6) Save the file as zoo11.fla.

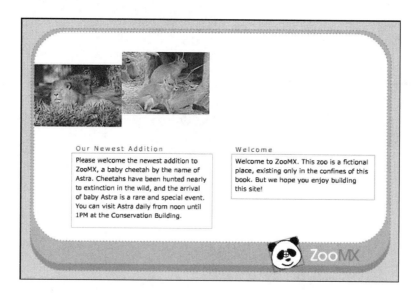

The movie is starting to shape up rather nicely! Let's keep moving—keep the file open while you continue to the next exercise.

EDITING SYMBOLS AND GROUPS

When you edit a symbol, every instance of that symbol is updated, including instances added to the stage in the main movie and instances that are nested inside of other symbols. Similarly, you can make changes to groups. However, if you make copies of the group and edit one of the copies, only the copy you edit will be changed. You will find it very useful to turn anything you plan to use more than once in a movie into a symbol.

In the next exercise you will edit a symbol and a group. Make sure you have zoo11.fla open.

1) Double-click the instance of the Bitmap Animation symbol on the stage.

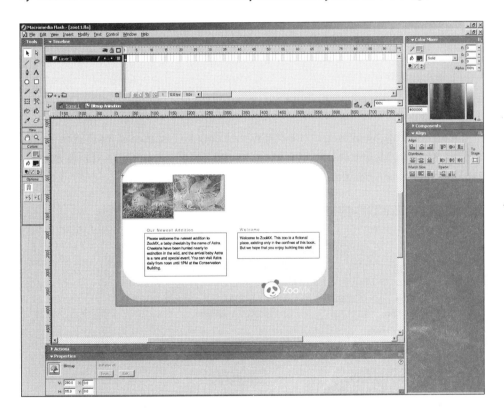

When you double-click the instance of the Bitmap Animation symbol, Flash switches to symbol-editing mode. You can tell you're in symbol-editing mode because the symbol's name appears in the information bar under the timeline. When you open a symbol in symbol-editing mode, you can edit the original symbol. Any changes you make in the original symbol will be reflected in every instance of that symbol used in the movie.

When you open a symbol in symbol-editing mode by double-clicking, the symbol appears in the context of the elements on the stage. The other elements on the stage are dimmed, indicating that they are not currently being edited. This editing mode is useful because it lets you see how your changes will look in the context of the other elements.

There are other ways to open a symbol in symbol-editing mode. From the Library panel you can select a symbol, click the Options menu control, and choose Edit. You can also right-click (Windows) or Control-click (Macintosh) the symbol, either on the stage or in the Library panel, and choose Edit. If you want to work within the library, you can even double-click the icon to the left of the symbol's name, or the graphic at the top of the Library panel, to open the symbol in symbol-editing mode. There are other ways to open a symbol, and as you explore Flash you will undoubtedly find more.

You should notice that the layer name is Layer 1. Don't let that confuse you—the time spent naming all your layers has not been wasted. This Layer 1 refers to the single layer inside the Bitmap Animation symbol. Movie clips, graphic symbols, and buttons have their own timelines, complete with layers.

2) Locate the frog.jpg bitmap in the library, and drag an instance of it onto the stage. Use the Property inspector to position it at X: 280 and Y: 20. Add an instance of the fish.jpg bitmap, and position it at X: 420 and Y: 0.

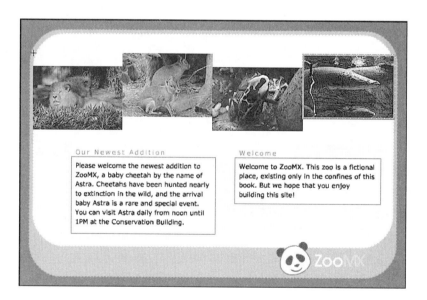

When you add the frog.jpg and fish.jpg bitmaps to the Bitmap Animation, you can see how they will affect the main movie.

3) Click the Scene 1 icon.

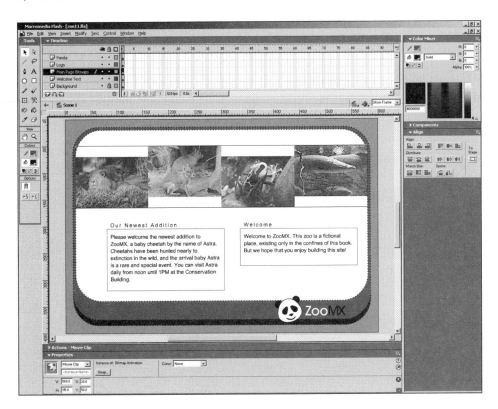

Clicking the Scene 1 icon takes you back to the main movie. The Scene 1 icon is at the left of the symbol's name in the information bar under the timeline. You can also click the Back button in the information bar to go back to the main timeline, or you can choose Edit > Edit Document to return to the main movie.

4) Right-click (Windows) or Control-click (Macintosh) the Background layer, and choose Lock Others. Double-click the group in that layer.

When you choose the Lock Others option, all the layers except the Background layer are locked. This is important, because you don't want to mess up anything on the stage, and you don't want to accidentally edit something other than the contents of the Background layer.

When you double-click a layer, an icon labeled Group appears, indicating that you are editing a group. You can now edit any part of the group without disturbing the rest of the movie.

5) Choose Edit > Select All. Shift-click the white rectangle to deselect it.

Just as you can select multiple items by holding down the Shift key and clicking each element, you can deselect an element by keeping the Shift key down and clicking the element. Right now you want to select everything except the white rectangle in the center, and it's much easier to Shift-click than to click everything except the white rectangle.

6) Choose Edit > Cut. Click the Scene 1 icon.

The Cut command copies whatever you have selected to the Clipboard, and then removes it from the screen. You should end up with just the white rectangle on the stage—that's going to be the background now.

When you click the Scene 1 icon, you are returned to the main movie—remember there are other ways to go to the main menu, so you can use whatever method you like.

7) Add a new layer named Frame above the Main Page Bitmaps layer. Choose Edit › Paste in Place.

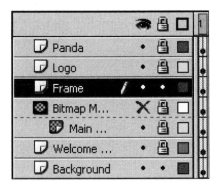

Make sure the new Frame layer goes above the Main Page Bitmaps layer, but below the Logo and Panda layers. When you choose the Paste in Place command, whatever is currently on the Clipboard (the stuff you cut in the last step) is pasted onto the stage in the same position from which it was copied originally. The Paste command, which is also in the Edit menu, pastes whatever is in the Clipboard onto the center of the currently displayed area. So if you've moved the stage around, the Paste command will give you a result very different from Paste in Place.

When you paste the graphics you cut from the group in the Background layer, they should overlap the right and left edges of the Bitmap Animation symbol. If for some reason the graphics do not overlap, make sure the Frame layer is above the Main Page Bitmaps layer.

TIP *The shortcut key for the Paste in Place command is Control+Shift+V (Windows) or Command+Shift+V (Macintosh).*

8) Save the file as zoo12.fla.
It's almost time to start animating! Before you do, make sure to save your movie. In the next exercise, you'll pick up a few tips for keeping track of where everything in the movie is located. Then, in Lesson 4, you will start adding animation to your movie.

USING THE MOVIE EXPLORER

The Movie Explorer provides a hierarchical tree view of every element in your Flash movie. You can filter which categories of items in the movie are displayed in the Movie Explorer, as you will learn in this exercise. You can search, replace text and fonts, and find every instance of any symbol. You can also copy the contents of the Movie Explorer as text to the Clipboard or print the display list in the Movie Explorer.

You should still have zoo12.fla open from the last exercise.

1) Choose Window > Movie Explorer. Select only the Show Text and Show Buttons, Movie Clips, and Graphics buttons.

The Movie Explorer opens. Take a moment to look at the Movie Explorer. Move the pointer over each part—you should see Tooltips when you move over the buttons that are across the top of the Movie Explorer.

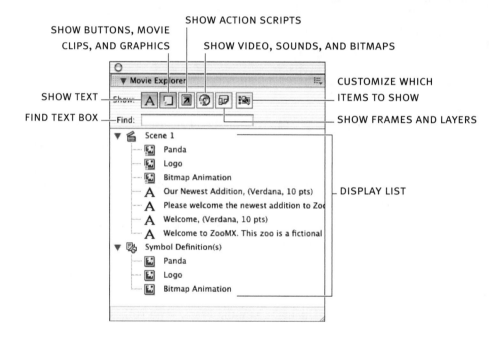

You can turn on a filter by clicking its button. If the Show Text and Show Buttons, Movie Clips, and Graphics buttons are already selected, don't click them. If any other buttons are selected, click them to deselect. Right now, you only want the Show Text and Show Buttons, Movie Clips, and Graphics buttons selected.

The buttons filter the categories of items in the Display List, which is the hierarchical tree view of the filtered elements. When you click the Show Text and Show Buttons, Movie Clips, and Graphics buttons, only these elements appear in the Display List. Move your mouse over each of the other filter buttons to see its Tooltips. The button on the far right, Customize which Items to Show, opens the

102

Movie Explorer Settings dialog box, in which you can select any combination of items to show in the Display List.

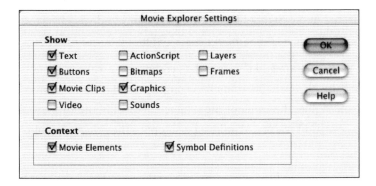

The Display List is currently split into two major categories—Scene 1 and Symbol Definition(s). The Scene 1 category lists all the elements currently in the movie. If you click an item in the Scene 1 category, the instance on the stage is selected, as long as it's in an unlocked, visible layer. The Symbol Definition(s) category lets you open the symbols for editing—it refers to each symbol, and not the instances on the stage. But it does list only the symbols that are listed in the Scene 1 category.

2) Click the Options menu control in the top-right corner of the Movie Explorer.
The Movie Explorer has many commands available via the Options menu. Take a look at some of the options.

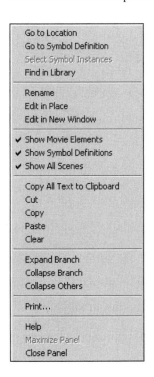

USING SYMBOLS AND THE LIBRARY

The Go to Location command makes the movie jump to the selected location (layer, scene, or frame) in the movie, while the Go to Symbol Definition command selects the symbol definition, in the Symbol Definition(s) category, for the symbol selected. If you have a symbol selected in the Symbol Definition(s) category and you choose Select Symbol Instances, Flash selects the symbol instance(s) in the Scene 1 category.

You can use the Find in Library command to select the symbol in the Library panel. If the Library panel is not already open, choosing this command will open it. The Rename command lets you change the name of the selected symbol in the Library. If you choose Edit in Place or Edit in New Window, Flash opens the selected symbol in symbol-editing mode.

A particularly useful command in the Options menu is Print. You can use this command to make a printed copy of the hierarchical structure in the Display List.

Take some time to explore some of the other commands in the Movie Explorer. As you use Flash, you will find that these commands make working with complex movies much easier.

3) Click the Show Frames and Layers filtering button.

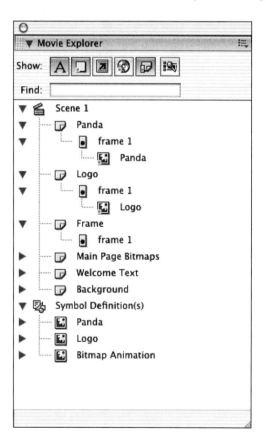

The Display List should change dramatically. Now, instead of showing a list of all the symbols in the movie, the Display List shows how the elements in the movie are arranged by layers and frames. Each of the layers in the main movie is listed under the Scene 1 category. Right now you have only one frame in each layer, but that single frame is also listed, nested under each layer. Finally, you can see which instance is in each layer. Notice that the Frame layer doesn't look as if it has anything—that's because while it does have contents in the layer, they aren't in the Movie Explorer because the filter only shows Text, Buttons, Movie Clips, and Graphics. But aren't the contents of the Frame layer graphics? Technically yes, but they're graphics that aren't part of a symbol.

4) Click the Show Frames and Layers filtering button again. Now click the Show Video, Sounds, and Bitmaps button.

When you click the Show Frames and Layers filtering button the second time, the Movie Explorer's display list switches back to the view you saw originally. After you click the Show Video, Sounds, and Bitmaps button, if you look closely you should notice that a plus sign (+) or expand triangle appears to the left of the Bitmap Animation symbol in the Symbol Definition(s) category.

5) Click the plus sign (+) (Windows) or the expand triangle (Macintosh) next to the Bitmap Animation symbol.

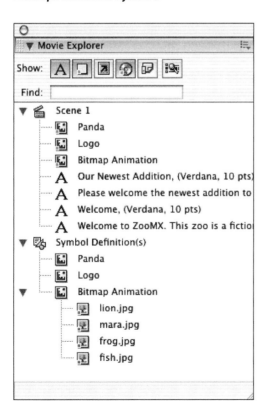

When you click a plus sign or expand triangle in the Movie Explorer, the item next to the plus sign expands, and you can see the filtered contents of that item. In this case, you're filtering for Video, Sounds, and Bitmaps, so you'll see information about the bitmaps in the Bitmap Animation symbol. To collapse a symbol definition, click the minus sign (–) or the expand triangle next to the expanded definition.

6) Click the Lock/Unlock All Layers icon at the top of the timeline. Double-click the Welcome in the Movie Explorer. When the text becomes editable, change it to Welcome to ZooMX, and press Enter (Windows) or Return (Macintosh).

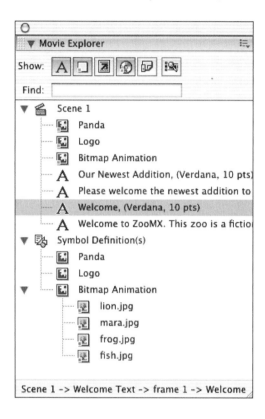

You have to click the Lock/Unlock All Layers icon to unlock all the layers in the movie. If you click the icon and locks appear next to the name of each layer, click the icon again to make the locks disappear. You need the layer unlocked because you can't modify elements in locked layers, and the text you want to select is in a locked layer. You also could have unlocked only the Welcome Text layer, but it is quicker and easier to unlock all layers if you're not sure which layer contains the item you want to select.

You can change the text on the stage, and even symbols on the stage, from within the Movie Explorer. When you modify the text, the change takes place not only in the Movie Explorer but also on the stage. You can modify the properties of just about anything in the Movie Explorer. If you decide that you'd like to use a different font, for example, you can select the text in the Movie Explorer and then change the font in the Property inspector. Notice that when you select anything in the Movie Explorer, the contents of the Property inspector change to display the properties for whatever you have selected.

7) Save your movie as zoo13.fla.

You're done for now. Take a quick break, because in the next lesson you're going to be working on animation for your movie. You'll have the contents of your movie moving around in no time.

WHAT YOU HAVE LEARNED

In this lesson, you have:

- Imported assets into the movie (pages 74–79)

- Created a symbol containing imported bitmaps (pages 79–82)

- Explored the Library panel and organized your assets (pages 83–88)

- Opened an existing movie as a library (pages 88–91)

- Added instances of symbols to the movie (pages 91–96)

- Learned how to edit symbols and groups (pages 97–101)

- Used the Movie Explorer (pages 102–107)

creating animation

LESSON 4

Animation is the process of creating a change over time. Animation can be an object moving from one place to another or scaling from one size to another. A change of color or transparency over time is animation, too. The change can be a morph from one shape to another. Any change of position or appearance that occurs over time is animation.

In Macromedia Flash, you achieve animation by changing the contents of successive frames over a given period. This process can include any of the changes above, in any combination.

Chrissy Rey

You're going to add some animation to the ZooMX Web site.

Flash provides two methods for creating an animation sequence in the timeline: *frame-by-frame animation* and *tweened animation*. To create Flash animation frame by frame, you change the contents of successive frames. You create the image in every frame, although your modifications might be barely noticeable between frames. In tweened animation, you create starting and ending frames and let Flash create the frames in between. Because of its interactive capabilities, Flash can also create dynamic animation that is controlled with ActionScript. You'll learn about ActionScripts in Lesson 7.

WHAT YOU WILL LEARN

In this lesson, you will:

- Create a frame-by-frame animation
- Reverse a sequence of frames
- Extend the time that content is displayed on the stage
- Distribute the contents of a single layer to multiple layers
- Create a motion tween
- Add a mask
- Use a motion guide
- Create a shape tween

APPROXIMATE TIME

This lesson takes approximately one hour to complete.

LESSON FILES

Media Files:
None

Starting Files:
Lesson04/Starting/zoo13.fla

Completed Project:
Lesson04/Completed/zoo19.fla

CREATING A FRAME-BY-FRAME ANIMATION

The most basic form of animation is frame-by-frame animation. Because this type of animation employs unique artwork in each frame, it is ideal for complex animations, such as facial expressions that require subtle changes. Frame-by-frame animation is also useful for making dramatic changes in a short period of time—in a slide show, for example.

Frame-by-frame animation does have drawbacks. Drawing a unique image for each frame can be tedious and time-consuming. And all those unique drawings contribute to a larger file size.

Let's start with a simple frame-by-frame animation.

1) Open zoo13.fla.

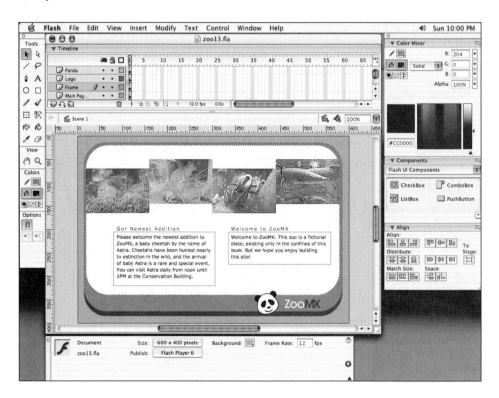

This is the same file you completed at the end of Lesson 3, so if you still have that file open, you can get started. If you don't have it open, you can find it in the Lesson04/Starting folder on the CD-ROM.

2) Select the Panda layer, and choose Insert › Blank Keyframe.

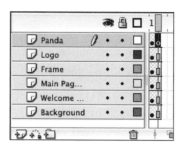

A hollow dot should appear on the timeline in frame 2 of the Panda layer. This hollow dot signifies an empty keyframe in the timeline. A solid black dot signifies a keyframe with something on the stage. In frame 1 of the Panda layer, there's an instance of the Panda symbol on the stage.

A *keyframe* marks a point on the timeline where the contents of a layer change. In this case, the change is from a keyframe containing something (the panda) to a keyframe containing nothing. If you'd like to see what the keyframe looks like, you can choose Control > Play to play the animation.

When you add a blank keyframe to the Panda layer, Flash automatically adds a single frame to each of the other layers. Inserting a frame does not change the animation in a layer; it only extends the animation for a longer period.

Up to this point, you've known the timeline as the place where Flash keeps all your layers, but it's really much more. The timeline enables you to create animation by changing the contents of the stage over time. One way to think of the timeline is as a graph. The *y*-axis of the timeline shows the name of each layer. The *x*-axis, across the top of the timeline, indicates the frame number. Each hash mark indicates a frame, and the numbers over the first frame, and every five subsequent frames, help you find a frame in the "graph." The point at which the two axes intersect is a frame. So, each square in the "graph" is a frame.

3) Select frame 2 of the Logo layer. Shift-click frame 2 of the Background layer; this selects frame 2 in all the layers in between. Select Insert › Blank Keyframe.

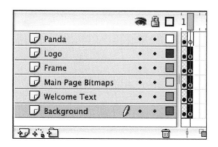

CREATING ANIMATION

You can select a frame by clicking the frame in the timeline. Don't click the number at the top of the timeline—the number simply indicates the number of each frame.

When you select a frame, look at the numbers at the bottom of the timeline. You should see the current frame number, as well as the frame rate for the movie, which you set in the Document Properties dialog box (Modify > Movie). The third number indicates the amount of time that would have elapsed by the time you reach this frame. Right now the number should be 0.1, which indicates that in frame 2 of the animation, 0.1 seconds have elapsed.

When you select frame 2 of the Logo layer, then hold down the Shift key and select frame 2 of the Background layer, Flash selects frame 2 in the Logo, Frame, Main Page Bitmaps, Welcome Text, and Background layers. This great feature lets you select multiple adjacent frames, either layer by layer or in a single layer. Simply click the first frame in the span you want, and then hold down the Shift key and click the last frame you want in the span.

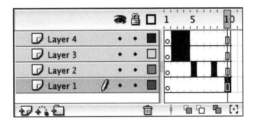

You can also select non-adjacent frames in the timeline. Just click the first frame you want to select, then hold down the Ctrl (Windows) or Command (Macintosh) key and click the next frame you want. If you continue to hold down the Ctrl or Command key, you can keep selecting additional frames.

In Lesson 1, you learned that Flash lets you use frame-based or span-based selection in the timeline. In frame-based selection, which you're using right now, you can select individual frames in the timeline. In span-based selection, you can click a frame, and the entire frame sequence, from one keyframe to the next, is selected. The Span Based setting is located in Flash's Preferences dialog box.

4) Select the blank keyframe in frame 2 of the Panda layer, and drag an instance of the Panda symbol from the Library to the stage.

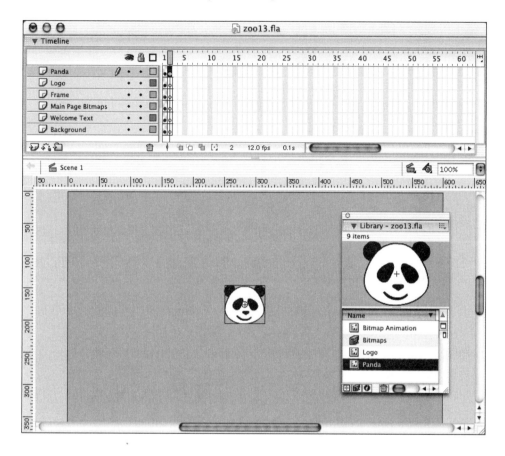

You can select the keyframe in frame 2 of the Panda layer by clicking it.

Before you add the instance of the symbol, make sure the Panda layer is unlocked—otherwise you won't be able to add the instance. It's also a good idea to make sure it's the only layer that's unlocked, so you don't accidentally add the instance of the Panda movie-clip symbol to the wrong layer. Just right-click (Windows) or Control-click (Macintosh) the name of the layer and choose Lock Others from the drop-down menu.

After you've added the instance of the Panda symbol to the keyframe in frame 2 of the Panda layer, the hollow dot that indicated an empty keyframe becomes a solid black dot. That block dot indicates there's something in the keyframe, namely the Panda symbol.

5) Use the Transform panel to set this instance of the Panda symbol to 200% of its original height and width. Then use the Align panel to center this instance horizontally and vertically on the stage.

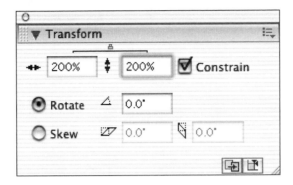

You've used both the Transform and Align panels before. If you can't find them on the screen, look in the Window menu. You can choose Window > Transform to open the Transform panel and Window > Align to open the Align panel.

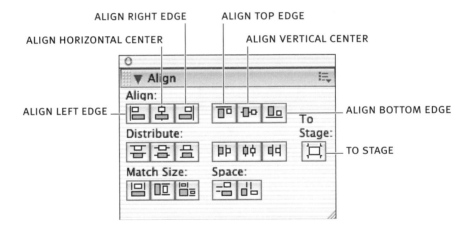

To center a selected element on the stage, you can use the Align panel. Select the element you want to align, and click the To Stage button. Then click the Align Horizontal Center and Align Vertical Center buttons, and whatever you have selected will be centered on the stage. You can also use the Align panel to position elements along the left, right, top, and bottom edges of the stage. Keep the To Stage button selected, and then click the Align Left Edge, Align Right Edge, Align Top Edge, or Align Bottom Edge button to position the element where you want it. You can even select multiple elements, by Shift-clicking each one, and align them all at once using this method.

6) Select frame 1 of the Panda layer, then hold down the Shift key and select frame 2 of the Background layer. Choose Modify > Frames > Reverse.

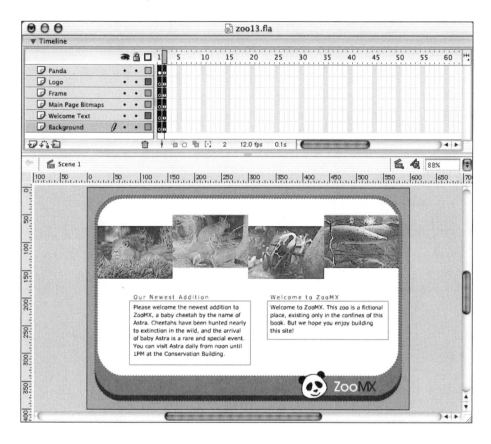

You can reverse the frames in an animation using the Modify > Frames > Reverse command. You can use this command to reverse any number of frames in an animation sequence. Right now you just have two frames, so it'll simply swap the order of the frames. You can reverse a sequence of frames as long as there are keyframes at the beginning and end of the sequence. Select the entire sequence of keyframes and choose Modify > Frames > Reverse. Remember, you can click the first frame, and then hold down the Shift key and click the last frame to select a sequence of frames.

7) Drag the playhead back and forth between frames 1 and 2. Save the file as zoo14.fla.

The *playhead* is the red rectangle above the timeline. It moves through the timeline to indicate the current frame displayed on the stage. To display a frame on the stage, move the playhead to the frame on the timeline. Drag the playhead back and forth between frames 1 and 2 to see what you have accomplished in this step. The animation should start with only an instance of the Panda symbol on the stage, and end in frame 2 with all of the content you added in Lesson 3.

EXTENDING STILL IMAGES

Once you've added some content to your movie, you might want the content to appear on the stage for more than just a split second. You can add content to a keyframe, and extend the time that it's displayed on the stage, by adding frames after it. Inserting a frame does not change the animation in a layer; it only extends the animation for a longer period. The contents of the frame that you just added are identical to those of the preceding frame in the same layer.

1) Drag the playhead over frame 1. Click the playhead to make sure you don't have any frames selected, and then add ten frames to every layer after frame 1 by pressing the F5 key ten times.

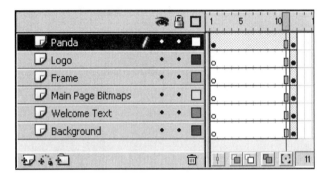

Remember, the playhead is the red rectangle at the top of the timeline. A red line extends through each layer beneath the playhead, so you'll always know where it is. When you drag the playhead to frame 1 and then click the playhead, you won't actually have any frame selected. You're going to add some motion to the movie, so you need a few extra frames over which to perform that motion. When you added ten frames after frame 1, the contents of frame 2 moved to frame 12. The contents of frames 2 through 11 are identical to the contents of frame 1, because all you did was add some frames. Remember that frames only increase the time in your movie; they don't change the animation (except for expanding the time).

TIP *You can tell exactly which frame the playhead is located on by checking the current frame number at the bottom of the timeline.*

2) Drag the playhead to frame 1, and choose Control › Play.

You can get an idea of what the movie will look like by using the Control > Play command. Instead of using the Control > Test Movie command to export the file, the Control > Play command plays the animation. You can watch the playhead move across the timeline as the movie plays.

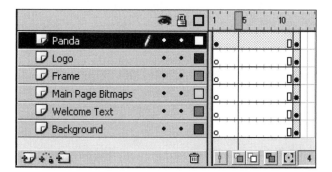

Notice when you play the movie that the Panda symbol instance appears for the first 11 frames, and then all the content you added in Lesson 3 appears in the final frame.

The movie plays at whatever frame rate is set in the Document Properties dialog box (Modify > Document). Right now the frame rate is 12 frames per second (fps). That means that 12 frames are displayed every second, so each frame is displayed for approximately 0.08 seconds.

3) Save the movie as zoo15.fla

You still have a lot to do with this movie, so save the file and get ready to add more animation.

CREATING A MOTION TWEEN

Motion tweening is useful for animating symbols. As its name suggests, motion tweening typically is used to move an element from one place to another, but it can do much more than that. You can use motion tweening to scale, rotate, and skew elements, and to change the color settings and transparency of a symbol over time. You can apply motion tweening to only one element on a layer, so when you want to tween multiple elements, you must use multiple layers.

117

1) Select frame 12 of the Main Page Bitmaps layer, and double-click the instance of the Bitmap Animation symbol on the stage.

TIP *You may find it useful to hide every layer except the Main Page Bitmaps layer. Just right-click (Windows) or Control-click (Macintosh) the Main Page Bitmaps layer, and choose Hide Others in the drop-down menu. Then drag the playhead to frame 12 and double-click whatever is on the stage. That should take you into the Bitmap Animation symbol, but you should still be able to see the stage.*

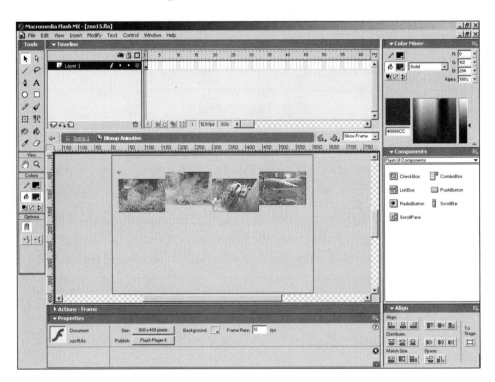

When you double-click the instance of the Bitmap Animation symbol on the stage, Flash switches to symbol-editing mode. You are going to make some changes to this symbol, and it will be useful to see how the changes look in the context of the rest of the movie. You should still see the contents of every layer in the movie while you're in symbol-editing mode.

2) Choose Edit > Select All to select all the bitmaps in the symbol. Now choose Modify > Distribute to Layers.

When you create a motion tween, you must first place each element you want to animate in a separate layer. The Distribute to Layers command makes it easy to create separate layers.

The Distribute to Layers command, which is new in this version of Flash, lets you select elements in one or more layers and distribute each of them to its own layer. In this case, you selected four elements; Flash will create four new layers and place each element in one of the layers. When you distribute symbols or bitmaps, Flash also names each new layer after whatever is distributed to it. So you should end up with layers named lion.jpg, mara.jpg, frog.jpg, and fish.jpg. The layer that contained all the distributed elements stays, but it's empty. Leave the empty layer, which is probably named Layer 1, alone. You will use this empty layer in Lesson 5.

NOTE *Don't worry if your layer names don't contain the .jpg extension. That is perfectly OK—the extension is dependent on your system and won't affect the animation in any way.*

3) Select the lion.jpg bitmap on the stage, and convert it to a graphic symbol named Lion Bitmap. Do the same for the mara.jpg, frog.jpg, and fish.jpg bitmaps, naming the new symbols Mara Bitmap, Frog Bitmap, and Fish Bitmap.

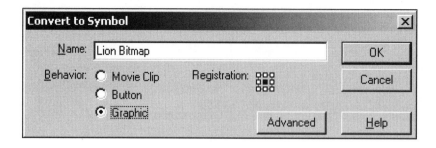

You can convert the lion.jpg bitmap to a graphic symbol by selecting it and choosing Insert > Convert to Symbol. In the Convert to Symbol dialog box, type *Lion Bitmap* in the Name box, and set the Behavior to Graphic. Set the Registration to the top left or center, and then click OK. Repeat this process for the other bitmaps in the movie clip, giving each one the appropriate name.

TIP *Be sure to have only one bitmap selected when you choose Insert > Convert to Symbol. This command puts everything you currently have selected into a single symbol. To avoid mistakes, you may find it useful to lock any layer you're not currently working with, especially when you're first getting started with Flash.*

Graphic symbols are great for static images you plan to use more than once. For any motion tween, you need to use a graphic at least twice—once in the initial position and once in the final position. The graphics will be moving through the motion tween, but the contents of the symbol are actually static. Using the Graphic behavior for symbols results in a smaller file size.

It's important to place each of the bitmaps into a symbol before you proceed, or you might end up with some strangely named symbols in your library! Flash expects symbol instances in each endpoint of a motion tween, and if you don't have one at the endpoint when you perform the next step, Flash makes one for you.

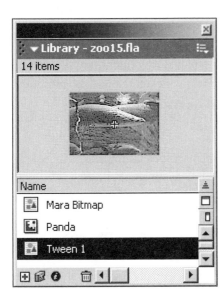

NOTE *If you ever end up with a bunch of symbols named Tween 1, Tween 2, and so on, and you can't remember making them, you probably tried to apply a motion tween to a frame containing something other than a symbol instance. If you should find unknown symbol names, just use the Undo command to go back to the point before you created the motion tween.*

4) Select frame 6 in each layer, and insert a keyframe. Select frame 1 in each layer, except the empty layer, and choose Insert > Create Motion Tween.

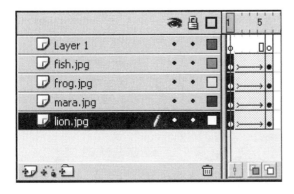

Click in frame 6 of the topmost layer, Shift-click frame 6 in the bottommost layer, and then choose Insert > Keyframe. Make sure you insert a keyframe and not a blank keyframe. When you insert a blank keyframe, you remove any content from the stage in that frame on that layer. If you insert a keyframe, the new keyframe contains the same contents as the previous keyframe in the same layer.

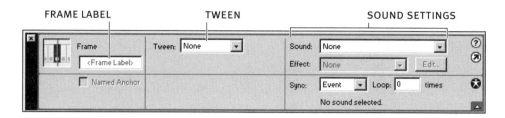

Notice that as you select each keyframe, even if you select all the frames at once, the Property inspector displays the settings for a frame. The settings include Frame Label, Tween, and several sound settings. You'll take a look at the Frame setting in Lesson 5, and you'll work with the sound settings in Lesson 6.

After you choose Insert > Create Motion Tween, a small arrow should appear between frames 1 and 6 of the lion.jpg, mara.jpg, frog.jpg, and fish.jpg layers, indicating that a motion tween has been created. The frames in the motion tween are shaded.

Notice that after you create the motion tween, the Property inspector changes. All the properties for the motion tween appear, including Tween, Scale, and Ease. The Tween setting should be set to Motion, since the selected frames have a motion tween applied to them. If you modify the size of either the initial or final instance in your motion tween and select the Scale option, Flash automatically scales the intermediate frames. The Ease setting allows you to modify the rate of change between tweened frames, and you can select any number between –100 and 100. Negative values simulate acceleration, and positive values simulate deceleration. Setting the Ease value to 0 makes the rate of animation constant.

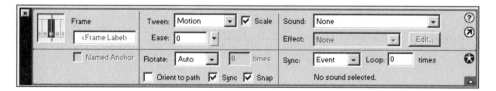

The properties for a motion tween also include Rotate. You can set the Rotate value to None to prevent rotation, Auto to rotate the tweened element once in the direction requiring the least motion, CW to rotate the element clockwise, and CCW to rotate the element counterclockwise. If you choose CW or CCW, the Times field lets you enter a number, which corresponds to the number of times the element will rotate in the indicated direction.

When you create a motion tween, you must have at least two keyframes. The first keyframe contains the initial state of the symbol to be animated, and the last keyframe contains the final state of that symbol. To create the motion tween, Flash interprets the state of the symbol in the in-between frames. You have to make sure to use instances of the same symbol in both the initial and final states. The properties, including the X, Y, Width, and Height, of each instance can be different. Right now the initial and final states of the motion tween are identical—you'll change that in the next step.

Before you continue, check your library to make sure you don't have any symbols named Tween 1 or something similar. If you do, you probably forgot to convert one of the bitmaps to a symbol.

TIP *If you ever need to convert a keyframe back to a frame, just select that keyframe and choose Insert > Clear Keyframe.*

5) Drag the Lion Bitmap symbol instance off the left side of the stage. Move the Mara Bitmap, Frog Bitmap, and Fish Bitmap symbol instances so that they are off the top, bottom, and right sides of the stage, respectively.

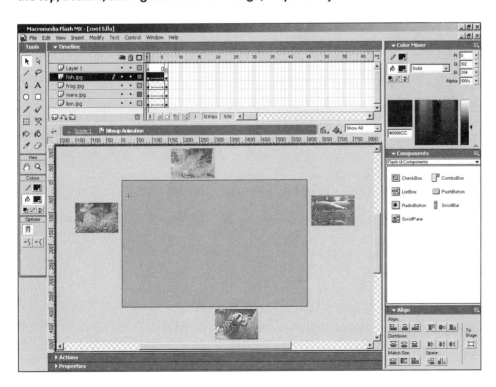

CREATING ANIMATION

As you move each graphic symbol in frame 1, drag the playhead between frames 1 and 6 to see how the animation changes. You should notice that Flash automatically updates the movie clip's animation, creating a smooth animation from each graphic symbol's new initial state to its final state.

In this exercise, you're using a motion tween to animate the movement of elements from one position to another. But you can use motion tweens to do much more. You can animate changes in scale, rotation, and skew. If you use a symbol in both the initial and final states, as you did in this exercise, you can also animate changes in color and transparency.

NOTE *You can only animate changes in color and transparency when using symbol instances because those settings are only available in the Property inspector for symbol instances. The Property inspector allows you to animate changes in color and transparency only for symbols. You can't apply color effects directly to bitmaps.*

TIP *It's almost always a good idea to convert anything you're going to use in a motion tween to a symbol.*

6) Drag the playhead to frame 1, and choose Control > Play. Save the file as zoo16.fla.

You now have a nice animation. It's actually relatively complex, with elements moving on several different layers. But as you can see, Flash makes creating such complex animations simple.

You may notice as you play the movie that the animated bitmaps appear outside the frame in the Frame layer. You'll add a mask to fix that in the next exercise.

NOTE *If you choose Control > Test Movie to see the animation, you might not be able to see it. That's because by default, Flash movies loop. So the movie will get to the last frame and then jump back to the first frame and continue to play. If you want to stop the looping in the Test Movie window, choose Control > Loop. If there's a check next to the command, the movie will loop. If the Loop command is not checked, the movie will play once and then stop.*

USING A MASK

You can use a mask layer to create a hole through which the contents of one or more underlying layers are visible. You can group multiple layers below a single mask layer to create sophisticated effects. You cannot mask layers inside buttons.

1) Click the Scene 1 icon, or choose Edit > Edit Document. Lock all the layers in the movie, select frame 12 of the Background layer, and choose Edit > Copy Frames.

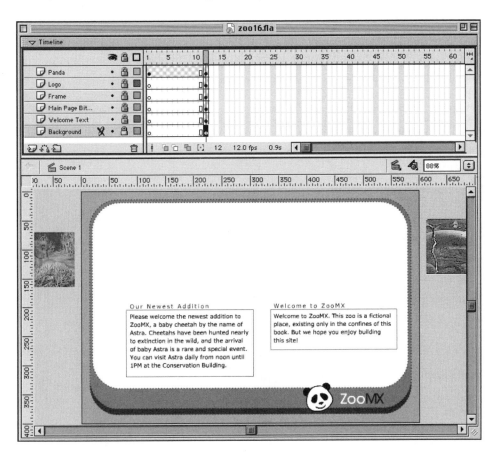

When you click the Scene 1 icon to return to the main movie, notice that the bitmaps in the Main Page Bitmaps layer appear off the sides of the stage. That means that when you publish your movie in Lesson 12, the bitmaps will appear off the edges of the movie. When the instance of the Bitmap Animation plays, the bitmap instances will move to the middle of the stage, as they appeared before you added your motion tween.

You can lock all the layers in the movie by clicking the Lock/Unlock All Layers icon at the top of the timeline. Click the icon until a lock appears to the right of each layer's name. Locking the layers will prevent you from accidentally moving anything around.

The Background layer contains only a white rectangle. That white rectangle is exactly the shape we want to use for our mask—you want to modify the movie so the Bitmap Animation appears only inside the confines of the contents of the Frame layer, and the shape in the Background layer will do nicely. When you copy the frame, you don't have to unlock the layer.

2) Add a new layer, named Bitmap Mask, above the Main Page Bitmaps layer. Select frame 1 of the new layer, and choose Edit > Paste Frames.

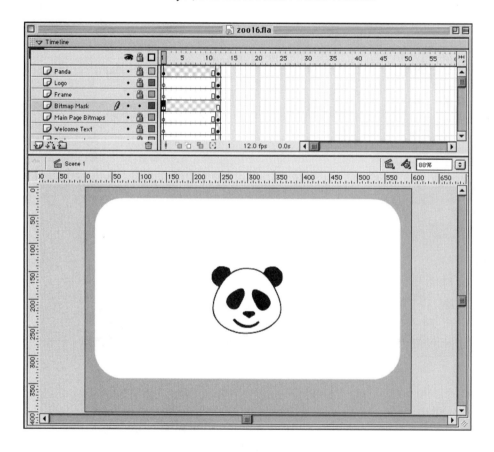

When you paste the frame, the contents of the frame that you copied appear in the Bitmap Mask layer.

NOTE *If you don't name the new layer Bitmap Mask before you paste the frame into it, the layer name will be set to Background. This is a handy feature of the Edit > Paste Frames command.*

3) Right-click (Windows) or Control-click (Macintosh) the name of the Bitmap Mask layer, and choose Mask.

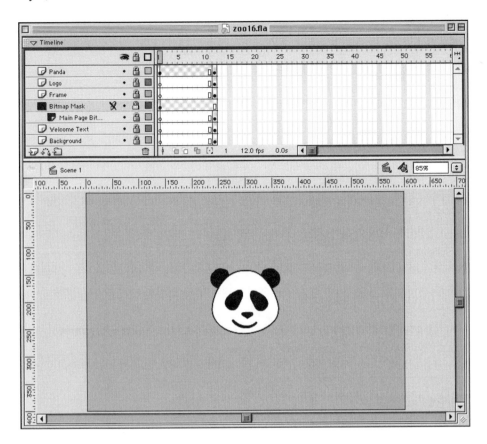

This step turns the Bitmap Mask layer into a mask for the layer below it, which is the Main Page Bitmaps layer. Only the area covered by the rectangle in the Bitmap Mask layer (the mask layer) shows through in the Main Page Bitmaps layer (the masked layer). Flash locks the mask and masked layers automatically. Icons identify the mask and masked layers in the timeline.

You can mask more than one layer with a single mask layer. Move the layer under any mask or masked layer; right-click (Windows) or Control-click (Macintosh) the layer's name and choose Properties from the drop-down menu. In the Layer Properties dialog box, set the layer's Type to Masked, and click OK.

4) Drag the playhead to frame 12.

You shouldn't be able to see the contents of the Main Page Bitmaps layer anymore. The bitmaps are still there, you just can't see them because the layer is masked and the bitmaps are outside the mask.

5) Choose Control › Test Movie. Save the movie as zoo17.fla.

When you test the movie, it's going to loop over and over. You probably want to see how the mask affected everything, so choose Control > Loop to make the movie stop looping. Notice when you select Loop, the Bitmap Animation starts when the movie reaches the last frame. Also notice that the Bitmap Animation plays over and over. You'll learn how to stop both the main movie and the Bitmap Animation from looping in Lesson 5.

Your movie is coming along nicely now. It's getting more and more complex, so now is another great time to save.

USING A MOTION GUIDE

You can use a motion guide to force a tweened symbol to follow a specified path. This technique is great for simulating motion along a curved or irregular line.

In the following exercise, you'll learn how to create a motion tween that follows a path, or motion guide, to move the Panda symbol on a curved path. You'll also learn how to use onion skinning to see multiple frames of your animation at the same time.

1) Insert a keyframe in frame 6 of the Panda layer. With the frame 6 keyframe selected, choose Insert › Create Motion Tween.

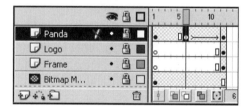

You should be a pro at making motion tweens by now! So this step should be pretty easy. All you have to do is select frame 6 in the Panda layer, and choose Insert > Keyframe or press F6. Then make sure you have the new inserted keyframe selected and choose Insert > Create Motion Tween.

TIP *You can also right-click (Windows) or Control-click (Macintosh) the keyframe you want to use, and choose Create Motion Tween to create a motion tween.*

NOTE *Make sure you don't accidentally insert a blank keyframe in frame 6. A blank keyframe eliminates the contents of the Panda layer in that frame, which is not what you want.*

2) Right-click (Windows) or Control-click (Macintosh) the name of the Panda layer, and choose Add Motion Guide from the drop-down menu.

NOTE *Make sure you choose Add Motion Guide, and not Guide. These are two very different commands.*

A new layer called Guide: Panda appears above the Panda layer. A motion-guide icon appears to the left of the name, and the Panda layer is indented below it.

TIP *Another way to add a motion guide is to select the frame you want to guide and choose Insert > Motion Guide.*

3) Lock every layer except the Panda and Guide: Panda layers, and click the Onion Skin button at the bottom of the timeline.

ONION SKIN   ONION SKIN OUTLINES

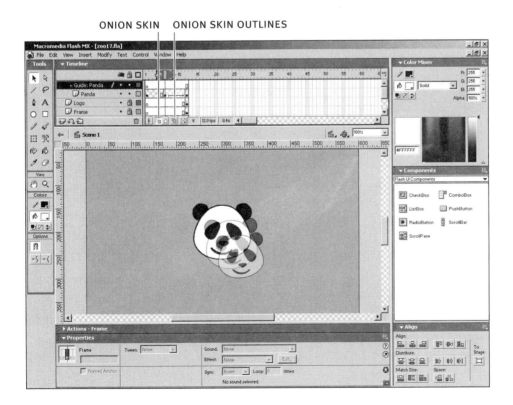

Flash's onion skin feature lets you view multiple frames at the same time. You need to specify which frames you want to view before you can use this feature. The onion skin markers appear at the top of the timeline. These markers show you which frames are included in the onion skin.

In addition to the onion skin feature, Flash has an onion skin outline feature. This feature lets you see the outlines of multiple frames at one time. This is very useful if you have complex graphics in the frames you want to view. The color of the outline corresponds to the square at the right of each layer's name, next to the lock and hide controls.

NOTE *It's important to make sure the Panda and Guide: Panda layers are unlocked before you proceed. You cannot view onion skins for layers that are locked or hidden.*

4) Select frame 1 of the Guide: Panda layer, and drag the right onion skin marker to frame 12.

The contents of frames 1 through 12 of the Panda layer should be visible. Notice that there is one instance of the Panda symbol in the middle of the stage, and six dimmed copies that appear to move toward the bottom-right corner of the stage. When you work with onion skins, the contents of the unlocked and unhidden frames beneath the playhead appear in full color. The contents of the other visible frames, as indicated by the onion skin markers, appear dimmed. If you want to view the outlines of each frame's contents instead of the actual contents, you can click the Onion Skin Outlines button in step 3.

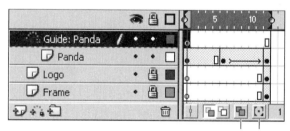

EDIT MULTIPLE FRAMES   MODIFY ONION MARKERS

The Edit Multiple Frames and Modify Onion Markers buttons can be used in conjunction with the Onion Skin and Onion Skin Outline buttons to make working with multiple frames even easier. After you have enabled either the Onion Skin or Onion Skin Outlines feature, you can click the Edit Multiple Frames button to modify the contents of all the frames within the onion skin markers. When you

130

click the Modify Onion Markers button, a menu appears that allows you to modify the display of the onion skin markers. The Always Show Markers option lets you display the onion skin markers in the timeline whether or not onion skinning is enabled. You can select the Anchor Onion option to lock the markers in their current positions in the timeline. The Anchor Onion option prevents the markers from moving with the playhead, as is the default. You can select Onion 2, Onion 5, or Onion All to display 2, 5, or all frames on either side of the current frame.

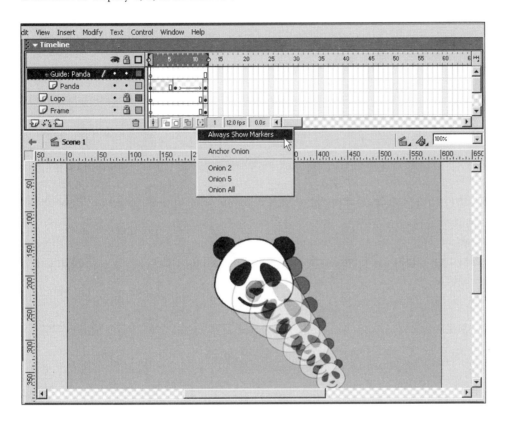

N O T E *Remember that only unlocked and unhidden layers will appear onion skinned. This is actually very useful, because you can lock or hide layers you don't want to work with while onion skinning is enabled.*

5) Select the line tool, and set the Stroke Color to red (#FF0000).

You're going to create a line that will be your motion guide.

T I P *When you create a motion guide, you may find it useful to make the line height 4 or large, so that it's easy to see.*

6) Draw a line from the center of the Panda symbol instance in the center of the stage to the center of the instance near the bottom right of the stage.

Make sure you still have frame 1 of the Guide: Panda layer selected before you start drawing; otherwise you're going to end up with a motion guide that doesn't guide anything. Just click the center of the Panda symbol instance in the center of the stage, drag to the center of the Panda symbol instance near the bottom-right side of the stage, and then release. You should end up with a straight line that goes from the first instance to the second instance. Don't worry if it's not perfect—you can go back and adjust the endpoints in just a bit.

The line you just drew is the motion guide. It's just a straight line right now, so it shouldn't have changed your animation too much, if at all. When you drew the line, you might have seen the onion skinned contents of the Panda layer shift slightly. If they did, it's OK. In fact, it's a good thing, because it means you drew your line with the endpoints touching the centers of both the initial and final instances of the Panda symbol. But don't worry if the line didn't touch the endpoints, because you'll learn how to fix that in the next step.

7) Using the arrow tool, drag the line to change it to a curve.

You can use the arrow tool to modify the shape of a straight line. Select the arrow tool, and move the pointer near the middle of the line. When the icon changes to an arrow with a curved line next to it, drag the line you created to the left. Don't click and drag, as that will select the line and move it to the left. Rather, you need to just start dragging. If it doesn't work on the first try, press Ctrl+Z (Windows) or Command+Z (Macintosh) and try again.

TIP *If you accidentally select the line, just press Ctrl+Shift+A (Windows) or Command+ Shift+A (Macintosh) to deselect it.*

When you've created the curve, the onion skinned contents of the Panda layer should follow the curve. If for some reason the animation doesn't follow the curve, don't panic. It just means that one or both of the line's endpoints isn't touching the center of the initial or final instance in the animation. Use the arrow tool to drag each endpoint around until it touches the center. As before, don't click the line first, just move the pointer near the endpoint of the line until the icon changes to an arrow with a right angle next to it. Then drag that endpoint to the center of the instance.

If, after you fiddle around with the endpoints, the animation doesn't follow the curve of the line, don't despair! Turn off onion skinning by clicking the Onion Skin button, and move the playhead to frame 6. Use the arrow tool to drag the endpoint of the curved line until it snaps to the center of the Panda symbol instance in that frame. Then drag the playhead to frame 12 and do the same thing.

NOTE *Make sure the Snap to Objects button in the Options section of the toolbox is pressed. With Snap to Objects selected, the endpoints of the line snap to other objects on the stage.*

TIP *If after positioning the endpoints of the line your animation still doesn't follow the guide, make sure the curved line is in the correct layer. It must be in the Guide: Panda layer, or the motion guide won't work.*

8) Play the movie. If you like what you see, turn off the onion skin and save the movie as zoo18.fla.

You can turn off the onion skin by clicking the Onion Skin button.

The motion guide that appears in the Guide: Panda layer will only appear while you're authoring the file. It won't appear when you export the movie. If you'd like to check, choose Control > Test Movie to see what the exported movie will look like. You should notice that the line does not appear in the finished animation.

Now that you have motion tweening down, it's time to explore another type of tweening: *shape tweening*. Before you move on, make sure to save your movie, just in case you need to go back.

CREATING A SHAPE TWEEN

Shape tweening is useful for morphing shapes between endpoints. Flash can shape-tween only shapes, not groups, symbols, or editable text. If you want to tween a group, symbol, or editable text, you must first break it up completely (choose Modify > Break Apart until everything has been turned into a shape).

You can shape-tween multiple shapes in a layer, but for the sake of organization, putting each shape in its own layer is easier.

1) Choose Insert > New Symbol. In the Symbol Properties dialog box, set the Name to Shape Animation and the Behavior to Movie Clip, and click OK.

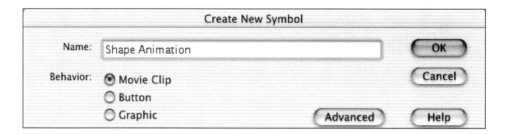

You are going to create another movie clip. This time the movie clip won't have anything in it at first. Any time you want to create a new, empty symbol, choose Insert > New Symbol.

When you choose Insert > New Symbol, a dialog box appears. The dialog box is titled Create New Symbol, but we're going to call it the Symbol Properties dialog box. It's almost identical to the dialog box you used to create symbols earlier in this lesson and in Lesson 3. When you create a new symbol, initially you don't need to worry about the Registration since you will add all the content to the symbol after it has been created. The symbol is initially empty.

As you use Flash more, you might find it useful to use shortcut keys to perform commands found in the menu. The shortcut key for the New Symbol command is Ctrl+F8 (Windows) or Command+F8 (Macintosh).

When you click OK, Flash switches to symbol-editing mode for the new Shape Animation movie clip. The movie clip is completely empty, and you're going to add some content to it.

2) Name the default layer (Layer 1) Shapes. Use the rectangle tool to draw a 25-by-25 pixel rectangle on the stage, and then use the Align panel to center the rectangle horizontally and vertically on the stage.

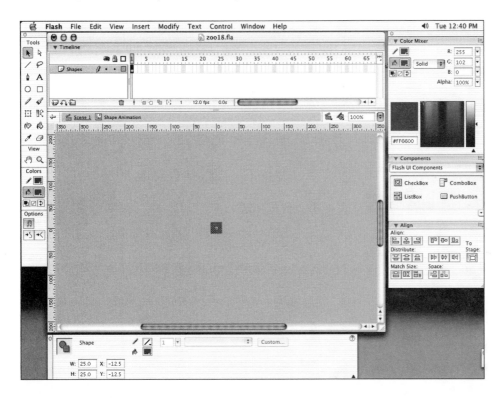

This new, empty symbol starts out with a single layer and a blank keyframe. Double-click the name of the symbol to edit it, and name it Shapes.

It's time to get back to those drawing skills you used in Lesson 2. The rectangle can look however you want, as long as it's 25 pixels wide and 25 pixels high. The one in the figures and source files on the CD-ROM has no outline, and its fill color is #FF6600 (orange). Both the outline and fill color can be set in the Property inspector once the rectangle tool is selected. The rectangle also has a Corner Radius of 0, so its corners are nice and sharp.

135

> **TIP** *If you hold down the Shift key as you draw the rectangle, Flash will constrain the shape to a perfect square.*

Once you've drawn the rectangle, use the arrow tool to select it. Then click the To Stage button in the Align panel. Finally, click the Align Horizontal Center and Align Vertical Center buttons to align the rectangle to the center of the stage.

> **TIP** *You might find it easier to simply draw a rectangle, select it with the arrow tool, and then use the Property inspector to set its Width and Height to 25, and X and Y to –12.5. As with many things in Flash, there are a number of ways to achieve the same effect, using different commands and tools, so use the combination that is most effective for you.*

3) Insert a blank keyframe in frame 12. Select that frame, and use the oval tool to draw a 25-by-25 oval on the stage. Center the oval horizontally and vertically on the stage.

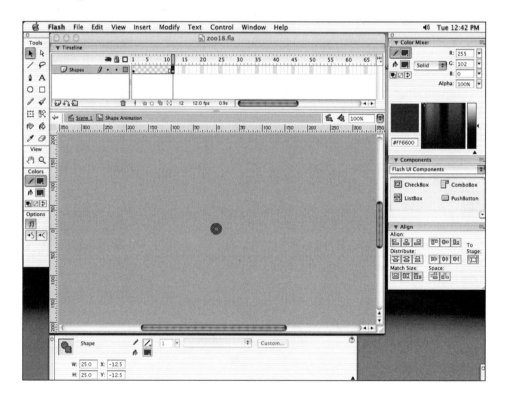

Be sure to insert a blank keyframe, not keyframe. You want a blank keyframe because you want to place an oval in this frame. Select frame 12, and choose Insert > Blank Keyframe or press F7.

As with the rectangle, you can make the oval look however you want, as long as it's 25 pixels wide and 25 pixels high. The oval used in the figures and the source files that accompany this book has no outline and has a fill color of #FF6600. Once you've drawn the oval, you can use the Property inspector to set its Height and Width to 25 each. Then use the Align panel or Property inspector to place it in the center of the stage.

TIP *If you hold down the Shift key as you draw the oval, Flash will constrain it to a perfect circle.*

4) Insert another blank keyframe in frame 24, and use the drawing tools to draw a 25-by-25 triangle on the stage, centering it horizontally and vertically on the stage.

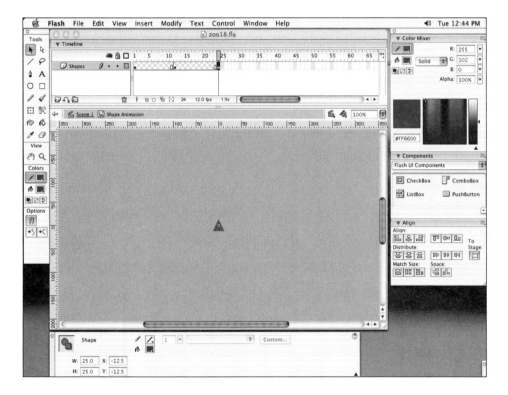

Once again, you need to make sure to add a blank keyframe so you don't duplicate the contents of the previous keyframe in frame 24. Select frame 24, and choose Insert > Blank Keyframe or press F7.

Drawing a triangle might be a little more complicated than drawing an oval or rectangle. Flash does not have a triangle tool, but don't let that bother you—it's still pretty easy to do. Just use the tools that are available to create a triangle like the one in the figure above. Let's take a quick look at a few methods.

The triangle in the figures and source files was drawn using the pen tool. Select the pen tool from the toolbox, and set the Fill Color in the Property inspector to the color you'd like (#FF6600 in the source files). You can set the color to anything—you're going to delete it from the stage, so the color doesn't matter, though it is much easier to draw the triangle if you make the stroke color very different from the fill color. Once you have selected a fill color and a stroke color, click about 15 pixels above the center of the stage. Hold down Shift and click again about 15 pixels below and to the left of the center. Still holding down the Shift key, click a third time about 15 pixels below and to the right of the stage's center. Then click once more on your starting point. Flash should close the shape, creating a triangle that has the fill color you selected. Now you can delete the outline of the triangle by switching to the arrow tool, double-clicking the stroke that creates the outline, and pressing the Delete or Backspace key.

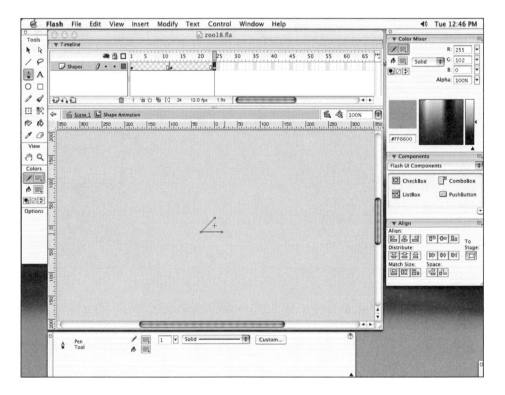

TIP *Holding down the Shift key as you draw straight lines with the pen tool will constrain those lines to 45-degree angles.*

Another way to draw the triangle is by using the line or pencil tool. Use one of these tools to draw the shape, and then use the paint bucket tool to add the fill color inside the shape. Finally, use the arrow tool to select and delete the outline.

TIP *If you use the pencil tool to draw a triangle, make sure that Pencil Mode, in the Options section of the toolbox, is set to Straighten. You may also find it useful to select the Recognize Lines drawing setting, in the Editing panel of the Preferences dialog box, to Tolerant. Then if you draw something that merely resembles a triangle, Flash will do a good job of turning it into a triangle.*

You can also use the rectangle tool, with a little help from the line tool, to draw a triangle. Select the rectangle tool, set the Fill Color to the color you want, and turn off the Stroke. Then draw a rectangle on the stage, holding down the Shift key as you draw to constrain it to a perfect square. Next, switch to the line tool, and draw a line that goes from the rectangle's top-left corner to the bottom-right corner. Select the top-right side of the rectangle, and press Delete or Backspace to remove it from the stage. Then select the stroke you added to create the remaining rectangle, and delete it as well. Finally, select the remaining rectangle, and use the free transform tool to rotate it so that it looks like the triangle in the figure at the start of this step.

TIP *If you only want to rotate an element using the free transform tool, you can click the Rotate and Skew button in the Options section of the toolbox. You can also constrain the rotation of a selected element to 45-degree angles by holding down the Shift key as you rotate the element.*

Once you've drawn the triangle, use the Property inspector to set its width and height to 25 pixels each. Then use the Align panel or Property inspector to center the triangle on the stage.

5) Select frame 1. Hold down Alt (Windows) or Option (Macintosh) and drag frame 1 to frame 36.

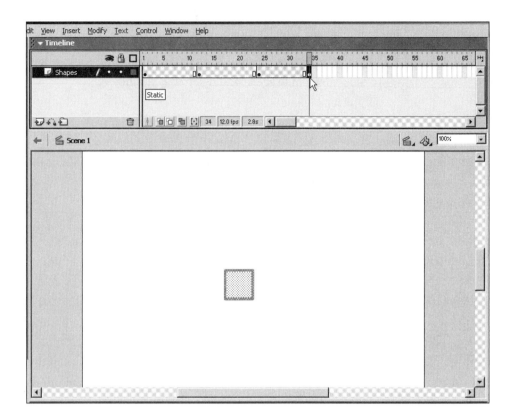

This step can be a little tricky, so be careful. First click frame 1 and release the mouse button. Then hold down the Alt key (Windows) or Option key (Macintosh), and click and drag to frame 36. If you release the Alt or Option key, Flash doesn't copy the frame to the new location but moves it instead. That's not what you want.

Alt-dragging (Windows) or Option-dragging (Macintosh) a keyframe is much like using the Copy Frames and Paste Frames commands. It's just a bit faster.

6) Insert keyframes in frames 6, 18, and 30. Select each of the keyframes one at a time and set the tween to shape, and set the Tween to Shape in the Property inspector.

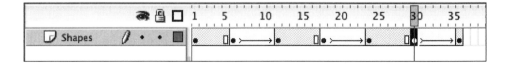

Select frames 6, 18, and 30, and press F6 to insert keyframes. Be sure to insert keyframes, not blank keyframes.

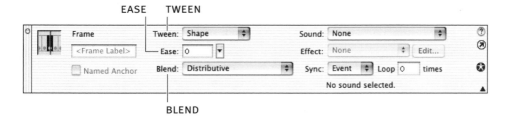

After you insert each keyframe, make sure you still have a keyframe selected, and choose Shape from the Tween drop-down menu in the Property inspector. Notice that two additional settings appear in the Property inspector. The Ease setting allows you to modify the rate of change between tweened frames. The rate can be set to any number between –100 and 100. Negative values simulate acceleration, and positive values simulate deceleration. By default, Ease is set to 0, so the rate of the animation will be constant. Blend, a third setting, can be set to either Distributive or Angular. Distributive smooths the more irregular intermediate shapes, while Angular preserves corners and straight lines in the intermediate shapes. You should only use Angular if the shapes you're tweening between have sharp corners and straight lines; otherwise Flash automatically reverts to Distributive. Feel free to play around with these settings to see how they modify the shape tween.

NOTE *Don't select the Motion option from the Tween drop-down menu. If you do accidentally select it, Flash turns the shape in the selected frame into a symbol, which you absolutely do not want. Remember, you can only shape tween shapes.*

After you set Tween to Shape, the frames between the selected frame and the next keyframe should be shaded green, and an arrow should appear between the keyframes. This indicates that you have added a shape tween.

7) Choose Control > Loop Playback, and then choose Control > Play. Save the movie as zoo19.fla.

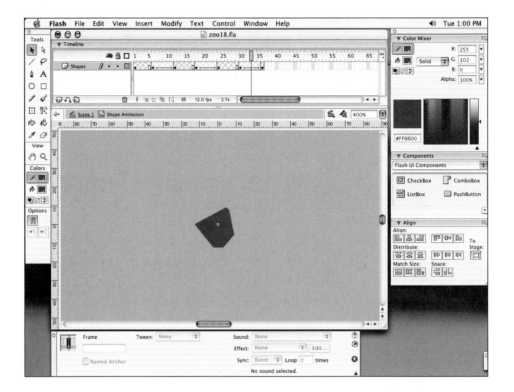

As the animation plays, you should see that Flash created intermediate shapes to tween from one shape to the next. Because you chose Control > Loop Playback, Flash will play the animation repeatedly. Pay special attention to the transition between the triangle and rectangle near the end of the animation—right now it's a little chaotic, but you'll add some shape hints in the next exercise to make it look a little smoother.

You can stop the animation by choosing Control > Stop, or by pressing the Enter (Windows) or Return (Macintosh) key.

ADDING SHAPE HINTS

When you tween between complex shapes, you may notice that Flash sometimes creates complex intermediate shapes. You can use shape hints to minimize this complexity and to control the way the intermediate shapes appear. You do this by adding shape hints to identify which points correspond in the initial and final shapes. You should still be inside the Shape Animation symbol in zoo19.fla when you start this step.

1) Select frame 30 of the Shapes layer, and choose Modify > Shape > Add Shape Hint.

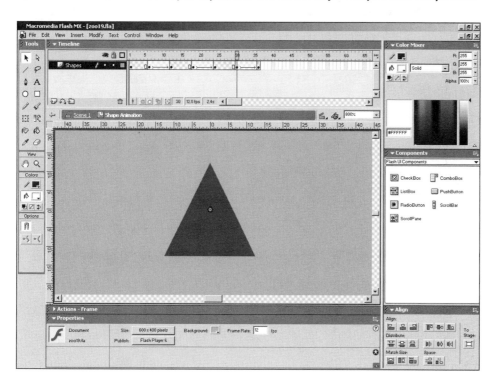

When you choose Modify > Shape > Add Shape Hint, a small red circle containing the letter *a* appears in the center of the stage. This circle is a shape hint. You can add up to 26 shape hints, going from *a* through *z*.

NOTE *Because the shape hint is in the center of the stage, you might not be able to see the letter. When you move the shape hint in the next step, you should be able to see the letter.*

TIP *If you accidentally add a shape hint that you don't need, you can remove it by dragging it off the stage. You can remove all the shape hints in the currently selected frame by choosing Modify > Shape > Remove All Hints. This command will work only if you have the starting frame selected.*

2) Drag the shape hint to the top point of the triangle.

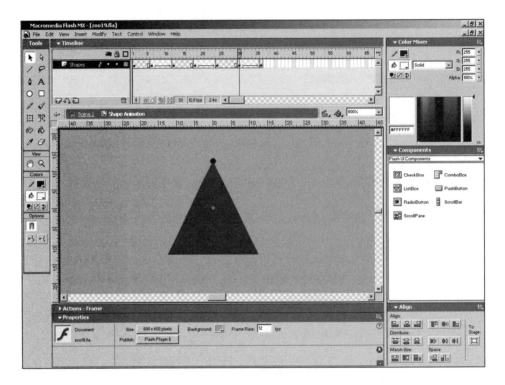

When you added the shape hint in the last step, Flash should have automatically switched to the arrow tool. Using the arrow tool makes it easier to drag the shape hint around on the stage. As you drag the shape hint, you should notice that it snaps to the edges of the triangle. If it doesn't, click the Snap to Objects button in the Options section of the toolbox.

3) Select frame 36 of the Shapes layer. Drag the shape hint to the top of the rectangle, placing it in the same position as the shape hint in frame 30.

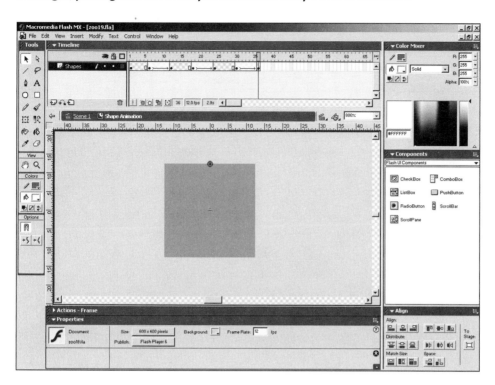

When you select frame 36, you should see a shape hint containing the letter *a* in the center of the stage. It might be hidden by the center of the symbol, so look carefully. Drag the shape hint to the top of the rectangle. The shape hint should snap to the edge of the rectangle and also should turn green, indicating that it's an ending shape hint.

NOTE   *Starting shape hints are yellow, and ending shape hints are green. If a shape hint is not attached to the edge of a shape (curve), it will appear red.*

4) Select frame 30 of the Shapes layer. Press Ctrl+Shift+H (Windows) or Command+Shift+H (Macintosh). Drag the resulting shape hint to the bottom of the triangle.

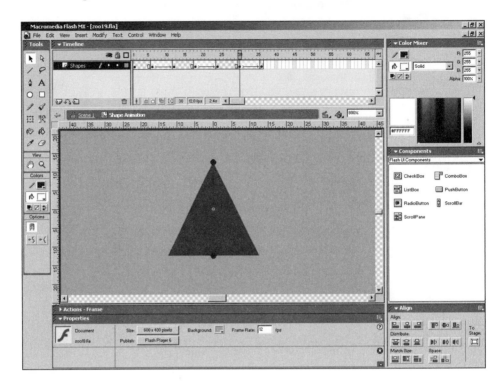

When you select frame 30 again, you should notice that the shape hint containing the letter *a* is now yellow.

Pressing Ctrl+Shift+H (Windows) or Command+Shift+H (Macintosh) adds another shape hint. This shape hint contains the letter *b*, and appears in the middle of the stage. Move it to the bottom edge of the triangle.

5) Select frame 36 of the Shapes layer and move the shape hint that corresponds with the one you added in the last step to the bottom of the rectangle.

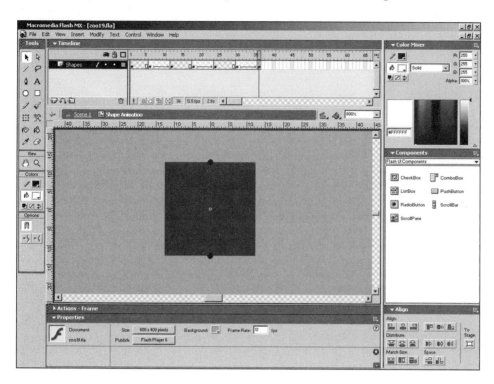

When you switch to frame 36, you should see a shape hint containing the letter *b* in the center of the stage. Move the shape hint to the bottom edge of the rectangle.

TIP *If you are working with shape hints and you don't see them on the stage, choose View > Show Shape Hints. The shape hints for the currently selected frame, if there are any, will appear.*

6) Choose Control > Play. Save the movie as zoo20.fla.

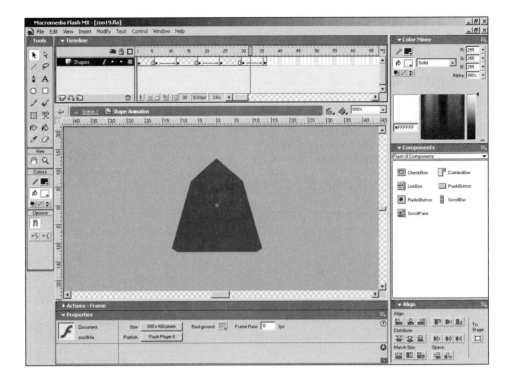

When you play the animation, you should see that the transition between the triangle and rectangle shapes has changed significantly. The top corners of the rectangle should appear to grow out of the side of the triangle, and the top and bottoms should stay in place.

If you'd like to see what your movie looks like now, choose Control > Test Movie. Be sure to choose Control > Loop Playback to stop the looping playback or the movie will loop repeatedly. You haven't added the Shape Animation symbol yet, so don't be alarmed if you don't see it.

WHAT YOU HAVE LEARNED

In this lesson, you have:

- Created a frame-by-frame animation and reversed the sequence of frames (pages 110–115)

- Extended a still image in the timeline by adding frames (pages 116–117)

- Distributed the contents of a single layer to multiple layers (pages 117–124)

- Created several motion tweens (pages 125–128)

- Added a mask to display contents of a layer only in a particular area of the stage (pages 128–134)

- Used a motion guide to make a motion tween follow a curved path (pages 134–142)

- Created a shape tween to animate from one shape to another, and added shape hints to control the intermediate shapes (pages 143–148)

adding basic
interactivity

So far, you have created a movie with a timeline that plays sequentially, one frame after the other. That's all well and good, but you're probably impatient to get to all this interactivity stuff you keep hearing about. Not to worry—interactivity is the subject of this lesson.

In Flash, you can set up your movie to be interactive. When you reach a particular frame, and you click a button or move the mouse pointer over it, press a key, or enter information in a text box, an event is triggered. To make interactivity possible, you assign actions to a frame or an object, such as a button or movie clip. *Actions* are sets of instructions written in ActionScript, Flash's full-fledged scripting language.

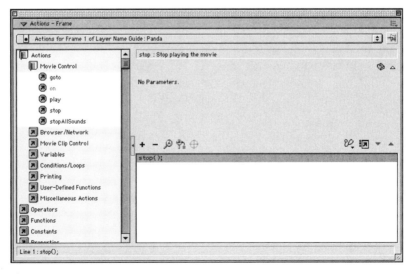

The Actions panel is useful for adding interactivity.

Chrissy Rey

WHAT YOU WILL LEARN

In this lesson, you will:

- Explore the Actions panel

- Add actions to frames to control the timeline

- Create a button and add actions to an instance of the button

- Create and use a template

- Add actions to open a URL and send an email

APPROXIMATE TIME

This lesson takes approximately one hour to complete.

LESSON FILES

Media Files:

Lesson05/Assets/visitorinfo.swf

Lesson05/Assets/assets.fla

Starting Files:

Lesson05/Starting/zoo20.fla

Completed Project:

Lesson05/Completed/zoo23.fla

Lesson05/Completed/Zoo Template.fla

Lesson05/Completed/visitorinfo1.fla

EXPLORING THE ACTIONS PANEL

You can attach actions to buttons, movie clips, or frames by using the Actions panel. Actions can do everything from making the movie stop playing to loading data from an external file. The actions are added to the Actions panel as ActionScript. In this exercise, you'll discover what's available in the Actions panel.

You should have zoo20.fla from the last lesson open. If you closed the file, you can open the file from the Lesson05/Starting folder on the CD-ROM. Just make sure to save it to your hard drive before you continue.

1) Choose Window > Actions.

ACTIONS TOOLBOX   PARAMETERS PANE   OPTIONS MENU CONTROL

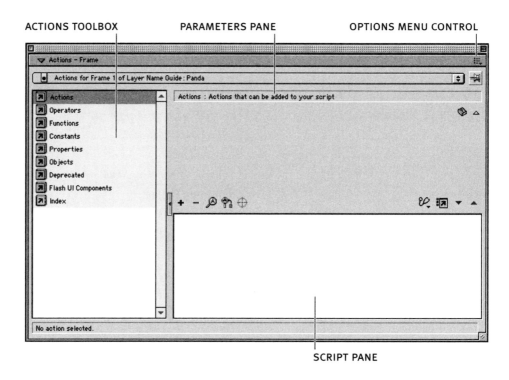

SCRIPT PANE

You've just opened the Actions panel.

On the left side of the Actions panel is the Actions toolbox. The Actions toolbox contains all the pieces of ActionScript you can add to your movie. On the bottom-right side of the Actions panel is the script pane, where the ActionScript is created. Above the script pane is the parameters pane. If you don't see the parameters pane, click the Options menu control and choose Normal Mode from the Options menu. When you're editing in normal mode, the parameters pane prompts you for the parameters (arguments) needed for each action.

2) If necessary, click Actions in the Actions toolbox to expand the category.

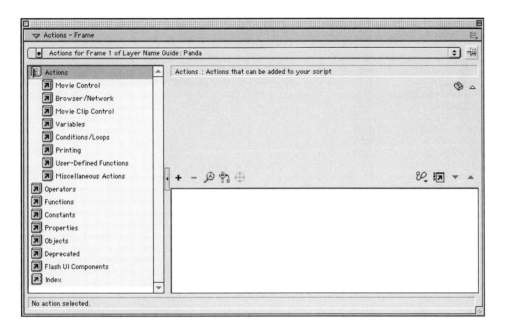

The Actions toolbox is divided into categories: Actions, Operators, Functions, Constants, Properties, Objects, Deprecated, Flash UI Components, and Index. Most of these categories are further divided into subcategories. For example, the Actions category is divided into Movie Control, Browser/Network, Movie Clip Control, Variables, Conditions/Loops, Printing, User-Defined Functions, and Miscellaneous Actions.

You are not restricted to using the actions listed in the Actions toolbox. You can import an external file into the script pane, and in expert mode you can write your own script directly in the script pane. You can also export the ActionScript in the script pane to an external file, and edit the file outside of Flash.

3) Click the Movie Control category in the Actions toolbox.

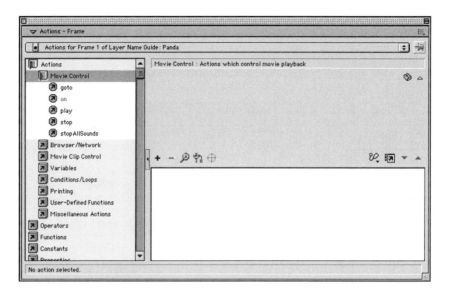

When you click the Movie Control category, it expands to reveal five actions: `goto`, `on`, `play`, `stop`, and `stopAllSounds`. Each of the actions in the Actions toolbox should be grayed, and the Actions panel's title is simply Actions. That's because you don't currently have any frames, movie clips, or buttons selected.

TIP *If you select an element that cannot have actions applied to it, for example a group, the script pane will read, "Current selection cannot have actions applied to it."*

4) Move your pointer over each of the actions listed in the Movie Control category of the Actions toolbox.

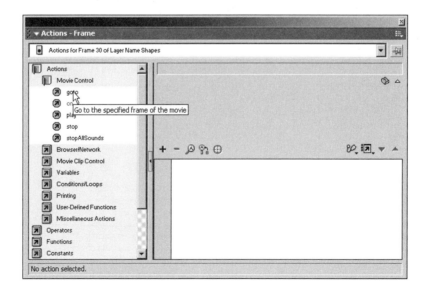

As you move your pointer over each action, a Tooltip should appear. The Tooltip gives a brief explanation of the action's function. For example, the Tooltip for `goto` is: "Go to the specified frame of the movie." If you click an action, the same information appears in the parameters pane.

NOTE *If you click an action and don't see its description in the parameters pane, click the Arrow button in the top-right corner of the parameters pane.*

5) Click the `goto` action in the Actions toolbox and then click the Reference button.

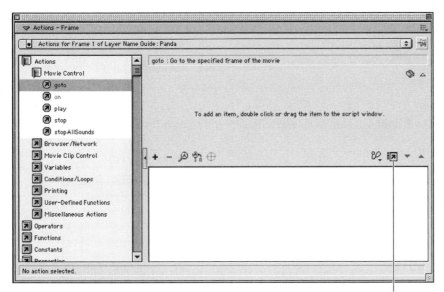

REFERENCE BUTTON

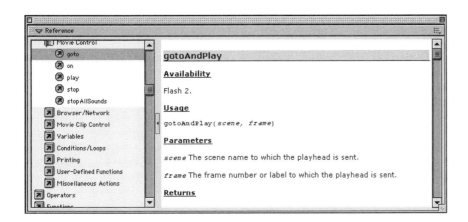

ADDING BASIC INTERACTIVITY

The Reference button is on the top-right side of the Actions panel. When you click it, the Reference panel opens, revealing a detailed description of the selected action. Take a few moments to explore the Reference panel. You'll see that it is divided into categories identical to those in the Actions panel. Close the panel when you've finished exploring, but remember that you can open it again by simply clicking the Reference button in the Actions panel.

TIP *You can also open the Reference panel by pressing Shift+F1.*

Another useful reference when working with ActionScript is the ActionScript Dictionary. If you purchased the boxed version of Flash, you should have received a copy of the dictionary in the package, as part of the documentation. You can view an HTML version by choosing Help > ActionScript Dictionary. You can also use Appendix D in this book if you need a quick reference.

6) Click the Options button and select View Line Numbers from the drop-down menu.

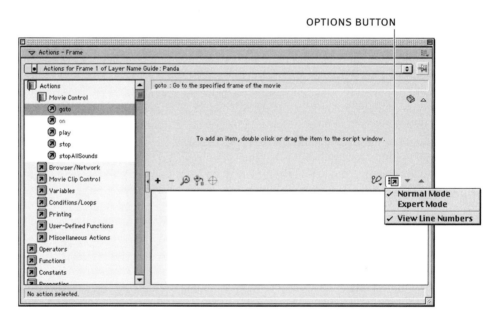

To make it easier to refer to the bits of code you're going to add to the movie over the course of this lesson and several later lessons, select the View Line Numbers option. If you click the Options button and View Line Numbers is already checked, you don't need to select it. When you select the View Line Numbers option, the Actions panel won't change, but when you start adding ActionScript to the script pane, you'll see that Flash displays the line numbers.

7) Click the Options menu control in the upper-right corner of the Actions panel, and choose Preferences from the drop-down menu.

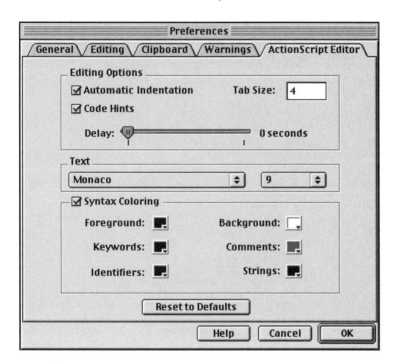

The Preferences option opens the Preferences dialog box, which is the same dialog box that opens when you choose Edit > Preferences. The Preferences dialog box opens with the ActionScript Editor tab selected.

The Editing Options section of the ActionScript Editor panel has four settings: Automatic Indentation, Code Hints, Tab Size, and Delay. When the Automatic Indentation option is selected, as it is by default, Flash automatically indents the ActionScript in the script pane in expert mode. You can also enter an integer in the Tab Size box to set the number of spaces by which you want the ActionScript to be indented. When Code Hints is selected, Flash displays syntax, method, and event-completion hints in both expert and normal modes. The Delay slider specifies the amount of time Flash will wait before displaying a code hint—you can change this setting by moving the slider.

The Text section of the panel lets you modify the display of the ActionScript in the script pane. You can change the font and the font height. If you find that the font displayed in the script pane is too small, just open the Preferences panel and change the font height.

The Syntax Coloring section lets you modify the color of the text in the script pane. If the Syntax Coloring option is selected, you can set colors for the foreground, background, keywords, comments, identifiers, and strings in the script pane, if it is not selected, you can set the colors for only the foreground and background. You can change a color by clicking a color box and choosing a color from the color palette.

NOTE *Don't worry if some of the terms found in the ActionScript Editor panel, such as Keywords and Comments, are unfamiliar. You'll learn more about them in Lesson 8.*

Click OK when you've finished exploring the ActionScript Editor panel of the Preferences dialog box. You haven't changed anything in the movie at this point, so it's not necessary to save the file before you continue.

USING ACTIONS TO CONTROL THE TIMELINE

You're ready to start adding interactivity to your Flash movie. You'll start by adding a couple of Stop actions. This may sound like un-interactivity, but it's a good first step.

You should still have zoo20.fla open before you begin.

1) Add a new layer, named Actions, to the main timeline. Place the Actions layer at the top of the layer stacking order.

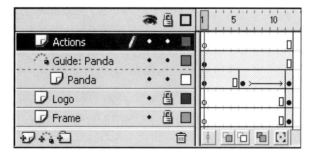

Throughout the rest of this book, you will notice references to the main movie's timeline, or the main timeline. The main timeline is not part of any symbol—it's the one you see when you first open a movie. You can reach this timeline from inside any symbol by choosing Edit > Edit Document. If the Edit Document command is not available, you are already in the main timeline.

It's usually a good idea to add your ActionScript to a separate layer in each timeline. That way, if you run into problems with your ActionScript, you'll know just where to fix it.

2) Select frame 12 of the Actions layer and add a keyframe. With the new keyframe selected, double-click the `stop` action in the Actions toolbox.

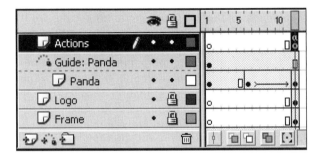

A small *a* should appear in frame 12 of the Actions layer. This *a* indicates that an ActionScript is applied to this frame. If you don't see the *a* in frame 12, check frame 1. If the *a* appears in frame 1, you added the action to the wrong frame. Make sure you added a keyframe to frame 12, and select that keyframe, before you try to add the **stop** action.

When you add actions to the timeline, you can add them only to keyframes. Keyframes not only mark changes in the contents of the movie, as you learned in Lesson 4, but they also mark changes in the interactivity (ActionScript). Whenever you add something to your movie at a certain point in time, as measured by the timeline, you need to add a keyframe.

To add the **stop** action, make sure you select frame 12 of the Actions layer. Look at the Property inspector—it should indicate that you have a frame selected. Then make sure the Actions panel is open—it should still be open from the last exercise. You should also make sure the Actions panel's title is Actions – Frame, which indicates you are about to add ActionScript to a frame. Finally, double-click the **stop** action in

159

the Actions toolbox. It's inside the Movie Control category, in the Actions category. When you double-click the action, it should appear in the script pane.

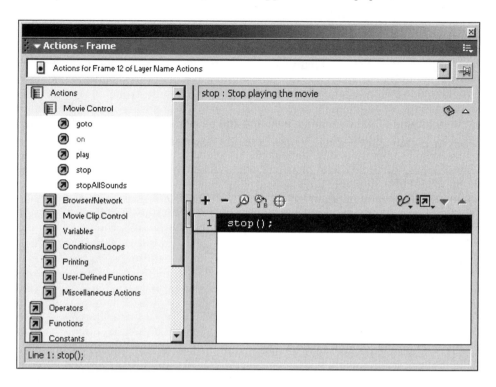

Take a look at the script pane after you add the action. There should be a single line, displaying the text **stop();**. The **stop** portion of the script should be pretty easy to understand—that's the action. But what about the **();**? That's ActionScript's punctuation. The parentheses ("(" and ")") enclose any parameters that the preceding action might have, and the semicolon (";") marks the end of a line of ActionScript. Parameters are extra information the action might need in order to perform properly— the **stop** action doesn't have any parameters, it just stops the movie, but many of the other actions do.

TIP *You can also add the action by clicking the Add a New Item to the Script button, and then choosing Actions > Movie Control > stop. Notice when you choose this option, there's also a keyboard shortcut listed in Windows. You can click the script pane and then press that keyboard shortcut to add the ActionScript as well.*

By adding a **stop** action to the keyframe in frame 12, you're telling Flash to stop when it gets to that point. So the Flash movie will play for about 2 seconds, and then stop.

Take a quick look at some of the other actions listed in the Movie Control category—move the pointer over each one to get a brief description. The `goto` action tells the timeline to go to a specific frame, and either stop or play from there. The `on` action is for use with buttons, as you'll learn in the next exercise. You can use the `play` action to make a stopped timeline play.

3) Choose Control > Test Movie.

When you test the movie, you should see that as expected, the movie stops when it gets to frame 12. This keeps you from having to choose Control > Loop in the Test Movie window.

So you have the main timeline stopping at frame 12. But what about that Bitmap Animation movie clip? It's still looping away, ignoring the fact that the main timeline has stopped. That's because the Bitmap Animation is a movie clip, and movie clip timelines are independent of other timelines.

As you learned in Lesson 3, movie clips are basically mini-movies. They can contain interactions, sounds, and other movie clips, as well as vector graphics, bitmaps, and graphic symbols. The timeline of a movie clip is completely independent of any other timeline, so you can place a movie clip containing 20 frames inside a movie clip containing only one frame, and the entire 20-frame movie clip will still play, unless there's an ActionScript telling it to do otherwise.

A graphic symbol's timeline is tied to the timeline it's inside of, unlike movie clips. So if you place a 20-frame graphic symbol inside a 1-frame movie clip, only the first frame of the graphic symbol will play. If you had used Graphic behavior for the Bitmap Animation, instead of Movie Clip behavior, only the first frame of the symbol would appear.

Close the Test Movie window when you're finished, so you can get back and make some changes in zoo20.fla.

4) Open the Bitmap Animation symbol in symbol-editing mode. Change the topmost layer's name to Actions.

You can open the Bitmap Animation symbol in symbol-editing mode by double-clicking the icon to the left of its name in the Library. Or you can click the Edit Symbols button under the timeline and choose the Bitmap Animation symbol from the menu that appears. If you have the Actions panel expanded, you may have to collapse it to see the contents of the symbol. For now, just click the panel's title bar to collapse it.

Once again you're going to add your ActionScript to a single layer in this movie clip, called Actions. Remember, it's a good practice to place all your actions in a single layer in each timeline, and the timeline for the Bitmap Animation movie clip is no exception. It's a good idea to place the Actions layer at the top, or bottom, of the layer stacking order to make it easy to find. In this case, you need to change the name of the empty layer, which is called Layer 1 or something similar in your Bitmap Animation symbol, to Actions. Double-click the existing name and type a new name in its place.

5) Select frame 6 of the Actions layer and double-click the `stop` **action in the Actions toolbox of the Actions panel.**

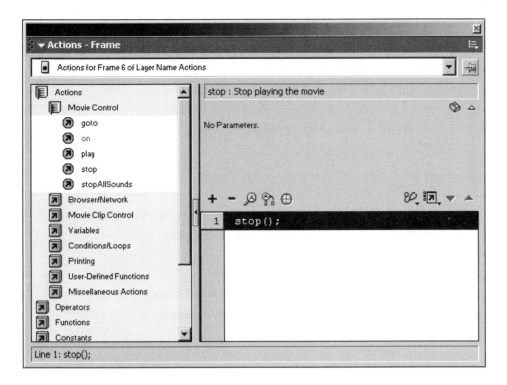

You should already have a keyframe in frame 6 of the Actions layer. If not, be sure to add one before you add the **stop** action. If you don't add the keyframe, the action will be added to frame 1 and the movie will stop in frame 1, which means you won't see any of the animation.

As before, you can locate the stop action in the Movie Control category of the Actions category.

Adding a **stop** action to the last frame of the main timeline stopped that timeline, but it didn't stop the Bitmap Animation movie clip from looping continuously. Adding a **stop** action to the last frame of the Bitmap Animation movie clip should prevent looping. Remember that movie clip timeline's run independently from the timelines they're inside of, so stopping one timeline will not stop the other.

6) Choose Control > Test Movie. Save the file as zoo21.fla.

When you test the movie this time, the main movie should stop at frame 12, and then the instance of the Bitmap Animation symbol should stop when it reaches frame 6.

Close the Test Movie window when you're done, and save the movie as zoo21.fla. Now that you've made the movie stop, you're going to add more ActionScript to make it go again.

CREATING A BUTTON

You've already worked with both movie clip and graphic behaviors for symbols. Now it's time to look at a symbol with button behavior. As you learned in Lesson 3, button symbols are useful for creating interactive buttons. Each button symbol can have different graphics for each button state—Up, Over, and Down. Plus you can specify a hit area for the button. As you'll learn in this exercise, the timeline for a button looks quite different from any you've seen before.

Make sure you have zoo21.fla open when you start this exercise.

1) Choose Insert › New Symbol. When the Symbol Properties dialog box opens, type *Visitor Info Button* and set the Behavior to Button. Click OK.

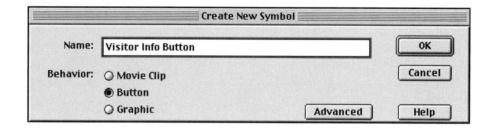

Once again you're making a brand new, empty symbol. So when you click OK, Flash will switch to symbol-editing mode for the new Visitor Info Button symbol. But once you get to symbol-editing mode, things should look quite different. The timeline for a button symbol is different from that of the main timeline, a movie clip, or a graphic symbol.

When the new symbol opens in symbol-editing mode, you should see that the timeline has four named frames or states: Up, Over, Down, and Hit. Each frame corresponds with a button state. The Up state is how the button first appears on the screen. The Over state becomes visible when you move the pointer over a button on the stage. When you click a button, the Down state is revealed. The Hit state is not visible in your movie; it defines the active area of a button. The active area can be larger or smaller than the visible button and can even have a different shape. Button symbols can have shapes, groups, graphic symbols, movie clips, and sounds in the first three frames. You can place all these, except sounds, in the Hit frame.

164

LESSON 5

If you want to animate any of the states for your button, you can add a movie clip to that state. As you learned in the previous exercise, movie clip timelines are independent of the timelines they're inside. That means you can place an animated movie clip in a single keyframe inside a button, for example the Over state, and the movie clip will play as long as that state is active, unless there's an ActionScript inside the movie clip to make it do otherwise.

You can also add sounds to the Up, Over, and Down states of a button. The sound, or sounds, will play when the state is active. You'll learn more about adding sounds to Flash, including buttons, in Lesson 6.

2) Select the text tool and add a text box containing the text *visitor info* to the stage in the Up frame. Use the Align panel to center it horizontally and vertically on the stage.

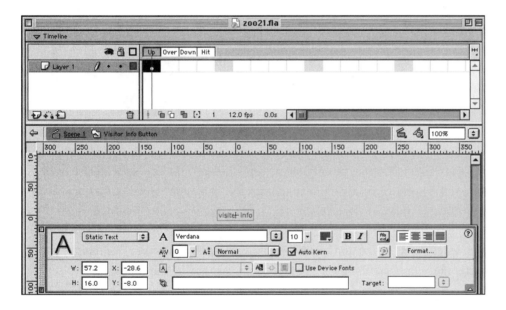

In the Property inspector, set the Font to Verdana, Font Size to 10, Text (fill) Color to #CC0000, and Character Spacing to 2. Make sure the Text Type is set to Static Text and create a text box containing the words *visitor info* to the Up frame. Then select the text box and use the Align panel to center it horizontally and vertically on the stage.

3) Select the Over frame and insert a keyframe. Select the text box in that frame and set its Text (fill) Color to #FF6600 (orange).

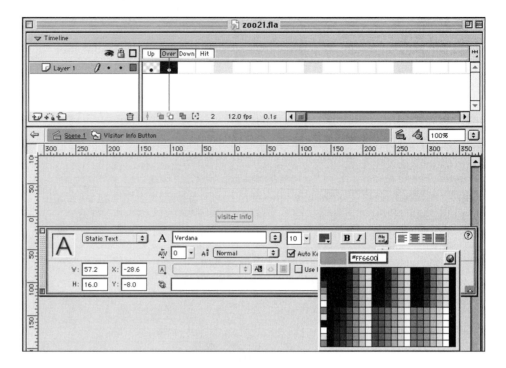

Whatever you add to the Over frame will appear when you move the mouse over the button instance. So for the text visitor info button, the color #CC0000 (red) will change to #FF6600 (orange) when you move the mouse over the button.

4) Select the Hit frame and insert a keyframe. Use the rectangle tool to draw a rectangle approximately the same size as the text box in that frame.

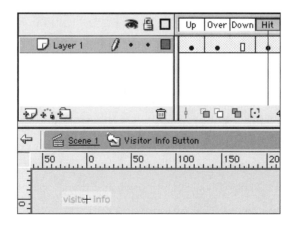

This is a very important step. Without a Hit area, you'd have a hard time clicking the button. When you add the rectangle, you can use any color for the fill—just make sure the rectangle does have a fill. The Hit state is not visible in your movie, so the color of the rectangle doesn't matter. You don't need a stroke outline for the rectangle, so you can set the stroke to No Color. Then just draw the rectangle over the text box that should still be in the Hit frame.

If you forget to add a Hit frame to this button, the text in the preceding keyframe (the Over frame) will act as the hit area. That means the shapes of the letters in the words visitor info will act as the hit area. Using only the shapes of the letters would make it very difficult to hit the button.

NOTE *If you add an animated movie clip to the Hit frame of a button, only the first frame of the movie clip will act as the Hit state. Adding an animation will not create an animated Hit state.*

5) Save the movie as zoo22.fla.

Now you just have to add an instance of your button to the movie and add some ActionScript to it.

ADDING ACTIONS TO A BUTTON INSTANCE

Now that you've made a button, it's time to add the button to the movie and add some ActionScript to it. Actions that are added to a keyframe are triggered when that keyframe is reached in the timeline. Actions that are added to a button are activated when an event, specified in the ActionScript added to the button, is triggered. You don't want to add ActionScript to the keyframes inside a button, rather, you want to add it to an instance of the button that has been added to a movie clip or the main timeline. You shouldn't add button instances to graphic symbols or other button symbols, as the button might not work as expected.

1) Choose Edit > Edit Document. Add a new layer, named Menu. Place the Menu layer below the Actions layer, but above all of the other layers.

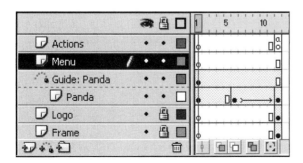

You should still have zoo22.fla open. Most likely you're still inside the new Visitor Info Button symbol, so go to the main timeline. You can go to the main timeline by choosing Edit > Edit Document or you click the Scene 1 icon.

Right now, you are going to add a button to this new layer, and later you will add a menu to this layer.

2) Insert a keyframe in frame 12 of the Menu layer. With the new keyframe selected, add an instance of the Visitor Info Button to the stage. Use the Property inspector to set the X to 100 and Y to 350.

You can find the Visitor Info Button symbol in the library. Make sure the correct frame is selected, and then drag an instance of the symbol onto the stage. Use the Property inspector to set the X and Y properties for this instance of the symbol.

3) Add a blank keyframe to frame 13 of the Actions, Bitmap Mask, Bitmap Animation, and Welcome Text layers. Add a frame to frame 13 of all the other layers.

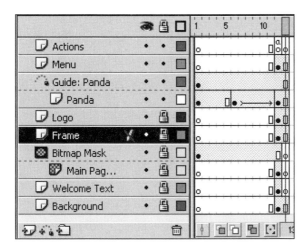

When you add a blank keyframe to frame 13 of the Bitmap Mask, Bitmap Animation, and Welcome Text layers, you ensure that the contents of those layers do not appear in that frame. There's nothing in the Actions layer, but you need to add a keyframe to frame 13 of the Actions layer so you can add a frame label, which you'll do next. Adding frames to frame 13 of all the other layers merely extends the length of those layers' animations, so you'll still see the logo, panda, background, and frame.

4) Select frame 12 of the Actions layer and type _home_ in the Frame label box in the Property inspector. Then select frame 13 of the Actions layer and type _blank_ in the Frame label box in the Property inspector.

FRAME LABEL

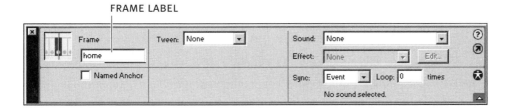

When you select a keyframe, you should see one of the settings in the Property inspector is the Frame label. You can add frame labels to identify keyframes in the timeline. Adding a label is useful for targeting frames with ActionScript.

TIP _Keep your frame labels short as they are exported with the movie and can add to the file's size._

After you type the frame label, press Enter or Return to apply it. When you add the frame label to frame 13, a small red flag should appear in the keyframe you had selected. This red flag indicates that the keyframe contains a frame label. The flag may not appear in frame 12 because the *a* indicating there's ActionScript in that frame is taking up all the space.

TIP *If you'd like to see both the frame label flag and the ActionScript indicator, you can change the view of the timeline. Click the Frame View button in the top-right corner of the timeline, and choose Medium or Large.*

FRAME VIEW BUTTON

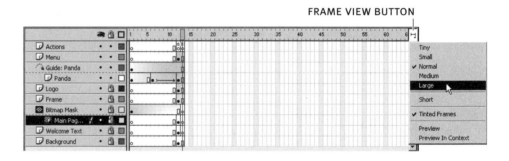

If there's enough room between frames containing labels, you'll see the frame labels in the timeline to the right of each red flag. Otherwise you can move the pointer over the frame containing the label, and a Tooltip should appear indicating the label's name.

You can also add frame comments to keyframes. Comments are useful for making notes for you and other. For example, you might want to add a comment indicating which frame should have content added to it. Unlike frame labels, frame comments aren't exported with the movie, so you can make them as long as necessary. To make a frame comment, add two slashes (//) before the text in the Frame label setting. When you add a frame comment to the timeline, two green slashes (//) appear in the timeline before the text in the comment, similar to the red flag for a frame label.

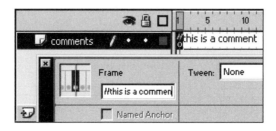

5) Select the instance of the Visitor Info Button in frame 12 of the Menu layer. Double-click the goto action in the Actions panel.

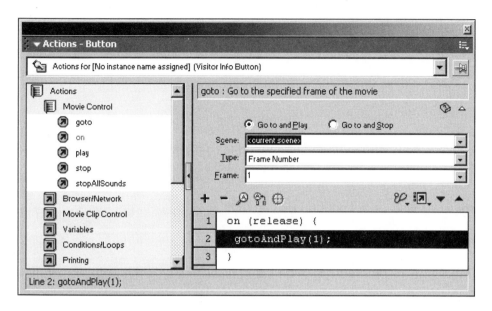

Make sure you have the instance of the Visitor Info Button in frame 12 selected—you can check the Property inspector to verify the selection. The title of the Actions panel should be Actions – Button. This indicates that you have a button instance selected.

When you double-click the goto action, which is in the Movie Control category of the Actions category, Flash adds the following ActionScript to the script pane:

```
on (release) {
  gotoAndPlay(1);
}
```

The first line of this ActionScript tells Flash to do something on (release), which means that when the mouse button is pressed and released, everything inside the curly braces ({}) should happen. This is known as an event handler—the contents of the curly braces are triggered when the event, or events, specified in the parentheses occurs. All actions added to button instances must be contained in an event handler. The events that can trigger ActionScript on a button are press, release, releaseOutside, rollOut, rollOver, dragOut, dragOver, keyPress. You can use the keyPress event to trigger actions when a key is pressed.

The next line tells Flash to gotoAndPlay(1);. This line tells Flash to go to frame 1 and play the movie from there. The action portion of this line, gotoAndPlay, tells Flash what to do. The parameters portion, (1), modifies the action—it provides

171

additional information to Flash so it can perform the `gotoAndPlay` function. The last part of this line, the semicolon (;) lets Flash know this line of code has ended. You don't need semicolons at the end of the first and last lines in this script—the curly braces ({}) suffice.

TIP *If you can't see all the ActionScript listed above in the script pane, try to increase the size of the Actions panel. You should also see a scroll bar on the right side of the Actions panel—you can use the scroll bar to scroll through the script pane.*

6) Select the line that says `gotoAndPlay(1);`. **Select the Go to and Stop option in the parameter pane. Set the Type to Frame Label and the Frame to blank.**

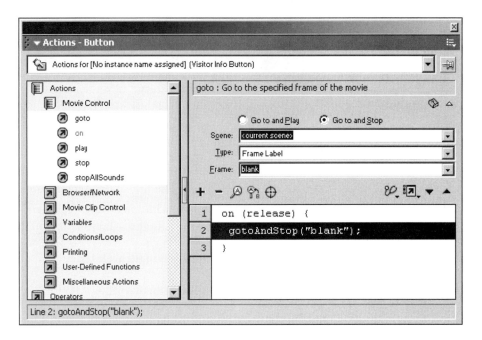

Your ActionScript should now look like this:

```
on (release) {
  gotoAndStop("blank");
}
```

With only a few simple changes, you modified the ActionScript so that when the mouse button is released, the movie goes to and stops at the frame labeled blank.

The Type can be set to Frame Number, Frame Label, Expression, Next Frame, or Previous Frame. If you set Type to Frame Number, you can only set the value in the Frame setting to a number. In order to achieve the same effect as the ActionScript above, you could set the Type to Frame Number and then set the Frame to 13, but what happens if you need to add more frames to your movie, and frame 13 is no longer frame 13? You would have to go back and change the ActionScript—this example illustrates the usefulness of frame labels.

The Next Frame and Previous Frame types change the appearance of the ActionScript in the script pane dramatically. Setting the Type to Next Frame changes the ActionScript to `nextFrame();`, while setting it to Previous Frame changes it to `prevFrame();`. These actions do not require parameters, as they simply tell the timeline to jump to the next or previous frame.

When you set the Type to Frame Label, the Frame setting has a drop-down menu containing all the labeled frames in the timeline, so you can select the necessary frame label from the menu. Or you can type the frame label into the box.

7) Choose Control > Test Movie to test your work. Save the movie as zoo23.fla.

When you test the movie, clicking the Visitor Info button should make the movie jump to the frame labeled blank, and the Bitmap Animation and Welcome Text should disappear.

NOTE *If you have any trouble clicking the button, make sure you added a rectangle to its Hit frame.*

When you close the Test Movie window, you can also test the ActionScript added to the button by clicking Control > Enable Simple Buttons. Then when you move the playhead to frame 12 and click the button, the playhead should jump to frame 13. Just be sure to turn off Enable Simple Buttons if you want to use the arrow tool to select a button.

8) Save the movie before you continue and keep it open for the next exercise.

CREATING A TEMPLATE

When you work on a large project, as you're doing over the course of this book, you might find it useful to create templates to maintain consistency across the various pieces of the project. You can save a Flash movie as a template, and then use the template to create a new Flash document. The template can contain special layers, called guide layers, which you can use to position the elements in your template-based movies. They can also contain comments, to provide information to others using the template.

1) Delete the Menu, Guide: Panda, Bitmap Mask, Main Page Bitmaps, and Welcome Text layers.

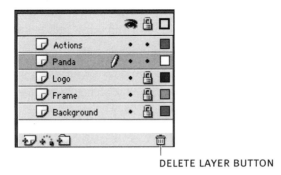

DELETE LAYER BUTTON

You can delete a layer by selecting it, and clicking the Delete Layer button at the bottom of the timeline. If you want to delete all these layers at one time, click the first one, hold down Ctrl (Windows) or Command (Macintosh), and click each of the other layers. After you delete the layers listed, your movie should have only the Actions, Panda, Logo, Frame, and Background layers remaining.

Before the end of this exercise, you are going to save this file as a template, and you don't need the content in the layers you just deleted. You saved the file as zoo23.fla in the last exercise, so you'll be able to open the file to get back to work on the Web site. But you need to make a template so you can create additional content that will be loaded into this movie later.

2) Remove frames 1 through 12 of every layer. Select frame 1 of the Actions layer and change the frame label to *//This is the ZooMX template.*

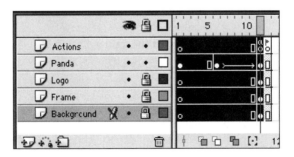

Select frame 1 of the Actions layer, and then Shift click frame 12 of the Background layer. You should have frames 1 through 12 of every layer selected. Once you have the layers selected, choose Insert > Remove Frames to remove frames 1 through 12 of each layer. Frame 13 should take the place of frame 1.

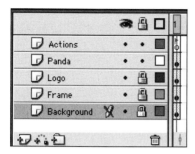

After frames 1 through 12 have been removed, the label in frame 1 of the Actions layer should be info. You don't necessarily need that frame label for movies based on the template you're creating, so you can change the label to a comment. When you create a new movie based on this template, you can add whatever labels the new movie might require. Remember, a frame comment is simply a label preceded by two slashes (//). So typing *//This is the ZooMX template* in the Frame label setting in the Property inspector should create a comment.

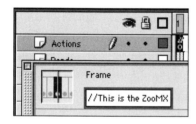

TIP *Don't forget to press Enter or Return after you type the comment in the Frame label setting.*

3) Select the Panda layer and click the Insert Layer Folder button. Name the new layer folder Guides.

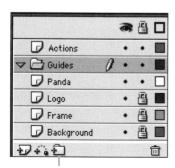

INSERT LAYER FOLDER BUTTON

Add the layer folder by clicking the Insert Layer Folder button at the bottom of the timeline. Alternatively you could choose Insert > Layer Folder. Once the layer folder has been added, rename the folder the same way you rename a layer.

Layer folders make it easy to organize the layers in your Flash movie. You can place layers inside the folders, and then expand and collapse them, without affecting what you see on the screen. You can also lock or hide all the layers in a folder by locking or hiding the folder.

4) Move the Panda, Logo, Frame, and Background layers into the Guide folder.

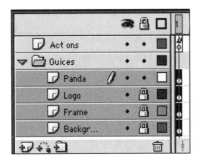

Make sure you keep the layers in the same order they were in before moving them. You can move them quickly and easily by clicking the topmost layer (Panda), and then Shift click the bottommost layer (Background). Then drag all the layers into the Guides layer folder—the layer folder should highlight, indicating that you've dragged something into it. When the folder is highlighted, release the mouse and the layers should appear inside the layer folder.

5) Right-click (Windows) or Control-click (Macintosh) the Panda layer and choose Guide. Repeat this step for the Logo, Frame, and Background layers.

When you choose Guide a small icon should appear to the left of the layer name, indicating that it's now a guide layer. Guide layers are not exported in your Flash Player movie and do not add weight to the final file size. Guide layers are different from the guides you added in Lesson 2. Guides can be straight lines, and they are not actually contained on a layer. Guide layers can contain graphics of any shape, which you can use as visual aids for drawing complex art in Flash.

You can now use the Panda, Logo, Frame, and Background guide layers to place elements in your Flash movie. The contents of the guide layers appear only while you are editing; they will not appear in the finished movie. If you want to test this, choose Control > Test Movie—you should see only the orange color of the stage.

6) Unlock and unhide every layer and then lock the Guides layer folder. Click the triangle to the left of the Guide layer folder's name to collapse the folder. Select the Guides layer folder and add a new layer named Content.

You can unlock every layer by clicking the Lock/Unlock All Layers icon at the top of the timeline until every layer is unlocked. Remember, a small lock icon appears to the right of a layer's name when it's locked, so just make sure there are no lock icons next to the layer names. You can click the Show/Hide All Layers icon at the top of the timeline until every layer is visible. A small X will appear to the right of a hidden layer's name, under the Show/Hide All Layers icon. Just make sure no X's appear there. After every layer is unlocked and unhidden, lock the Guides layer folder. All the layers inside the folder should be locked.

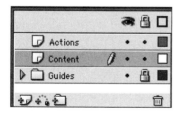

ADDING BASIC INTERACTIVITY

When you collapse the folder, the layers inside the folder disappear from the timeline, but their contents do not vanish. Since the folder and all the layers inside it are locked, you won't be able to change the contents of these layers. Having the folder locked but still visible makes the contents of the Guides folder useful for positioning elements on the stage.

Finally you need to add a new layer above the Guides folder. You are going to use the new layer to place the content for movies based on the template you're about to create.

NOTE *When you add the layer, it should appear above the Guides layer folder, not inside it. If you accidentally place the new layer inside the Guides layer, make sure you drag it out of the Guides layer before you continue.*

7) Choose File > Save as Template. When the Save as Template dialog box opens, set the Name to Zoo Template and Category to Flash TFS. Click Save.

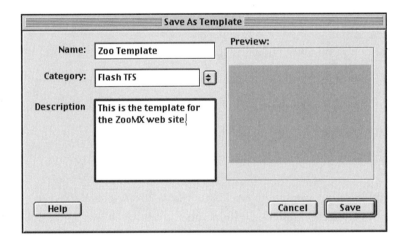

You just made a template! You can use this template to create other Flash movies. Because you have a layer folder full of guide layers in the template, you can position elements in movies that use the template so they'll look good in the context of the ZooMX Web site. This template will be important in future exercises, as much of the remaining content for the site will be created in new movies.

8) Close the movie.
You're finished with the template, so you can close it. You're going to create a movie based on the template in the next exercise.

USING ACTIONSCRIPT TO OPEN A WEB PAGE

You can use ActionScript to open another Web page by using the `getURL` action. The `getURL` action, as its name implies, gets a URL. This action works much like the anchor (<a>) tag in HTML.

1) Choose File > New From Template. In the New Document dialog box, select Flash TFS from the Category list. Make sure the Zoo Template is selected in the Category Items and click Create.

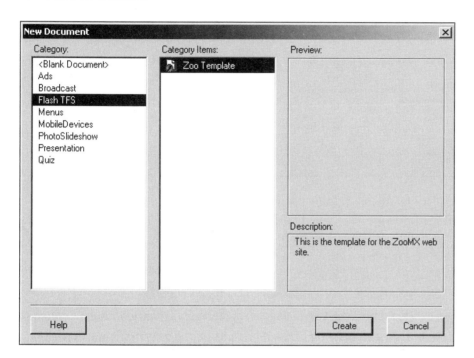

A new movie appears, containing all the elements you added to the Zoo Template in the previous exercise.

Notice that the New Document dialog box has a number of other templates available. Flash comes with several templates. Some of them are pretty complex, and very useful, so you might want to spend some time looking at them.

2) Select the Contents layer and import visitorinfo.swf from the Lesson05/Assets folder on the CD-ROM.

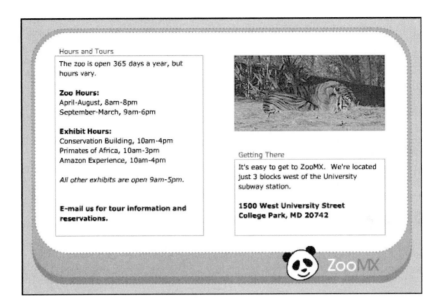

To import the file, choose File > Import and browse to the Lesson05/Assets folder. Select visitorinfo.swf, and click Open. The visitorinfo.swf file contains some text and graphics. You can use your drawing skills to re-create the contents of this file. Just use the figure above as a guide.

3) Open assets.fla from the Lesson05/Assets folder as a library. With the Contents layer selected, drag an instance of the Directions Button onto the stage. Place it in the bottom-right corner of the Getting There box.

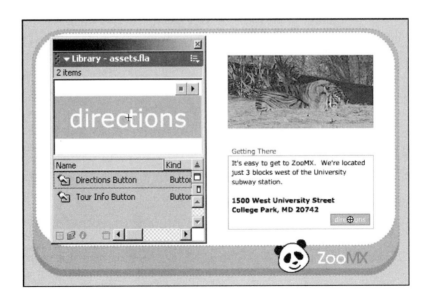

To open a file as a library, choose File > Open as Library, locate the file, and click Open. The assets.fla file contains two symbols—Directions Button and Tour Info Button. You already know how to create buttons, so if you'd like to try to make these buttons on your own you can. Or, just use the buttons from the assets.fla library.

4) Make sure you have the instance of the Directions Button selected. Expand the Browser/Network category in the Actions panel and double-click the getURL action.

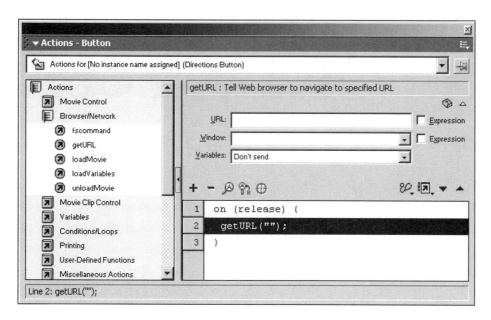

The getURL action is located inside the Browser/Network category, which is inside the Actions category in the Actions panel. When you double-click this action, the following should appear in the script pane:

```
on (release) {
  getURL("");
}
```

As with the Visitor Info Button, Flash automatically adds an event handler to the button. Adding an event handler only happens when you use the Actions panel in Normal Mode—if you were in Expert Mode, only the getURL action would have been added.

Right now, this bit of ActionScript can be translated to read, "When the user releases the mouse button, go to the URL contained within the quotation marks." Nothing appears inside the quotation marks, so you need to add that next.

5) Select the line containing getURL("");. **Set the URL to** *http://www.mapquest.com/directions*. **From the Window pop-up menu, choose _blank.**

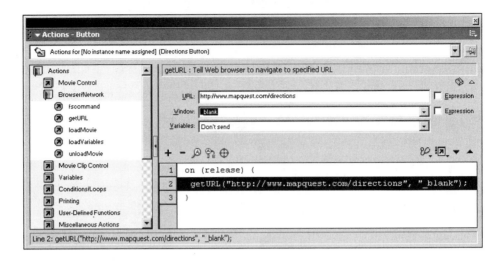

The ActionScript in the script pane should now look like this:

```
on (release) {
  getURL("http://www.mapquest.com/directions", "_blank");
}
```

The getURL action has three parameters: URL, Window, and Variables. The URL parameter can be any URL, including an email URL (mailto:). The Window parameter can be one of the windows listed in the pop-up menu (_self, _blank, _parent, or _top) or any other window named by JavaScript, VBScript, or a frameset. The Variables parameter specifies whether any variables set in the Flash movie should be sent via GET or POST. You don't have any variables in this movie, so leave this at the default setting "Don't send."

When the user clicks the instance of the Directions Button symbol and releases the mouse button, Flash will open a new browser window (_blank) and go to the URL http://www.mapquest.com/directions.

6) Add an instance of the Tour Info Button to the bottom-right corner of the Hours and Tours box in the Contents layer. With this instance selected, double-click the getURL action in the Actions panel. Set the URL to *mailto:tours@zoo-mx.com? subject=Tour% 20Info.*

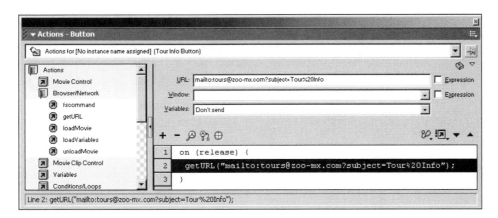

The ActionScript should look like this:

```
on (release) {
    getURL("mailto:tours@zoo-mx.com?subject=Tour%20Info");
}
```

When the user clicks this button, Flash will open the default mail client to send an email. The email will automatically have tours@zoo-mx.com in the To field, and the subject will be set to Tour Info.

7) Save the file as visitorinfo1.fla in the FlashTFS folder on your hard drive. Choose Control > Test Movie.

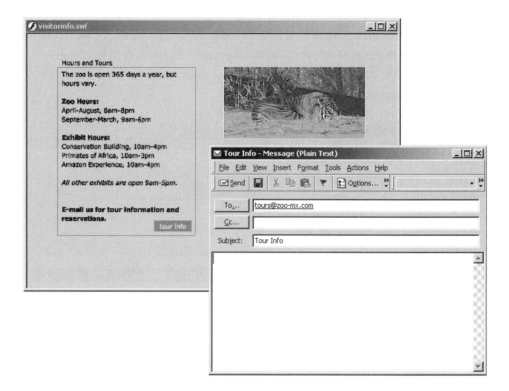

Make sure to save the file before you test the movie. When you choose Control > Test Movie, Flash exports a copy of the movie using the name of the saved file. So Flash will create a file called visitorinfo.swf in the FlashTFS folder on your hard drive. You'll use this file later.

When you test the movie, you'll see that the contents of the Guides layer folder do not appear. Only the assets in the Contents layer will be visible.

Try clicking each of the buttons you added to the movie. When you click the Directions button, Flash should open a browser window taking you to MapQuest. If you click the Tour Info button, Flash should open a new email, with the To and Subject already filled in.

WHAT YOU HAVE LEARNED

In this lesson, you have:

- Explored the Actions panel (pages 152–158)

- Added actions to frames to control the timeline (pages 158–163)

- Created a button and added actions to an instance of the button (pages 164–173)

- Created and used a template (pages 173–178)

- Added actions to open a URL and send an email (pages 179–184)

using sound and video

The use of sound and video in Macromedia Flash movies will enhance your presentations (think silent movie versus talkies). Although it is not always necessary, sound adds another dimension to your presentation and, when used effectively, can make the viewer's experience more enjoyable. Flash can also import a variety of video formats, all of which can be embedded into your Flash movies.

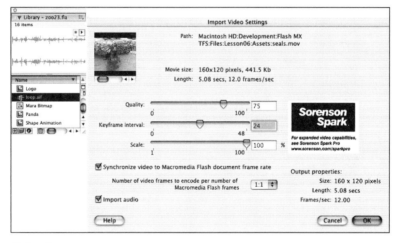

The ZooMX Web site wouldn't be complete without sound and video.

Chrissy Rey

WHAT YOU WILL LEARN

In this lesson, you will:

- Import a sound file and add it to the timeline

- Modify sound properties

- Add sounds to a button

- Customize a sound's effects

- Import a video file and add it to the movie

APPROXIMATE TIME

This lesson takes approximately
30 minutes to complete.

LESSON FILES

Media Files:

Lesson06/Assets/loop.aif

Lesson06/Assets/loop.wav

Lesson06/Assets/assets.fla

Lesson06/Assets/feature.swf

Lesson06/Assets/seals.mov

Lesson06/Assets/seals.flv

Starting Files:

Lesson06/Starting/zoo23.fla

Completed Project:

Lesson06/Completed/zoo28.fla

Lesson06/Completed/feature1.fla

IMPORTING SOUNDS

Before you can include sound files in your Flash movie, you need to import them into the library just as you import artwork. When you import a sound, it gets added to your current movie library. You can use numerous instances of the same sound throughout your movie, just as you can use multiple instances of a symbol.

You should start this lesson with zoo23.fla open—it's the file you saved in the last lesson, so you should be able to find it in the FlashTFS folder on your hard drive. If it's not there, you can open zoo23.fla from the Lesson06/Starting folder on the CD-ROM. Just be sure to save it to your hard drive before you continue.

1) Insert a new layer, name it Soundtrack, and drag it to the bottom of the layer-stacking order.

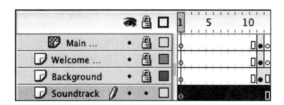

It is usually a good idea to put sounds in a separate layer, or layers; they're easier to find and modify that way.

2) Choose File > Import to Library. When the Import to Library dialog box opens, browse to the Lesson06/Assets folder, and import loop.wav or loop.aif.

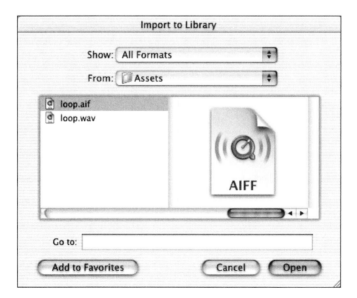

The sound file is imported directly into the current Flash library, where it is stored with your symbols and any bitmaps you imported. You can use a sound multiple times in the same movie, so you only need one copy of a sound file in your library.

TIP *You can also bring the loop.wav or loop.aif file into your movie by opening assets.fla in the Lesson06/Assets folder as a library. You should find loop.wav and loop.aif in the library.*

Flash imports different sound formats depending on whether you have QuickTime 4 or later installed. Without QuickTime 4 installed, you can only import MP3 sounds in Windows and on a Macintosh. And, if you do not have QuickTime installed, you can also import WAV sounds in Windows and AIFF sounds on a Macintosh. If QuickTime 4 is installed, you can import sound-only QuickTime movies and Sun AU sound files. QuickTime also lets you import Sound Designer II, WAV, and System 7 sounds on a Macintosh, and AIFF sounds in Windows.

NOTE *Once a sound is imported into a Flash movie, you can copy the sound to other Flash libraries, regardless of whether you're using Windows or a Macintosh. You don't even have to have QuickTime installed.*

Flash does not create sound files for you, but many other programs do. The sounds included on the CD-ROM were created using Sonic Foundry's Acid Pro 3.0. Acid Pro is a timeline-based editor, that lets you mix sound loops together to create your own music. You can export your mixes in a number of different formats, including MP3. Appendix C lists several other programs that let you create music, as well as a number of resources for sounds and music loops.

3) Open the Library, and locate the loop.wav or loop.aif sound.

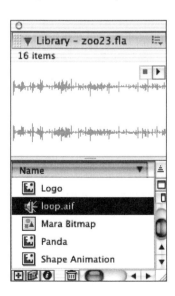

You can preview your sound before you add it to the movie by clicking the Play button in the top-right corner of the library.

4) Save your work as zoo24.fla in the FlashTFS folder on your hard drive.

Now that you have sound in your library you can add it to the movie.

ADDING SOUNDS TO THE TIMELINE

Importing a sound only adds it to the library. For the sound to play in your movie, you must place it on the timeline. Adding a sound to your movie is relatively easy, but it is important to place the sound in the frame where you want the sound to begin. To prevent one sound from overwriting another, you should create a new layer for each sound you want in your movie.

1) Select the Soundtrack layer of zoo24.fla, and drag a copy of loop.wav or loop.aif from the library to the stage.

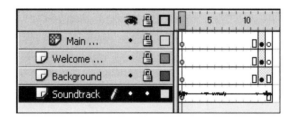

The sound is added to the first, and only, keyframe of the Soundtrack layer, and graphic representation (waveform) of the sound appears in the timeline. The sound doesn't actually appear on the stage, but you have to drag it to the stage in order to add it to the movie.

When you add a sound to the timeline, it can only be added to a keyframe. So be sure to place a keyframe in the frame you want to use as the starting point for the sound before you try to add the sound. If you already have a sound in a keyframe, and you add another sound to the same keyframe, the second sound simply replaces the first.

NOTE *You can add a sound to a keyframe that contains graphic content, without replacing the graphic content. It is a little harder to find the sound later, as the keyframe indicating content on the stage might hide the graphic representation of the sound. It's usually a good idea to add your sounds to a unique layer, or layers, set aside just for sounds.*

2) Drag the playhead to frame 1 and choose Control > Play.

When you play the movie, you hear the sound play once.

NOTE *If Control > Loop Playback is checked, you'll hear the sound more than once. Choose Loop Playback to deselect and you'll only hear the sound play once.*

3) Save your movie in the FlashTFS folder as zoo25.fla.

Next, you're going to make the sound fade in and loop a few times.

MODIFYING SOUND PROPERTIES

After you have a sound in your movie, you can use the Property inspector to apply a preset sound effect or customize a sound effect by using Flash's basic editing capabilities. You'll also use the Property inspector to define the sound type as a streaming or event sound.

Streaming sounds are synchronized with the timeline. Each piece of the sound is linked to a specific frame in the movie. *Event sounds* are synchronized with a specific keyframe or event, such as clicking a button. An event sound plays independently of the timeline. So in a sense, streaming sounds are analogous to graphic symbols and event sounds are analogous to movie clips. You'll learn more about the different types of sound synchronization as you work through this exercise.

1) Select frame 1 of the Soundtrack layer. Make sure the Sound name in the Property inspector is set to loop.wav or loop.aif.

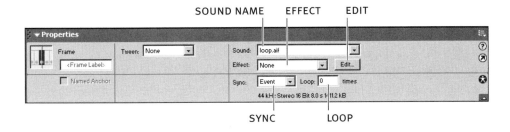

NOTE *On some systems, the Sound name might be simply loop. That's fine.*

You can select any sound you've imported into the movie from the Sound pop-up menu. To remove an existing sound from a frame, choose None from the Sound menu.

2) In the Property inspector set the sound Effect to Fade In.

191

Choosing Fade In gradually increases the sound over its duration. (Fade Out does the opposite, gradually decreasing the sound.)

If you want to remove a sound effect, choose None in the Sound Effect setting.

Left Channel/Right Channel applies the sound to only the left or right channel, so the sound seems to be coming from only one speaker. Fade Left to Right/Fade Right to Left shifts sound from one channel to the other. You can specify Custom to create your own effect, which you'll learn more about in the next exercise.

3) Set the Sync to Stream.

The Property inspector's Sync setting can be set to Event, Start, End, or Stream. Event synchronizes the sound to an event, such as clicking a button or reaching its keyframe in the timeline. An event sound plays for its entirety and independently from the timeline. If you need the sound to play exactly with the timeline, do *not* choose this option. Event sounds play each time they are triggered, thus they can overlap.

Start is similar to Event, but sounds play to the end before playing again if they are triggered. End stops every occurrence of a specific event or start sound at the frame in which the End is located. To use the End feature, create an additional layer; insert a keyframe where you want the sound to end; into that keyframe insert the sound you want to stop; open the Sound panel; and set Sync to End. Because Event sounds run independently of the timeline, this procedure is the only way to guarantee that an event sound will stop at a specific frame.

Stream synchronizes the sound with the timeline. Streaming sounds end when there are no more frames in the timeline. Streaming sounds can be helpful for use as background sounds and for synchronizing a voice with animation.

4) Set the Loop to 0.

Finally, you set the number of times you want the sound to repeat in the Loop setting in the Property inspector. A sound cannot be looped forever, but it can be looped 99,999 times.

TIP *Looping a streamed sound is not wise, especially if the sound is large. If a streamed sound is set to loop, the size of the file increases to accommodate the additional frames of the looped sound. This does not apply to sounds that have their Sync set to Start, Stop, or Event, only to sounds that have a Sync setting of Stream.*

5) Drag the playhead to frame 1, and choose Control > Play.

When you play the movie, the sound fades in. But as soon as the animation reaches frame 12, the sound stops, because the streaming sound is synchronized with the movie's timeline. When the movie stops, the sound stops. And when the movie runs out of frames, the sound stops.

NOTE *If Control > Loop Playback is checked, the sound will start again when the movie loops back to frame 1. Just choose the Loop Playback command to deselect it and you'll hear the sound play only once.*

6) Select frame 1 of the Soundtrack layer. In the Property inspector, choose Start from the Sync setting, and type *3* in the Loop box. Play the animation again.

This time, the sound should play all the way through three loops. When you set Sync to Start, the sound starts playing in the frame in which it's triggered and keeps playing until it's completed or stopped.

7) Save the movie in the FlashTFS folder as zoo26.fla.

You now have a nice looping sound in your movie. Now it's time to add a sound to a button. This is done similarly to the previous step, only the timeline is a bit different.

ADDING SOUNDS TO A BUTTON

Adding sounds to buttons is similar to adding sounds to the timeline. By adding a keyframe and inserting the sound into that state of the button, you can place a sound in any of the three active states of the button: Up, Over, and Down. In the following exercise, you will add a sound to the Visitor Info Button you created in Lesson 5.

1) Open the Visitor Info Button symbol in zoo26.fla in symbol-editing mode. Name the existing layer Graphics, and add a layer named Sounds.

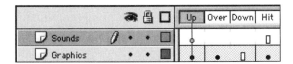

193

The simplest way to open a symbol in symbol-editing mode is to double-click the symbol's icon in the library. (You must click the icon, not the name; double-clicking the name only highlights the name.) You can also select the symbol's name in the library and then choose Edit from the Library window's Options menu. Or you can choose Edit > Edit Symbols and select the symbol in the library.

2) In the timeline, select the Down frame in the Sounds layer, and insert a keyframe.

Adding a keyframe to the Down state lets you add a sound that plays only when the button is clicked.

3) With the new keyframe selected, choose Window > Common Libraries > Sounds. Select a sound in the Sounds library, and drag it onto the stage.

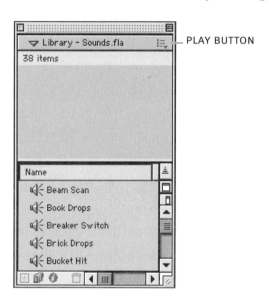

PLAY BUTTON

The sound you choose is the one you will hear when you click the Visitor Info Button. You can use any sound you like. If you'd like to test the sound, click the Play button in the top-right corner of the library.

4) In the Sound layer, select the Down frame. From the Sync pop-up menu in the Property inspector, choose Event.

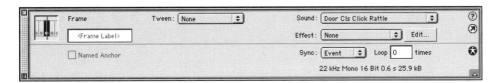

Remember that because event sounds play each time they are triggered, they can overlap. Each time you click the Visitor Info Button, the sound will play.

5) Choose Control > Test Movie. When Flash opens the movie in the Test Movie window, click the instance of the Visitor Info Button symbol.

If you click the button once, you hear the sound once. If you click the button more than once, the sound starts to overlap; it keeps getting triggered because the Sync for this sound is set to Event.

Close the Test Movie window when you've finished testing the button.

6) Open the Visitor Info Button symbol in symbol-editing mode, and change the Sync of the sound in the Down frame to Start. Test the movie again, and click the button.

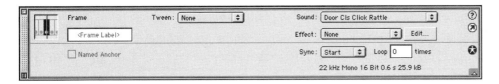

Sounds that have a sync setting of Start play all the way through when they are first triggered. If a sound of this type is triggered again before it finishes playing, it won't start playing again. So when you keep clicking the button, the sound will not overlap.

7) Save your movie in the FlashTFS folder as zoo27.fla.

Working with sounds in Flash has been fairly painless so far. Now you're going to get into something more complicated: customizing sound effects.

CUSTOMIZING SOUND EFFECTS

Clicking the Edit button in the Sound panel opens the Edit Envelope dialog box, where you can modify existing sound effects and create your own custom effects. You can use the Edit Envelope dialog box, to change the in point and out point of the sound, as well as control the volume of each sound channel. If you want to do to perform a more complex sound edit, you'll need another program such as Macromedia's SoundEdit and Sonic Foundry's Sound Forge.

1) Select frame 1 of the Soundtrack layer in zoo27.fla, and click the Edit button in the Property inspector.

The Edit Envelope dialog box opens. This dialog box has several controls you can use to customize your sounds, as well as three windows. The top window controls the sounds for the left channel. The bottom window controls the sounds for the right channel. The center window—a bar between the channel windows—is the timeline for the sound.

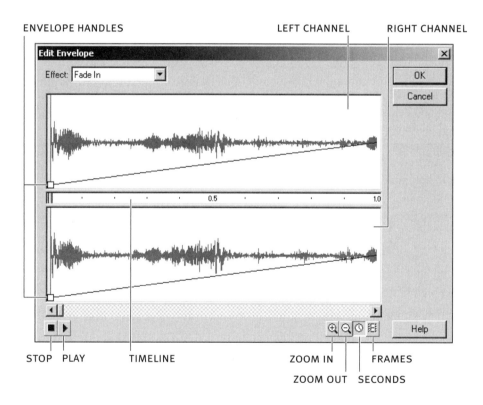

2) Click the Zoom Out button in the bottom-right corner of the Edit Envelope dialog box until you can see one complete loop of the sound file.

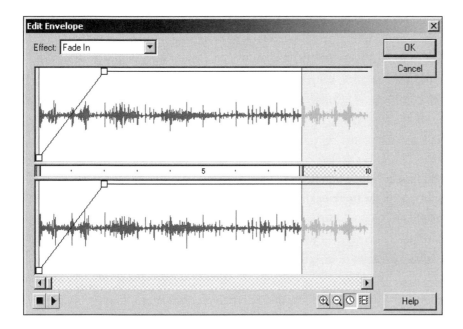

The end of the loop is marked by a vertical line. Right now the sound fades in, starting at no volume and ending at full volume. This end of the loop setting is indicated by a solid black line (the envelope line) that goes from the bottom to the top of each channel. The line indicates the volume of the sound in that channel. Each line features two white squares called envelope handles at either end. You can move the envelope handles to change the volume in each channel.

3) From the Effect drop-down menu, choose Fade Left to Right.

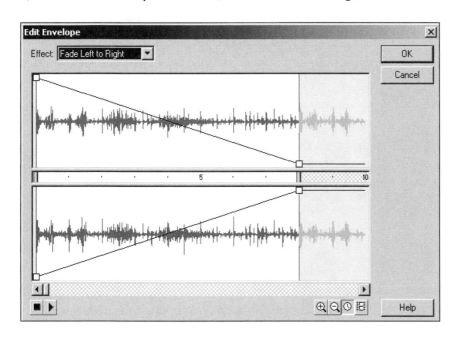

197

The envelope handles move to new positions. The first envelope handle in the left channel is now at the top of that channel's window, indicating that the left channel starts at full volume. The line in that channel slopes down and eventually meets the bottom of the window, indicating that over the course of the first loop, that channel fades out to no volume. The opposite is true of the right channel; it starts at no volume and moves up to full volume. You can click the Play button in the bottom-left corner of the dialog box to test the sound.

4) Drag the first envelope handle in the right channel window to the top of that channel's window. Do the same for the second envelope handle in the left channel window.

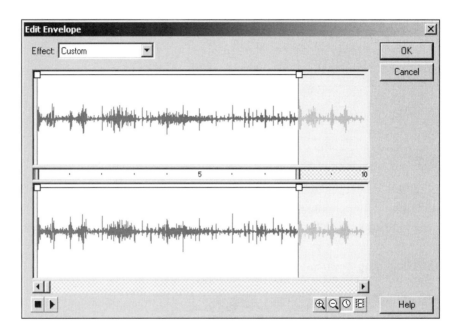

Now both channels start at full volume, and continue to play at full volume for the duration of the sound. You can click the Play button in the Edit Envelope dialog box to make sure.

5) Click the envelope line between the existing envelope handles in the left channel.

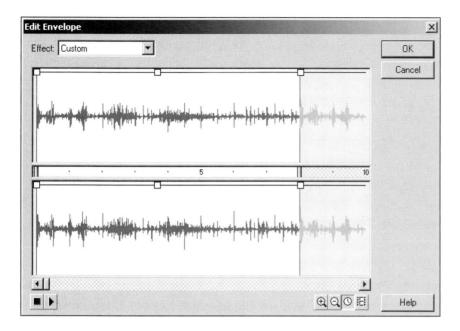

When you click the envelope line, in either channel Flash adds another handle to both channels. You can have up to eight envelope handles in each channel.

6) Drag the envelope handle you just added off the top of the left channel window.

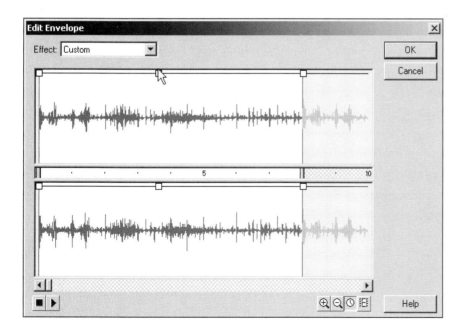

When you drag an envelope handle that is not an end point (the first or last envelope handle) off the channel, it removes that envelope handle from both channels.

7) Click OK, and save your movie as zoo28.fla in the FlashTFS folder.

Now that you're a sound effects pro, it's time to move on to some video. You will learn more about working with sound in Lesson 12. You can close zoo28.fla, since you're going to work with a new file in the next exercise.

IMPORTING VIDEO

As with sound and artwork, you must import video files into your Flash movie before you can use them. When you import a video file, it is added to your current movie's library. You can then use instances of the same video file throughout your movie. In the next exercise you will import some video into a movie clip. You will then add that movie clip to the main timeline.

1) Choose File > New From Template. In the New Document dialog box, select Flash TFS from the Category list, make sure the Zoo Template is selected, and click Create.

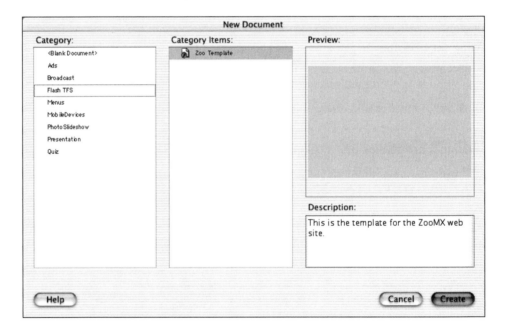

You're going to make a new file, based on the template you created in Lesson 5.

2) Select the Contents layer and import feature.swf from the Lesson06/Assets folder on the CD-ROM that comes with this book.

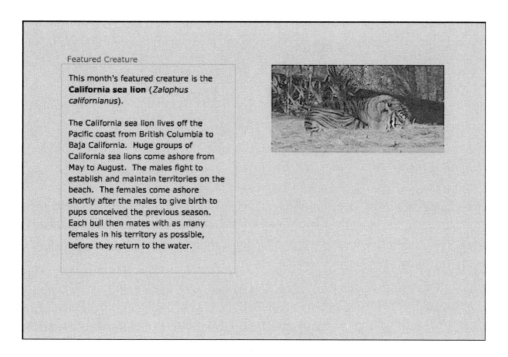

To import the file, choose File > Import and in the Import dialog box browse to the Lesson06/Assets folder. Select feature.swf, and click Open. The feature.swf file contains text and graphics. You can use your drawing skills to recreate the contents of this file. Just use the figure above as a guide.

3) Create a new, empty movie clip named Video Clip.

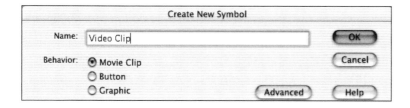

You are going to place the video you import into this movie clip. To create the movie clip, choose Insert > New Symbol, or press Ctrl+F8 (Windows) or Command+F8 (Macintosh). When the Symbol Properties dialog box opens, set the Name to Video Clip and the Behavior to Movie Clip. Then click OK, and Flash opens the new symbol in symbol-editing mode.

4) Choose File › Import. When the Import dialog box opens, browse to the Lesson06/ Assets folder, and import seals.mov. When the Import Video dialog box opens, choose "Embed video in Macromedia Flash document" and click OK.

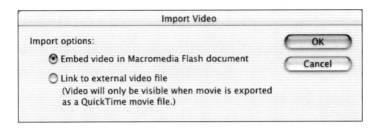

When you attempt to import a QuickTime movie into Flash, you have the option of embedding the movie in the Flash document, or linking to the external video file. If you choose to link to the external file, the video will only be visible when you export the Flash movie as a QuickTime file.

With QuickTime 4 installed, Flash can import Audio Video Interleaved (AVI), Digital Video (DV), Motion Picture Experts Group (MPEG), and QuickTime Movie (MOV) file formats in both Windows and on a Macintosh. On a Windows computer with DirectX 7 or higher installed, you can import Windows Media File (WMV or ASF), AVI, and MPEG file formats. You can also import Macromedia Flash Video format (FLV) directly into Flash in Windows and on a Macintosh. FLV files are created when you export a video clip from Flash.

Flash imports and exports video using the Sorenson Spark codec, which is an algorithm that controls how multimedia files are compressed and decompressed. Additional video codecs, may be supported on your system. If you try to import a file that is not supported on your system, Flash will display a warning message.

NOTE *If for some reason you are unable to import seals.mov, try to import seals.flv from the Lesson06/Assets folder. The file is saved in Macromedia Flash Video format, and you should be able to import it regardless of your system's setup. If you import seals.flv, you can skip to step 7 in this exercise.*

5) In the Import Video Settings dialog box, set the Quality to 75, Keyframe interval to 24, and Scale to 100%.

When you attempt to import most video files, the Import Video Settings dialog box should open.

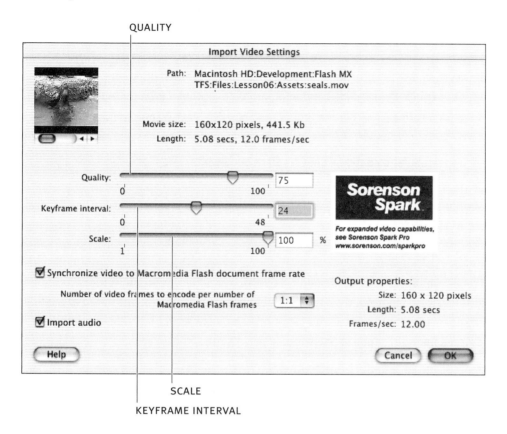

QUALITY

SCALE

KEYFRAME INTERVAL

The Quality setting specifies the level of compression for the video. A smaller value in this setting will import the video at a lower quality and higher compression; a higher setting will import the video at a higher quality and lower compression (larger file size). You can set this value by dragging the slider, or typing a number between 0 and 100 in the space provided.

The Keyframe interval controls the frequency of keyframes in the video clip. A video keyframe is a frame that contains complete data, while the frames between store only the data that changes from the preceding frame. A keyframe interval of 24 will store a keyframe every 24 frames in the video clip. Smaller intervals store more complete frames, resulting in a larger file size. Drag the slider to modify this setting, or type a number between 0 and 48 in the Keyframe interval box.

NOTE *Video keyframes don't necessarily correspond to Flash keyframes.*

The Scale setting modifies the video's pixel size. You can set the Scale as low as 1% and as high as 100%. You can't use the Scale setting to make the video larger than its original size. A smaller pixel size reduces the file size of the imported video clip. Drag the slider to set the Scale, or type a number between 1 and 100 in the Scale box.

6) Make sure the "Synchronize video to Macromedia Flash document frame rate" option is checked, and deselect the Import Audio option. Leave the Number of video frames to encode per number of Macromedia Flash frames setting at 1:1.

☑ Synchronize video to Macromedia Flash document frame rate

Number of video frames to encode per number of
Macromedia Flash frames   [1:1 ▲▼]

☐ Import audio

The Synchronize video to Macromedia Flash document frame rate setting, when selected, lets you match the speed of the imported video clip to the speed of the Flash movie. So if the frame rate of your Flash movie is set to 12 frames per second (fps) the imported video clip will also play at 12 fps.

When the Import Audio setting is selected, Flash imports the video clip's audio track. If you leave Import Audio selected, and import the audio track, the file size will increase. If the audio codec used in the audio track is not installed on your system, you will not be able to import it. Flash will display a warning telling you so; you can then import the video without sound, or modify the original video file so it uses an audio codec supported on your system.

The Number of video frames to encode per number of Macromedia Flash frames setting specifies the ratio of imported video frames to Flash frames. The default setting is 1:1, which will encode one video frame per Flash frame. If you change the setting to 1:2, one imported video frame will be encoded for every two Flash frames which can result in choppier playback.

When you click OK, a message should appear asking if you'd like to expand the timeline to fit the frames of the video clip. Click Yes, otherwise only the first frame of the video will appear in the finished file.

The video clip will be imported. Flash should expand the timeline to fit the frames of the video clip.

7) Choose Edit > Edit Document to return to the main timeline. Select the Contents layer and add an instance of the Video Clip symbol to the stage. Use the Property inspector to set the X and Y of this instance to 321 and 196, respectively.

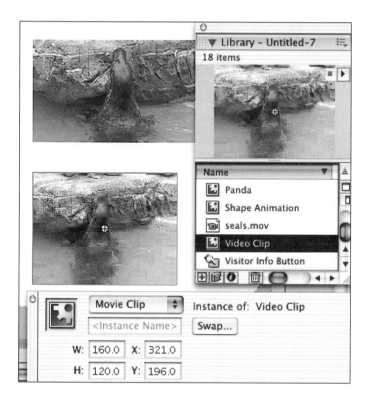

TIP *You can also return to the main timeline by clicking the Scene 1 icon.*

You should be able to locate the Video Clip movie clip symbol in the Library (Window > Library). Select the Contents layer and drag an instance of the movie clip onto the stage. With the Video Clip movie clip instance selected, use the Property inspector to position it precisely on the stage.

8) Choose Control › Test Movie.

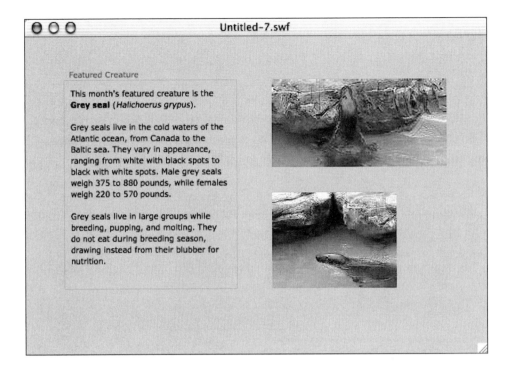

When you test the movie, you should see that the video clip, which is inside the Video Clip symbol, plays as part of the Flash movie. Notice that when the video reaches the end, it loops back to its first frame and plays again. If you'd like to make the movie stop at the last frame, you can simply add a keyframe in the last frame and add a `stop` action.

9) Save the file as feature1.fla in the FlashTFS folder on your hard drive.

You now have some sound and video in your project. In Lesson 12, you will learn more about working with sound and video.

WHAT YOU HAVE LEARNED

- Imported a sound file and added it to the timeline (pages 188–191)
- Modified a sound's properties (pages 191–193)
- Added sounds to a button (pages 193–195)
- Customized a sound's effects (pages 196–200)
- Imported a video file and added it to the movie (pages 200–206)

programming with ActionScript

At this point, you should be comfortable using the Flash basics. You've gotten to know the panels and tools, worked in the timeline and on the stage, used layers and simple ActionScript, and created everything from simple graphics to working buttons. But Flash can do so much more. This lesson gives you a taste of the power of Flash.

You can use ActionScript to create complex interaction.

```
26 for (var i=0; i<menu.length; i++) {
27     menuClip.attachMovie("mpiece", "item" + i, ++cDepth);
28     menuClip["item"+i].mtext = menu[i];
29     menuClip["item"+i]._y = menuClip.top._height + menuClip
30     menuClip["item"+i].useHandCursor = false;
31     menuClip["item"+i].onRollOver = function () {
32         this.t.backgroundColor = 0xFF6600;
33         this.t.textColor = 0xFFFFFF;
34     }
35     menuClip["item"+i].onRollOut = function () {
36         this.t.backgroundColor = 0xFFFFFF;
37         this.t.textColor = 0xCC0000;
38     }
39 }
40 menuClip.attachMovie("minmax", "minmax", ++cDepth);
41 menuClip.minmax.useHandCursor = false;
42 menuClip.minmax._y = 0;
43 menuClip.minmax._x = menuClip.top._width - menuClip.minmax.
44 menuClip.minmax.maximized = true;
45 menuClip.minmax.onPress = function () {
46     if (this.maximized) {
47         this.maximized = false;
```

Chrissy Rey

Here you will learn the basics of programming with ActionScript. If you don't have any experience programming, you may feel a bit overwhelmed at first with all the code in this lesson. Don't give up! It may take some time to understand all the concepts. You might find it useful to read through the lesson a couple of times before you go to the next lesson. Be sure to read the explanations—don't just type the code to make the project work!

WHAT YOU WILL LEARN

In this lesson, you will:

- Use ActionScript to create a drop-down menu
- Add a dynamic text box and use a variable to give it content
- Create and use an array
- Modify text boxes using the `TextField` object's properties
- Create a loop to repeat several lines of ActionScript
- Use several of the `MovieClip` object's methods, properties, and event handlers
- Control the appearance of your menu with a conditional statement

APPROXIMATE TIME

This lesson takes approximately two hours to complete.

LESSON FILES

Media Files:
Lesson07/Assets/assets.fla

Starting Files:
Lesson07/Starting/zoo28.fla

Completed Project:
Lesson07/Completed/zoo34.fla

USING VARIABLES

A *variable* is a placeholder for information. Think of it as a container. The container (variable) is always the same, but the contents (value) can change. You can change the contents of a variable to record information about what a user has done, record values that change as the movie plays, or evaluate whether a condition is true or false. You can use variables to make updating your movie easy; every place where the variable is used, Flash fills in its value.

One place you can use the value of a variable is a *dynamic text box*, which can display dynamically updated text such as scores and stock quotes. To assign the value of a variable to a dynamic text box, you give the variable and the dynamic text box the same name.

1) Open zoo28.fla.

You should start this lesson with zoo28.fla open. It's one of the files you saved in the last lesson, so you should be able to find it in the FlashTFS folder on your hard drive. If it's not there, you can open the file from the Lesson07/Starting folder on the CD-ROM. Just make to save it to your hard drive before you continue.

2) Select frame 12 of the Menu layer. Select the instance of the Visitor Info Button in frame 12, and press Backspace or Delete to remove it. Right-click (Windows) or Control-click (Macintosh) the name of the Menu layer, and choose Hide Others.

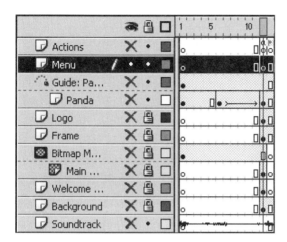

You are going to use ActionScript to create a menu in this layer, so you should remove the button now.

Since you want to concentrate on the menu you're building, it'll be easier to work in the movie if only the Menu layer is visible. So it's a good idea to hide all the other layers in the movie so that their contents won't distract you and you won't accidentally select something in another layer.

3) Select the text tool from the toolbox. In the Property inspector set the Text Type to Dynamic Text. Modify the remaining properties so that the Property inspector looks like the figure below.

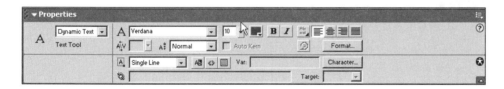

When you select the text tool from the toolbox, the Property inspector should display the Text properties. The Text Type is the setting on the far left. Set the Text Type to Dynamic Text, which allows you to add a text box that displays content generated by ActionScript. Set the Font to Verdana, the Font Size to 10, and the Text (fill) Color to red (#CC0000). You also need to set the Line Type to Single Line. This

211

ensures that the text box you create in the next step will allow users to type text only in a single line. You will add a multiline text box later in this lesson.

Compare the Property inspector with the figure above, and make sure the rest of the settings are the same.

Notice that choosing Dynamic Text causes the settings in the Property inspector to change. The Line Type setting becomes available, and the Variable setting appears along with the Character button. The Use Device Fonts option disappears, and the Auto Kern option becomes disabled. The left half of the figure below shows the Property inspector when Static Text is selected; the right half shows the Property inspector after you choose Dynamic Text.

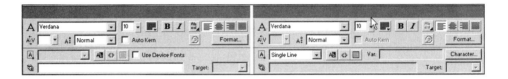

4) Make sure frame 12 of the Menu layer is selected. Create a text box on the stage by clicking and dragging to the desired width.

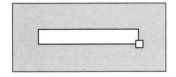

The text box should be approximately 100 pixels wide.

NOTE *Be sure to resize the text box by double-clicking and dragging the handle on the right side of the text box. Don't use the Property inspector to resize the text box, as that will resize the text inside the text box. You want the text to have a font size of 10, and resizing the text box using the Property inspector may result in strange-looking text.*

5) Use the arrow tool to select the text box you just drew. In the Property inspector, type *mtext* in the Variable text box.

When you switch to the arrow tool, the text box should be selected automatically.

The Variable setting in the Property inspector is the variable name associated with the text box. It's set in the text box labeled Var. A variable is a container for a value. The container you just created is a text box called mtext. You're going to use ActionScript to provide a value for that container.

6) Select frame 1 of the Actions layer, and open the Actions panel if it's not already open. Click the Options menu control in the top-right corner of the Actions panel, and choose Expert Mode.

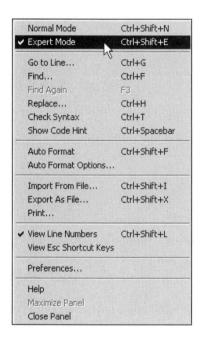

TIP *If you can't find the Actions panel, choose Window > Actions to open it. You can also use the keyboard shortcut F9 to open this panel.*

When you switch the Actions panel to Expert Mode, the Actions toolbox is still on the left side of the panel, but the parameters pane disappears. A few extra buttons also appear above the script pane.

In expert mode you can enter ActionScript directly into the script pane, much as you would add JavaScript or C++ in a text editor. You can use the Actions toolbox and the Add button to add ActionScript to the script pane. Expert mode also lets you check for syntax errors, automatically format code, and use code hints—just click the Check Syntax, Auto Format, or Show Code Hint buttons to trigger one of these very useful features. You will use all three later in this lesson.

7) Make sure you still have frame 1 of the Actions layer selected. Click in the script pane, and type `mtext = "guestbook";`.

The following ActionScript should now appear in line 1 of the script pane:

```
mtext = "guestbook";
```

Notice that this ActionScript appears in line 1. If you don't see the line number on the left of the ActionScript in the script pane, click the Options button near the right side of the Actions panel, and choose View Line Numbers. You should also see the line number, total number of lines, and current column position of the pointer at the bottom of the Actions panel.

This ActionScript sets the "container" to `mtext`, which is the name you gave the variable in the dynamic text box. It also sets the contents of the container to `"guestbook"`, using the assignment operator (=). The quotes around the contents indicate that the value is a string, which is a type of data that the variable can hold.

TIP *You can click the Check Syntax button above the script pane, and Flash will check the code to make sure the syntax is correct. If there are any errors, a window will open, indicating where those errors might be.*

The value of a variable, or what the "container" holds, can be one of several types of data. For `mtext`, the variable's value is a string, which is a sequence of characters such as letters, numbers, and punctuation marks. Variables can also hold numbers, which can be manipulated using arithmetic operators such as addition (+) and subtraction (−). You'll learn more about operators later in this lesson. The value of a variable can also be a Boolean, which is a value that is either true or false. Movie clips are considered data types in Flash, as you will learn later in this lesson. Variables can have a null

214

value, which means "no value." A variable can have an undefined value, which happens when the variable has not yet been assigned a value.

Variables can refer to objects, which are collections of properties and methods. Each property in an object has a name and value, and the value can be any data type. Each method of an object describes what the object does. For example if you had a `Seal` object, that object might have a method called `swim`. The `swim` method of the `Seal` object tells the seal to swim. You can often pass arguments, or additional information, to a method of an object, to modify how it works. Using the `Seal` object example, you might pass an argument called `speed`, with a value of 20, to the `swim` method. The argument would cause the seal to swim at a speed of 20 knots. You'll learn much more about objects throughout this lesson.

NOTE *The type of data a variable contains affects how the variable's value changes when the variable is assigned in ActionScript.*

The semicolon (;) at the end of the line of ActionScript you just added is punctuation for ActionScript. It lets Flash know you've reached the end of a line. It's not required, but it's good practice to add a semicolon at the end of a line of code. You will see that ActionScript has other punctuation, such as curly braces ({ and }).

8) Choose Control > Test Movie.

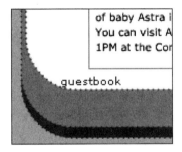

When you test the movie, the word *guestbook* should appear somewhere on the stage. The value of the `mtext` variable you created in frame 1 of the Actions layer is passed to the text box with the same variable name. When you're finished, close the test-movie window.

9) Save the file as zoo29.fla in the FlashTFS folder on your hard drive.
The text box on the stage isn't quite a menu, but you are going to use it to create one.

USING ARRAYS

Arrays are lists of variables. Each "line" of the list can contain a single variable, the value of which can be anything (string, number, object, another array, and so on). After you have created an array, you reference a line of the array by giving the name of your array and then the line number, which is actually called the *index* and always starts at 0, inside square brackets like this:

```
MyArray[2];
```

In the next exercise, you will create an array to contain all the items you are going to have in your menu. You should start this exercise with zoo29.fla open.

1) Select frame 1 of the Actions layer. In the Actions panel, modify the code so you have a variable called menu, with a value of new Array();.

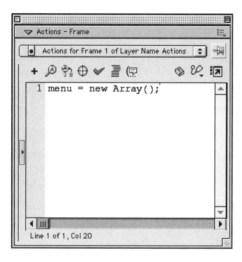

The ActionScript attached to frame 1 of the Actions layer should now look like this:

```
menu = new Array();
```

This sets the value of the menu variable to a new Array object. Remember, an object is a collection of properties and methods. An Array object is a collection of properties and methods that refer to an array. An array is a list of variables, or elements, and each element in that list is considered a property of the Array object. The Array object also has a length property, which lets you know how many elements are in the array.

The Array object is one of the many objects built into ActionScript. An ActionScript has several methods, or special functions, that let you handle an array. For example, the Array object has a reverse method, which lets you reverse the order of the elements in the array.

216

The new portion of the ActionScript is a special operator that lets you create a new object. The operator is typically followed by a constructor function, which is a special function that defines the properties and methods of a new object. The constructor function in this case is **Array()**, which refers to the built-in **Array** object. So in essence, this code creates a new copy of the **Array** object. The constructor function can optionally have arguments passed to it in the parentheses. In the **Array** object, the optional arguments are the length of the new array or the elements you want to add to the new array. The name of the new object is **menu**. The **menu** object has all the built-in properties and methods of the built-in **Array** object.

TIP *The code in this step has a space before and after the assignment operator (=). This space is not required, but it does make it easier to read the code.*

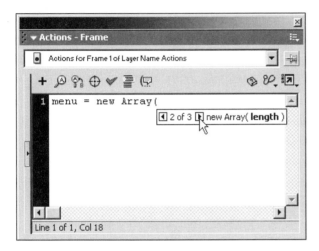

As you typed the code in this step, you may have noticed that a Tooltip popped up after you typed the open parenthesis ((). That Tooltip is a code hint, which displays the complete syntax for the code that Flash thinks you're typing. Notice that there are two arrow buttons in the Tooltip—these appear when there's more than one possible syntax for the code. Click the arrow buttons to scroll through the possibilities. When you type the closing parenthesis ( )), the Tooltip should disappear.

NOTE *If for some reason you didn't see a Tooltip, click the Options menu control in the Actions panel and choose Preferences. Make sure the Show Code Hint option is selected, and click OK.*

NOTE *If you find that the code in the Actions panel is too small to read, you can modify its size. Click the Options menu control at the top-right side of the Actions panel and choose Preferences. You can then change the font size in the Text area of the Preferences dialog box.*

2) Type "home", "featured creature", "visitor info", "map", "games", "guestbook" **inside the parentheses.**

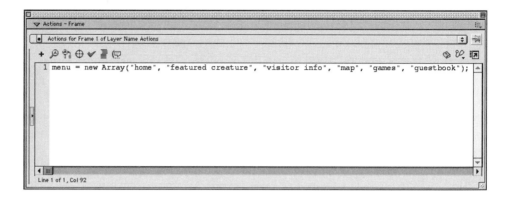

Your ActionScript should now look like this:

```
menu = new Array("home", "featured creature", "visitor info", "map",
"games", "guestbook");
```

When you use the `Array()` constructor function, as you did in step 2, you can type either the length of the new array or a list of the elements inside the parentheses. Or you can leave the parentheses empty. In this case, you added six elements to the array: `"home"`, `"featured creature"`, `"visitor info"`, `"map"`, `"games"`, and `"guestbook"`. Notice that each of the elements in this array is surrounded by quotation marks, which indicates that each element is a string.

TIP *The space between each element in the array is optional, but it does help make the code more readable.*

3) Add a second line to the script pane, and type mtext = menu[0];.

You can add a second line by going to the end of the first line and pressing Enter or Return. Then just type the code. Your ActionScript should end up looking like this:

```
menu = new Array("home", "featured creature", "visitor info", "map",
"games", "guestbook");
mtext = menu[0];
```

Once again you added the `mtext` variable, but this time its value is quite different. Instead of setting the value to a string, you set it to one of the elements in the `menu` array, namely `menu[0]`. This refers to the element in the `menu` array that has an index of 0, which is the first element (`"home"`). The second element in the array (`"featured creature"`) has an index of 1, the third has an index of 2, and so on.

4) Choose Control > Test Movie.

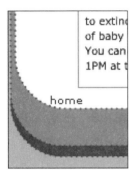

When you test the movie, the word *home* should now appear in the dynamic text box that has the variable name `mtext`.

Close the Test Movie window when you're finished.

5) Select frame 1 of the Actions layer, and modify the ActionScript so the `mtext` variable has a value of `menu[3]`.

Your ActionScript should now look like this:

```
menu = new Array("home", "featured creature", "visitor info", "map",
"games", "guestbook");
mtext = menu[3];
```

Now the value of the `mtext` variable is another element in the `menu` array. This time it's the one that has an index of 3, which is the fourth element (`"map"`).

219

6) Choose Control > Test Movie.

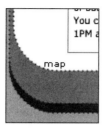

This time, when you test the movie, the word *map* should appear in the text box.

Close the Test Movie window when you're finished.

7) Select frame 1 of the Actions layer, and modify the menu **array so each element is on its own line.**

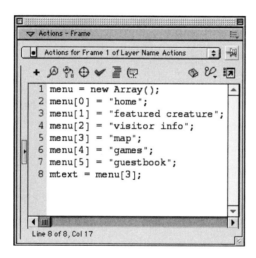

This is actually much easier than it sounds! All you have to do is delete the arguments (all of the elements) in the Array constructor function, so the first line of ActionScript will look like this:

```
menu = new Array();
```

Then you can add a new variable name/value pair for each element. The variable name is the name of the array, followed by the index number of the element inside of square brackets ([and]). The value is the element. Don't forget that the index numbers start at 0, and make sure to put quotes around each value so Flash knows it's a string. For the first element, you would type this:

```
menu[0] = "home";
```

Your ActionScript should be:

```
menu = new Array();
menu[0] = "home";
menu[1] = "featured creature";
menu[2] = "visitor info";
menu[3] = "map";
menu[4] = "games";
menu[5] = "guestbook";
mtext = menu[3];
```

There's no need to test the movie again, unless you want to double-check your work. You didn't actually change the array, you just split it into several lines, making it a bit easier to read and modify. You will make some major changes to the menu array in Lesson 11, and this step is preparation for those modifications.

8) Save the file as zoo30.fla in the FlashTFS folder on your hard drive.

You still don't have a menu, but you have an array that contains all of the text for your menu. Over the course of the next two exercises you'll use more ActionScript to dynamically add several instances of a movie clip, each of which will contain one element from the array.

USING THE TEXTFIELD OBJECT

Flash has several built-in objects, which you can use to customize many aspects of your movies. One of the built-in objects is the TextField object. Every instance of a dynamic or input text box in Flash is a copy of the TextField object. The TextField object has a number of properties, including background, backgroundColor, border, and borderColor. You can use these properties to customize the look of your text boxes with ActionScript, as you'll do in the next exercise.

Start this exercise with zoo30.fla from the last exercise open.

1) Select the dynamic text box in frame 12 of the Menu layer, and choose Insert > Convert to Symbol. When the Symbol Properties dialog box opens, type *Menu Piece* in the Name text box, set the Behavior to Movie Clip, and set the Registration to the top-left corner.

You are going to use the dynamic text box as the basis for each piece of the menu. But before you do, you have to place the dynamic text box inside a movie clip. You are going to use ActionScript to dynamically attach instances of the movie clip containing the dynamic text box to the movie.

It's important that you set the Registration for this new movie clip to the top-left corner. The ActionScript you'll add to create the menu will be based on the assumption that the registration point for the Menu Piece movie clip is in the top-left corner of the symbol. If it's not, the menu may look strange. If you complete the menu and it looks a little off, check to make sure the top-left corner of the dynamic text box is at the center of the Menu Piece symbol. The dynamic text box should look like the figure below.

2) Click the Advanced button in the Symbol Properties dialog box. In the expanded dialog box, select the "Export for ActionScript" option and type *mpiece* in the Identifier text box. Make sure the "Export in first frame" option is also selected, and click OK.

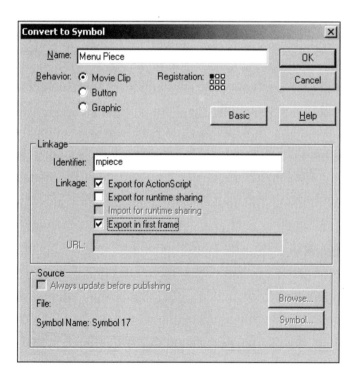

When you click the Advanced button in the Symbol Properties dialog box, several additional options appear in the dialog box, including the Linkage settings.

Before you can attach a movie clip directly from the library, you need to set the movie clip to export with the movie. By default, symbols that are not on the stage are not exported with the movie. There's currently an instance of the Menu Piece movie clip on the stage, but you will remove that instance by the end of this exercise. So first you need to select the "Export for ActionScript" option in the Linkage area of the Symbol Properties dialog box. When you select this setting, Flash automatically selects the "Export in first frame" option—leave this option selected, or the symbol must be added to the stage in order to export it with the movie.

Once the movie clip is set to be exported with the movie, you have to give it an identifier. An identifier is simply a name that Flash can use to reference the exported movie clip in ActionScript, since there is no instance of the movie clip in the movie, and thus no instance name for the movie clip. When you select the "Export for ActionScript" option, the Identifier field becomes editable. Type *mpiece* in that field, so Flash knows to call this movie clip mpiece when it's time to attach it to the movie.

3) Open the Menu Piece movie clip in symbol-editing mode. Select the text box on the stage, and set its instance name to t.

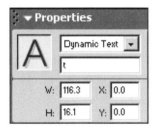

You can open the Menu Piece movie clip in symbol-editing mode by double-clicking on the instance that was created on the stage in the last step. Or you can open the library, locate the Menu Piece movie clip, and double-click the icon to the left of that symbol's name.

In order to use the built-in `TextField` object, which you're going to do in the next step, you need to give the dynamic text box an instance name. That way Flash knows which text box the ActionScript should modify. In this case, the instance name of the text box, which is set in the Property inspector, should be `t`.

4) Name the existing layer Text, and add a new layer above it named Actions. Select frame 1 of the new Actions layer, and add the following ActionScript to the Actions panel:

```
t.background = true;
t.border = true;
t.borderColor = 0xCC0000;
```

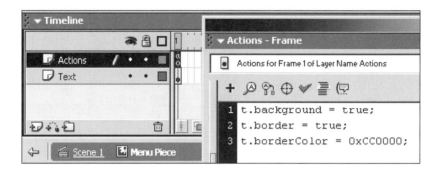

When you used the built-in Array object to create a new array in the last exercise, you had to use the new operator and a constructor function:

```
menu = new Array();
```

You do not need to use the built-in TextField object in Flash. You simply need a text box, or text field in the movie. The instance name of the text box is the name of the object, so the TextField object in this case is called t. It would be like adding this code:

```
t = new TextField();
```

You don't have to add this code, though, because Flash "knows" that you have a TextField object when you add a dynamic text box to the movie.

NOTE *All dynamic and input text boxes are instances of the TextField object.*

TIP *Click the Insert a Target Path button to open the Insert Target Path dialog box. Select the movie clip, text field, or button you want to use as your object, be sure the Notation is set to Dots, set the Mode to Relative, and click OK. See the figure on the following page.*

224

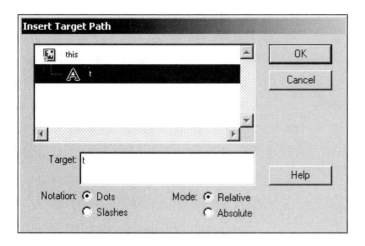

Once you've added a new object to the movie, you can access its built-in properties using dot syntax. Simply type the name of the object, followed by a dot, and then followed by the property you want to modify or read. In the ActionScript you just added, the name of the object is **t**, and the properties are **background**, **border**, and **borderColor**.

You can use dot syntax to target anything with an instance name, such as a text box or a movie clip. A dot syntax target path looks much like a file path on your computer, except the slashes (/) or colons (:) are replaced with dots (.). So if you refer to the **fish** instance, which is inside the **seal** instance, you would use **seal.fish**.

Dot syntax target paths can be absolute or relative. Dot syntax uses two special aliases, **_root** and **_parent**. The **_root** alias refers to the main timeline (root), and the **_parent** alias refers to the timeline in which the current movie clip is nested.

In addition to using dot syntax to identify target paths, ActionScript uses dot syntax to refer to properties of an object. State the name of the object (or the target path of a movie clip), followed by a dot, and name the property you want to reference. For example, if you want to reference the **speed** property of an object called **cheetah**, you would reference **cheetah.speed**.

Referring to a method of an object works almost the same way. Methods have arguments, or parameters, that are placeholders for values passed to the method. These arguments follow the name of the method in parentheses, using the following syntax: **methodName(arguments)**. To use dot syntax to refer to a method of an object, you would first state the name of the object (or the target path of a movie clip), followed by a dot and then the method. For example, if you want to reference the **eat** method of the `cheetah` object with no arguments, you would reference `cheetah.eat()`. If you want to pass an argument called `victim` with a value of `"antelope"`, the syntax would be `cheetah.eat("antelope")`. The `victim` argument is specified in the definition of the object method.

Properties are basically like variables—they can hold values. In the `background` property of the built-in `TextField` object, the value can be a Boolean, which means it can be either `true` or `false`. Setting it to `true` will cause a background to appear behind the text box. By default, that background will be white. The border property's value can also be a Boolean. Setting this value to `true` will cause a border to appear around the text box. The default color for this border is black. Finally, the `borderColor` property can have a number value. In this case, the value should be a hexadecimal number. Setting this value to the hexadecimal number 0xCC0000 will create a dark red border around the text box.

5) Return to the main movie's timeline, and delete the Menu layer. Choose frame 1 of the Actions layer, and add the following ActionScript to the Actions panel:

```
// create a new movie clip to hold the menu
this.createEmptyMovieClip("menuClip", 1);
menuClip._visible = false;
cDepth = 0;
```

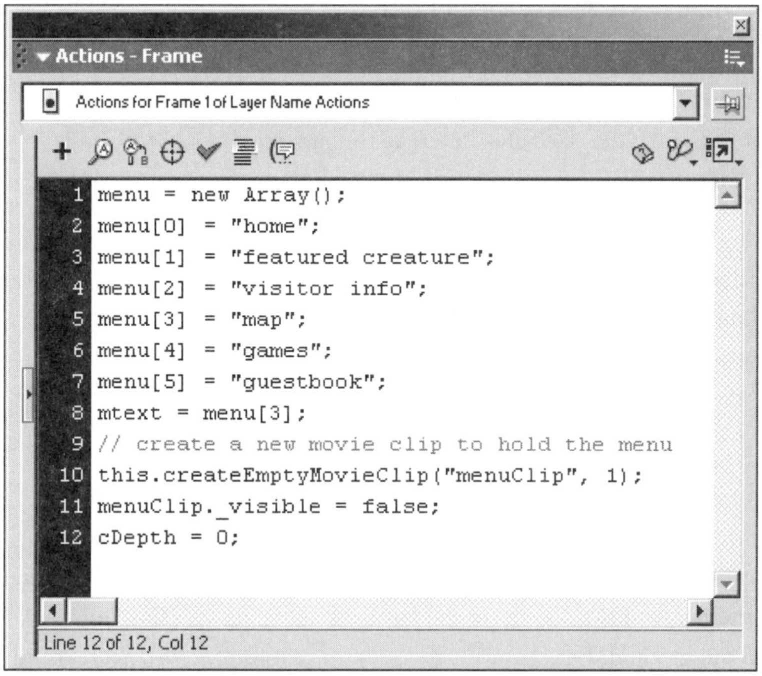

Actions - Frame
Actions for Frame 1 of Layer Name Actions
menu = new Array();
menu[0] = "home";
menu[1] = "featured creature";
menu[2] = "visitor info";
menu[3] = "map";
menu[4] = "games";
menu[5] = "guestbook";
mtext = menu[3];
// create a new movie clip to hold the menu
this.createEmptyMovieClip("menuClip", 1);
menuClip._visible = false;
cDepth = 0;
Line 12 of 12, Col 12

You don't need the Menu layer anymore, because you're going to use ActionScript to add the menu to the movie. Select the Menu layer, and click the Delete Layer button at the bottom of the timeline.

The first line of this ActionScript is a comment. When you add it to the Actions panel, the comment is highlighted in gray. The comment reminds you what a particular piece of ActionScript does, and it's helpful for other programmers who might need to use your code.

The next line of ActionScript creates a new, empty movie clip. The `createEmptyMovieClip` portion of this code is a method of the `MovieClip` object, another built-in object in Flash. Every movie clip added to the stage is considered an instance of the `MovieClip` object, so as with the `TextField` object, you don't have to use a constructor function to make a copy. The `createEmptyMovieClip` method, as its name might suggest, creates a new, empty movie clip inside its object. In this case, the object is `this`, which refers to the current timeline.

The arguments for the `createEmptyMovieClip` method are the instance name of the new movie clip and its depth. In this code, you set the instance name to `"menuClip"`, which will become a new instance of the `MovieClip` object once the movie clip is added. The depth is the z-index, or stacking order, of the attached movie clip. Attached movie clips are always higher in the stacking order than anything else in the movie. For this bit of code, the depth is set to 1. The depth value can be any positive number, and the higher the number, the higher in the stacking order the movie clip will be.

The `MovieClip` object has a number of properties, one of which is the `_visible` property. This property determines whether or not the referenced movie clip is visible on the screen. A Boolean value of `true` makes the movie clip visible, while `false` makes it disappear. In this case, you'll set the `_visible` property of the `menuClip` object (movie clip) to `false`, so it will not appear on the screen. Why go through the hassle of adding it if it's not visible? Because you don't want the menu to appear on the screen until you're ready! You'll add more code later to make the menu appear.

Finally, you added a line of code that initializes a variable called `cDepth`. The value of this variable is a number, namely 0. It's a good idea to initialize variables before you use them so you don't end up with undefined values later. You will use this variable to set the depths of several movie clips later in the code.

6) Add the following ActionScript:

```
// attach an instance of mpiece
menuClip.attachMovie("mpiece", "top", ++cDepth);
menuClip.top.mtext = "menu";
```

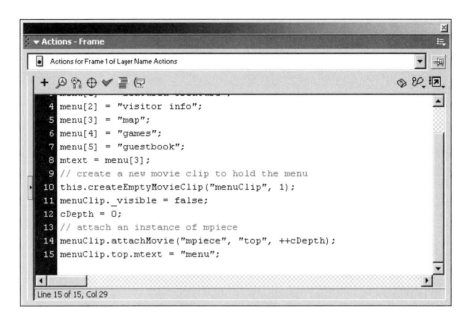

You should add this ActionScript following the script already in frame 1 of the Actions layer. Just add a new line and start typing.

Once again, the first line of this ActionScript is a comment. It's there to remind you, or another programmer, what's going on.

The next line of code uses another method of the MovieClip object: attachMovie. As you already know, a method needs an object—in this case, menuClip, which refers to the movie clip you created in the last step.

The arguments for the attachMovie method are idName (the identifier for the attached movie clip), newName (the new instance name of the attached movie clip), and depth (the depth of the attached movie clip). You set the identifier for the Menu Piece movie clip to mpiece when you created it. The instance you attach inside the menuClip movie clip will have an instance name of top when this code is run. Finally, the depth is the z-index, or stacking order, of the attached movie clip. In this case, you're using a variable (cDepth), but it has the increment operator in front of it. That changes the value of the variable cDepth by 1 before it returns a value. When you use the increment operator, you can increase the value of the affected variable by 1. You initialized cDepth at 0, so this code will set the depth (the value of cDepth) to 1. It will keep the new value of cDepth in memory for the next time that variable is used.

Be sure to put the values for the `idName` and `newName` arguments in quotation marks. You want the string `"mpiece"` to be used for the `idName` argument and the string `"top"` to be used for the `newName` argument. If you forget the quotation marks, Flash tries to use the values of variables called `mpiece` and `top` for those arguments. Because no such variables exist, your ActionScript won't work. The value for the `depth` argument doesn't need quotation marks, because it's a variable.

Finally, the last line of code sets the `mtext` variable inside the attached movie clip to `"menu"`. So when the instance of the Menu Piece movie clip is attached inside the movie clip instance named `menu`, the word *menu* should appear inside. In the next step you'll modify the text box so it has a unique background color and text color.

7) Add this ActionScript:

```
// set the background color and text color of the text field
menuClip.top.t.backgroundColor = 0xCC0000;
menuClip.top.t.textColor = 0xFFFFFF;
```

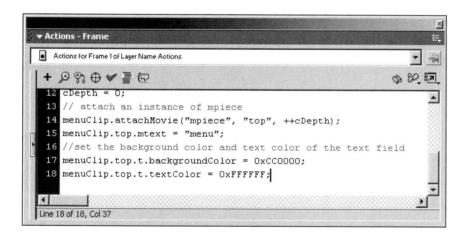

Add this ActionScript to frame 1 of the Actions layer, following the code already there.

As before, the first line of this code is a comment. You'll see quite a few comments throughout this lesson. It's very useful to add comments to your code as you learn ActionScript so you can remember what all those strange lines of code do the next time you look at them.

The next line of code uses the `backgroundColor` property of the built-in `TextField` object. It sets the background color of the `t` instance, which is inside the `top` instance, which is nested in the `menuClip` instance, to a dark red color (#CC0000). In step 4 of this exercise, you set the `background` property of the text field named `t` to `true`—the background property must be `true` in order for the color set by the `backgroundColor` property to be visible.

229

PROGRAMMING WITH ACTIONSCRIPT

The last line of code sets the `textColor` property of the built-in `TextField` object, which is applied to the dynamic text box with an instance name of `t`. The `textColor` property, as its name suggests, sets the text color of the affected text box. So this code will set the text color of the `t` text box to white (#FFFFFF).

8) Save the file as zoo31.fla in the FlashTFS folder on your hard drive.

Since the menu movie clip is invisible (`_visible` is `false`) right now, there's no point in testing because you won't be able to see anything. If you'd like to check your work anyway, just go back and comment out the line that sets the `menuClip`'s `_visible` property to `false`—add two slashes (//) at the start of that line. Then test the movie to see what happens. Remember to remove the two slashes from the start of the line before you continue.

Make sure you save your work at this point! You've added a lot of ActionScript and significantly changed the movie.

WORKING WITH LOOPS IN ACTIONSCRIPT

Sometimes you need to apply the same ActionScript several times. Rather than writing the ActionScript each time, you can use an ActionScript-based loop to repeat the same ActionScript a set number of times. ActionScript has several different actions to create loops: `for`, `for…in`, `while`, and `do while`. In the following exercise you will add a `for` statement to your movie to add several instances of the Menu Piece movie clip. You will also customize the appearance of each Menu Piece instance using the `for` statement. You should still have zoo31.fla from the last exercise open when you start this exercise.

1) Add this code to frame 1, following the ActionScript already in the script pane:

```
for (var i=0; i<menu.length; i++) {
}
```

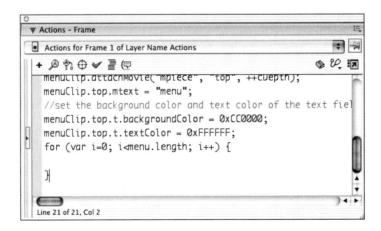

Select frame 1 of the Actions layer, and add this code to the script pane in the Actions panel. It should follow the code already in frame 1.

The first and last lines of code create a loop:

```
for (var i=0; i<menu.length; i++) {
}
```

This is a `for` statement, which is a loop with a built-in counter. The syntax for a `for` statement is as follows:

```
for (initial expression; condition; post expression) {
}
```

Any code inside the curly braces of the `for` statement will run as many times as the `condition` is true.

The `initial expression`, which is `var i=0` in the code you added, initializes the built-in counter for the `for` statement. It sets the value of a variable named `i` to an initial value of `0`. The `var` before the variable assignment simply tells Flash that this is a local variable—it will exist only inside the `for` statement. That way, if you use a variable named `i` in another part of the code, it won't be affected by this variable named `i`. The `post expression`, which is `i++` in your code, tells the `for` statement what to do to the counter each time it runs through the `for` statement. So in the case of the ActionScript you added, the counter is a variable named `i`, which starts with a value of `0`, and is changed by an increment of 1 each time the `for` statement is run (`i++`).

NOTE *When you used the increment operator (++) before, it was placed before the name of the variable, which increases the value of the variable by 1 and returns the new value. In this* for *statement, the increment operator follows the name of the variable and changes the variable's value by an increment of 1, but it returns the value before it was incremented.*

The `condition` is a logical expression that determines how many times the `for` statement is run. The statement runs as long as the `condition` expression is true. In this case, the condition checks to see if `i` is less than the value of `menu.length`, which is the `length` property of the `menu` array. The `length` property of the built-in `Array` object, of which the `menu` array is a copy, checks to see how many elements are in the array. The `menu` array has six elements, so `menu.length` has a value of `6`. If you add or remove elements from the `menu` array, the value of `menu.length` changes accordingly. Once the value of `i` reaches `6`, the condition is no longer true, and the `for` statement will not run anymore.

2) Inside the for **statement's curly braces (**{ **and** }**) add the following code:**

```
menuClip.attachMovie("mpiece", "item"+i, ++cDepth);
menuClip["item"+i].mtext = menu[i];
menuClip["item"+i]._y = menuClip.top._height + menuClip["item"+i]._height*i;
```

After you add the code, the for statement should look like this:

```
for (var i=0; i<menu.length; i++) {
menuClip.attachMovie("mpiece", "item"+i, ++cDepth);
menuClip["item"+i].mtext = menu[i];
menuClip["item"+i]._y = menuClip.top._height + menuClip["item"+i]._height*i;
}
```

Don't let this code intimidate you! It may appear to be very complex, but after you break it down, you'll see that it's actually rather simple.

The first line attaches an instance of the Menu Piece movie clip inside the menuClip instance, giving it a new instance name of "item"+i. So the first time through the for statement, when i is 0, the instance name will be item0. The second time through, it will be item1, and so on. The depth for the attached movie clip is the incremented value of cDepth. You already increased the value of cDepth by one once, when you attached the top instance, so the first time through the for statement, it should have a value of 2, and it will increase by one more each time the for statement runs this code.

The second line of code sets the value of the `mtext` variable inside the attached movie clip to a value from the `menu` array. This second line sets up your ActionScript to use the dynamically generated instance name for the attached Menu Piece movie clip. Notice that no dot follows the word `menuClip`. Flash understands the value inside the brackets (`["item"+i]`) as though the dot were used. This syntax is known as *associative array syntax*, which is one way of placing expressions in the target path of an object. The element from the `menu` array that the `mtext` variable is assigned depends on the value of `i`. If `i` is 0, then the first element in the array is used. If it's 3, then the fourth element in the array is used.

The last line of code you added in this step sets the `_y` property of the attached movie clip. The `_y` property is one of the many properties of the `MovieClip` object; the attached movie clip instance is a copy of the `MovieClip` object. It refers to the *y* position of the movie clip, relative to the timeline it's inside of. So in this case, it's the *y* position relative to the `menuClip` movie clip. This value is set to an expression, which bases the *y* position on the height—the `_height` property—of the `top` movie clip, plus the height of the attached movie clip times the value of `i`. This ingenuous bit of code places each attached movie clip below the one before it.

NOTE *While the coordinate system on the main timeline starts at the top-left corner of the stage, the coordinate system for a movie clip starts at its registration, or center point. So 0,0 on the main timeline is at the top-left corner of the stage, and 0,0 in a movie clip is the registration for the movie clip.*

3) Select frame 12 of the Actions layer, and add:

```
menuClip._visible = true;
```

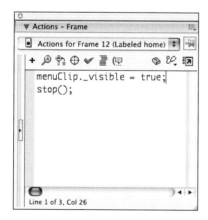

Select frame 11 of the Actions layer, and make sure you have the Actions panel open. Then type the code in the script pane—it should still be in Expert Mode.

This code sets the instance of the `menuClip` movie clip's `_visible` property to `true`. When the movie reaches frame 11, the menu becomes visible on the screen.

4) Choose Control › Test Movie.

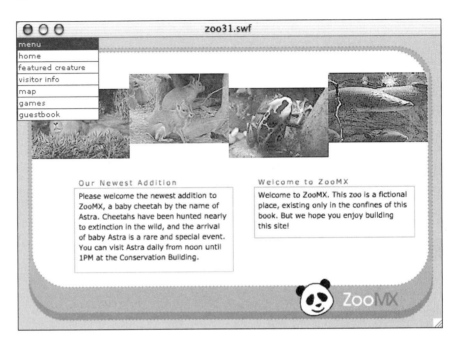

When you test the movie, a menu should appear on the screen when the movie reaches frame 11. The top of the menu should have a red background, with the word *menu* in white. The rest of the menu items should have a white background with red text. The text should correspond to the elements in the `menu` array. Each menu item should have a red border.

5) Save the file as zoo32.fla in the FlashTFS folder on your hard drive.

You still have quite a bit to do to your menu. So save your work, just in case you have to go back to this version.

USING MOVIECLIP METHODS AND EVENT HANDLERS

As you have learned, each instance of a movie clip is a copy of the `MovieClip` object. Thus you can use the properties and methods of the `MovieClip` object to programmatically control every movie clip in your movie. You can also use the `MovieClip` object's event handlers, which are special bits of code that trigger code at the occurrence of events such as the mouse moving or a movie clip being pressed. In the following exercise you will use not only several methods and event handlers of the `MovieClip` object, but also some of its properties. Start this exercise with zoo32.fla open.

1) Select frame 1 of the Actions layer. Add a new line after line 14, and add the following ActionScript:

```
menuClip.top.useHandCursor = false;
```

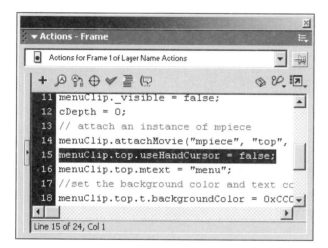

You should still have the Actions panel open from the last exercise. Just add a new line following line 14, and type this ActionScript.

This bit of code sets the `useHandCursor` property of the top movie clip to `false`. The `useHandCursor` property is another property of the built-in `MovieClip` object. You're going to add button events to the top movie clip during this exercise. By default, adding events to a movie clip will make a hand cursor appear when you move the mouse over the movie clip, but you don't want that to happen.

menu	menu
home	home
featured creature	featured creature
visitor info	visitor info
map	map
games	games
guestbook	guestbook

2) Add another new line, and add the following ActionScript:

```
menuClip.top.onPress = function () {
  menuClip.startDrag();
}
```

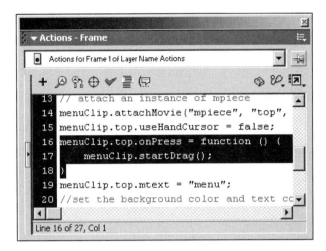

You should add this ActionScript after the code you added in the last step. Insert a new line and start typing. The second line of code in this step does not have to be indented, but indenting it will make the code a bit more readable.

The built-in `MovieClip` object has several event handlers, one of which is `onPress`. The `onPress` event handler is invoked when the object is pressed. In this case, the object is the `top` movie clip, which is nested in the `menuClip` movie clip.

When the event handler is invoked, it runs the function assigned to it. In this case, the function assigned to the `onPress` event handler simply tells Flash to start dragging the `menuClip` movie clip—this is the `startDrag` method of the built-in `MovieClip` object.

TIP *The `MovieClip` object has several event handlers, including `onPress`, `onRelease`, `onRollOver`, and `onLoad`—all of which should be self-explanatory. A complete list of the `MovieClip` object's event handlers can be found in Appendix D.*

3) Add the following ActionScript:

```
menuClip.top.onRelease = function () {
  menuClip.stopDrag();
}
menuClip.top.onReleaseOutside = function () {
  menuClip.stopDrag();
}
```

236

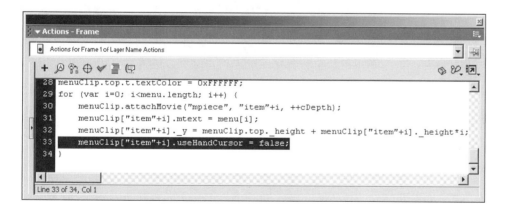

```
18 }
19 menuClip.top.onRelease = function () {
20     menuClip.stopDrag();
21 }
22 menuClip.top.onReleaseOutside = function () {
23     menuClip.stopDrag();
24 }
25 menuClip.top.mtext = "menu";
```

Line 19 of 33, Col 1

Type this code in the script pane, immediately following the code you added in the last step. This code sets up the `onRelease` and `onReleaseOutside` event handlers for the top movie clip. It tells Flash to stop dragging the `menuClip` movie clip when the `onRelease` or `onReleaseOutside` event occurs.

4) Add a new line after line 32, and add the following ActionScript:

```
menuClip["item"+i].useHandCursor = false;
```

```
28 menuClip.top.t.textColor = 0xFFFFFF;
29 for (var i=0; i<menu.length; i++) {
30     menuClip.attachMovie("mpiece", "item"+i, ++cDepth);
31     menuClip["item"+i].mtext = menu[i];
32     menuClip["item"+i]._y = menuClip.top._height + menuClip["item"+i]._height*i;
33     menuClip["item"+i].useHandCursor = false;
34 }
```

Line 33 of 34, Col 1

You should add this code inside the `for` statement that adds the menu items. Once the code is added, the `for` statement should look like this:

```
for (var i=0; i<menu.length; i++) {
menuClip.attachMovie("mpiece", "item"+i, ++cDepth);
menuClip["item"+i].mtext = menu[i];
menuClip["item"+i]._y = menuClip.top._height + menuClip["item"+i]._height*i;
menuClip["item"+i].useHandCursor = false;
}
```

This last line of ActionScript simply sets the useHandCursor property of each menu item to false.

5) Add another new line, and then add the following:

```
menuClip["item"+i].onRollOver = function () {
  this.t.backgroundColor = 0xFF6600;
  this.t.textColor = 0xFFFFFF;
}
menuClip["item"+i].onRollOut = function () {
  this.t.backgroundColor = 0xFFFFFF;
  this.t.textColor = 0xCC0000;
}
```

Add this code right after the line you added in the previous step.

This ActionScript adds onRollOver and onRollOut event handlers to each of the Menu Piece movie clips added by the for statement. So when you roll over a menu item, the background color of the t text box will become orange, and the text will become white. When you roll out of the menu item, the background color of the t text box will become white, and the text color will become red.

NOTE *The this in the code refers to the instance of the Menu Piece movie clip that contains the t text box.*

The completed for statement should look like this:

```
for (var i=0; i<menu.length; i++) {
  menuClip.attachMovie("mpiece", "item" + i, ++cDepth);
  menuClip["item"+i].mtext = menu[i];
  menuClip["item"+i]._y = menuClip.top._height + menuClip["item"+i]._height*i;
  menuClip["item"+i].useHandCursor = false;
  menuClip["item"+i].onRollOver = function () {
    this.t.backgroundColor = 0xFF6600;
    this.t.textColor = 0xFFFFFF;
  }
    menuClip["item"+i].onRollOut = function () {
    this.t.backgroundColor = 0xFFFFFF;
    this.t.textColor = 0xCC0000;
  }
}
```

6) Choose Control > Test Movie. Save the file as zoo33.fla in the FlashTFS folder on your hard drive.

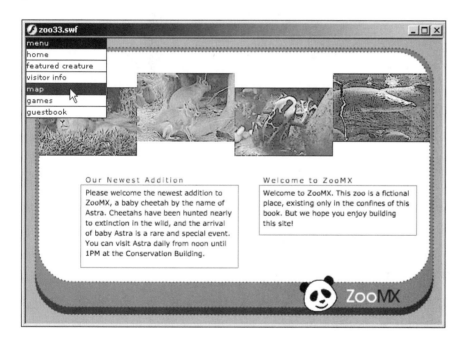

When you test the movie, you should now be able to drag and drop the menu by clicking and dragging the topmost menu item (the **top** instance, which has the text *menu*). The colors of the text and background in each of the subsequent menu items should change colors as your pointer moves over them.

Now you need to add a bit more code, to maximize and minimize the menu. You'll do that next.

239

USING A CONDITIONAL STATEMENT

Conditional statements check to see if a condition is true before performing the enclosed ActionScript. If the condition is not true, the ActionScript enclosed by the conditional statement is not performed. Using conditional statements makes it easy to create special circumstances for certain actions. For example, if you want a button to trigger an event only when a variable is false, you can add a conditional statement to do that. The conditional statements in ActionScript usually start with the `if` action, but they can include `else if` statements and `else` statements. You will add a conditional statement to your menu in the following exercise, which starts with zoo33.fla open.

1) Open assets.fla in the Lesson07/Assets folder as a library. Open the library for the current movie, and drag a copy of the Min Max Clip symbol from the assets.fla library into the current library.

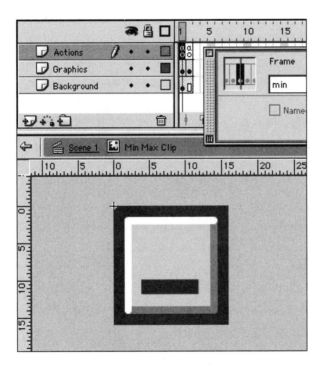

The Min Max Clip symbol is a movie clip. Open it in symbol-editing mode if you'd like to take a look. It's relatively simple, consisting of two frames. The first frame of the movie clip contains a graphic that indicates the user can minimize the menu. This frame also has a `stop` action (in the Actions layer), and its Frame label is min. The second frame has a graphic that indicates the user can maximize the menu. It also has a `stop` action, and its Frame label is max.

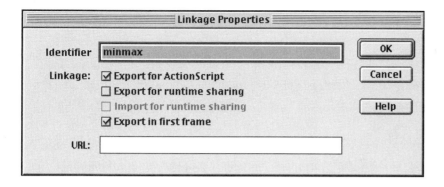

The Min Max Clip you added to the current library already has its Linkage properties modified in the assets.fla library. The Min Max Clip has an Identifier of minmax and is set to export in the first frame of the movie. If you'd like to check these settings, right-click (Windows) or Control-click (Macintosh) the name of the symbol in the library, and choose Linkage. The Linkage Properties dialog box will open.

If you opened the Min Max Clip symbol in symbol-editing mode, be sure to return to the main movie before you continue.

2) Select frame 1 of the Actions layer, and make sure you have the Actions panel open. Add the following ActionScript at the end of the current script pane contents:

```
menuClip.attachMovie("minmax", "minmax", ++cDepth);
menuClip.minmax.useHandCursor = false;
menuClip.minmax._y = 0;
menuClip.minmax._x = menuClip.top._width - menuClip.minmax._width;
menuClip.minmax.maximized = true;
```

```
   Actions - Frame
   Actions for Frame 1 of Layer Name Actions
   +  ⌕  ⚘  ⊕  ✓  ☰  ⊟                                          ⬦ ℓ 🔁
38          menuClip[item+1].onRollOut = function () {
39              this.t.backgroundColor = 0xFFFFFF;
40              this.t.textColor = 0xCC0000;
41          }
42  }
43  menuClip.attachMovie("minmax", "minmax", ++cDepth);
44  menuClip.minmax.useHandCursor = false;
45  menuClip.minmax._y = 0;
46  menuClip.minmax._x = menuClip.top._width - menuClip.minmax._width;
47  menuClip.minmax.maximized = true;

   Line 47 of 47, Col 34
```

This ActionScript should go after all the other ActionScript attached to frame 1 of the Actions layer.

Most of this code should be somewhat familiar to you. The first line attaches an instance of the Min Max Clip symbol to the `menuClip` instance. It gives the attached symbol an instance name of `minmax`, and sets its depth to the incremented value of `cDepth`. Then the code sets the `useHandCursor` property for the attached movie clip to `false` and sets its `_y` property to `0`. Next the ActionScript sets the `_x` property of the `minmax` instance to the width (`_width`) of the `top` instance minus the width of the attached `minmax` instance. Finally, it initializes the `maximized` variable in the `minmax` movie clip's timeline with a value of `true`. The `maximized` variable is not part of any built-in object in Flash: it's a unique variable that will be used later in this lesson.

3) Now add the following ActionScript:

```
menuClip.minmax.onPress = function () {
}
```

```
39        this.t.backgroundColor = 0xFFFFFF;
40        this.t.textColor = 0xCC0000;
41    }
42 }
43 menuClip.attachMovie("minmax", "minmax", ++cDepth);
44 menuClip.minmax.useHandCursor = false;
45 menuClip.minmax._y = 0;
46 menuClip.minmax._x = menuClip.top._width - menuClip.minmax._width;
47 menuClip.minmax.maximized = true;
48 menuClip.minmax.onPress = function () {
49
50 }
```

This code, which simply sets up the `onPress` event handler for the `minmax` movie clip, should follow the code you added in the last step.

4) Inside the `onPress` event's function, add this ActionScript:

```
if (this.maximized) {
  this.maximized = false;
  this.gotoAndStop("max");
  for (var i=0; imenu.length; i++) {
    menuClip["item"+i]._visible = false;
  }
}
```

```
45 menuClip.minmax._y = 0;
46 menuClip.minmax._x = menuClip.top._width - menuClip.minmax._width;
47 menuClip.minmax.maximized = true;
48 menuClip.minmax.onPress = function () {
49     if (this.maximized) {
50         this.maximized = false;
51         this.gotoAndStop("max");
52         for (var i=0; i<menu.length; i++) {
53             menuClip["item"+i]._visible = false;
54         }
55     }
56 }
```

This code should be typed inside the curly braces you added in the last step, so the
onPress event handler should look like the following:

```
menuClip.minmax.onPress = function () {
  if (this.maximized) {
    this.maximized = false;
    this.gotoAndStop("max");
    for (var i=0; i<menu.length; i++) {
      menuClip["item"+i]._visible = false;
    }
  }
}
```

The ActionScript you just added contains an if statement, which is also called a
conditional statement. The syntax for an if statement is:

```
if (condition) {
}
```

If the condition is true, the code inside the curly braces is run. If the condition is not
true, the code inside the curly braces is ignored.

The condition for this if statement is maximized. You already initialized the maximized
variable with a value of true for the minmax instance in step 2 of this exercise, so the
condition for this if statement will also be true when the onPress event is first invoked.

When the condition for the if statement is true, the maximized variable is set to
false. Then the this object (the minmax instance) is told to go to the frame labeled
max. Next, a for statement sets the _visible property of each of the Menu Piece
movie clips that were added by the previous for statement (all of the Menu Piece
instances, except the top instance) to false, which simply hides them.

5) Following the `if` statement, add this ActionScript:

```
else {
  this.maximized = true;
  this.gotoAndStop("min");
  for (var i=0; imenu.length; i++) {
    menuClip["item"+i]._visible = true;
  }
}
```

```
49        if (this.maximized) {
50            this.maximized = false;
51            this.gotoAndStop("max");
52            for (var i=0; i<menu.length; i++) {
53                menuClip["item"+i]._visible = false;
54            }
55        } else {
56            this.maximized = true;
57            this.gotoAndStop("min");
58            for (var i=0; i<menu.length; i++) {
59                menuClip["item"+i]._visible = true;
60            }
61        }
```

Line 65 of 65, Col 2

You can add this code immediately following the `if` statement. The first line of this code can be added on the last line of the `if` statement, so the resulting code looks like this:

```
if (this.maximized) {
  this.maximized = false;
  this.gotoAndStop("max");
  for (var i=0; i<menu.length; i++) {
    menuClip["item"+i]._visible = false;
  }
} else {
  this.maximized = true;
  this.gotoAndStop("min");
  for (var i=0; i<menu.length; i++) {
    menuClip["item"+i]._visible = true;
  }
}
```

The code you just added runs when the condition for the `if` statement is not `true`. This code basically does the opposite of the code that's run when the `if` statement's condition is `true`. It sets `maximized` to `true`, tells the `minmax` instance to go to the frame labeled min, and then sets the `_visible` property of each of the Menu Piece movie clips in the `for` loop to `true`.

```
48  menuClip.minmax.onPress = function () {
49      if (this.maximized) {
50          this.maximized = false;
51          this.gotoAndStop("max");
52          for (var i=0; i<menu.length; i++) {
53              menuClip["item"+i]._visible = false;
54          }
55      } else {
56          this.maximized = true;
57          this.gotoAndStop("min");
58          for (var i=0; i<menu.length; i++) {
59              menuClip["item"+i]._visible = true;
60          }
61      }
62  }
```

The resulting `onPress` event handler for the `minmax` movie clip should look like this:

```
menuClip.minmax.onPress = function () {
  if (this.maximized) {
    this.maximized = false;
    this.gotoAndStop("max");
    for (var i=0; i<menu.length; i++) {
      menuClip["item"+i]._visible = false;
    }
  } else {
    this.maximized = true;
    this.gotoAndStop("min");
    for (var i=0; i<menu.length; i++) {
      menuClip["item"+i]._visible = true;
    }
  }
}
```

6) Choose Control > Test Movie.

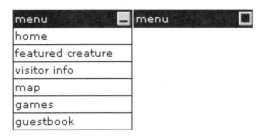

You should now be able to minimize and maximize the menu when you click the attached instance of the Min Max Clip. The menu isn't really becoming smaller or larger—the secret in this programmatic trickery is that you're just changing the visibility of all the menu items when you click the Min Max Clip.

7) Save your movie as zoo34.fla.

You now have a menu, but it doesn't actually make the movie do anything yet. You'll add that ActionScript in Lesson 11. If you had trouble with any of the concepts we've gone over in this lesson, you may find it useful to go back and read the explanations again. It's important that you understand the basics of programming in ActionScript before you continue to the "good" stuff!

WHAT YOU HAVE LEARNED

In this lesson, you have:

- Used ActionScript to create a drop-down menu (pages 210–246)

- Added a dynamic text box to the movie (pages 210–215)

- Created and used an array (pages 216–221)

- Modified the appearance of dynamic text boxes using the `TextField` objects (pages 221–230)

- Created a loop to repeat several lines of ActionScript (pages 230–234)

- Used several `MovieClip` methods, properties, and event handlers (pages 234–239)

- Used a conditional statement to show and hide the menu (pages 240–246)

using components

LESSON 8

Components are complex movie clips that contain ActionScript and graphical elements, and they can be customized with defined parameters when you create the Flash movie. Flash MX includes several user-interface (UI) components you can use to add simple interaction to Flash movies. Each component has a set of ActionScript methods that allow you to set parameters and additional options at runtime. The UI components included with Flash are CheckBox, ComboBox, ListBox, PushButton, RadioButton, ScrollBar, and ScrollPane. Each of these components can be found in the Components panel (Window › Components).

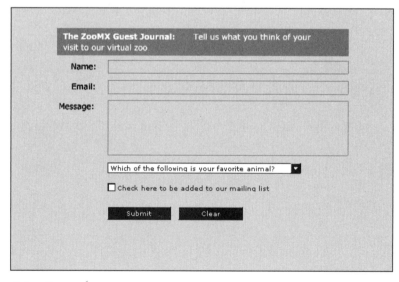

The guestbook for the ZooMX Web site uses several components.

Chrissy Rey

WHAT YOU WILL LEARN

In this lesson, you will:

- Add input text boxes to gather data from the user

- Add and customize several Flash UI components

- Customize a skin for one of the Flash UI components

- Use custom styles to modify the appearance of the Flash UI components

APPROXIMATE TIME

This lesson takes approximately one hour to complete.

LESSON FILES

Media Files:

Lesson08/Assets/guestbook.swf

Lesson08/Assets/check_black.swf

Starting Files:

None

Completed Project:

Lesson08/Completed/guestbook7.fla

ADDING INPUT TEXT BOXES

Flash's input text boxes, combined with the UI components you'll add later in this lesson, let you create graphically appealing forms and surveys. You can use input text boxes to collect information about your users, to give users a means of logging in to your Web site, to create order forms, and much more.

1) Create a new Flash movie based on the Flash TFS Zoo Template.

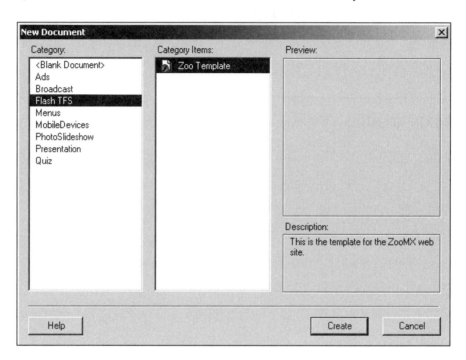

You've done this before, but here's a quick refresher. Choose File > New From Template. When the New Document dialog box opens, set the Category to Flash TFS and make sure the Zoo Template is selected. Click Create, and a new movie, based on the Zoo Template file, appears.

2) Select the Contents layer, and import guestbook.swf from the Lesson08/Assets folder on the CD-ROM.

250

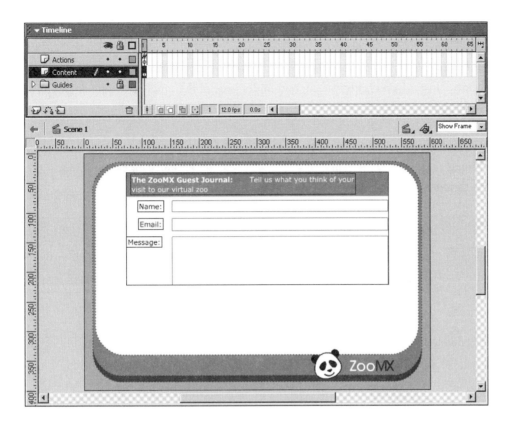

To import the file, choose File > Import and browse to the Lesson08/Assets folder. Select guestbook.swf, and click Open. The guestbook.swf file contains some text and graphics. You can re-create the contents of this file for more practice—just use the figure above as a guide.

The contents of the guestbook.swf file will act as a background for the guestbook entry form you will create as you work through this lesson.

3) Change the name of the Content layer to Background, and lock it. Add a new layer above the Background layer, and name it Text Boxes.

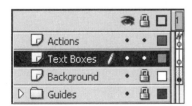

Double-click the name of the Contents layer to select it, and change the name to Background. Lock the Background layer by clicking the dot under the Lock/Unlock All Layers icon to the right of the layer's name. With the Background layer selected, click the Insert Layer button at the bottom-left side of the timeline to add a new layer. Name the new layer Text Boxes.

4) Select the text tool from the toolbox. In the Property inspector set the Text Type to Input Text. Modify the remaining properties so the Property inspector looks like the figure below.

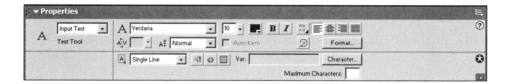

When you select the text tool from the toolbox, the Property inspector should display the text properties. The Text Type is the setting on the far left of the Property inspector. Set it to Input Text, as you are going to add a text box that visitors will be able to use to type a message. Make sure the Font is set to Verdana, the Font Size to 10, and the Text (fill) Color to black (#000000).

The Line Type should be set to Single Line. This will ensure that the text box you create in the next step will allow users to type text only in a single line. You will add a multiline text box later in this exercise, so you will be able to see the difference.

Compare the Property inspector with the figure above, and make sure the rest of the settings are the same.

5) Select the Text Boxes layer. Create a text box on the stage by clicking and dragging to the desired width.

The ZooMX Guest Journal: Tell us what you think of your
visit to our virtual zoo

Name:

Email:

Make the text box about the same width as the area labeled Name in the Background layer. These labeled areas will be called *text-box backgrounds* throughout the rest of this lesson.

252

6) Use the arrow tool to select the text box you just drew. Position the text box so that it's in the text box-background labeled Name. In the Property inspector, type *visitorName* in the Var text box.

When you switch to the arrow tool, the text box should be selected automatically.

The Var setting is the variable name associated with the text box. The variable for this text box is `visitorName`, and the value is going to be whatever the user types into the text box.

NOTE *Flash input text boxes are similar to HTML input text fields, only they're created in Flash, and not with HTML.*

Notice that the Property inspector has a Maximum Characters setting for the input text box. You can type a number in this setting to limit the number of characters a user can enter in the text box.

7) Create another text box for the text-box background labeled Email. Type *visitorEmail* in the Var text field to set the variable name for that text box.

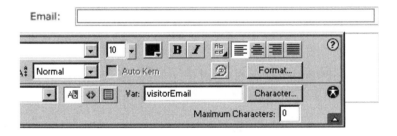

You should have two text boxes, each with a different variable name. It's very important that you give each text box a different variable name. If you accidentally use the same variable name for more than one text box, both text boxes will end up with the same text.

8) Add a third text box for the text-box background labeled Message. Set the Line Type for this text box to Multiline, and enter *visitorMessage* in the Var text field.

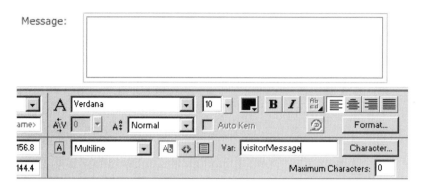

The third text box should be larger than the other two. You can make it the same size as the text-box background labeled Message by dragging down as you drag to the right.

When you set the Line Type for a text box to Multiline, Flash automatically wraps text to the next line. Notice that you can also set the text box to Multiline No Wrap, which places text on a new line only if you add a new line yourself (by pressing Return or Enter). There's also a Password option, which turns text typed into the text box into asterisks (*), as shown in the figure below.

****

9) Choose Control > Test Movie. When you've finished testing, close the Test Movie window, and save the file as guestbook1.fla in the FlashTFS folder on your hard drive.

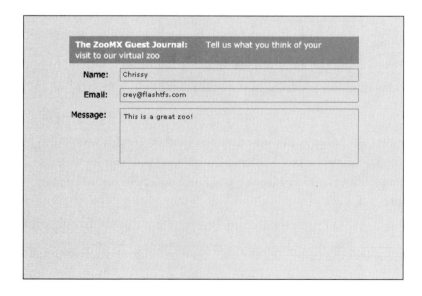

When you test the movie, it may look as if there isn't anything on the screen, other than the background you added. Try clicking each of the text-box backgrounds—the cursor should appear indicating that there is a text box. Type something in each text box to see how it looks. Type enough text to reach the end of the box to make sure the text in the multiline text box wraps.

Now that you have text boxes in the movie, it's time to add some components.

ADDING COMPONENTS

Input text boxes are limited to text-only information. HTML forms allow you to add check boxes, radio buttons, combo boxes, and more. Flash can now do the same, with the UI components included with the program. These UI components make it easy to create an interactive form.

In the next exercise you will add several UI components to guestbook1.fla, so make sure that file is still open.

1) Add a new layer above the Text Boxes layer, and name it Components. Lock the Text Boxes layer.

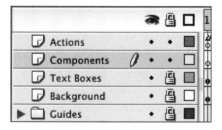

You don't want to accidentally mess up the contents of the Text Boxes layer, so lock the layer before you continue. In this exercise you are going to add the UI components to the new Components layer.

2) Drag an instance of the ComboBox component onto the stage. Use the Property inspector to set the Width of the ComboBox instance to 300. Then set the X and Y to 153 and 234, respectively. Type *animal* in the Instance Name text field.

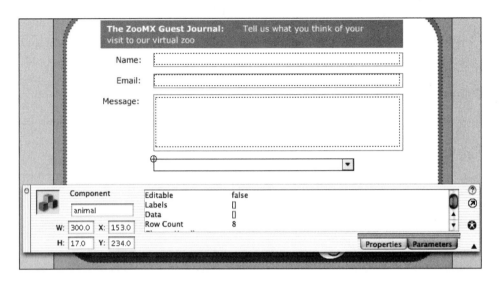

You'll find all of the components you need for this lesson in the Components panel. If you don't see the Components panel on the screen, choose Window > Components. It should be open if you haven't strayed from the panel set you created in Lesson 1.

When you add a component from the Components panel, you are actually adding an instance of a symbol—each component is a special movie clip. Just click the ComboBox component in the Components panel and drag it onto the stage. When you release the mouse, an instance of the ComboBox should appear on the stage.

Take a quick look at the library after you add the ComboBox component. You should see a new Flash UI Components folder. When you add a UI component from the Components panel, it is automatically added to the folder. If you open the Flash UI Components folder in the library, you should see the ComboBox component—notice the icon to its left, which indicates that it's a component, and not just a "plain" movie clip. Also notice a Component Skins folder inside the Flash UI Components folder. You'll take a look inside that folder later in this lesson.

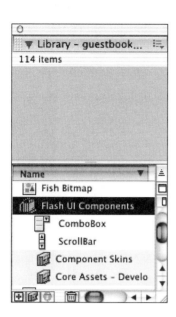

When you select a component, the Property inspector should have two tabs on the right side: Properties and Parameters. You can set the width, height, X, Y, and instance name values regardless of which tab is selected. If you click the Properties tab, you should see that Flash knows the selected component is a movie clip, as shown in the figure below. Because this movie clip is "special" you can also set a number of additional values in the Parameters tab panel. You'll do so later in this lesson.

NOTE *You can set the width but not the height of the ComboBox component. The height is determined by the font used in the component.*

The ComboBox you just added will eventually contain a list of animals. Users will pick their favorite animal from the list.

3) Drag an instance of the CheckBox component onto the stage, placing it under the ComboBox instance you just added. Set the CheckBox component's Width to 200. Set the X and Y to 153 and 265. Finally, type *mailList* in the Instance Name text box.

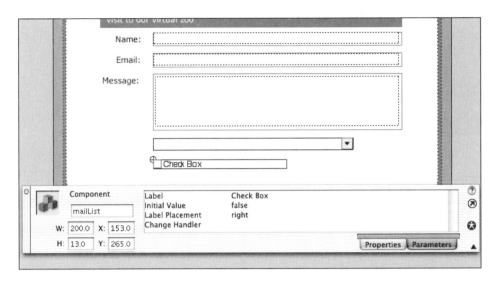

You can add the CheckBox component the same way you added the ComboBox component. Make sure the Components layer is selected, and drag the CheckBox component from the Components panel onto the stage.

As with the ComboBox component, the Property inspector displays both the Properties and Parameters tabs when the CheckBox component is selected. You'll modify the properties in the Parameters tab later in this lesson.

The CheckBox component you just added lets users indicate whether they want to be added to the zoo's mailing list.

4) Drag an instance of the PushButton component onto the stage. Set the X and Y for the instance of the PushButton component to 153 and 300, and type *submit* in the Instance Name text box.

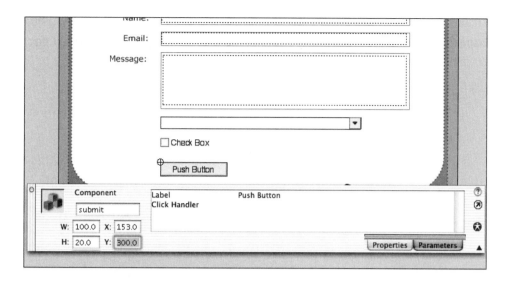

The PushButton instance you just added will act as a submit button for the form you're creating. You'll add a Clear button next.

Take a look in the library—you should see that there are now several components in the Flash UI Components folder.

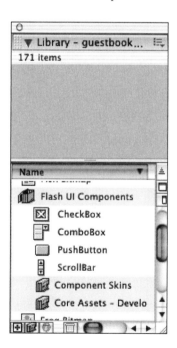

259

5) Add another instance of the PushButton component to the stage, using the Property inspector to position it at X: 265 and Y: 300. Type *clear* in the Instance Name text box.

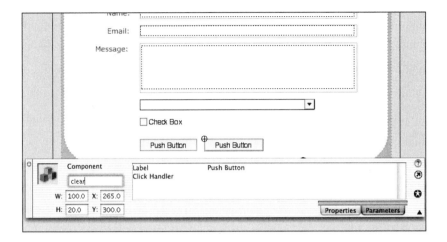

When you add a second instance of the PushButton component to the movie, Flash doesn't add another copy to the library—there should still be just one PushButton component. But if you were to add a modified version of the PushButton component, for example a customized one, Flash would ask if you'd like to replace the existing component, as shown in the figure below.

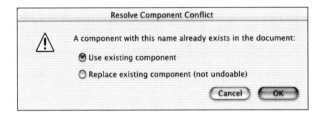

This instance of the PushButton component will act as a Clear button for your form. It will reset all the values in the form to their initial settings.

6) Save the movie as guestbook2.fla.

Now that you have some components in your movie, it's time to set their parameters. Make sure to save the movie as guestbook2.fla in the FlashTFS folder on your hard drive before you continue.

USING THE COMBOBOX COMPONENT

The ComboBox component lets you add a scrollable drop-down list to your Flash movie. Once you have added an instance of the ComboBox component, you can modify several values in the Property inspector to customize that instance and have the combo box contain the information you want to display. When you select a component instance, the Property inspector displays two tabs—Properties and Parameters. The Parameters allow you to customize the contents of the component instance—in the case of a ComboBox instance, the labels, data, and more.

1) Select the instance of the ComboBox component on the stage, and look at the Property inspector.

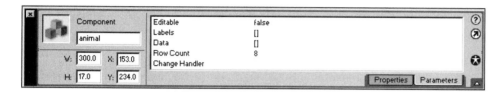

Make sure the Parameters tab is selected in the Property inspector. You should see several settings, including the usual Width, Height, X, Y, and Instance Name. The extra settings are called parameters. The ComboBox component's parameters are `Editable`, `Labels`, `Data`, `Row Count`, and `Change Handler`.

The parameters for a component are all specified in the component's Component Definition. You can see these parameters—and modify them, if you're feeling brave—by right-clicking (Windows) or Control-clicking (Macintosh) the component in the library and choosing Component Definition. The Component Definition dialog box opens, displaying the parameters and a few other settings.

261

Parameters are really just variables used in the ActionScript built into each component. If you look at the parameters in the Component Definition dialog box, you'll see that each one has a Name, Variable, Value, and Type setting. The Name is the label that appears in the Property inspector when the component is selected. The Variable is the name used in the ActionScript built into the component. The Value is the default value for the parameter, and the Type is the type of data required for the parameter. Types that can be used are Default, Array, Object, List, String, Number, Boolean, Font Name, and Color. Notice that many of these Types correspond with the data types a variable can hold—that's because each of the parameters is a variable.

2) Select the Labels parameter in the Property inspector, and click the Edit button that appears on the far right. In the Values dialog box that opens, type the following values for the Labels setting: *Which of the following is your favorite animal?, Cheetah, Elephant, Gorilla, Mara, Orangutan, Sea Lion, Yeti.*

When you select the Labels parameter, an Edit button should appear at the far right. Click the Edit button to open the Values dialog box.

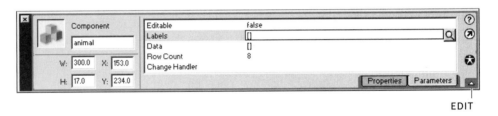

EDIT

The Labels parameter provides the labels that appear when the combo box is viewed in the exported movie. This parameter contains an array, so you can give it multiple values. Remember, an array is simply a list of variables.

DELETE   MOVE DOWN

ADD   MOVE UP

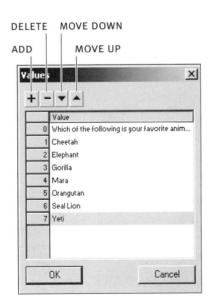

You can add a value to the Values dialog box by clicking the Add (+) button. Then click the name and edit the new value. Notice when you add the first value, a 0 appears next to it. The 0 is that value's index for the array. If you need to remove a value, simply select it and click the Delete (-) button. You can also change the order of the values by clicking the Move Up and Move Down buttons. When you've finished adding values, click OK to close the Values dialog box.

After you click OK, notice that the first value you entered in the Values dialog box appears in the ComboBox instance on the stage. If it doesn't appear, choose Control > Enable Live Preview. When that command is checked, the Flash UI components update automatically, so you can preview the components on the stage. You should also notice that the Property inspector displays the values you entered in the Values dialog box for the Labels parameter.

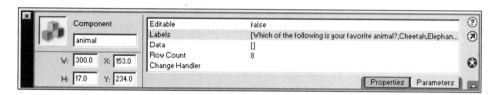

3) Double-click the Data parameter. In the Values dialog box, delete defaultValue, the first value (labeled 0). Add the following values: *cheetah, elephant, gorilla, mara, orangutan, sea lion, yeti*.

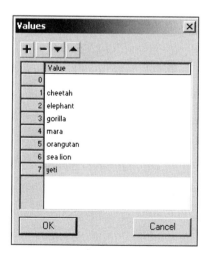

You can open the Values dialog box for the Data parameter the same way you opened it for the Labels parameter. Or you can double-click the default value at the right of the parameter's name. Both methods open the Values dialog box.

When you add the first value, make sure to delete the default value (`defaultValue`) listed, or that value will be used for the first option in the combo box.

The `Data` parameter, like the `Labels` parameter, contains an array and holds the values for the data array in the ActionScript that controls the ComboBox component. These values can be used in other parts of the movie, or they can be sent to the server, as you will do in Lesson 9. All the values in the `Data` and `Labels` parameters are strings.

4) Set the Row Count to 5.

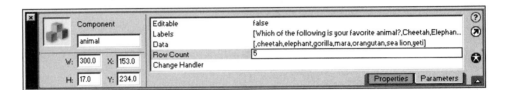

You can set the row count by clicking the default value to the right of that parameter and then typing the number 5 in the text box that appears. Press Enter or Return after you type the value to make sure that it takes effect.

The Row Count specifies the number of values shown in the combo box before a scroll bar appears. You have eight values in your combo box that you set in the `Labels` and `Data` parameters, so a scroll bar will appear. The scroll bar is an instance of the ScrollBar component that's automatically included with and controlled by the ComboBox component.

5) Choose Control > Test Movie.

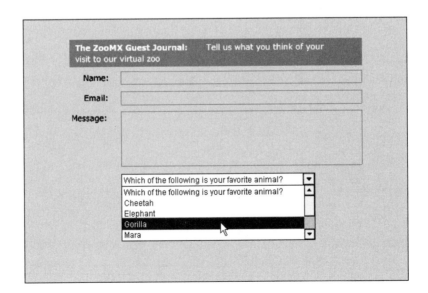

When you test the movie, click the combo box. You can use the scroll bar on the right side of the combo box to move through the options. Notice that each option is one of the values you listed in the Labels parameter.

The ComboBox component has several built-in keyboard controls. The Up and Down Arrow keys move the selection up or down one line in the scroll list. The Page Up and Page Down keys move the selection up or down one page. The size of the page is set by the Row Count parameter, so a single page in this combo box will be five items. The Home key selects the first item in the list, and the End key selects the last item in the list.

When you're finished testing the combo box, close the Test Movie window.

6) Save the file as guestbook3.fla in the FlashTFS folder on your hard drive.

You still have more UI components to customize. So save the file in the FlashTFS folder and keep it open for the next exercise.

USING THE CHECKBOX COMPONENT

The CheckBox component lets you add check boxes to your Flash movie. In this movie you have only a single check box, but you can use multiple instances of the CheckBox component if you need to. Like the ComboBox component, the CheckBox component has several parameters. You'll look at those parameters, and use them to customize your check box, in this exercise. Be sure you still have guestbook3.fla open from the last exercise before you start.

1) Select the instance of the CheckBox component on the stage. Type *Check here to be added to our mailing list* in the Label parameter text box.

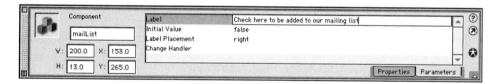

You can modify the Label parameter by clicking the default value on its right, and typing the new value in its place. Press Enter or Return after you type the new value, and it should appear on the stage. That is, part of it will appear on the stage—

the last few characters may be cut off, as illustrated in the figure below, because the CheckBox instance isn't wide enough for the label. You'll fix that in a moment.

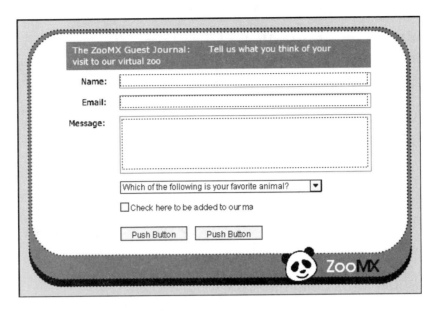

The `Label` parameter for the CheckBox can have a value of a string, not an array like the ComboBox. You want only a single label for the check box anyway, so that should suffice.

2) Make sure you still have the CheckBox component selected, and set its width to 300 in the Property inspector.

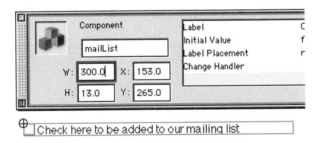

When you change the width of the CheckBox component instance to 300, the entire label should appear. As with the ComboBox, you can set the width of the CheckBox component, but not its height. The height is controlled by the font used for the label.

You don't have to modify the remaining parameters, as their default values are fine for now. Since you still have the CheckBox component selected, take a quick look at some of the other parameters. The `Initial Value` parameter specifies whether the check box is initially selected. When this parameter is set to `true`, the checkbox is selected initially. When it's set to `false`, it's not selected initially. The value for the `Initial Value` parameter is a Boolean. The `Label Placement` parameter, which has a list value type, lets you place the label for the check box on the right or left side. If you click the initial value for this parameter, a list should appear.

The `Change Handler` parameter, which you might have noticed in the ComboBox component's parameters, lets you specify a function that will run when the value of the component is changed. You don't need to add a Change Handler for either the ComboBox component or the CheckBox component; you are really only concerned with the values (data) specified by those components. However, the Change Handler parameter could be useful if you want to use a component to make something happen in the movie when an option is selected. For example, you could use the ComboBox component to make a menu. When an item in the drop-down list is selected, the function specified in the `Change Handler` parameter could tell the movie to go to a certain frame, based on which item in the list was selected.

3) Choose Control > Test Movie.

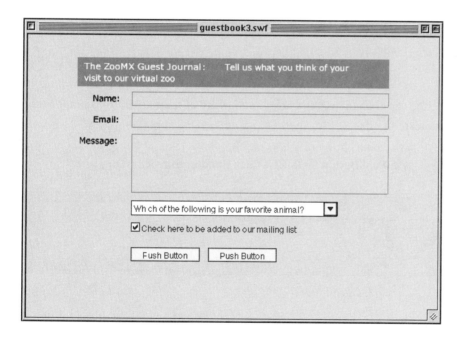

When you test the movie, you should be able to see the label you set for the check box. You can also click the check box to turn the check on and off. By default, the check box will not be checked.

4) Save the file as guestbook4.fla in the FlashTFS folder.

Now you need to modify the PushButton components you added to the movie.

USING THE PUSHBUTTON COMPONENT

The PushButton component lets you add standardized buttons to Flash movies. This component lets you add buttons that simulate form buttons in HTML. All you have to do is add the component to your movie, provide a label and Click Handler, and you're finished. In this exercise you will provide labels for the two PushButton instances you added earlier in this lesson.

1) Select the submit **PushButton instance, and change the** Label **parameter to** Submit.

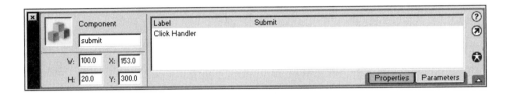

N O T E *Press Return or Enter after you type a parameter value. You can also press Tab to apply the new value and jump to the next parameter.*

Click the default value at the right of the Label parameter's name, and type your new value in the text box. If the label you add is too large for the button, it will be truncated. You can change both the height and width of the PushButton component to suit your taste.

2) Set the submit **PushButton instance's Click Handler to** processForm.

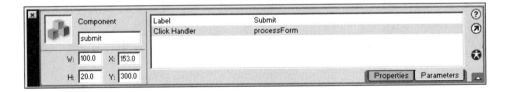

The Click Handler has the same function as the Change Handler for the CheckBox and ComboBox components, only it's triggered when the button is clicked. It simply assigns a function that should run when the button is clicked. The processForm function, which you will write in Lesson 9, handles the data in the form.

3) Select the `clear` PushButton instance, and set its Label to Clear.

You don't have to add a Click Handler for either `PushButton` instance yet. You'll do that in Lesson 9, when you modify the form you've created.

4) Set the `clear` PushButton instance's Click Handler to `processForm`.

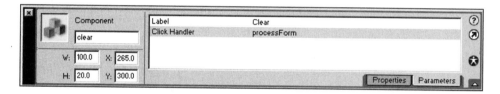

It's a good idea to use the same function for each instance of a component. It will be easier to update the code when it's all in one place. The function has to check to see which component instance triggered it—you'll learn how in Lesson 9.

5) Look at the PushButton instances on the stage. Save the file as guestbook5.fla in the FlashTFS folder.

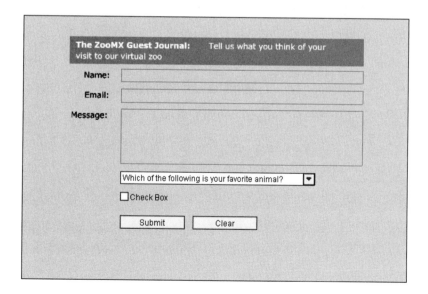

Both of the instances should have custom labels.

Now that you have your form set up, it's time to customize its appearance. Right now the components you've added are rather gray and boring. You can change their appearance to work better with the look of your Web site. You'll do that in the next two exercises.

CUSTOMIZING A COMPONENT SKIN

You can easily change the look of a component by modifying its *skin*. The skin is a graphic that's used by all the instances of a component. For example, every instance of the CheckBox component has a check that appears when it's selected. In this exercise, you will modify the appearance of a component skin. Start with guestbook5.fla open.

1) Open the fcb_check movie clip in symbol-editing mode.

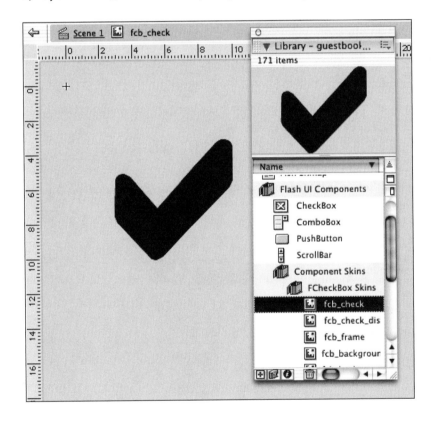

You'll find the fcb_check movie clip in the FCheckBox Skins folder, which is in the Component Skins folder inside of the Flash UI Components folder. You can open the movie clip in symbol-editing mode by double-clicking the icon on the left of its name.

The fcb_check movie clip is part of the CheckBox component. It controls the appearance of the check in the check box.

2) Double-click the instance of the fcb_check movie clip nested inside the fcb_check movie clip.

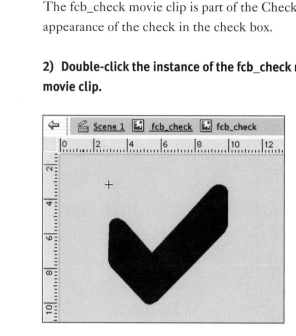

There are actually two fcb_check movie clips in the Flash UI Components folder. You opened one in the last step, and you just opened the other one in this step. The one you just opened is the graphic for the first one. The two clips have the same names, but are in different folders.

3) Select the check graphic in the element layer, and press Delete or Backspace.

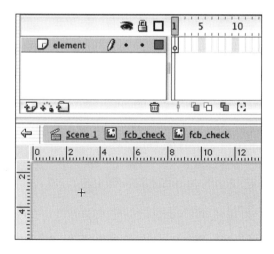

You're going to replace this check graphic with a custom graphic, but you need to remove the existing graphic first. After you delete the graphic, the element layer should be empty.

4) Import check_black.swf from the Lesson08/Assets folder.

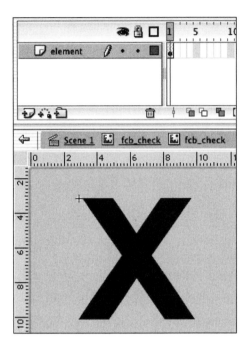

Choose File > Import and browse to the Lesson08/Assets folder. Locate check_black.swf in that folder, select it, and click Open. A small black X should appear on the screen. The top-left corner of the X should be located at the center of the symbol. If not, use the Property inspector to set the X and Y of the X graphic to 0 and 0.

If you want to add check boxes that can be disabled, you will also want to change the fcb_check_disabled in the FCheckBox Skins. The Lesson08/Assets folder contains another graphic, check_gray.swf, if you'd like to try this on your own.

5) Choose Control > Test Movie.

When you click the check box in the movie, an X should appear instead of a check. If you had multiple instances of the CheckBox component in your movie, each instance would contain an X when selected.

You can customize the look of your components using this same technique. When you opened the Component Skins folder, you probably noticed there were folders for other components: FPushButton Skins, FScrollBar Skins, and Global Skins. You can explore the movie clips in these folders and make additional changes if you'd like to further customize the skins.

If you mess up any components during your exploration, simply double-click the component in the Components panel. The Resolve Component Conflict dialog box will open and ask if you would like to use the existing component (the one you modified) or replace the existing component (with the original). Select "Replace existing component" and click OK, and your component will revert back to the original.

Close the Test Movie window when you're finished looking at the updated check box.

6) Choose Edit > Document to return to the main timeline. Save your movie as guestbook6.fla in the FlashTFS folder on your hard drive.
As you can see, customizing the skin of a component is pretty easy. Modifying the skin is useful if you want to change the shape of any part of the component. But as you'll learn in the next exercise, it's best to use ActionScript to change colors.

SETTING A COMPONENT STYLE

You can use ActionScript to apply styles to your Flash UI components, in order to customize their appearance to suit the look and feel of your movie. The FStyleFormat object lets you apply a style to specific component instances, while the globalStyleFormat object lets you apply a style to all components in your movie. These objects will not necessarily work for components other than the UI components included with Flash.

In the next exercise you will create a global style that will apply to all of the Flash UI components in your movie. You will then create another component style, using the FStyleFormat object, which you will apply to specific component instances. Start with guestbook6.fla open from the last exercise.

1) Open the Actions panel. Select frame 1 of the Actions layer, and add the following ActionScript:

```
// arrow color
globalStyleFormat.arrow = 0xFFFFFF;
```

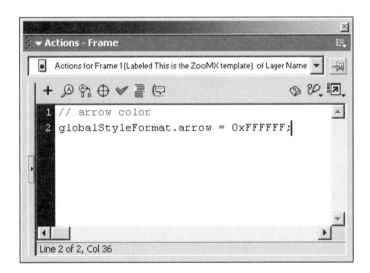

This ActionScript sets the arrow property of the globalStyleFormat object to 0xFFFFFF (white). The arrow appears in the button on the right side of the combo box. The globalStyleFormat object is accessible when you add a single instance of any Flash UI component to the movie, so you don't have to create a new object. A complete list of properties for the globalStyleFormat object can be found in the ActionScript Dictionary.

2) Now add this ActionScript:

```
// text styles
globalStyleFormat.textColor = 0xCC0000;
globalStyleFormat.textFont = "Verdana";
globalStyleFormat.textSize = 10;
globalStyleFormat.textSelected = 0xFFFFFF;
```

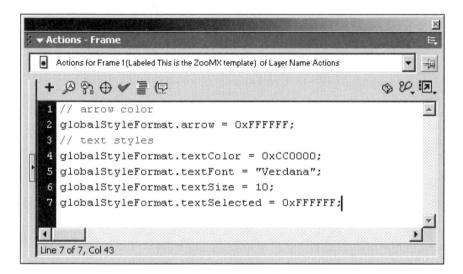

You should add this code to frame 1, following the code already there.

This ActionScript modifies the text properties of all the components in the movie. The **textColor** property sets the text color to red, the **textFont** property sets the font in each component instance to Verdana, and the **textSize** property sets the font size to 10 points. The **textSelected** property sets the color of selected text, which is text highlighted in the combo box, to white.

3) Add the following code:

```
// component colors
globalStyleFormat.face = 0xFF6600;
globalStyleFormat.darkshadow = 0x000000;
globalStyleFormat.highlight = 0xCC0000;
globalStyleFormat.highlight3D = 0xFFC055;
globalStyleFormat.shadow = 0xCC0000;
globalStyleFormat.selection = 0xFF9933;
```

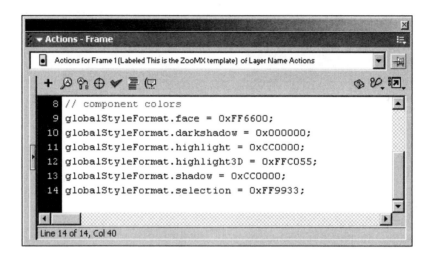

This ActionScript, which should be added to frame 1 following the code already there, modifies the colors for the buttons and outlines of each component. The `face` property modifies the main color of the component—for the PushButton component that's the main button color, and for the ComboBox component it's the color of the button on the right side of the combo box. In this case, the `face` will be orange. The `darkShadow` property, which is the color of the inner border or shadow of a component, is black. The `highlight` property sets the color of the inner border or darker shadow of a component to red when it is selected. The `highlight3D` property sets the color of the outer border or light shadow of a component to light orange when it is selected. The `shadow`, which is set to the same color as the `highlight`, sets the color of the outer border or light shadow of a component. Finally, the `selection` property sets the color of the selection bar that highlights an item in a list (such as the combo box) to orange.

4) Add the following code to frame 1:

```
globalStyleFormat.applyChanges();
```

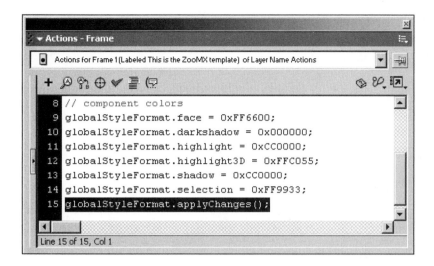

The `applyChanges` method of the `globalStyleFormat` object updates all properties in that object. If you didn't change a property, it will keep its default value. When you apply the changes, the components will appear with the new styles.

5) Choose Control > Test Movie

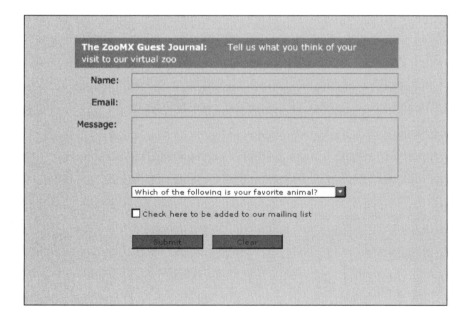

When you test the movie, the new property values you applied to the `globalStyleFormat` object should change the look of the components. They should now fit with the color scheme for the Web site.

277

You might notice one problem with the updated style—the text color in the buttons doesn't work well with the face color you applied. Close the Test Movie window so you can add an ActionScript to fix it.

6) Add the following ActionScript:

```
// modify push button style
pbStyle = new FStyleFormat();
pbStyle.textColor = 0xFFFFFF;
pbStyle.addListener(submit, clear);
```

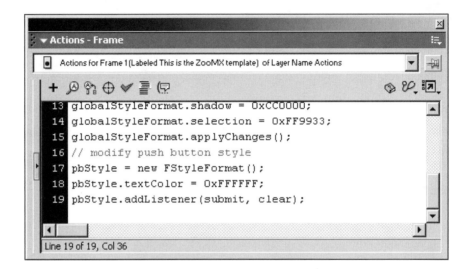

Add this code to frame 1, following the ActionScript already in that frame.

This simple bit of code uses the FStyleFormat object to apply a new text color to the submit and clear instances of the PushButton component. The first line is a comment, reminding you that this code is for the push buttons. The second line creates a new object, called pbStyle, based on the FStyleFormat object. The textColor property of the new pbStyle object is set to white. Finally, the last line uses the addListener method of the pbStyle object to apply the new style only to the submit and clear instances.

7) Choose Control > Test Movie.

When you test the movie, the text in the push buttons should be white. The text in the other components should remain black.

8) Save the movie as guestbook7.fla.

Your form is almost done. All you have left to do is add some ActionScript to send the data from the form to the server. You'll do that in Lesson 9.

WHAT YOU HAVE LEARNED

In this lesson, you have:

- Added input text boxes to gather data from the user (pages 250–255)
- Added and customized the ComboBox, CheckBox, and PushButton UI components (pages 255–270)
- Customized a skin for the CheckBox component (pages 270–273)
- Used the `globalStyleFormat` and `FStyleFormat` objects to modify the appearance of the Flash UI components (pages 274–279)

creating
dynamic content

You can create dynamic content in Flash with ActionScript. Using a variety of actions and methods, you can request information from server-side scripts. Those scripts can request information from a database and return the data to Flash. Flash doesn't care what language the scripts are written in, as long as the data is returned in a format it can understand. Some of the most commonly used languages for server-side scripts include ASP, Macromedia ColdFusion, PHP, and Perl.

In this lesson you will create an interactive map. The map is accompanied by a dynamically generated list of animals in the zoo. You can narrow the list to show animals from a specific location in the zoo by clicking parts of the map. You can

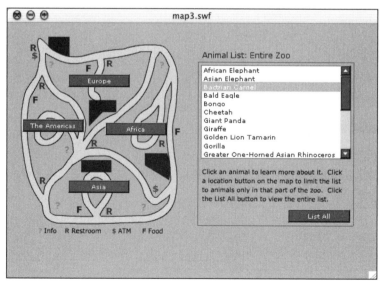

You can create dynamic content in Flash.

Chrissy Rey

also display additional information about each animal by clicking its name in the list. You will use the `LoadVars` object, dynamic text boxes, and several components to create this map.

In order to successfully complete this lesson, you should have an Internet connection. This lesson connects to several files on the Internet. If you do not have an Internet connection, you can build the files, but you will not be able to view the data or send data to the server.

WHAT YOU WILL LEARN

In this lesson, you will:

- Add a map and several component instances to the movie

- Learn how to use the ListBox UI component.

- Load variables from a data source on a server using the `LoadVars` object

- Display dynamic content in an instance of the ListBox component and a dynamic text box

- Learn how to use the ScrollBar component

- Use the `setEnabled` method to disable and enable a component instance

- Display dynamic content in an instance of the ComboBox component

- Send data from a Flash movie to a script on a server

APPROXIMATE TIME

This lesson takes approximately two hours to complete.

LESSON FILES

Media Files:

Lesson09/Assets/map.swf
Lesson09/Assets/style.as
Lesson09/Assets/assets.fla
Lesson09/Assets/map.php
Lesson09/Assets/animals.php
Lesson09/Assets/guestbook.php

Starting Files:

Lesson09/Assets/guestbook7.fla

Completed Project:

Lesson09/Completed/map5.fla
Lesson09/Completed/guestbook8.fla

SETTING UP THE MAP

In this exercise you will build the zoo map that you will use throughout this lesson. The graphic for the map has already been created, but you will add some PushButton components so that users will have a place to click. You'll also add a ListBox component to display the list of animals in the zoo.

1) Create a new Flash movie based on the Flash TFS Zoo Template.

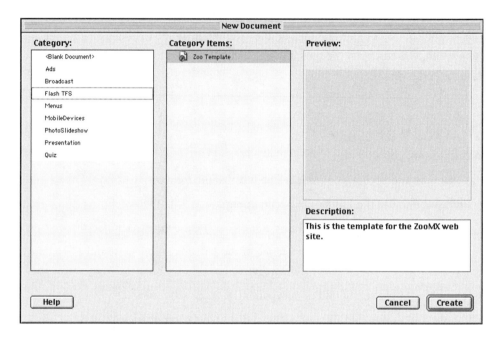

Choose File > New From Template. In the New Document dialog box, set the Category to Flash TFS and make sure the Zoo Template is selected. Click Create, and a new movie, based on the Zoo Template file, appears.

2) Select the Contents layer, and import map.swf from the Lesson09/Assets folder on the CD-ROM.

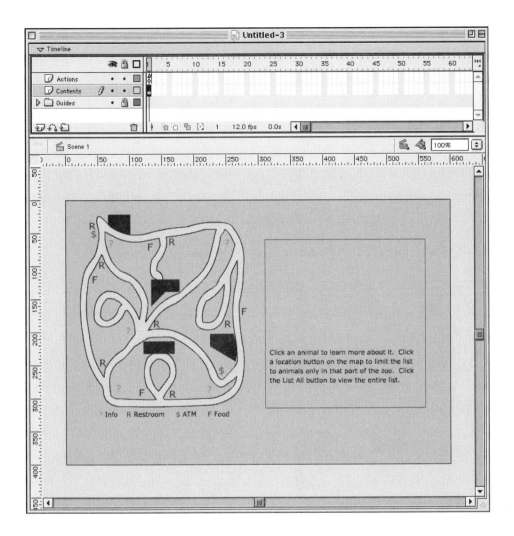

To import the file, choose File > Import and browse to the Lesson09/Assets folder. Select map.swf and click Open. This file contains the map graphic you'll use to let visitors know where the animals are located. You can re-create the contents of map.swf for more practice—just use the figure above as a guide.

3) Set the name of the Contents layer to Map, and lock it. Add two new layers above the Map layer, and name them Locations and List.

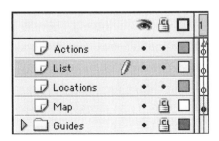

Double-click the name of the Contents layer to select it, and change its name to Map. Lock the Map layer by clicking the dot under the Lock/Unlock All Layers icon to the right of the layer's name. Then add a new layer called Locations, and place it above the Map layer in the layer stacking order. In the next step you are going to place the location markers—instances of the PushButton UI component—in the Locations layer. Next add the List layer above the Locations layer. In step 6 you're going to add an instance of the ListBox component to the List layer—by default this instance will display a list of all the animals in the zoo. When you click an instance of the PushButton component, the list will change to display only the animals in that part of the zoo.

4) Add five instances of the PushButton component to the Locations layer.

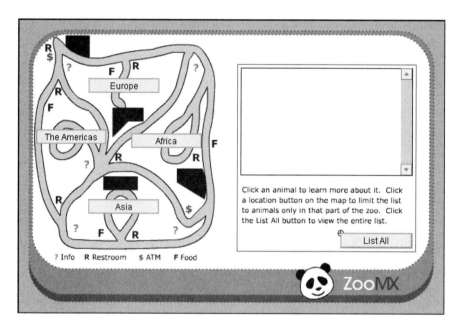

Make sure to select the Locations layer before you add any instances of the PushButton component. You can add a single instance of the PushButton component to the Locations layer, then press Ctrl+D (Windows) or Command+D (Macintosh) four times to make a total of five copies.

Each instance of the PushButton component will mark one area in the zoo. Use the Property inspector to set the instance names of the PushButton component instances to all, americas, africa, asia, and europe. Set the X and Y of the all instance to 455 and 290, and enter List All in the Label parameter field. Then set the X and Y of the americas instance to 25 and 150, and enter *The Americas* in the Label parameter field. Next set the X and Y of the africa PushButton instance to 160 and 155, and enter

Africa in the Label parameter field. Now set the X and Y of the asia instance to 100 and 245, and enter *Asia* in the Label parameter field. Finally, set the X and Y of the europe instance to 100 and 80, and enter *Europe* in the Label parameter field.

5) Set the Click Handler parameter for each instance of the PushButton component to getList.

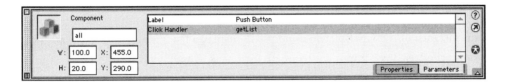

Now when you click any of the PushButton component instances, the getList function will be triggered. You haven't added this function yet, but you will in the next exercise.

TIP *You're finished working with the Locations layer, so it would be wise to lock it. You don't want to accidentally mess up anything as you work in the List layer.*

6) Add an instance of the ListBox component to the List layer. In the Property inspector type *animalList* in the Instance Name text box, and set the Width to 240, the Height to 150, X to 315, and Y to 65.

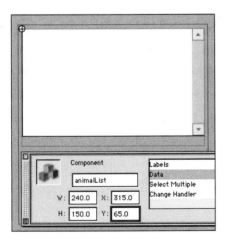

You can find the ListBox component in the Components panel. Make sure you have the List layer selected, click the ListBox component in the Components panel, and drag the component onto the stage.

Or you can double-click ListBox in the Components panel to add an instance of the component to the stage. Then use the Property inspector to modify its Name, Width, Height, X, and Y settings—just like any other UI component instance. In this case, type *animalList* in the Instance Name text box.

NOTE *Make sure the Instance Name is **animalList** and not **animalist** or **animaList**. You need both L's in the name in order for the code you'll add later in this lesson to work.*

This instance of the ListBox component will display a list of animals in the zoo. You can use the ListBox component to create list boxes, which will display lists of data. You can modify the parameters of each instance so that the user can select only single items or multiple items from the list. This component contains a copy of the ScrollBar component, which you'll work with later, so if there are more list items than can fit in the ListBox component's viewable area, a scroll bar will allow the user to scroll through the items.

Like the ComboBox component you worked with in Lesson 8, the ListBox component has several keyboard controls built in. The up and down arrow keys move the selection up or down one line in the scroll list. The Page Up and Page Down keys move the selection up or down one page. The size of the page is set by the height of the list box. The Home key selects the first item in the list, and the End key selects the last item in the list. You have to click an instance of the ListBox component to use these keyboard controls.

7) Set the `Change Handler` **for the instance of the ListBox component to** `getDetail`**.**

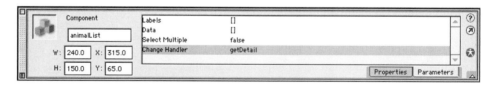

The ListBox component has only four parameters: `Labels`, `Data`, `Select Multiple`, and `Change Handler`. The `Labels` and `Data` parameters can contain arrays, much like the `Labels` and `Data` parameters for the ComboBox component you worked with in Lesson 8. Leave the `Labels` and `Data` parameters alone for this instance of the ListBox component—you'll add some ActionScript to add labels and data for this instance later in this lesson. The `Select Multiple` parameter can have a value of `true` or `false`—`true` allows the user to select more than one item in the list, while `false`, the default, allows the user to select only one item in the list. The Change Handler, which you should set to `getDetail`, is the function that will be called when you select an item in the list box. The function, which you will define later in this lesson, must be in the same timeline as the instance of the ListBox component.

8) Select frame 1 of the Actions layer, and add the following ActionScript to the Actions panel:

```
// arrow color
globalStyleFormat.arrow = 0xFFFFFF;
// text styles
globalStyleFormat.textColor = 0xCC0000;
globalStyleFormat.textFont = "Verdana";
globalStyleFormat.textSize = 10;
globalStyleFormat.textSelected = 0xFFFFFF;
// component colors
globalStyleFormat.face = 0xFF6600;
globalStyleFormat.darkshadow = 0x000000;
globalStyleFormat.highlight = 0xCC0000;
globalStyleFormat.highlight3D = 0xFFC055;
globalStyleFormat.shadow = 0xCC0000;
globalStyleFormat.selection = 0xFF9933;
globalStyleFormat.applyChanges();
// modify push button style
pbStyle = new FStyleFormat();
pbStyle.textColor = 0xFFFFFF;
pbStyle.addListener(americas, africa, asia, europe, all);
```

Actions – Frame

Actions for Frame 1 (Labeled This is the ZooMX template) of Layer Name Actions

```
 1  // arrow color
 2  globalStyleFormat.arrow = 0xFFFFFF;
 3  // text styles
 4  globalStyleFormat.textColor = 0xCC0000;
 5  globalStyleFormat.textFont = "Verdana";
 6  globalStyleFormat.textSize = 10;
 7  globalStyleFormat.textSelected = 0xFFFFFF;
 8  // component colors
 9  globalStyleFormat.face = 0xFF6600;
10  globalStyleFormat.darkshadow = 0x000000;
11  globalStyleFormat.highlight = 0xCC0000;
12  globalStyleFormat.highlight3D = 0xFFC055;
13  globalStyleFormat.shadow = 0xCC0000;
14  globalStyleFormat.selection = 0xFF9933;
15  globalStyleFormat.applyChanges();
16  // modify push button style
17  pbStyle = new FStyleFormat();
18  pbStyle.textColor = 0xFFFFFF;
19  pbStyle.addListener(americas, africa, asia, europe, all);
```

Line 19 of 19, Col 58

This ActionScript should look somewhat familiar to you. It's nearly identical to the ActionScript you used to modify the appearance of the components in Lesson 8.

If you don't want to type all this ActionScript in the Actions panel, you can import it from the Lesson09/Assets folder. Click the Actions panel's Options menu control, and select Import From File. When the Open dialog box appears, browse to the Lesson09/Assets folder, select style.as, and click Open. The ActionScript appears in the Actions panel.

9) Save the file as map1.fla in the FlashTFS folder on your hard drive.

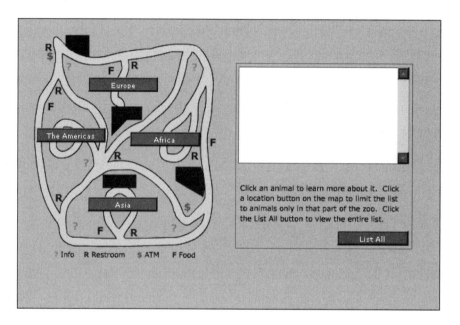

You can test the movie before you save it by choosing Control > Test Movie. You should see that each component uses the styles you specified in frame 1 of the Actions layer.

The map is set, and the movie is ready for some ActionScript to get data about the animals in each section of the zoo. Once you have the data, you'll use ActionScript to display the data in the instance of the ListBox component.

LOADING VARIABLES FROM A DATA SOURCE

Flash movies can load data from external data sources. You can use actions and methods to communicate with server-side scripts, XML files, and text files. The MovieClip object loads information into a movie, in a URL-encoded format, using the loadVariables, loadVariablesNum, loadMovie, and loadMovieNum methods. You can also use the `load` and `sendAndLoad` methods of the `LoadVars` object to get data from an external source. The `XML` and `XMLSocket` objects also have methods that let you communicate with external data sources, but the use of these objects is outside the scope of this book.

In the next exercise, you will use the `sendAndLoad` method of the `LoadVars` object to get data from a PHP file on a server. Depending on which instance of the PushButton component was clicked, the ActionScript you add might also send data to the PHP file, modifying its output. You should start this exercise with map1.fla open.

1) Select frame 1 of the Actions layer, and add the following ActionScript:

```
function getList(btn) {
  trace(btn._name);
}
dataURL = "http://www.flashtfs.com/data/";
```

Add this ActionScript before the ActionScript that you added in the previous exercise. Just add a new line before that code, and start typing.

This is the `getList` function you assigned as the Click Handler for each instance of the PushButton component. If you use the same chunk of code in several places in your movie, it can be useful to turn that chunk of code into a function, which is simply a reusable chunk of code. You can then refer to the function instead of rewriting the code each time you want to use it. A function can also be useful when you need to make changes to the code; you only have to do it in one place—the function itself.

The `getList` function has a single parameter, `btn`. When you click an instance of the PushButton UI component, it automatically sends the path of the instance, in dot syntax, along with the call to the function specified in the `Click Handler` parameter. For example, when you click the `asia` instance of the PushButton component, that instance calls the `getList` function as if you had added the following code to the `onPress` event for that symbol:

```
getList(_level0.asia);
```

The `_level0` portion of this code specifies the level of the `asia` instance. You'll learn about levels in Lesson 11.

The contents of the `getList` function are very simple right now. You've added only one line to the function:

```
trace(btn._name);
```

This code triggers the `trace` action. The single parameter for the `trace` action can be any expression. In this case, the expression is `btn._name`, which will return the `_name` property, or instance name, of whatever instance called the `getList` function. The `trace` action then displays the result in the Output window, as you'll see in the next step.

The last line of code you added sets the value of the `dataURL` variable to `http://localhost/flashtfs/data/`. This URL is part of the Flash TFS Web site— it contains several PHP scripts, which you will use to send and load data. You will use the `dataURL` variable later in this lesson.

2) Choose Control > Test Movie.

When you click one of the PushButton instances, a window should pop up displaying the instance name of the push button. That is the Output window, which is useful for displaying notes or messages when you test a movie. The window opens because the `trace` action, which is called as part of the `getList` function, prints something in the window. If the window is already open, the `trace` action simply prints its output in the open window—it won't open another window.

You can use `trace` actions throughout your ActionScript to check values and to make sure the values are being set properly. In this case, the `trace` action should output the instance name of the PushButton instance that you click. For example, if you click the `asia` instance of the PushButton component, the word *asia* should appear in the Output window.

3) Modify the `getList` function by adding the following ActionScript:

```
locData = new LoadVars();
if (btn._name != "all" && btn._name != undefined) {
  locData.location = btn._name;
}
locData.sendAndLoad(dataURL+"map.php", locData, POST);
```

You should add this code following the line containing the `trace` action. After you add the code, your `getList` function should look like this:

```
function getList(btn) {
  trace(btn._name);
  locData = new LoadVars();
  if (btn._name != "all" && btn._name != undefined) {
    locData.location = btn._name;
  }
  locData.sendAndLoad(dataURL+"map.php", locData, POST);
}
```

The first line of the code you just added creates a new instance of the built-in `LoadVars` object. This code should look somewhat familiar to you—you created several new object instances in Lesson 7. In this case, the constructor function that follows the `new` operator is `LoadVars()`. This code sets the name of the new instance of the `LoadVars` object to `locData`.

The next three lines of code add a little bit of logic to the `getList` function. This `if` statement checks to see if the instance name of the PushButton you clicked (`btn._name`) is not `"all"` and `undefined`. The inequality operator (`!=`) tests for inequality. So if the left side of the first expression (`btn._name`) is *not* equal to the right side (`"all"`), the expression will be true. The logical `"and"` operator (`&&`) requires that both expressions be true in order to make the `if` statement's condition true. So the ActionScript inside the `if` statement will only be triggered if the instance name of the PushButton that calls `getList` is neither `"all"` nor `undefined`. If the condition is true, the location variable in the `locData` instance of the `LoadVars` object you created is set to `btn._name`.

NOTE *As you learned in Lesson 7, undefined is a special value in Flash. It is used to indicate that the value of a variable has not been set. So if no instance of the PushButton component triggered the getList function, which could happen if you simply call the function from a frame, the instance name of btn would be undefined.*

NOTE *The location variable is not a built-in variable or property of the LoadVars object. See Appendix D for more information about the LoadVars object.*

The last line of code you added to the `getList` function uses the `sendAndLoad` method of the built-in `LoadVars` object to send the values of any variables in the `locData` instance of the object to a server-side script. If the instance name of the PushButton that called the `getList` function is neither `all` nor `undefined`, the `locData` object has a variable named `location`, with a value of the instance name of the button that called the function.

This method also requests the resulting data set and places it inside the `LoadVars` object named `locData`. The parameters for the `sendAndLoad` method are the URL of the script and the object that you want to receive the resulting data. In this case the URL parameter is `dataURL+"map.php"`, which translates to http://www.flashtfs.com/data/map.php. The object that will receive the data returned by the server is `locData`, which is the same object that sent the data.

> **NOTE** *When you view the Flash movie in your browser, as you will in Lesson 12, Flash might not be able to connect to the map.php file because Flash Player has some built-in security that disables connections to external data sources on other Web servers. But you should still be able to test the movie and view the data when you choose Control > Test Movie.*

Try viewing the URL specified in the URL parameter for the `sendAndLoad` method in your browser. The map.php file outputs a bunch of variable name/value pairs, in a format that Flash understands. When the file opens in your browser, choose View > Source (Microsoft Internet Explorer) or View > Page Source (Netscape Navigator) to view the source. The first couple of lines of the source should look something like this:

```
&common0=African Elephant&
&latin0=Loxodonta africana&
```

The first line of text generated by the PHP file creates a variable called `common0` with a value of `African Elephant`:

```
common0=African Elephant
```

This format is how you set up a variable in Flash, so that Flash understands the text from the PHP file as though it were a bunch of internal variables. The `&`'s in the text generated by the PHP file separate each of the variables.

If you're curious, take a look at the source code for the PHP script. Open map.php from the Lesson09/Assets folder in a text editor such as Notepad (Windows) or SimpleText (Macintosh). The code looks like this:

```php
<?php
  $link = mysql_connect("hostname", "username", "password");
  $query = "SELECT animals.* FROM animals";
  if (isset($location)) {
    $query .= ",locations WHERE locations.name='$location' AND locations.ID=animals.LID";
  }
  $query .= " ORDER BY animals.common";
  $result = mysql_db_query("zoomx", $query);
  $c = 0;
  while ($animals = mysql_fetch_array($result)) {
    $output .= "&common$c=$animals[common]&\r\n";
    $output .= "&latin$c=$animals[latin]&\r\n";
    $output .= "&description$c=$animals[description]&\r\n";
    $output .= "&image$c=$animals[image]&\r\n";
    ++$c;
  }
  echo($output);
  echo("&numAnimals=$c&");
?>
```

Don't worry if you don't understand all this code—you don't have to be a PHP guru to work with Flash! You might notice that some of it looks a lot like ActionScript— the two languages are actually quite similar. All this script does is connect to a MySQL database, get some records from that database, and then return the text you see when you view the source code in your browser. The script retrieves either all of the records in the database, or records for a specific location, depending on whether the $location variable (the location variable of the locData object, which was sent to the script) is set.

**4) Add a dynamic text box to the List layer. Set the variable for this text box to
`heading`, and set the X and Y to 315 and 40.**

NOTE *The text box should be at least 200 pixels wide, but it should not extend beyond the
right edge of the ListBox component instance in the List layer.*

Use the text tool to add this text box. When you select the text tool from the toolbox,
the Property inspector displays the text properties. Set the Text Type to Dynamic
Text. Make sure the Font is set to Verdana, the Font Size to 12, and the Text (fill)
Color to #CC0000 (red). You should also set the Line Type to Single Line, and make
sure the Selectable button is not clicked.

Compare the Property inspector with the figure above, and make sure the settings
are the same.

**5) Add the following ActionScript to the `if` statement in the `getList` function in the
Action layer:**

```
var subtitle = btn.getLabel();
```

```
Actions - Frame

Actions for Frame 1 (Labeled This is the ZooMX template) of Layer Name Actions

 1  function getList(btn) {
 2      trace(btn._name);
 3      locData = new LoadVars();
 4      if (btn._name != "all" && btn._name != undefined) {
 5          locData.location = btn._name;
 6          var subtitle = btn.getLabel();
 7      }
 8      locData.sendAndLoad(dataURL+"map.php", locData, POST);
 9  }
10  dataURL = "http://www.flashtfs.com/data/";
11  // arrow color
12  globalStyleFormat.arrow = 0xFFFFFF;
```

Line 6 of 30, Col 1

Add this code after the line already in the `if` statement. The function should look like this after you add the code:

```
function getList(btn) {
  trace(btn._name);
  locData = new LoadVars();
  if (btn._name != "all" && btn._name != undefined) {
    locData.location = btn._name;
var subtitle = btn.getLabel();
  }
  locData.sendAndLoad(dataURL+"map.php", locData, POST);
}
```

The code you just added sets up a new local variable named `subtitle`. A local variable exists only inside the function, so if for some reason you add a variable called `subtitle` to another part of your code, this variable's value will not affect that variable's value. You can make a variable local by adding the `var` action to the beginning of the line that declares the variable name and value.

The value for the subtitle variable is `btn.getLabel();`. Each instance of the PushButton component is actually an instance of the built-in `FPushButton` object, so you can use the methods for that built-in object. The `getLabel` method gets the `Label` value of the specified PushButton instance (`btn`). The `getLabel` function will return the `Label` parameter's value for any instance that triggers the `getList` function, as long as the instance's name is not `"all"` or `undefined`. For example, if you click the `americas` instance of the PushButton component, the `subtitle` variable will have a value of `"The Americas"`.

NOTE *Appendix D lists more of the `FPushButton` object's methods and properties.*

6) **Add this code after the `if` statement:**

```
else {
  var subtitle = "Entire Zoo";
}
```

Add this code following the curly brace (}) that ends the `if` statement. After you add the ActionScript, the function should look like this:

```
function getList(btn) {
  trace(btn._name);
  locData = new LoadVars();
  if (btn._name != "all" && btn._name != undefined) {
    locData.location = btn._name;
    var subtitle = btn.getLabel();
  } else {
    var subtitle = "Entire Zoo";
  }
  locData.sendAndLoad(dataURL+"map.php", locData, POST);
}
```

The `else` statement provides a value for the `subtitle` variable if the instance name of the PushButton that calls the `getList` function is `"all"` or `undefined`. If you click the `"all"` instance of the PushButton component, or you call the function from the timeline, the `subtitle` variable will have a value of `"Entire Zoo"`.

7) Now add the following code to the `getList` function:

```
heading = "Animal List: " + subtitle;
```

This code should be added after the `if` statement. Your almost-complete `getList` function should look like this:

```
function getList(btn) {
  trace(btn._name);
  locData = new LoadVars();
  if (btn._name != "all" && btn._name != undefined) {
    locData.location = btn._name;
    var subtitle = btn.getLabel();
  } else {
    var subtitle = "Entire Zoo";
  }
  locData.sendAndLoad(dataURL+"map.php", locData, POST);
  heading = "Animal List: " + subtitle;
}
```

This ActionScript sets the value of the `heading` variable, which is not a local variable (no `var` action). That's the variable name you set for the dynamic text box you added earlier in this exercise, so this line of code sets the value of the text displayed in that text box. The value of the `heading` variable depends on the value of the `subtitle` variable—the addition operator (+) adds the value of the `subtitle` variable to the string "Animal List: ". If the subtitle variable has a value of "Entire Zoo", the heading variable will have a value of "Animal List: Entire Zoo".

8) Choose Control > Test Movie. Save the file as map2.fla.

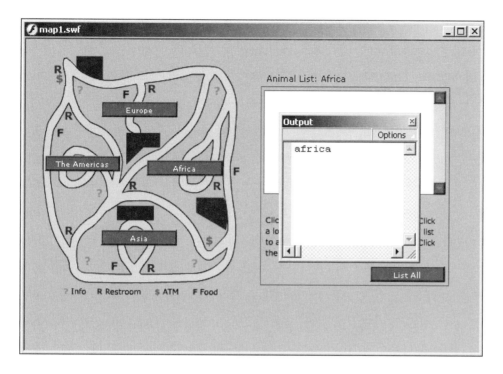

When you click one of the PushButton instances, the instance name should still appear in the Output window. Additionally, the dynamic text box that has a variable name of heading should change, depending on which button you click.

After you test each button, close the Test Movie window and save your file as map2.fla in the FlashTFS folder. Right now the ActionScript in the getList function only requests the data from the map.php file on the server. You still have to add more code to display the data that Flash receives when it's loaded. You'll do that in the next exercise.

DISPLAYING DYNAMIC CONTENT

Flash has requested the data from map.php, but before Flash can display that data, you must make sure it's fully loaded. You need to add another function, which will display the data when the onLoad event for the locData object occurs.

You should still have map2.fla open when you start this exercise.

1) Add another function to frame 1 of the Actions layer:

```
function showList(success) {
  if (success) {
  }
}
```

```
Actions - Frame

Actions for Frame 1 (Labeled This is the ZooMX template)  of Layer Name Actions

 1  function showList(success) {
 2      if (success) {
 3
 4      }
 5  }
 6  function getList(btn) {
 7      trace(btn._name);
 8      locData = new LoadVars();
 9      if (btn._name != "all" && btn._name != undefined) {
10          locData.location = btn._name;
11          var subtitle = btn.getLabel();
12      } else {
13          var subtitle = "Entire Zoo";
14      }
15      heading = "Animal List: " + subtitle;
16      locData.sendAndLoad(dataURL+"map.php", locData, POST);
17  }
18  }

Line 1 of 38, Col 1
```

Add this function before the **getList** function. This function will be called by the **getList** function, so you have to make sure the function is loaded before the code attempts to call it. Adding it before the **getList** function ensures that it is.

The **sendAndLoad** method of the **LoadVars** object requests the data from a specified URL, but you have to make sure the data has loaded before you can actually use it. The **showList** function, which has a parameter named **success**, specifies what to do when the data has loaded. If the value of **success** is **true**, the ActionScript you add inside the **if** statement will run.

NOTE *You have to add a little more code to the getList function to trigger the showList function. You'll do that later in this exercise.*

2) Inside the `if` statement add the following code:

```
animalList.removeAll();
for (var i=0; i<this.numAnimals; i++) {
trace(this["common"+i]);
animalList.addItem(this["common"+i], i);
}
```

```
▼ Actions - Frame                                              ≣
[■] Actions for Frame 1 (Labeled This is the ZooMX template) of Layer Name Actions  [↕] [-⋈]
[+ 🔍 ⅋ ⊕ ✔ ≣ ⎘]                                        ◈ 𝒶, 🗗
 1  function showList(success) {
 2      if (success) {
 3          animalList.removeAll();
 4          for (var i=0; i<this.numAnimals; i++) {
 5              trace(this["common"+i]);
 6              animalList.addItem(this["common"+i]);
 7          }
 8      }
 9  }
10  function getList(btn) {
11      trace(btn._name);
12      locData = new LoadVars();
13      if (btn._name != "all" && btn._name != undefined) {
14          locData.location = btn._name;
15          var subtitle = btn.getLabel();
16      } else {
17          var subtitle = "Entire Zoo";
18
Line 3 of 42, Col 1
```

The `showList` function should now look like this:

```
function showList(success) {
  if (success) {
    animalList.removeAll();
    for (var i=0; i<this.numAnimals; i++) {
      trace(this["common"+i]);
      animalList.addItem(this["common"+i], i);
    }
  }
}
```

The code you just added sets up the `animalList` instance of the ListBox component
to display the data from the server. All instances of the ListBox component are copies
of the built-in `FListBox` object, which has several methods, including `removeAll` and
`addItem`. This code takes advantage of both methods.

The first line of code you added, `animalList.removeAll();`, removes all the labels and data in the `animalList` instance of the ListBox component. If you already had values in that instance of the component, this new code wipes out the data.

The next block of code is a `for` statement. The `for` statement runs as long as `i` is less than `this.numAnimals`. In this case, `this` refers to the `locData` object, and `numAnimals` is a variable set in that object. The `numAnimals` variable is one of the many variables you will receive from the map.php file on the server—`numAnimal` simply provides the number of animals that is returned by the server.

Inside the `for` statement are two lines of code. The first line, `trace(this["common"+i]);`, writes the value of the `"common"+i` variable in the `locData` object each time the `for` statement is run. If `numAnimals` is 3, it will output the values of the `common0`, `common1`, and `common2` variables in the `locData` object. The second line uses the `addItem` method of the built-in `FListBox` object. This method can have two parameters: `label` and `data`. The `label` parameter for this code is the value you traced in the first line to the `animalList` instance of the ListBox component (the value of the `"common"+i variable`). The `data` value is the value of `i`. So the first `label` value will be `common0`, and the first `data` value will be `0`.

3) Add this code to the `getList` function:

```
locData.onLoad = showList;
```

302

You need to trigger the `showList` function when the `onLoad` event of the `getList` function occurs, in order to make the data appear. The `onLoad` event occurs when the data requested by the `sendAndLoad` method has loaded successfully, and it will return a value of `true`. The `getList` function should look like the following when you're finished:

```
function getList(btn) {
  trace(btn._name);
  locData = new LoadVars();
  if (btn._name != "all" && btn._name != undefined) {
    locData.location = btn._name;
    var subtitle = btn.getLabel();
  } else {
    var subtitle = "Entire Zoo";
  }
  heading = "Animal List: "+subtitle;
  locData.sendAndLoad(dataURL+"map.php", locData, POST);
  locData.onLoad = showList;
}
```

4) Add the following ActionScript:

```
getList();
```

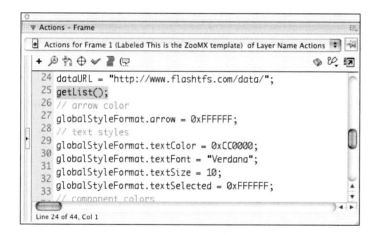

This code should follow the `dataURL` variable—you have to initialize the `dataURL` variable before you trigger the `getList` function, or Flash won't know where to find map.php.

TIP *Try adding this line of code before the `dataURL` variable to see what happens. You should get an error message when you test the movie. Be sure to move the call to the `getList` function after the `dataURL` variable before you save the movie, or that error will pop up, and the list box won't get the data it needs to display the animals.*

5) Choose Control > Test Movie. Save the movie as map3.fla in the FlashTFS folder.

When you test the movie, Flash will request map.php from the server when frame 1 calls the `getList` function. After the data has loaded, it will be displayed in the `animalList` instance of the ListBox component. When you click one of the location buttons, the `getList` function will be triggered and will display only the animals in that location, or all the animals if you click the List All button.

After you've finished testing everything, close the Test Movie window and save the file as map3.fla in the FlashTFS folder. Now that your animal list is working, it's time to add a bit more code to display the details for each animal.

USING THE SCROLLBAR COMPONENT

The ScrollBar component lets you add horizontal and vertical scroll bars to dynamic and input text boxes. You can display large amounts of text in a movie without having to display it all at once. You have already seen the ScrollBar component in your movies, even though you might not have realized it. It is part of the ListBox, ComboBox, and ScrollPane components.

In this exercise you will add a new symbol to display the details for an animal. The description for each animal is relatively long, so you will add a ScrollBar component to a dynamic text box inside the new symbol. You will also add some more ActionScript to display the details about each animal. Before you start this next exercise, open map3.fla if it isn't still open from the last exercise.

1) Open assets.fla from the Lesson09/Assets folder as a library. Open the map3.fla library (Window > Library), and drag copies of the Detail Clip and Close Clip symbols from the assets.fla library to the map3.fla library.

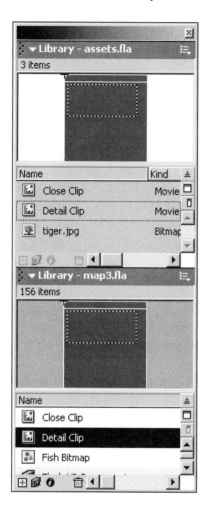

To open a file as a library, choose File > Open as Library, locate the file, and click the Open button. The assets.fla file contains two symbols (Close Clip and Detail Clip) and a bitmap (tiger.jpg). The bitmap is part of a Guide layer inside the Detail Clip movie clip, so it will be added to the map3.fla library when you add the Detail Clip symbol.

You will use the `attachMovie` method of the MovieClip object to add instances of the Close Clip and Detail Clip symbols to the movie, as you did with the Menu Piece movie clip in Lesson 7. You can check the Linkage settings for these two symbols by right-clicking (Windows) or Control-clicking (Macintosh) the symbol names in the map3.fla library and choosing Linkage. The Identifiers for the Close Clip and Detail

Clip symbols are `closeClip` and `detailClip`. You should also see that both symbols have the "Export for ActionScript" and "Export in first frame" options selected.

Close the assets.fla library when you're finished. Click the assets.fla library's Options menu control, and choose Close Panel.

2) Open the Detail Clip movie clip in symbol-editing mode. Select the text box in the Text Box layer, and set its Instance Name to *t* and Variable to `description`.

> **N O T E** *Make sure you open the* `Detail Clip` *symbol from map3.fla, and not from assets.fla.*

The Detail Clip movie clip is very simple. It has three layers: Text Box, Image Placeholder, and Background. You can use the skills you've learned to create your own Detail Clip in place of this one, but be sure to read through this entire step before you attempt to do so.

The Text Box layer contains a text box just over 200 pixels wide and almost 95 pixels high. This text box is dynamic and will display white Verdana text. The Line Type is set to Multiline, so any text that exceeds the width of the text box automatically wraps to the next line. The "Render text as HTML" button is selected for this text box—Flash can render some HTML tags in input and dynamic text boxes, and when you click this button, Flash knows it should render text as HTML for a particular text box.

Select the text box in the Text Box layer, and set its Instance Name to *t*. It's very important that you give this text box an instance name, as the ScrollBar component you're going to add in the next step must know which text-box instance it will work with. Set the Variable for this text box to `description`.

> **N O T E** *The following HTML tags are supported in Flash: <A>, <B>, <FONT COLOR>, <FONT FACE>, <FONT SIZE>, <I>, <P>, and <U>. Flash also recognizes the following HTML attributes: LEFTMARGIN, RIGHTMARGIN, ALIGN, INDENT, and LEADING.*

The Image Placeholder layer is a Guide layer and will not be exported with the Flash movie. In this movie, the Image Placeholder layer simply indicates where the image will appear. This layer is not required if you plan to make your own version of the Detail Clip symbol.

The Background layer contains some vector graphics, which were drawn using Flash's drawing tools. These graphics consist of two rectangles, both of which are surrounded by a white outline. The layer should be locked when you open the symbol, but you can unlock it and modify the graphics to suit your taste.

3) Make sure you have the Text Box layer selected, and drag an instance of the ScrollBar component onto the text box in that layer.

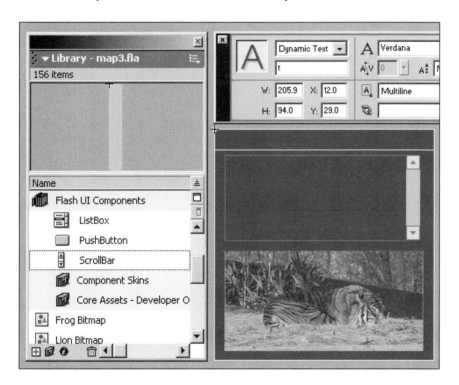

You can drag the instance of the ScrollBar component from the Flash UI Components folder in the map3.fla library. It was automatically added to the movie when you added the instance of the ListBox component earlier in this lesson.

When you drop an instance of the ScrollBar component onto a dynamic text box, the ScrollBar component automatically snaps to the right side of the text box.

4) Select the instance of the ScrollBar component, and look at the Property inspector.

Notice that Flash automatically set the `Target TextField` parameter for this instance of the ScrollBar component to `t`. Leave the `Horizontal` parameter at the default setting of `false`.

5) Choose Edit > Edit Document. Select frame 1 of the Actions layer, and add the `getDetail` function:

```
function getDetail(lb) {
}
```

```
10  function getList(btn) {
11      trace(btn._name);
12      locData = new LoadVars();
13      if (btn._name != "all" && btn._name != undefined) {
14          locData.location = btn._name;
15          var subtitle = btn.getLabel();
16      } else {
17          var subtitle = "Entire Zoo";
18      }
19      heading = "Animal List: " + subtitle;
20      locData.sendAndLoad(dataURL+"map.php", locData, POST);
21      locData.onLoad = showList;
22  }
23  getDetail(lb) {
24
25  }
26  dataURL = "http://www.flashtfs.com/data/";
27  getList();
```

Add this code after the `getList` function, but before the `dataURL` variable.

The Change Handler you assigned to the `animalList` instance of the ListBox component was `getDetail`. That function will be called any time you select an item in the list box. The `lb` parameter for the `getDetail` function is the dot-syntax path of the ListBox component that calls the function. Flash automatically passes this value to the function when it's called. You can add the following ActionScript to the `getDetail` function to test this out:

```
trace(lb);
```

NOTE *Make sure to set the parameter for the `getDetail` function to `lb` and not `1b`. That should be a lowercase l followed by a lowercase b. It stands for* list button.

6) Add the following code to the `getDetail` function:

```
var idNum = lb.getSelectedItem().data;
_root.attachMovie("detailClip", "detailClip", 1);
detailClip._x = 310;
detailClip._y = 60;
detailClip.description = "<b>"+locData["common"+idNum]+"</b><br>";
detailClip.description += "<i>"+locData["latin"+idNum]+"</i><br><br>";
detailClip.description += locData["description"+idNum];
```

```
15        var subtitle = btn.getLabel();
16     } else {
17        var subtitle = "Entire Zoo";
18     }
19     heading = "Animal List: "+subtitle;
20     locData.sendAndLoad(dataURL+"map.php", locData, POST);
21     locData.onLoad = showList;
22  }
23  function getDetail(lb) {
24     var idNum = lb.getSelectedItem().data;
25     _root.attachMovie("detailClip", "detailClip", 1);
26     detailClip._x = 310;
27     detailClip._y = 60;
28     detailClip.description = "<b>"+locData["common"+idNum]+"</b><br>";
29     detailClip.description += "<i>"+locData["latin"+idNum]+"</i><br><br>";
30     detailClip.description += locData["description"+idNum];
31  }
32  dataURL = "http://www.flashtfs.com/data/";
```

Line 24 of 53, Col 1

The `getDetail` function should look like the following:

```
function getDetail(lb) {
var idNum = item.getSelectedItem().data;
_root.attachMovie("detailClip", "detailClip", 1);
detailClip._x = 310;
detailClip._y = 60;
detailClip.description = "<b>"+locData["common"+idNum]+"</b><br>";
detailClip.description += "<i>"+locData["latin"+idNum]+"</i><br><br>";
detailClip.description += locData["description"+idNum];
}
```

This code may look complicated at first glance, but it's actually very simple.

The first line sets up a new local variable, named `idNum`, with a value of `item.getSelectedItem().data`. As you may recall from the last exercise, every instance of the ListBox component is actually a copy of the built-in `FListBox` object. The `getSelectedItem` method of the `FListBox` object returns the currently selected item from the list as an object, with `label` and `data` properties. In this case, you want the value of the `data` property. If you select the first item in the list, the value for this property will be `0` because when the `showList` function added all of the items to the list box (using `addItem`), it set the `data` parameter for the first item to `0` (see "Displaying Dynamic Content," step 2):

```
for (var i=0; i<this.numAnimals; i++) {
trace(this["common"+i]);
animalList.addItem(this["common"+i], i);
}
```

The next line of code attaches a copy of the Detail Clip movie clip to `_root`, using the `attachMovie` method. `_root` is a special property that specifies the main timeline of a movie. The main timeline of the movie can use the methods of the `MovieClip` object. This code sets the instance name of the attached movie clip to `detailClip` and gives it a depth of 1. If you don't remember how to use the `attachMovie` method, refer back to Lesson 7.

NOTE *The first parameter of the `attachMovieClip` object is the Identifier for the movie clip you want to attach. The Identifier for the Detail Clip symbol is `detailClip` (see figure below). Refer to step 1 of this exercise to see how to check the Identifier value.*

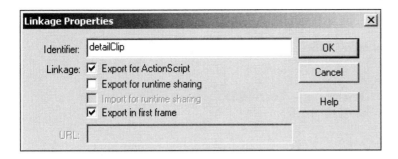

After Flash attaches an instance of the Detail Clip symbol, the next two lines of code set its _x and _y properties. The movie-clip instance will be positioned at 310, 60 on the main timeline.

The last three lines of code specify a value for the `description` variable in the attached `detailClip` instance:

```
detailClip.description = "<b>"+locData["common"+idNum]+"</b><br>";
detailClip.description += "<i>"+locData["latin"+idNum]+"</i><br><br>";
detailClip.description += locData["description"+idNum];
```

First the value of the `description` variable is set to `"<b>"+locData["common"+idNum]+"</b><br>"`. This takes the string `"<b>"`, adds the value of `locData["common"+idNum]`, and then adds the string `"</b><br>"`. The value of `locData["common"+idNum]` is the value of `"common"+idNum` in the `locData` object, which contains all the variables you loaded from the map.php file on the server. If you select the first item in the list, you would be selecting the value of the `common0` variable in the `locData` object. The variables starting with `common` contain the values for the common name of each animal in the list. So this code adds the common name for the selected animal in bold.

Next the value of `"<i>"+locData["latin"+idNum]+"</i><br><br>"` is added to the value of the `description` variable. This is done using the addition assignment operator (`+=`), which takes the current value of the `description` variable and adds the value following the operator. The value added is the string `"<i>"`, plus the value of `locData["latin"+idNum]`, plus the string `"</i><br><br>"`. This value adds the Latin name for the selected animal in italics, followed by two `<br>` tags.

Finally, the value of `locData["description"+idNum]` is added to the value of the `description` variable. This adds the description for the selected animal. The descriptions for the animals may be relatively long, which is why you added an instance of the ScrollBar component to the text box with the variable name `description`.

311

7) Add this code to the `getDetail` function:

```
detailClip.attachMovie("closeClip", "closeClip", 1);
detailClip.closeClip._x = 230;
detailClip.closeClip._y = 4;
detailClip.closeClip.onPress = function () {
  detailClip.removeMovieClip();
}
```

Add this code following the ActionScript already in the **getDetail** function. The
getDetail function should look like this after you've completed this step:

```
function getDetail(lb) {
var idNum = lb.getSelectedItem().data;
_root.attachMovie("detailClip", "detailClip", 1);
detailClip._x = 310;
detailClip._y = 60;
detailClip.description = "<b>"+locData["common"+idNum]+"</b><br>";
detailClip.description += "<i>"+locData["latin"+idNum]+"</i><br><br>";
detailClip.description += locData["description"+idNum];
detailClip.attachMovie("closeClip", "closeClip", 1);
detailClip.closeClip._x = 230;
detailClip.closeClip._y = 4;
detailClip.closeClip.onPress = function () {
  detailClip.removeMovieClip();
}
}
```

This code attaches an instance of the Close Clip movie clip inside the `detailClip` instance you added to the main timeline. It then sets the `_x` and `_y` properties for the Close Clip instance, which has an instance name of `closeClip`, and assigns a function to its `onPress` event. When the `onPress` event is triggered, the `removeMovieClip` method, which is a built-in method of the `MovieClip` object, removes the `detailClip` instance. You can only use the `removeMovieClip` method to remove dynamically attached or duplicated movie-clip instances.

8) Choose Control › Test Movie. Save the movie as map4.fla.

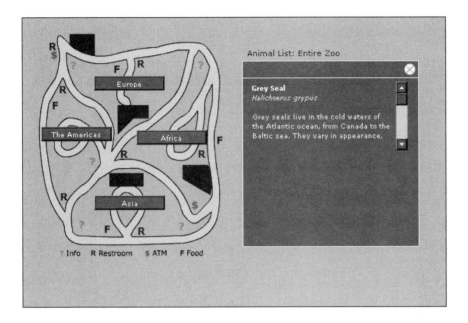

When you click an item in the list box, a window should appear, covering the list box, with the details for the animal you selected. You can close the window by clicking the Close Clip instance in the top-right corner of the window.

Notice the large space at the bottom of the window. You are going to add a dynamically included JPEG image in this space in Lesson 11.

You're almost finished with the map. You might notice that when you select an animal, attaching an instance of the Detail Clip symbol, you can still click other items in the list through the Detail Clip instance. You don't want this to happen, so in the next exercise you'll disable the `ListBox` component instance when the Detail Clip movie clip is opened.

Close the Test Movie window, and save your file as map4.fla in the FlashTFS folder on your hard drive when you've finished testing.

DISABLING A COMPONENT

As you saw in the last exercise, it's sometime necessary to disable a component. When you disable a component instance, that instance can no longer receive keyboard or mouse input. In this exercise you will disable the instance of the ListBox component so that it isn't clickable under the Detail Clip symbol. You will then reenable the list box when the Detail Clip movie clip is removed.

You should start this exercise with map4.fla still open.

1) Add this code to the `getDetail` function in frame 1 of the Actions layer:

```
animalList.setEnabled(false);
```

```
Actions - Frame

Actions for Frame 1 (Labeled This is the ZoomX template) of Layer Name Actions

23 function getDetail(lb) {
24     animalList.setEnabled(false);
25     var idNum = lb.getSelectedItem().data;
26     _root.attachMovie("detailClip", "detailClip", 1);
27     detailClip._x = 310;
28     detailClip._y = 60;
29     detailClip.description = "<b>"+locData["common"+idNum]+"</
30     detailClip.description += "<i>"+locData["latin"+idNum]+"</
31     detailClip.description += locData["description"+idNum];
32     detailClip.attachMovie("closeClip", "closeClip", 1);
33     detailClip.closeClip._x = 230;
34     detailClip.closeClip._y = 4;
35     detailClip.closeClip.onPress = function() {
36         detailClip.removeMovieClip();
37     }
38 }
39 dataURL = "http://www.flashtfs.com/data/";
40 getList();

Line 24 of 60, Col 1
```

Add this code to the beginning of the function—just add a new line and start typing. When you're finished, the `getDetail` function should look like this:

```
function getDetail(lb) {
animalList.setEnabled(false);
var idNum = lb.getSelectedItem().data;
_root.attachMovie("detailClip", "detailClip", 1);
detailClip._x = 310;
detailClip._y = 60;
detailClip.description = "<b>"+locData["common"+idNum]+"</b><br>";
detailClip.description += "<i>"+locData["latin"+idNum]+"</i><br><br>";
detailClip.description += locData["description"+idNum];
```

```
detailClip.attachMovie("closeClip", "closeClip", 1);
detailClip.closeClip._x = 230;
detailClip.closeClip._y = 4;
detailClip.closeClip.onPress = function () {
  detailClip.removeMovieClip();
}
}
```

Many of the Flash UI components, including the ListBox component, can be disabled using the `setEnabled` method. The `setEnabled` method is part of the `FlistBox` object; the ListBox component instance is a copy of the `FlistBox` object. The `setEnabled` method has a single parameter, the value for which can be true or false. If the value is `true`, the component instance is enabled. If the value is `false`, the component instance is disabled and cannot accept mouse or keyboard interaction.

2) Add the following ActionScript to the `getDetail` function:

```
detailClip.onUnload = function() {
  animalList.setEnabled(true);
};
```

This code should follow the line that attaches an instance of the Detail Clip movie clip. Your getDetail function should look like this after you've completed this step:

```
function getDetail(lb) {
animalList.setEnabled(false);
var idNum = lb.getSelectedItem().data;
_root.attachMovie("detailClip", "detailClip", 1);
detailClip.onUnload = function() {
  animalList.setEnabled(true);
};
detailClip._x = 310;
detailClip._y = 60;
detailClip.description = "<b>"+locData["common"+idNum]+"</b><br>";
detailClip.description += "<i>"+locData["latin"+idNum]+"</i><br><br>";
detailClip.description += locData["description"+idNum];
detailClip.attachMovie("closeClip", "closeClip", 1);
detailClip.closeClip._x = 230;
detailClip.closeClip._y = 4;
detailClip.closeClip.onPress = function () {
  detailClip.removeMovieClip();
}
}
```

The onUnload event of the built-in MovieClip object is triggered when the specified movie-clip instance is removed from the stage. When the removeMovieClip method is called by the instance of the Close Clip symbol inside the attached Detail Clip movie clip, the onUnload event will be triggered. This code enables the animalList ListBox instance, using the setEnabled method.

NOTE *Notice the semicolon (;) following the last curly brace in the code you just added. It's not required, but it's actually good syntax to add that semicolon because in essence, the code inside the curly braces is sort of like one long line of code. If you click the Auto Format button in the Actions panel, Flash will automatically add a semicolon after that curly brace.*

3) Choose Control > Test Movie.

Select an animal from the list. When the Detail Clip movie clip is attached, you should not be able to select other animals through it. When you're finished testing, close the Test Movie window.

4) Save the file as map5.fla in the FlashTFS folder on your hard drive.

You're finished with the map for now. Save it as map5.fla in the FlashTFS folder on your hard drive. You'll use this file again in Lesson 12.

SENDING DATA TO THE SERVER

Now it's time to get back to the guestbook you created in Lesson 8. You set everything to collect data from your visitors, but now you have to add ActionScript to send the data to the server.

1) Open guestbook7.fla from the FlashTFS folder on your hard drive.

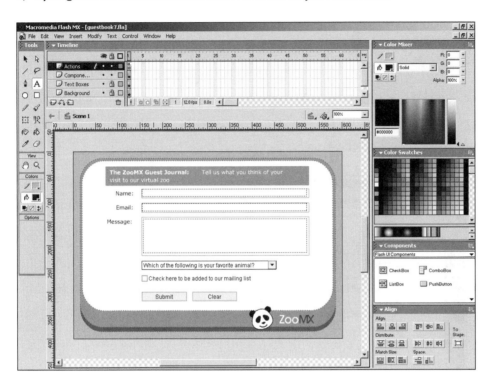

You created the guestbook7.fla file in Lesson 8 and should have saved it in the FlashTFS folder. If for some reason you can't find the file, you can open guestbook7.fla from the Lesson09/Starting folder. Make sure to save the file to the FlashTFS folder on your hard drive before you continue.

2) Select frame 1 of the Actions layer, and add the following ActionScript:

```
function showList(success) {
  if (success) {
    animal.removeAll();
    animal.addItem("Which of the following is your favorite animal?");
    for (var i = 0; i<this.numAnimals; i++) {
      animal.addItem(this["common"+i], this["ID"+i]);
    }
  }
}
function getList() {
  aList = new LoadVars();
  aList.load(dataURL+"animals.php", aList);
  aList.onLoad = showList;
}
dataURL = "http://www.flashtfs.com/data/";
```

TIP *If you don't want to type all this code, you can import it into the Actions panel. Just make a new line at the start of the code that's already there, and be sure the pointer is in that new line. Click the Options menu control in the Actions panel, and choose Import from File in the drop-down menu. In the Open dialog box, browse to the Lesson09/Assets folder, locate list.as, and click Open. Flash will import the code in list.as to the Actions panel.*

Add this ActionScript before any other code in the Actions panel. This code should look familiar—it's similar to the code you added to the map movie to add values to the ListBox component instance. In this case, you're adding values to the ComboBox component instance, using values loaded from the animals.php file on the server. The getList function creates a new LoadVars object named aList, and requests the data from the server using the load method. When the onLoad event is triggered, the showList function removes all the existing values from the animal instance of the ComboBox component and adds all the items returned by animals.php. Unlike what happens with the ListBox component instance in the map movie, the data value for each item in the animal ComboBox instance receives a value from the animals.php file. That value corresponds to the ID number of the selected animal in the database.

As you learned earlier in this lesson, Flash expects this format. When this data is loaded by the movie, Flash can use each of the variables in this external data source as a variable in the aList object.

You can find a copy of animals.php in the Lesson09/Assets folder. If you'd like to take a look at it, just open the file in a text editor.

```php
<?php
    $link = mysql_connect("hostname", "username", "password");
    $query = "SELECT common, ID FROM animals ORDER BY common";
    $result = mysql_db_query("zoomx", $query);
    $c = 0;
    while ($animals = mysql_fetch_array($result)) {
        $output .= "&common$c=$animals[common]&\r\n";
        $output .= "&ID$c=$animals[ID]&\r\n";
        ++$c;
    }
    echo($output);
    echo("&numAnimals=$c&");
?>
```

3) Add this code to the Actions panel:

```
getList();
```

You set up the **getList** function, but now you have to call it. Adding this line of code, which should follow the **dataURL** variable, will do just that. After you add this code, you can test your movie to make sure the combo box gets the values from the server.

4) Now add the following ActionScript:

```
function processForm(btn) {
  if (btn._name == "clear") {
    } else if (btn._name == "submit") {
  }
}
```

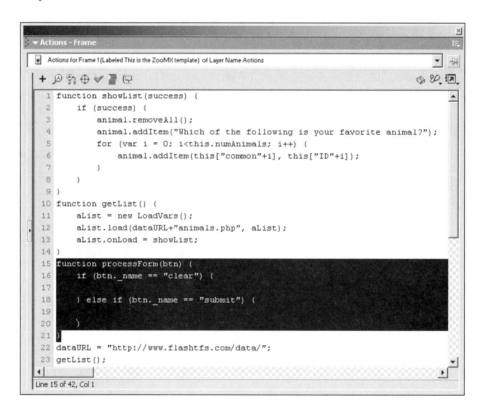

NOTE *This ActionScript should follow the* **getList** *function, but it should come before the* ***dataURL*** *variable.*

You already added instance names and click handlers to the PushButton instances in Lesson 8. The PushButton instance labeled **Submit** has an instance name of **submit**, and the PushButton instance labeled **Clear** has an instance name of **clear**.

The click handler for each instance is `processForm`. When the `processForm` function is called by either PushButton instance, the path of the clicked button is sent to the `processForm` function. The code you just added creates the `processForm` function—this function expects a parameter called `btn`, which is the path of the PushButton instance you clicked.

The `if` statement inside the `processForm` function checks to see which instance of the PushButton you clicked. If the instance name is `clear`, the `if` statement will run. If the instance name is `submit`, the `else if` statement will run. We're starting with the `clear` case because, as you'll see in the next step, it's much easier to write.

5) Add this ActionScript to the first part of the `if` statement inside the `processForm` function:

```
visitorName = "";
visitorEmail = "";
visitorMessage = "";
animal.setSelectedIndex(0);
mailList.setValue(false);
```

After you add this code, the `processForm` function should look like this:

```
function processForm(btn) {
  if (btn._name == "clear") {
    visitorName = "";
    visitorEmail = "";
    visitorMessage = "";
    animal.setSelectedIndex(0);
    mailList.setValue(false);
  } else if (btn._name == "submit") {
  }
}
```

This code is pretty simple. It sets the values of the `visitorName`, `visitorEmail`, and `visitorMessage` variables to "", which effectively removes any value that might be in the text boxes assigned those variable names. Then it sets the selected index for the `animal` instance of the ComboBox component to `0`, using the `setSelectedIndex` method of the built-in `FcomboBox` object. The argument for this method is the index number you want the component instance set to—using `0` will set it to the first item in the list, which is the default value. Finally, using the `setValue` method of the built-in `FCheckBox` object, the code sets the value of the `mailList` instance of the CheckBox component to `false`.

6) **Add the following code inside the** `else if` **statement:**

```
formData = new LoadVars();
formData.vname = visitorName;
formData.email = visitorEmail;
formData.message = visitorMessage;
formData.AID = animal.getSelectedItem().data;
if (mailList.getValue()) {
  formData.mlist = 1;
} else {
  formData.mlist = 0;
}
formData.action = "add";
```

After you add the code, the processForm function should look like this:

```
function processForm(btn) {
  if (btn._name == "clear") {
    visitorName = "";
    visitorEmail = "";
    visitorMessage = "";
    animal.setSelectedIndex(0);
    mailList.setValue(false);
  } else if (btn._name == "submit") {
    formData = new LoadVars();
    formData.vname = visitorName;
    formData.email = visitorEmail;
    formData.message = visitorMessage;
    formData.AID = animal.getSelectedItem().data;
    if (mailList.getValue()) {
      formData.mlist = 1;
    } else {
      formData.mlist = 0;
    }
    formData.action = "add";
  }
}
```

The code you just added should look familiar. You simply created a new instance of the LoadVars object, named formData. Then you set the values of the vname, email, message, AID, and mlist variables of the new formData object. The values of these variables will be set to the values of the visitorName, visitorEmail, and visitorMessage variables. Those variables are set by the corresponding text boxes in the movie. The AID variable will have a value of animal.getSelectedItem().data, which is simply the data value for the selected item in the animal instance of the ListBox component. Finally, if the mailList instance of the CheckBox component is selected (checked), mailList.getValue() will be true, and the mlist variable will be set to 1. Otherwise the mlist variable will be set to 0.

The last line of the code that was added in this step of this code creates another variable in the formData object. This variable, named action, is used by the guestbook.php script on the server. It lets the PHP script know that you want to add a record to the database.

7) Add the following ActionScript after the code you just added:

```
formData.sendAndLoad(dataURL+"guestbook.php", formData);
formData.onLoad = showResult;
```

Add this code to the else if statement, following the code you added in the last step. This ActionScript simply sends the data in the formData object to the guestbook.php file on the server. The onLoad event then triggers the showResult function, which you'll add next. The completed processForm function should look like this:

```
function processForm(btn) {
  if (btn._name == "clear") {
    visitorName = "";
    visitorEmail = "";
    visitorMessage = "";
    animal.setSelectedIndex(0);
    mailList.setValue(false);
  } else if (btn._name == "submit") {
    formData = new LoadVars();
    formData.vname = visitorName;
    formData.email = visitorEmail;
    formData.message = visitorMessage;
```

```
    formData.AID = animal.getSelectedItem().data;
    if (mailList.getValue()) {
      formData.mlist = 1;
    } else {
      formData.mlist = 0;
    }
formData.action = "add";
    formData.sendAndLoad(dataURL+"guestbook.php", formData);
    formData.onLoad = showResult;
  }
}
```

8) Add the `showResult` **function to the Actions panel:**

```
function showResult(success) {
  if (success) {
    trace("record added");
  }
}
```

CREATING DYNAMIC CONTENT

This function should be added before the processForm function. The showResult function is very much like the showList function in the map movie. Instead of actually showing a result if the variables in the formData object loaded successfully, this function simply writes the string "record added" in the Output window when you test the movie.

9) Choose Control > Test Movie. Save the file as guestbook8.fla when you're finished.

When you test the movie, you should be able to use both the Submit and Clear buttons. Try typing some values in the text boxes, and select an animal from the list. Then click each button to see what happens.

NOTE *If you would like to see the values you added to the database using the guestbook movie, point your browser to www.flashtfs.com/data/guestbook.php?action=view. The results may look like gibberish, but if you view the source code and scroll to the bottom, you should see your own entry.*

WHAT YOU HAVE LEARNED

In this lesson, you have:

- Added a map and several component instances and learned how to use the ListBox UI component. (pages 282–288)

- Loaded variables from a data source on a server using the `LoadVars` object (pages 288–299)

- Displayed dynamic content in an instance of the ListBox component and a dynamic text box (pages 299–304)

- Learned how to use the ScrollBar component (pages 304–313)

- Used the `setEnabled` method to disable and enable a component instance (pages 314–316)

- Sent data from a Flash movie to a script on a server (pages 317–326)

creating printable movies

LESSON 10

You can use Flash's printing capabilities to allow users to print parts of your Flash site. For the ZooMX Web site, users might want to print a copy of the map so they'll know just where to go when they arrive at the zoo. Using the `print` action, you can easily give your site's visitors this capability.

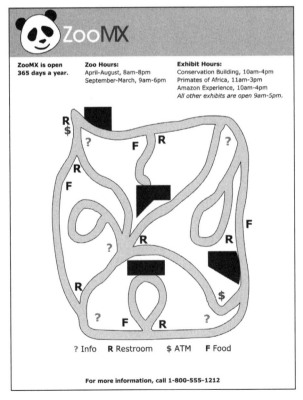

You can use ActionScript to print portions of your Flash movie.

Chrissy Rey

WHAT YOU WILL LEARN

In this lesson, you will:

- Print Flash content using the Flash Player's contextual menu

- Disable the Print command in the Flash Player's contextual menu

- Use the `print` and `printAsBitmap` actions to print a specific movie clip in Flash

- Specify printable frames

- Specify a print area

APPROXIMATE TIME

This lesson takes approximately 30 minutes to complete.

LESSON FILES

Media Files:

Lesson10/Assets/assets.fla

Starting Files:

Lesson10/Starting/map5.fla

Completed Project:

Lesson10/Completed/map8.fla

PRINTING FROM THE FLASH PLAYER CONTEXTUAL MENU

You can use the Print command in the Flash Player's contextual menu (called the *shortcut menu* in Windows) to print the contents of any Flash movie. This command only prints frames in the main movie's timeline and does not let you print any color effects. You can activate the Flash Player contextual menu by right-clicking (Windows) or Control-clicking (Macintosh) in the Flash movie.

1) Open map5.fla from the FlashTFS folder.

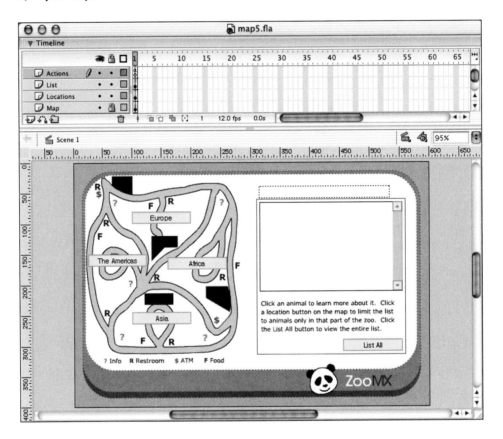

You should have created map5.fla in Lesson 9. If you can't find the file in the FlashTFS folder on your hard drive, use the file in the Lesson10/Starting folder on the CD-ROM. Open the file and save it in the FlashTFS folder on your hard drive before you continue.

2) Choose Control > Test Movie.

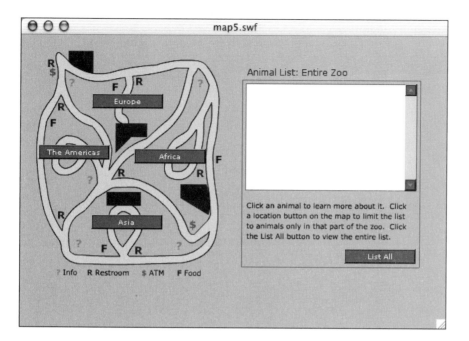

You can only access the Flash Player contextual menu when the movie is playing in the Flash Player. When you choose Control > Test Movie, Flash exports a copy of the Flash movie and plays it back in the Flash Player. The Flash Player plays the movie in the Test Movie window.

3) Right-click (Windows) or Control-click (Macintosh) in the movie. Choose Print from the contextual menu.

331

Take a look at some of the commands available in this menu. Choosing Print opens your system's default Print dialog box. The following figures illustrate the Print dialog boxes for Windows 2000, Mac OS 9.x, and Mac OS X.

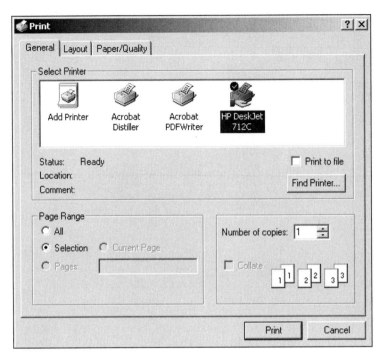

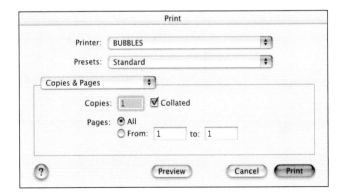

4) When the Print dialog box opens, use the default settings to print the Flash movie.

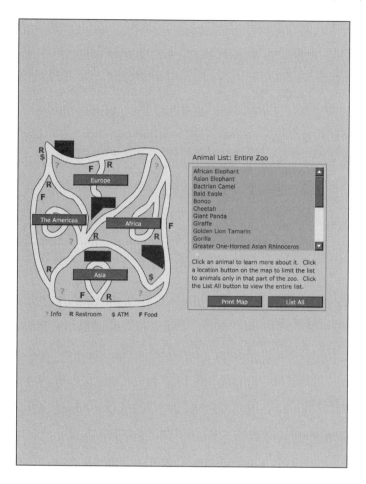

Try to print the movie in color if you can.

When you look at the printed movie, you should see the content on the main timeline of the movie. It probably doesn't look very good, and may be somewhat distorted on the page.

Only one page should have printed, as you have only one frame in the main timeline of the movie. See what happens if you add another frame to the main timeline—just be sure to choose File > Revert before you continue to the next exercise.

You don't have to save your file before you continue, as you haven't actually made any changes to the movie. Keep map5.fla open for the next exercise.

DISABLING THE PRINT COMMAND

If you decide that you don't want to let users print a movie through the limited Print command in the Flash Player contextual menu, you just need to label a frame in the main timeline !#p, which will disable the Print command in the Flash Player contextual menu. The !#p label only needs to appear in the main timeline once to disable printing for the entire movie. When you disable the Print command in the Flash Player contextual menu, you can still print content from the movie using ActionScript.

1) Select frame 1 of the Actions layer, and enter *!#p* in the Frame label box.

When you select frame 1 of the Actions layer, you should see that the Frame label is currently set to *//This is the ZooMX template*. You added this comment label in Lesson 5, when you created the template that map5.fla is based on. Delete that label, and replace it with *!#p*.

2) Choose Control > Test Movie.

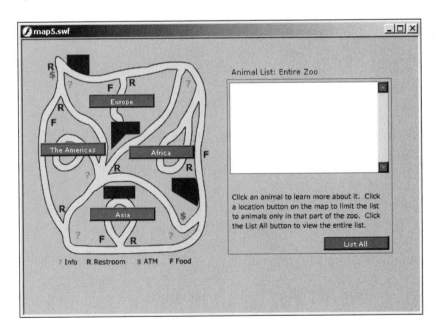

When the Test Movie window opens, the movie is once again displayed in the Flash Player.

334

3) Right-click (Windows) or Control-click (Macintosh) the movie to display the contextual menu.

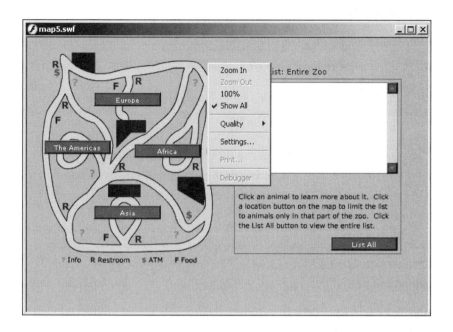

The Print command is disabled. You can also disable printing from the Flash Player contextual menu by disabling the appearance of the contextual menu altogether. You'll do that in Lesson 12.

4) Save the movie as map6.fla in the FlashTFS folder.

Now that the Print command in the Flash Player contextual menu is disabled, it's time to add some ActionScript that will let users print specific parts of the Flash movie. Be sure to save your file as map6.fla in the FlashTFS folder on your hard drive before you continue.

PRINTING WITH ACTIONSCRIPT

Your site might contain important information your visitors would like to print. They can use the Print command in their browsers, but that command often isn't adequate for printing Flash content. You can use ActionScript's printing capabilities to exercise greater control over the look of the printed content.

1) Select the Locations layer in map6.fla. Make sure this layer is unlocked, and add an instance of the PushButton component.

You are going to use this instance of the PushButton component to print a map.

2) Select the instance of the PushButton component you just added, and set its instance name to *pMap*, the Label to `Print Map`, and the Click Handler to `printContent`. Set the X to 345 and Y to 290.

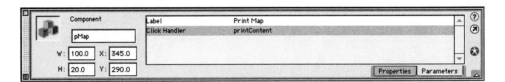

You should be a pro at adding instances of the PushButton component by now! This instance of the component is a little different from the other instances in the map movie, as it has a different Click Handler. Be sure to set the Click Handler for this new instance to `printContent`, and not `getList`.

You should also be sure to set the instance name of this new PushButton instance to pMap. The instance name of this button will be very important when you add the `printContent` function.

Since this is another instance of the PushButton component, you should change the ActionScript that modifies the style for the PushButton components. The following line should be near the end of the ActionScript in frame 1 of the Actions layer:

```
pbStyle.addListener(americas, africa, asia, europe, all);
```

Modify the line so it looks like this:

```
pbStyle.addListener(americas, africa, asia, europe, all, pMap);
```

```
    46  // text styles
    47  globalStyleFormat.textColor = 0xCC0000;
    48  globalStyleFormat.textFont = "Verdana";
    49  globalStyleFormat.textSize = 10;
    50  globalStyleFormat.textSelected = 0xFFFFFF;
    51  // component colors
    52  globalStyleFormat.face = 0xFF6600;
    53  globalStyleFormat.darkshadow = 0x000000;
    54  globalStyleFormat.highlight = 0xCC0000;
    55  globalStyleFormat.highlight3D = 0xFFC055;
    56  globalStyleFormat.shadow = 0xCC0000;
    57  globalStyleFormat.selection = 0xFF9933;
    58  globalStyleFormat.applyChanges();
    59  // modify push button style
    60  pbStyle = new FStyleFormat();
    61  pbStyle.textColor = 0xFFFFFF;
    62  pbStyle.addListener(americas, africa, asia, europe, all, pMap);
```

Line 62 of 62, Col 1

336

3) Add a new layer to the movie, and name it Printable Content. Open assets.fla from the Lesson10/Assets folder as a library, select the Printable Content layer, and drag a copy of the Printable Map symbol from the assets.fla library onto the stage.

It doesn't matter where in the layer stacking order the Printable Content layer goes, as long as it's above the Guides layer folder. In the files on the CD-ROM, the Printable Content layer is just under the Actions layer.

To open a file as a library, choose File > Open as Library, locate the file, and click Open. Make sure you have the Printable Content layer selected, and drag the Printable Map symbol from the assets.fla library onto the stage. If the Resolve Library Conflict dialog box opens, choose the Replace Existing Items option and click OK. This dialog box will probably appear, because the Printable Map symbol contains instances of the Logo and Panda symbols, which are already in the current movie's library.

The Printable Map symbol is a nicely formatted map, suitable for printing on a color printer. The map is easy for a visitor to read, and lists the zoo's hours. You will add some ActionScript to the movie that will allow the map to be printed.

Close the assets.fla library when you're finished adding the Printable Map symbol to map6.fla.

TIP *You may find it easier to hide all of the layers except the Print Content layer as you continue with this lesson.*

Take a moment to open the Printable Map symbol in symbol-editing mode. Unlock the Map layer; select the text that displays the hours, and look at the Property inspector. You should notice that the Use Device Fonts option is selected. This means that for this symbol, Flash will not embed the font specified in the Property inspector but instead will use the font from the user's system. It also means that the font will not be anti-aliased, or slightly blurred to make the edges look smooth. This is actually very important for printing. You don't want fuzzy text in the printed content. If you use the device fonts, the text will come out better when you print it.

NOTE *If you select Use Device Fonts, and the user doesn't have the font you specify in the Property inspector on his or her computer, the default font will be used. For a font such as Verdana, the system's default sans-serif font, which may be Arial or something similar, will be used and may affect the appearance of the printed content.*

When you're done looking at the Printable Map symbol, lock the Map layer and return to the main timeline by choosing Edit > Edit Document.

4) Select the instance of the Printable Map layer you just added to the movie, and set its X and Y to 0 and 0. Set its instance name to *cMap*.

In order to make a movie clip printable, it must be on the stage, and it must have an instance name. Don't worry that the movie clip covers all the other content in your movie—you'll take care of that in the next step.

Notice that the instance name you set for this instance of the Printable Map symbol is very similar to the instance name you gave the PushButton that will call the printContent function. You'll take advantage of that when you add the printContent function later in this exercise.

NOTE *Before a movie clip or level can be printed, it must be fully loaded. You will learn how to make a preloader, to ensure that your movies and movie clips are fully loaded, in Lesson 12.*

5) With the instance of the Printable Map movie clip on the stage selected, add the following ActionScript to the Actions panel:

```
onClipEvent(load) {
  this._visible = false;
}
```

When you select an instance of a movie clip, any ActionScript you add to the Actions panel is applied directly to that instance of the movie clip. In order to apply ActionScript directly to an instance of a movie clip, you must use the onClipEvent event handler. This is similar to using the on event handler on an instance of a button, as you did in Lesson 5. The onClipEvent event handler has the following syntax:

```
onClipEvent(movieEvent) {
  statement(s);
}
```

The movieEvent parameter, which specifies the event that triggers the statement(s) inside the curly braces, can be load, unload, enterFrame, mouseMove, mouseDown, mouseUp, keyDown, keyUp, or data. When load is specified, the statement(s) inside the curly braces of the event handler are initiated as soon as the movie clip appears in the timeline. The unload event initiates the statement(s) in the first frame after the movie clip is removed from the timeline. Specifying enterFrame triggers the statement(s) continually at the movie's frame rate. The mouseMove, mouseDown, and mouseUp events trigger the statement(s) every time the mouse is moved, pressed, or released. The keyDown and keyUp events initiate the statement(s) when a key is pressed or released. Finally, you can specify data to trigger the statement(s) when data is received by the movie clip via loadVariables or loadMovie.

The ActionScript you added to the instance of the Printable Map symbol occurs on the load event. So the statement inside the onClipEvent event handler's curly braces will run when the instance of the movie clip appears on the timeline. The statement that is run is this._visible = false;, which simply sets this instance of the movie clip to be invisible.

6) Select frame 1 of the Actions layer, and add the following ActionScript:

```
function printContent(btn) {
  var pc = "c" + btn._name.slice(1, btn._name.length);
  print(pc, "bmax");
}
```

Add this code before any other ActionScript in the Actions panel. This is the `printContent` function called by the pMap instance of the PushButton component.

In the first line of the `printContent` function you're creating a new local variable, named pc, which has a value of `"c" + btn._name.slice(1, btn._name.length);`. This line of code sets the value to the string `"c"` plus the value of `btn._name.slice(1, btn._name.length);`, which is the instance name of the PushButton that calls the function, minus the first letter of that instance name. So when you call the `printContent` function with the pMap button, the pc variable has a value of cMap.

The first line of code of the `printContent` function uses the `slice` method, which belongs to the built-in `String` object. Any string, such as an instance name, is a copy of the `String` object. The `slice` method simply takes the string (in this case pMap) and extracts a slice from it. It has the following syntax:

```
String.slice(start, end);
```

The start parameter specifies the starting index of the extracted slice, and the end parameter specifies the ending index for the extracted slice. For the code you just added, the start parameter is 1. The index of a string starts at 0, so setting start to 1 tells the `slice` method to start extracting the slice at the second character in the string, which happens to be M for `btn._name` when the `printContent` function is called by the pMap instance of the PushButton component. The end parameter for the code you added is `btn._name.length`. This returns the length of the string, which for `btn._name` is 4 when the `printContent` function is called by the pMap instance of the PushButton component. So the `slice` method will stop extracting the slice at the fourth character index, which happens to be the end of the string. The `slice` method extracts the string Map when it's done.

The next part of the function triggers the `print` action. The `print` action has the following syntax:

```
print(target, boundingBox);
```

The target parameter can be a movie clip or level. You'll learn about levels in Lesson 11—for now you'll just print movie clips. For the `printContent` function, the target you will print is the movie clip that has an instance name equal to the value of the local pc variable. The boundingBox parameter designates the boundaries of the printable area. Both of these parameters are required for the `print` action to work. You'll learn more about setting the printable area later in this lesson—for now just set this parameter to `"bmax"`.

The **print** action prints the targeted movie clip as vectors. When you print as vectors, Flash prints the content at the high quality. However, printing as vectors does not preserve color effects, such as transparency. You have to print the content as a bitmap in order to preserve those settings. You will learn how to print as a bitmap later in this exercise.

NOTE *In order to take advantage of ActionScript's print capabilities, users must have the Flash Player 4.0.20 (Macintosh) or 4.0.25 (Windows) or later installed. You can set up a detection scheme to determine which version of the Flash Player a user is running.*

7) Choose Control > Test Movie.

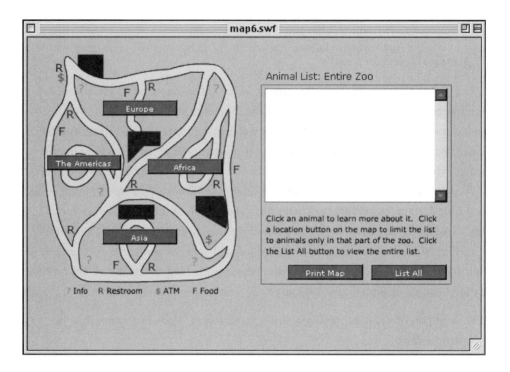

When you test the movie, the Printable Map symbol should not be visible, but that doesn't mean it can't be printed! Click the Print Map button; your system's Print dialog box should open. Use the default settings to print a copy of the map. If at all possible, print the map in color—it should look something like the figure on the next page.

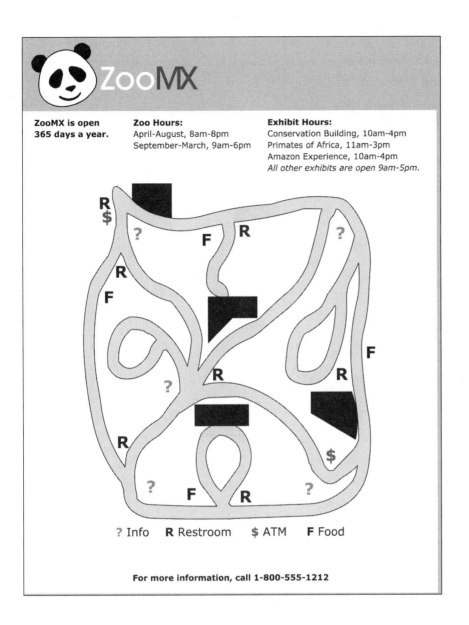

ZooMX

ZooMX is open 365 days a year.

Zoo Hours:
April-August, 8am-8pm
September-March, 9am-6pm

Exhibit Hours:
Conservation Building, 10am-4pm
Primates of Africa, 11am-3pm
Amazon Experience, 10am-4pm
All other exhibits are open 9am-5pm.

? Info   **R** Restroom $ ATM   **F** Food

For more information, call 1-800-555-1212

When you target a movie clip or level for printing, all of the frames in that timeline are printed by default. The Printable Map movie clip has only a single frame. Try adding two frames to every layer in the Printable Map movie clip, and test the movie again to see what happens. You'll find that a page will print for every frame in the movie clip, and you will end up with three pages, as illustrated by the figure below. Each page will have the same content, unless you modify the content of the frames you added.

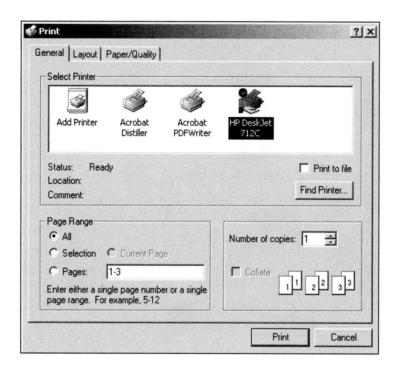

You can specify frames for printing by giving them a special label. Just select the frame you want to designate as printable, be sure it has a keyframe, and label that frame #p in the Property inspector. Then when you print the timeline, only the frames that have the #p label will be printed. Try it—add a keyframe to frame 2 of the Map layer in the Printable Map movie clip, set its label to #p, and test the movie again. When you print the map this time, only a single page should print, even though there are three frames in the movie clip.

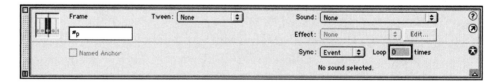

When you've finished testing the features of the print action, you can still get your original Printable Map movie clip back. Open assets.fla in the Lesson10/Assets folder as a library, and drag the Printable Map movie clip from that library into the current movie's library (the map6.fla library). The Resolve Library Conflict dialog box will open. Select the "Replace existing items" option and click OK. The original Printable Map movie clip will now appear in the map6.fla library, replacing the one you added frames to. Be sure to return to the main timeline when you're done (Edit > Edit Document).

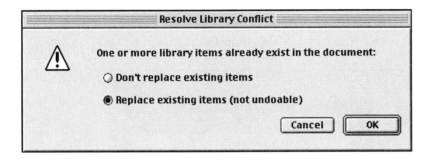

8) Change the `printContent` function so the movie clip is printed as a bitmap instead of vectors.

This is easier than it may sound. The `print` action prints content as vectors. You only need to change this action to one that prints as a bitmap. That action is `printAsBitmap`. Yes, it really is that simple!

When you make the change, the code should look like this:

```
function printContent(btn) {
  var pc = "c" + btn._name.slice(1, btn._name.length);
  printAsBitmap(pc, "bmax");
}
```

```
1  function printContent(btn) {
2      var pc = "c" + btn._name.slice(1, btn._name.length);
3      printAsBitmap(pc, "bmax");
4  }
5  function showList(success) {
6      if (success) {
7          animalList.removeAll();
8          for (var i = 0; i<this.numAnimals; i++) {
9              trace(this["common"+i]);
10             animalList.addItem(this["common"+i], i);
11         }
```

Line 3 of 66, Col 1

When you print Flash content as a bitmap, any color effects you might have applied to the printed content are preserved. However, the quality is usually lower than when the same content is printed as vectors.

9) Choose Control > Test Movie. Save the movie as map7.fla.

When you test the movie, click the Print Map button again. Use the default settings in your system's Print dialog box to print the movie, and take a look at the result. Does it look better or worse? It should look something like the figure below.

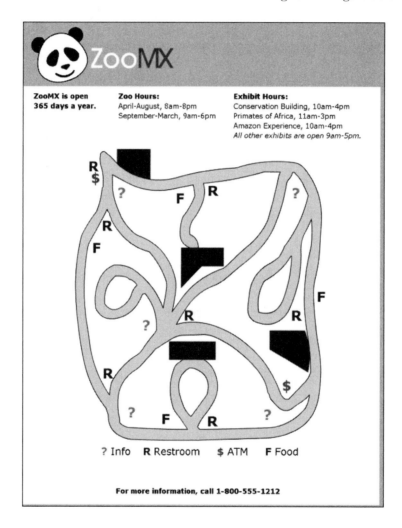

The resulting printout is probably lower in quality than the one you printed as vectors. If that's the case, and since there aren't any color effects in the Printable Map movie clip to worry about, close the Test Movie window and locate the `printContent`

function in frame 1 of the Actions layer. Change the function so that it will print content as vectors:

```
function printContent(btn) {
  var pc = "c" + btn._name.slice(1, btn._name.length);
  print(pc, "bmax");
}
```

When you're done, save the movie as map7.fla in the FlashTFS folder on your hard drive. Now that you know a little bit about printing, let's take a look at some of the other options available to you.

SPECIFYING A PRINT AREA

You can use the `boundingBox` parameter of the `print` action to specify a print area. This can be useful, for example, if you want to create a letter-size printout when your movie is 550 by 400 pixels. You just need to specify a print area for the printable content, and Flash will create your printout at whatever size you want. You will learn how in the following exercise. Start this exercise with map7.fla open from the last exercise.

1) Open the Printable Map movie clip in symbol-editing mode.

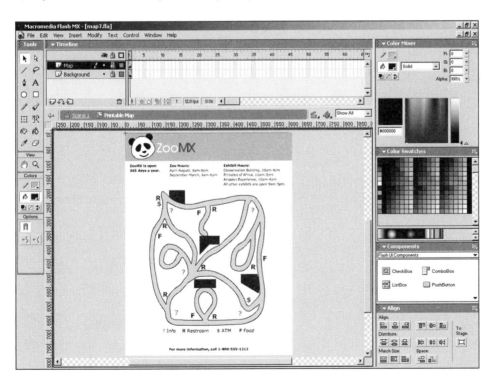

CREATING PRINTABLE MOVIES

Double-click the instance of the Printable Map symbol on the stage, or select the instance and choose Edit > Edit Symbols.

2) Add a new layer, named Label. Select frame 2 of the new layer and insert a keyframe. Select frame 2 of the Background layer and insert a frame.

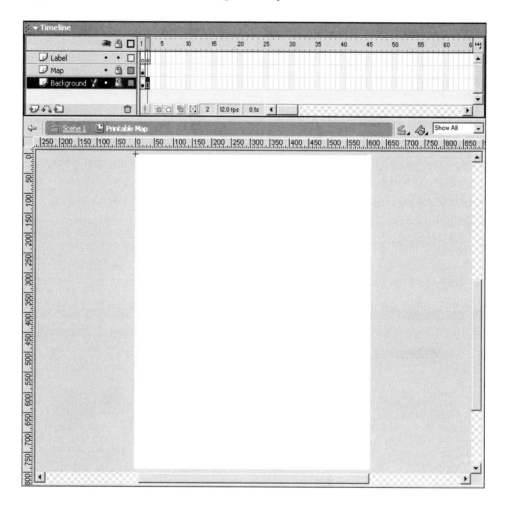

Place the new Label layer at the top of the layer stacking order. You're going to add labels to this layer, and it's a good idea to place labeled frames where they are easy to see and find.

After you add the new layer, select frame 2 of new layer and choose Insert > Keyframe. There should already be an empty keyframe in frame 1, and when you insert a keyframe in frame 2, you will have two empty keyframes in the Label layer.

Select frame 2 of the Background layer, and choose Insert > Frame. You don't need to add a keyframe to this layer; you only want the content from the previous frame (frame 1) to continue for two frames.

3) Select frame 1 of the Labels layer, and set the Frame label to #p.

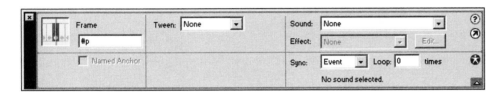

The #p label specifies a frame as printable. When you specify a frame (or frames) as printable, only that frame (or frames) will be printed by the print action. Any frame(s) that are not labeled with a #p will be ignored by the print action.

4) Select frame 2 of the Labels layer, and set the Frame label to #b.

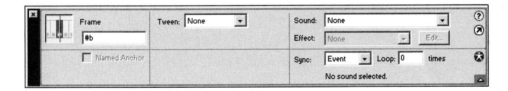

The #b label specifies that a frame contains the shape you would like to use as your print area. In other words, this frame will act as the bounding box for your printed movie clip. Frame 2 of the Background layer contains a large white rectangle, which is 612 pixels wide by 792 pixels high—approximately the size of a piece of letter-size paper (8.5 inches wide by 11 inches high).

NOTE *You can specify only a single frame in a timeline as the bounding box. You should not label more than one frame #b.*

Test the movie to see how it looks. The printed movie clip probably still doesn't look quite right (see the figure below). You have to make one more change before everything is in perfect working order. You'll do that in the next step.

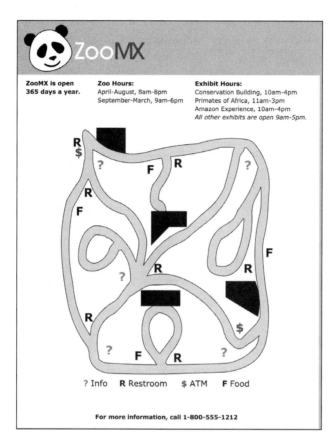

5) Click the Scene 1 icon, and select frame 1 of the Actions layer in the main timeline. Change the boundingBox **parameter for the** print **action in the** printContent **function to** "bmovie".

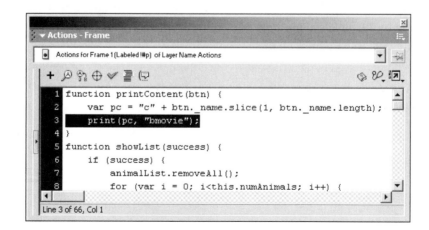

After you make this change, the `printContent` function should look like this:

```
function printContent(btn) {
  var pc = "c" + btn._name.slice(1, btn._name.length);
  print(pc, "bmovie");
}
```

The `boundingBox` parameter of the `print` function can have one of three settings: `"bmovie"`, `"bframe"`, or `"bmax"`.

The `"bmovie"` setting you used in the `printContent` function lets you use the shape in the frame labeled #b as the bounding box for the printed content. The contents of frame 2 of the Background layer will act as the print area for the Printable Map movie clip. That works out wonderfully, because that shape is approximately the same size as a sheet of letter-size paper.

If you set the `boundingBox` to `"bmovie"` and didn't label a frame in the targeted movie clip or level with #b, Flash simply uses the dimensions of the movie as the printable area. Try removing the #b label from frame 2 of the Printable Map movie clip to see what this looks like, or take a look at the figure below.

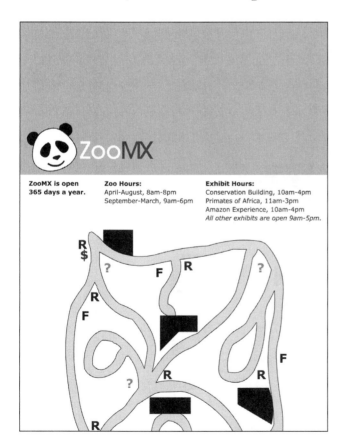

Setting the `boundingBox` parameter to `"bframe"` will set the print area to the bounding box of the contents of each frame. Flash will scale the contents of each frame to fit the printed page.

The `"bmax"` setting uses the maximum area of all printable frames in the timeline as the print area. So if you have three printable frames, one with a 300-by-200 object, another with a 200-by-300 object, and a third with a 200-by-200 object, the print area will be 300 by 300 pixels.

NOTE *When you use the* `"bmax"` *and* `"bframe"` *settings for the* `boundingBox` *parameter, frames labeled #b in the targeted timeline will be ignored.*

6) Choose Control > Test Movie, and click the Print Map button.

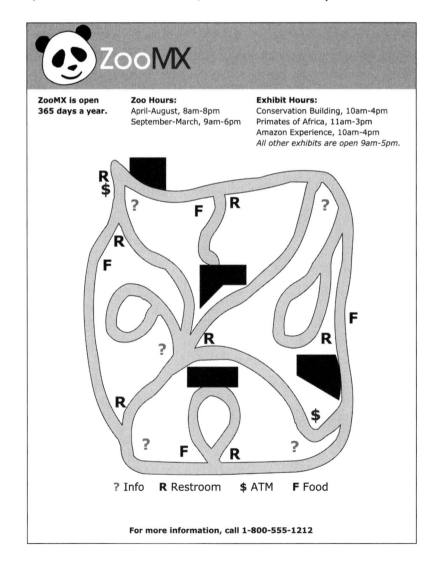

When you print the map this time, it should fit quite nicely on the printed page. After you print a copy of the map, close the Test Movie window.

NOTE *The background color for your movie is orange, but the map should have printed with a white background. This is not the default behavior for Flash; rather, the large rectangle in the Background layer acts as the background for the printed content. If you change the color of the rectangle shape, the color in the printed map will reflect that change.*

7) Save the movie as map8.fla in the FlashTFS folder.
You're now a printing pro! If you would like to work through some additional tutorials on printing, be sure to visit the Flash TFS Web site.

WHAT YOU HAVE LEARNED

In this lesson, you have:

- Printed Flash content using the Flash Player's contextual menu (pages 330–333)

- Disabled the Print command in the Flash Player's contextual menu (pages 334–347)

- Specified a print area (pages 347–353)

optimizing
Flash content

Broadband Internet connections, while more widespread now, are still not ubiquitous. So there's a good chance that some of your Flash site's visitors will not be viewing it over high-speed connections. In fact, depending on your audience, some of your visitors will be using a somewhat slow dial-up connection. If that's the case, you must make sure that the file sizes for your site are as small as possible. You can do that by optimizing the content using some of the methods outlined in this lesson.

Optimizing content should lead to a smaller file size.

Chrissy Rey

WHAT YOU WILL LEARN

In this lesson, you will:

- Use the Bandwidth Profiler to see which parts of a movie require preloading

- See how to preview your movie as it might play if it were downloaded over a modem line

- Optimize the assets in a Flash movie to reduce the file size

- Export a Flash movie as a .swf file

- Load a .swf file into a movie

- Load a JPEG image into a movie

APPROXIMATE TIME

This lesson takes approximately one hour to complete.

LESSON FILES

Media Files:

None

Starting Files:

Lesson11/Starting/feature1.fla
Lesson11/Starting/guestbook8.fla
Lesson11/Starting/map8.fla
Lesson11/Starting/visitorinfo1.fla
Lesson11/Starting/zoo34.fla

Completed Files:

Lesson11/Completed/feature2.fla
Lesson11/Completed/guestbook9.fla
Lesson11/Completed/main1.fla
Lesson11/Completed/map10.fla
Lesson11/Completed/visitorinfo2.fla
Lesson11/Completed/zoo37.fla

USING THE BANDWIDTH PROFILER

Before you publish your movie, you should check to see how your users might view it on the Web. You can do this in Flash by using the Bandwidth Profiler in test-movie mode.

The Bandwidth Profiler provides a graphical representation of your movie's size by frame. You can use the Debug menu to choose a modem speed for the Bandwidth Profiler to emulate. Any item above the red line will cause some download-performance issues at the modem speed you choose from the Debug menu.

1) Open zoo34.fla from the FlashTFS folder, and choose Control > Test Movie.

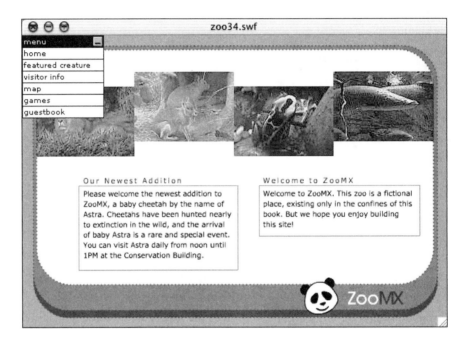

You created zoo34.fla in Lesson 7. If you cannot find a copy of this file in the FlashTFS folder on your hard drive, you can find it in the Lesson11/Starting folder on the CD-ROM.

2) Choose View > Bandwidth Profiler to open the Bandwidth Profiler.

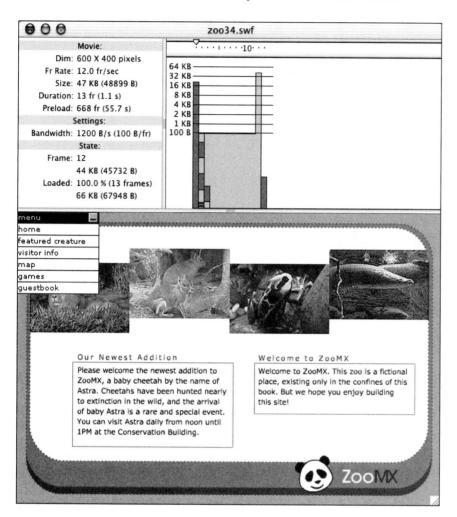

If this menu option is checked, the Bandwidth Profiler is already open. The left side of the Bandwidth Profiler contains basic movie information: dimensions, file size, length, and frame rate. The right side contains a graph showing the size of the file in each frame. The red line in the graph indicates whether a given frame streams in real time at the current modem speed set in the Control menu. If a bar extends above the red line, the movie must wait for that frame to load.

Notice that right now, the bar extends above the red line in a couple of places. The bar(s) mean that Flash will have to pause to load the content for those frames before the movie can play. You should also take note of the file size, which is listed in the area to the left of the graph. At this point, the movie should be approximately 47 KB. In the next exercise you will optimize the movie to bring that file size down.

TIP *Now that you have set up the test movie to show the Bandwidth Profiler, each movie you test will include this feature. To toggle the profiler on and off, choose View > Bandwidth Profiler.*

3) Choose Debug > 56k (4.7 KB/s); then choose View > Show Streaming.

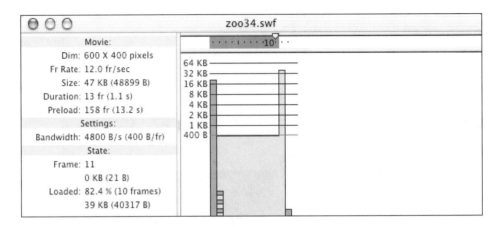

A green bar appears at the top of the Bandwidth Profiler to indicate how much of the movie has been loaded. When you turn on the Show Streaming option, the movie plays as though you're using a modem to look at the Web, at the same speed you chose from the Debug menu. You should see that the green bar stops moving at places where the bar(s) extend above the red line.

Don't rely solely on the Bandwidth Profiler to test your movie's performance. You should always test your movie over a variety of Internet connections, and on different computers and operating systems. You should also generate a size report when you publish your movie, as you will see later in this lesson.

4) Close the Test Movie window.
You haven't made any changes, so you don't need to save the movie at this point.

OPTIMIZING ASSETS
The larger the movie file, the longer the download time. When you identify frames that are too large to stream efficiently, as indicated by the Bandwidth Profiler, you might want to optimize your movie. You can take several steps to prepare your movie for optimal playback. As part of the publishing process, Flash automatically performs some optimizing on movies, including detecting duplicate shapes on export and placing these shapes in the file only once, and converting nested groups to single groups. In the following exercise, you will do a few things to optimize your movie and reduce the file size, making the download time much less.

1) Right-click (Windows) or Control-click (Macintosh) the Frame layer, and choose Hide Others from the contextual menu. Right-click or Control-click the Frame layer again, and choose Lock Others.

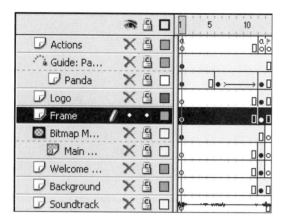

When you choose Hide Others and Lock Others from the contextual menu, all of the layers except the Frame layer should be hidden and locked. This will make it easier to work with.

2) Select frame 12 and choose Edit > Select All. In the Property inspector, set the Stroke Style to Solid. Choose Control > Test Movie.

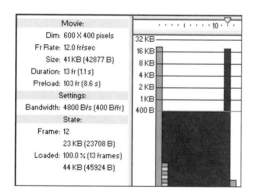

One of the many things you can do to reduce the file size of your Flash movie is reduce the amount of vector information in it. A dotted line requires considerably more information, and thus a greater file size, than a solid line. So by simply changing the outline around the graphics in the Frame layer, you can significantly reduce the size of your file. When you test the movie, the Bandwidth Profiler should now indicate that your file is approximately 41 KB.

3) Close the Test Movie window. Locate the loop.aif or loop.wav sound in the current movie's library. Double-click the icon to the left of the sound to open the Sound Properties dialog box.

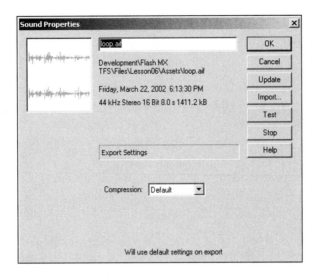

Graphic elements aren't the only thing to consider when it comes to optimization. Sounds can also add a significant amount of file size. You can modify the compression settings for each of your sounds individually using the Sound Properties dialog box. You can also modify the compression settings for all of the sounds in the movie at one time using the Publish Settings dialog box, as you'll learn in Lesson 12.

TIP *You can also open the Sound Properties dialog box by selecting a sound and clicking the Properties button at the bottom of the Library panel.*

PROPERTIES BUTTON

4) In the Sound Properties dialog box, set the Compression to MP3 and the Bit Rate to 16 Kbps. Click OK.

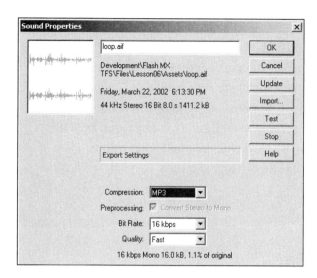

The loop.aif or loop.wav sound plays when the movie starts playing. You can apply compression, which normally sacrifices too much sound quality, because the distortion that occurs with the compression doesn't adversely affect this sound. If you were to set the bit rate to 8 Kbps, you might find that the sound distortion is unacceptable. You can test the compression settings, and get some idea of the finished size of the compressed sound, by clicking the Test button in the Sound Properties dialog box.

The Sound Properties dialog box provides a lot of information about a selected sound. It displays the sound's original location on the file system when it was imported, as well as the last date and time the file was updated (which you can access using the Update button) or imported (available by using the Import button or by choosing File > Import). The sample rate, bits, sound length, and original sound file size are also displayed in the Sound Properties dialog box.

In addition to displaying properties for a sound, you can use the Sound Properties dialog box to modify the Compression setting for individual sounds. By default, sounds are exported using the settings in the Publish Settings dialog box, which you'll work with in Lesson 12. However, you may find that some sounds require a little tweaking to decrease the file size, or to simply increase the quality (and file size) of a particular sound.

The Compression setting has five options: Default, ADPCM, MP3, Raw, and Speech. All of these, except Default, have additional settings you can modify in the Sound Properties dialog box. The Raw option exports the sound without compression.

When you use ADPCM (Adaptive Differential Pulse Code Modulation) Compression, which is most useful for short sounds, the Preprocessing, Sample Rate, and ADPCM Bits settings appear. Deselect the Preprocessing option to keep stereo sounds stereo—otherwise this option will convert stereo sounds to mono. The Sample Rate setting controls the sound fidelity. A lower sample rate results in a lower-quality sound and smaller file size, while a higher sample rate results in a higher-quality sound and larger file size. You can't increase the sample rate above the sound's original rate. The Sample Rate can be set to 5 kHz (very low quality), 11 kHz, 22 kHz, or 44 kHz (CD quality). The ADPCM Bits setting represents the number of bits used in ADPCM encoding—a lower number results in a smaller file size and lower quality, while a higher number results in a larger file size and higher quality.

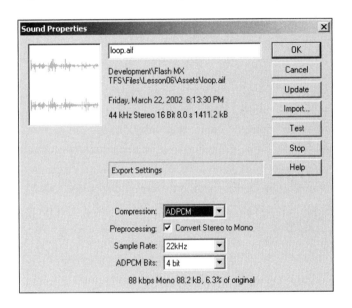

MP3 compression is ideal for longer streaming sounds in Flash. When you select this option from the Compression menu, the Preprocessing, Bit Rate, and Quality settings appear. The Preprocessing option is the same for MP3 compression as it is for ADPCM compression, but it is only enabled if you select a Bit Rate of at least 20 Kbps. The Bit Rate setting represents the bits per second in the compressed sound. You should use a Bit Rate of at least 16 Kbps for music, but keep in mind that while a higher value for this setting will result in better sound quality, it will also result in a larger file size. The Quality setting determines the speed at which the sound is compressed, and it also affects the sound's quality. Setting the Quality to Fast results in a lower quality sound that is compressed at a faster rate. Medium results in a better quality sound that's compressed at a somewhat slower rate. Finally, Best results in the highest quality sound, but it's compressed at a much slower rate.

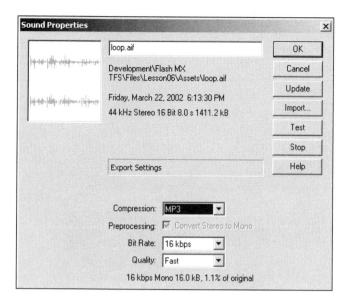

Speech compression is intended for sounds containing speech. If you choose this option from the Compression menu, the Preprocessing and Sample Rate settings appear. These settings are the same as those settings for ADPCM compression.

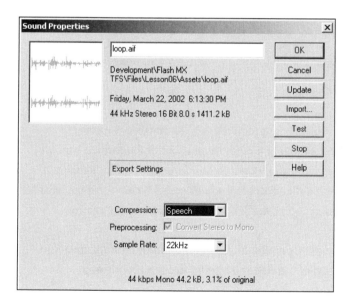

5) Choose Control > Test Movie.

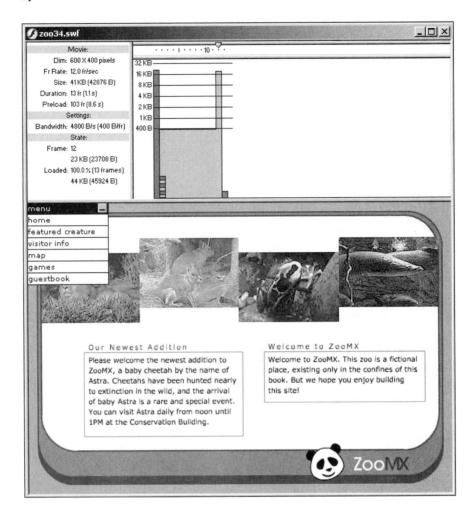

In this case the file size was probably not reduced. That's because the settings you provided in the Sound Properties dialog box for the loop.aif or loop.wav sound are the default compression settings for the whole movie, as you'll learn in Lesson 12. It's useful to know how to access the individual sound-compression settings, because you may find that some sounds require higher quality and lower compression.

6) Close the Test Movie window. Open the Bitmaps folder in the library, and double-click the icon to the left of the fish.jpg bitmap to open the Bitmap Properties dialog box.

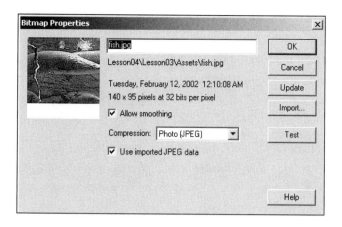

Bitmaps can add significantly to the size of your file. It's a good idea to optimize your images before you import them into Flash, but once the images are inside, you can optimize them even further using the Bitmap Properties dialog box.

7) Deselect the "Use imported JPEG data" option, and set the Quality to 50. Click OK.

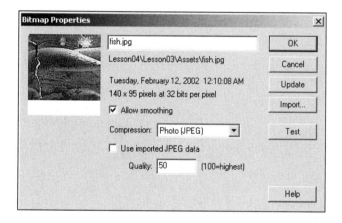

You can use the Bitmap Properties dialog box to modify the compression settings for each individual bitmap in your library. The lower the value in the Quality setting, the smaller the file size in the movie. Of course, if you set the Quality too low, you may end up with a grainy bitmap image. So you have to use this setting wisely.

You can preview the bitmap with the new Quality setting, and get an idea of how much the imported bitmap will add to the movie's file size, by clicking the Test button. Then the compressed bitmap size and percentage of original file size are displayed at the bottom of the Bitmap Properties dialog box.

NOTE *You cannot set all the compression for all the imported bitmaps at once in the Publish Settings dialog box. You'll learn more about this in Lesson 12.*

365

The Bitmap Properties dialog box works similarly to the Sound Properties dialog box. It displays information about the imported bitmap, such as its file name, original location on the hard drive, dimensions, resolution, and when it was last imported or updated. The Bitmap Properties dialog box also has a few settings you can use to modify the compression and appearance of an imported bitmap in Flash. Take a moment to look at those settings before you continue to the next step.

There are two Compression settings for imported bitmaps: Lossless (PNG/GIF) and Photo (JPEG). Lossless compression is great for images that have relatively few colors and simple shapes. With lossless compression, none of the data for the image is discarded when it's compressed. Photo compression is for complex images, such as photographs and images with gradient fills. When you select the JPEG option from the Compression menu and deselect the "Use imported JPEG data" option, a Quality setting text box appears. You can enter a number between 0 and 100—the larger the number, the better the quality and the larger the file size. If you leave the "Use imported JPEG data" option selected, Flash will use the quality that was set for the JPEG when it was created in an image editor such as Macromedia Fireworks.

8) Choose Control > Test Movie. Save your file as zoo35.fla in the FlashTFS folder on your hard drive.

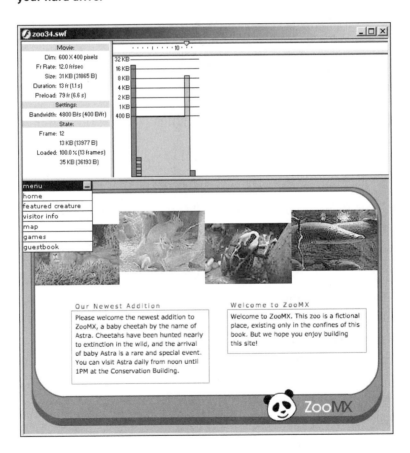

When you test the movie, check the Bandwidth Profiler to see how much changing the Quality setting for the fish.jpg bitmap reduced the size of the movie. Try playing with the Quality settings for all the bitmaps in the Bitmaps folder—see how much you can reduce the file size without adversely affecting image quality.

Keep the optimized version of your movie open for the next exercise.

NOTE *All of the imported bitmaps have been optimized in zoo35.fla in the Lesson11/ Intermediate folder on the CD-ROM. You can duplicate this by repeating steps 6 and 7 for every bitmap in the library.*

EXPORTING FLASH MOVIES

Every time you choose Control > Test Movie, Flash creates a .swf file in the same directory as the .fla file. So if you look in your FlashTFS folder, you'll see several .swf files, each of which was created when you tested a movie. This procedure is just one way to create a .swf file. Another way to create a .swf file, as well as files in several other formats, is to export your movie by using the Export Movie command. You can use this command to give the .swf file a name other than the name of the .fla file.

In this exercise, you are going to break the zoo movie into three separate movies: the base movie (Actions, Background, and Soundtrack layers), the home-page movie (Bitmap Mask, Main Page Bitmaps, and Welcome Text layers), and the overlay movie (Guide: Panda, Panda, Logo, and Frame layers). You will then export two of those movies as .swf files.

You should start this exercise with zoo35.fla open from the previous exercise.

1) Select frame 12 of the Bitmap Mask, Main Page Bitmaps, and Welcome Text layers, and choose Edit > Copy Frames. Create a new movie based on the Flash TFS Zoo Template, select frame 2 of the Contents layer in the new movie, and choose Edit > Paste Frames.

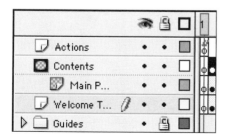

Select only frame 12 of the Bitmap Mask, Main Page Bitmaps, and Welcome Text layers. You can do this by clicking frame 12 of the Bitmap Mask layer, and then

Shift-clicking frame 12 of the Welcome Text layer. Then choose Edit > Copy Frames to copy these frames from the timeline.

You've created many new movies based on the Flash TFS Zoo Template throughout the course of this book, so this part should be easy for you. Just choose File > New From Template, and select the appropriate template. When the new movie appears, select frame 2 of the Contents layer. There's currently no keyframe in frame 2 of the Contents layer, but don't worry about that. When you choose Edit > Paste Frames, the frames you copied from zoo35.fla are pasted in frame 2. The Bitmap Mask layer is renamed Contents—you can change the name back to Bitmap Mask if you want.

NOTE *If the Resolve Library Conflict dialog box opens, choose the "Replace existing items" option and click OK.*

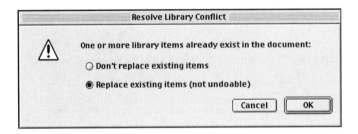

2) **Insert a keyframe in frame 2 of the Actions layer and add a `stop` action to that frame. Set the Frame label for the keyframe in frame 2 of the Actions layer to rf.**

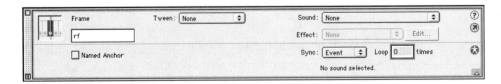

You are going to use the rf frame label in Lesson 12, when you learn how to make a preloader for your project. You can add the stop action by typing *stop();* in the Actions panel.

NOTE *Make sure to add the* stop *action to frame 2 of the Actions layer, and not frame 1.*

3) Choose File > Export Movie. In the Export Movie dialog box, browse to the FlashTFS folder on your hard drive, type *main.swf* in the File Name (Windows) or Save As (Macintosh) text box, and click Save. Save the movie as main1.fla in the FlashTFS folder on your hard drive.

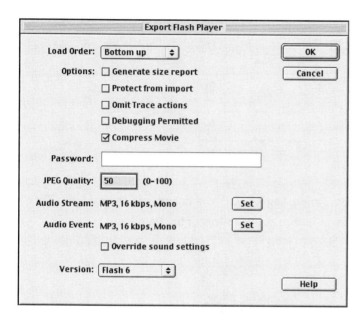

When you export the movie as a Flash Player movie, all the interactivity and sound in the movie are preserved. Notice that you can save the movie as several file types, including QuickTime, Animated GIF, and JPEG. Most of these file types will not preserve the interactivity and sound of your movie.

Before the movie is exported, the Export Flash Player dialog box opens. You can leave all these settings at their defaults and click OK. You'll look at some of the export options later in this lesson and in Lesson 12, when you publish your finished site.

4) Return to zoo35.fla and delete the Bitmap Mask, Main Page Bitmaps, and Welcome Text layers. Then delete frame 13 of every remaining layer.

TIP *Choose Window > zoo35.fla to return to that file.*

Since the contents of the Bitmap Mask, Main Page Bitmaps, and Welcome Text layers are now in main1.fla, you no longer need those layers in zoo35.fla. Just select all of the layers at once, and click the Delete Layer button at the bottom of the timeline.

You also don't need frame 13 of every layer. This frame acted as a blank frame to demonstrate the use of the `gotoAndStop` action. But now it's no longer necessary, so you can remove it. Just drag the playhead to frame 13, and choose Insert > Remove Frames. That should remove only frame 13 from every layer in the movie. When you've completed this step, the timeline should look like the figure below.

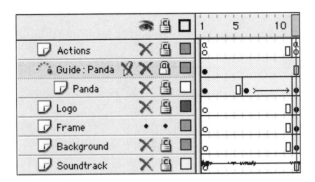

5) Select the Guide: Panda, Panda, Logo, and Frame layers, and choose Edit > Cut Frames. Click the Delete Layer button at the bottom of the timeline.

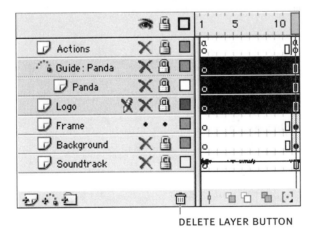

DELETE LAYER BUTTON

You've already broken out the Bitmap Mask, Main Page Bitmaps, and Welcome Text layers into a separate home-page movie (main1.fla). Now you need to break the Guide: Panda, Panda, Logo, and Frame layers into another separate overlay movie. Select all these layers at once—you can simply click the Guide: Panda layer and then Shift-click the Frame layer. Be sure to select the entire timeline for each layer, not just a single frame. Choose Edit > Cut Frames to remove the frames from this movie. Since the frames from these layers are gone, you should delete these layers before you move on to the next step.

6) Create a new Flash movie based on the Flash TFS Zoo Template. Choose Insert › New Symbol. In the Symbol Properties dialog box, set the Name to Top Clip and the Behavior to Movie Clip. Click OK.

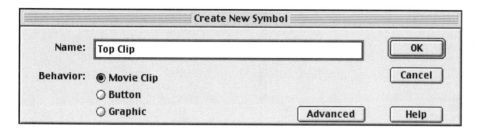

When you click OK, Flash enters symbol-editing mode for the new Top Clip movie clip. You are going to place the frames you cut in the last step inside this new symbol. Make sure it's a movie clip, because you're not going to add enough frames in the main timeline of the new movie to play every frame in the Top Clip symbol.

7) Select frame 1 of the Layer 1 layer, and choose Edit › Paste Frames. Add a new layer, named Actions, and insert a keyframe in frame 12. Add a `stop` action to that keyframe.

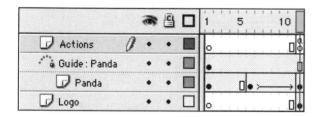

When you paste the frames you cut from the zoo35.fla into the new Top Clip symbol, the layer names that corresponded with the layers in the zoo35.fla movie should appear in the Top Clip symbol.

As you learned in Lesson 5, movie clips will loop continuously unless you use ActionScript to stop them. You don't want this animation to repeat endlessly, so add a new layer, named Actions, to the Top Clip movie clip. Select frame 12 of the new Actions layer, and choose Insert > Keyframe (F6). Select that frame, and add a `stop` action in the Actions panel. Since the Actions panel is in expert mode, you can just type *stop();* in the Actions panel.

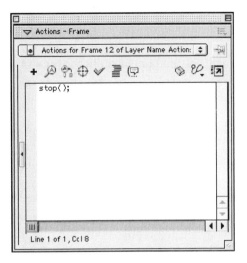

8) Choose Edit > Edit Document. Insert a keyframe in frame 2 of the Contents layer, and place an instance of the Top Clip symbol in that frame, centering it horizontally and vertically on the stage.

When you choose Edit > Edit Document, you'll be taken to the main timeline. You can also click the Scene 1 icon under the timeline to return to the main timeline. Once you're in the main timeline, select frame 2 of the Content layer, and insert a keyframe (Insert > Keyframe or F6). Open the Library panel and drag an instance of the Top Clip symbol onto the stage. Use the Align panel to center the instance of the Top Clip symbol horizontally and vertically on the stage.

NOTE *Make sure to select the To Stage button in the Align panel to center the Top Clip symbol.*

9) Add a keyframe to frame 2 of the Actions layer, and add a `stop` action. Label frame 2 rf. Repeat step 3 to export the movie as top.swf and save the movie as top1.fla.

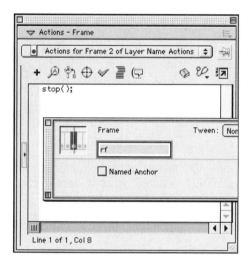

This step is the same thing you did for the main1.fla movie in step 2 of this exercise. Make sure to select frame 2 of the Actions layer, and add a **stop** action in the Actions panel. You can do this by typing *stop();* in the Actions panel. Then with frame 2 still selected, set the Frame label (in the Property inspector) to rf.

When you're ready to export the movie, choose File > Export Movie. In the Export Movie dialog box, browse to the FlashTFS folder on your hard drive, and save the file as top.swf. When the Export Flash Player dialog box opens, leave the settings at their defaults and click OK.

10) Return to zoo35.fla, and delete frames 2 through 11 of every layer. Save the file as zoo36.fla in the FlashTFS folder on your hard drive.

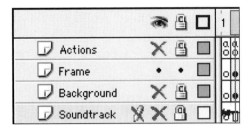

You can quickly return to zoo35.fla by choosing Window > zoo35.fla. After you delete frames 2 through 11 of every layer, the movie should have only two frames left.

LOADING MOVIES

Throughout this book you have made several movies that were not part of the main zoo movie. In the next exercise you will load these movies into the main movie. This is another technique you can use to create a more enjoyable experience for users—instead of having to download one enormous file containing everything, visitors can download the content they want to see. In this exercise you'll use the loadMovieNum action to load .swf files into the main movie. The loadMovieNum action lets you load a .swf file into a level of the Flash Player while the original movie is still playing. In this project, the original movie is the zoo36.fla movie (zoo36.swf when it's exported). The movies you are going to load will be the movies you created in previous lessons, including the map and guestbook you worked on in Lesson 9.

You should still have zoo36.fla from the last exercise open when you start this exercise.

1) Select frame 1 of the Actions layer. Modify the menu array so it looks like the following:

```
menu = new Array();
menu[0] = ["home", "main.swf"];
menu[1] = ["featured creature", "feature.swf"];
menu[2] = ["visitor info", "visitorinfo.swf"];
menu[3] = ["map", "map.swf"];
menu[4] = ["games", "games.swf"];
menu[5] = ["guestbook", "guestbook.swf"];
```

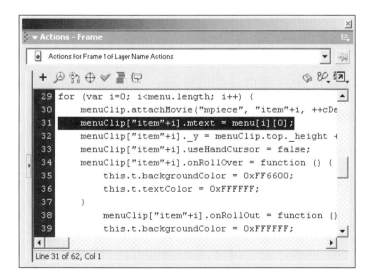

```
1  menu = new Array();
2  menu[0] = ["home", "main.swf"];
3  menu[1] = ["featured creature", "feature.swf"];
4  menu[2] = ["visitor info", "visitorinfo.swf"];
5  menu[3] = ["map", "map.swf"];
6  menu[4] = ["games", "games.swf"];
7  menu[5] = ["guestbook", "guestbook.swf"];
8  mtext = menu[3];
9  // create a new movie clip to hold the menu
10 this.createEmptyMovieClip("menuClip", 1);
11 menuClip._visible = false;
```

When you modify the menu array as instructed, you are creating a multidimensional array. That means that each element in the array contains an array. In this case, each menu array element will have two elements of its own. It's sort of like writing this:

```
menu[0] = new Array("home", "main.swf");
```

This gives the `menu[0]` element of the menu array two elements: `"home"` and `"main.swf"`. The first element provides the text for the menu item, while the second element will be the .swf file that loads when the menu item is clicked.

2) Modify line 31 of the ActionScript in frame 1 of the Actions layer so it uses the first element in each item in the menu array for the text in each menu piece:

```
menuClip["item"+i].mtext = menu[i][0];
```

```
29 for (var i=0; i<menu.length; i++) {
30     menuClip.attachMovie("mpiece", "item"+i, ++cDe
31     menuClip["item"+i].mtext = menu[i][0];
32     menuClip["item"+i]._y = menuClip.top._height +
33     menuClip["item"+i].useHandCursor = false;
34     menuClip["item"+i].onRollOver = function () {
35         this.t.backgroundColor = 0xFF6600;
36         this.t.textColor = 0xFFFFFF;
37     }
38         menuClip["item"+i].onRollOut = function ()
39         this.t.backgroundColor = 0xFFFFFF;
```

375

This code is in the `for` statement that's about halfway down in the Actions panel. It should look like the following when you've made your change:

```
for (var i=0; i<menu.length; i++) {
  menuClip.attachMovie("mpiece", "item"+i, ++cDepth);
  menuClip["item"+i].mtext = menu[i][0];
  menuClip["item"+i]._y = menuClip.top._height +
menuClip["item"+i]._height*i;
  menuClip["item"+i].useHandCursor = false;
  menuClip["item"+i].onRollOver = function () {
    this.t.backgroundColor = 0xFF6600;
    this.t.textColor = 0xFFFFFF;
  }
    menuClip["item"+i].onRollOut = function () {
    this.t.backgroundColor = 0xFFFFFF;
    this.t.textColor = 0xCC0000;
  }
}
```

Since each element in the menu array now contains an array, referring to `menu[i]` in the `for` statement will refer to an array. You want to refer to the first element in the `menu[i]` array. You can do this by referencing the first index in that array, which is 0.

3) Add a new line after line 41 in the Actions panel, and add the following ActionScript:

```
menuClip["item"+i].swf = menu[i][1];
menuClip["item"+i].onPress = function() {
  loadMovieNum(this.swf, 2);
};
```

Click the Auto Format button in the Actions panel, and Flash will automatically indent your ActionScript where appropriate. Flash will also add semicolons at the ends of any lines that should have one.

The for statement that creates all the menu pieces should now look like the following:

```
for (var i = 0; i<menu.length; i++) {
  menuClip.attachMovie("mpiece", "item"+i, ++cDepth);
  menuClip["item"+i].mtext = menu[i][0];
  menuClip["item"+i]._y = menuClip.top._height+menuClip["item"+i]._height*I;
  menuClip["item"+i].useHandCursor = false;
  menuClip["item"+i].onRollOver = function() {
    this.t.backgroundColor = 0xFF6600;
    this.t.textColor = 0xFFFFFF;
  }
  menuClip["item"+i].onRollOut = function() {
    this.t.backgroundColor = 0xFFFFFF;
    this.t.textColor = 0xCC0000;
  }
  menuClip["item"+i].swf = menu[i][1];
  menuClip["item"+i].onPress = function() {
    loadMovieNum(this.swf, 2);
  };
}
```

The first line of the ActionScript you just added initializes a new variable, called swf, in the instance of the Menu Clip movie clip named "item"+i. The value of the new swf variable is set to the value of the second element in the *i*th array element—the value of i is set by the for statement.

The next part of the code you added sets the onPress event for the menu piece. When the instance of the Menu Clip movie clip is pressed, the loadMovieNum action is triggered. The loadMovieNum action has the following syntax:

```
loadMovieNum(url, level);
```

The url argument contains the URL of the .swf file that you want to load. The level is much like a layer. Levels have a stacking order. The movie that Flash Player loads (the movie you're working with) is in level 0. In this case, you are loading this.swf, which refers to the value of the swf variable in each menu item, into level 2, so it will be above the current movie in the level stacking order.

4) Open visitorinfo1.fla from the FlashTFS folder. Move frame 1 of the Contents layer to frame 2.

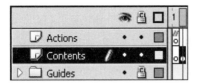

You made the visitorinfo1.fla file in Lesson 5—you should have a copy of it in the FlashTFS folder. If you can't find visitorinfo1.fla in the FlashTFS folder, there's a copy of it in the Lesson11/Starting folder on the CD-ROM.

To move frame 1 of the Contents layer to frame 2, you can copy and paste the frame. Or you can select frame 1, release the mouse, and then click and drag the selected frame to frame 2. Use whichever method is easier—just make sure frame 1 ends up empty and all of your content is in frame 2.

5) Add a keyframe to frame 2 of the Actions layer in visitorinfo1.fla. Add a stop action to this new keyframe, and set the Frame label to rf. Export the movie as visitorinfo.swf in the FlashTFS folder, and save the file as visitorinfo2.fla in the FlashTFS folder.

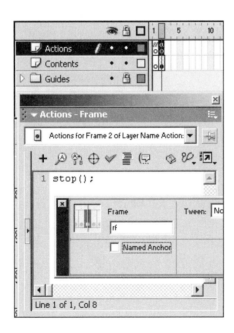

Select frame 2 of the Actions layer in visitorinfo1.fla, and choose Insert > Keyframe or press F6. Select the new keyframe, and add a **stop** action in the Actions panel by typing *stop( )*. After you add the `stop` action to frame 2, be sure to set the Frame label, in the Property inspector, to rf. This Frame label will be very important in Lesson 12, when you create a preloader for your project.

Now it's time to export the movie. Choose File > Export Movie. In the Export Movie dialog box, browse to the FlashTFS folder on your hard drive, enter visitorinfo.swf in the File Name (Windows) or Save As (Macintosh) box, and click Save. When the Export Flash Player dialog box opens, leave the settings at their defaults and click OK.

When you're done exporting the movie, save the .fla file as visitorinfo2.fla in the FlashTFS folder. You're going to work with that file again in Lesson 12.

6) Repeat steps 4 and 5 for feature1.fla, map8.fla, and guestbook8.fla from the FlashTFS folder.

If you can't find these files in the FlashTFS folder, you can find copies of them in the Lesson11/Assets folder on the CD-ROM.

Move frame 1 of the Contents layer in feature1.fla to frame 2. Then add a keyframe to frame 2 of the Actions layer, add a stop action in that keyframe, and set the Frame label for that keyframe to rf. Export feature1.fla, which you created in Lesson 6, as feature.swf. Save feature1.fla as feature2.fla—you're going to work with that file again in Lesson 12. Save the .fla file in the FlashTFS folder on your hard drive, which is the same place where you should save the .swf file.

TIP *You can easily switch between multiple open movies using the Window menu. Just choose Window and the name of the open .fla file you'd like to work with, as illustrated by the figure below.*

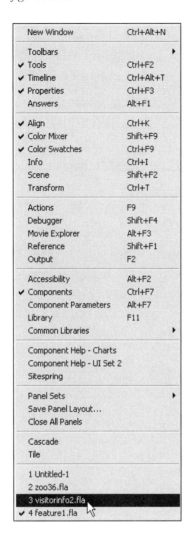

When you're ready to modify guestbook8.fla, things will be a bit more complicated than they were for feature1.fla. For guestbook8.fla, you should move frame 1 of the Actions, Components, Text Boxes, and Background layers to frame 2 of that movie. Make sure that you move the Actions that were in frame 1 of the original movie to frame 2; otherwise you'll find that parts of the movie will not work correctly. Add a `stop` action to the end of the ActionScript in frame 2. Finally, set the Frame label for frame 2 of the Actions layer to rf. Export the movie as guestbook.swf and save the file as guestbook9.fla.

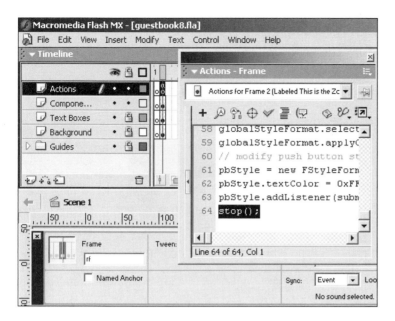

Modifying map8.fla is also a little more complicated. For map8.fla, move frame 1 of the Actions, Printable Content, List, Locations, and Map layers to frame 2. Add the **stop** action at the end of the ActionScript in frame 2. The label in frame 2 is already !#p, which disables the Print command in the Flash Player contextual menu—change that label to rf.

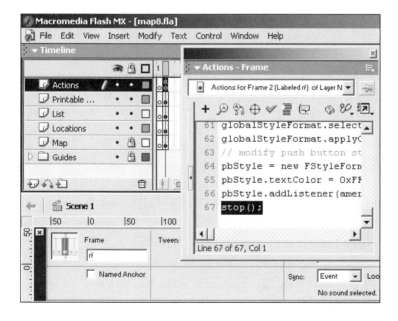

OPTIMIZING FLASH CONTENT

7) Return to zoo36.fla and choose Control > Test Movie.

When you test the movie, you should notice that the contents of the top1.fla file, which you exported as top.swf, do not appear. The contents of main1.fla, which you exported as main.swf, also don't appear unless you click the home menu item. That's because you haven't added ActionScript to load those movies when the Web site appears. You'll do that in Lesson 12.

Click each of the menu items. All except the games menu item should load a movie into level 2. When the movies load into level 2, they will obscure the menu, so you might have to move the menu off to the side so you can keep selecting items from it. You will fix that in Lesson 12, so the menu will appear above all of the loaded movies.

TIP *If you forgot to add a* stop *action in frame 2 of any of the loaded movies, the loaded movie may flicker. To fix the flickering, open the offending movie's .fla file and add a* stop *action to frame 2 of the Actions layer. Then export the movie to the FlashTFS folder, using the appropriate name, and test zoo36.fla again.*

8) Close the Test Movie window, and save the file as zoo37.fla.

When you're finished testing the menu, close the Test Movie window. Save the file as zoo37.fla in the FlashTFS folder on your hard drive. You're done with this file for this lesson, so you can close it.

LOADING JPEG IMAGES

In Flash MX, you can use ActionScript to load JPEG images into the Flash Player. Loading JPEG images is nearly identical to loading .swf files in Flash—the only difference is that the URL you specify is the URL of a .jpg file. Like .swf files, .jpg files can be loaded into levels in Flash. You can also load both .jpg and .swf files into movie clips. In the following exercise, you'll use the `loadMovie` method of the `MovieClip` object to load .jpg files into a movie-clip instance.

1) Open map9.fla from the FlashTFS folder.

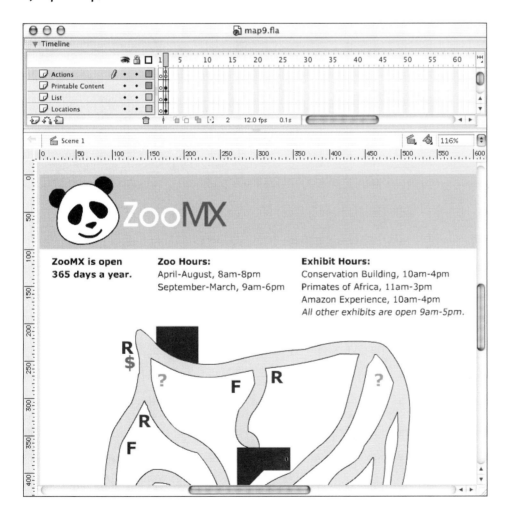

You're going to use some ActionScript to load a JPEG file into this movie.

TIP *If you already have this file open from the previous exercise, choose Window > map9.fla to switch to it.*

2) Select frame 2 in the Actions layer, and add the following ActionScript to the getDetail function:

```
detailClip.createEmptyMovieClip("imgClip", 2);
detailClip.imgClip._x = 12;
detailClip.imgClip._y = 135;
```

```
▼ Actions - Frame
  [•] Actions for Frame 2 (Labeled rf)  of Layer Name Actions            [▼] [⇥]
  + 🔎 ⭢ ⊕ ✔ ☰ 🖵                                            🖺 🕮 🔳
28  function getDetail(lb) {
29      animalList.setEnabled(false);
30      var idNum = lb.getSelectedItem().data;
31      _root.attachMovie("detailClip", "detailClip", 1);
32      detailClip.onUnload = function() {
33          animalList.setEnabled(true);
34      };
35      detailClip._x = 310;
36      detailClip._y = 60;
37      detailClip.description = "<b>"+locData["common"+idNu
38      detailClip.description += "<i>"+locData["latin"+idNu
39      detailClip.description += locData["description"+idNu
40      detailClip.attachMovie("closeClip", "closeClip", 1);
41      detailClip.closeClip._x = 230;
42      detailClip.closeClip._y = 4;
43      detailClip.closeClip.onPress = function() {
44          detailClip.removeMovieClip();
45      }
46      detailClip.createEmptyMovieClip("imgClip", 2);
47      detailClip.imgClip._x = 12;
48      detailClip.imgClip._y = 135;
49  }
50
51
  Line 45 of 70, Col 1
```

You should add this ActionScript to the end of the getDetail function. After you've added it, the function should look like this:

```
function getDetail(lb) {
  animalList.setEnabled(false);
  var idNum = lb.getSelectedItem().data;
  _root.attachMovie("detailClip", "detailClip", 1);
  detailClip.onUnload = function() {
    animalList.setEnabled(true);
  };
  detailClip._x = 310;
  detailClip._y = 60;
  detailClip.description = "<b>"+locData["common"+idNum]+"</b><br>";
  detailClip.description += "<i>"+locData["latin"+idNum]+"</i><br><br>";
  detailClip.description += locData["description"+idNum];
  detailClip.attachMovie("closeClip", "closeClip", 1);
  detailClip.closeClip._x = 230;
  detailClip.closeClip._y = 4;
  detailClip.closeClip.onPress = function() {
    detailClip.removeMovieClip();
  };
  detailClip.createEmptyMovieClip("imgClip", 2);
  detailClip.imgClip._x = 12;
  detailClip.imgClip._y = 135;
}
```

This simple bit of code creates a new, empty movie clip named imgClip inside of the detailClip instance. The code then places the imgClip movie clip at specific X and Y coordinates.

3) Now add this ActionScript to the getDetail function:

```
detailClip.imgClip.loadMovie(dataURL + "images/" + locData["image"+idNum]);
```

```
45        detailClip.removeMovieClip();
46    }
47    detailClip.createEmptyMovieClip("imgClip", 2);
48    detailClip.imgClip._x = 12;
49    detailClip.imgClip._y = 135;
50    detailClip.imgClip.loadMovie(dataURL + "images/" + locData["image"+idNum]);
51 }
52  dataURL = "http://www.flashtfs.com/data/";
53  getList();
```

Line 48 of 71, Col 1

Add this code in a new line immediately after the ActionScript you added in the last step.

This ActionScript uses the `loadMovie` method of the built-in `MovieClip` object to load a JPEG image into the imgClip movie clip. The `loadMovie` method is similar to `loadMovieNum`, except that instead of loading a movie into a level, it loads the movie into a movie clip. Both `loadMovie` and `loadMovieNum` can load .swf files and JPEG images.

The URL of the image to be loaded is `dataURL + "images/" + locData["image"+idNum]`. This concatenates the value of the `dataURL` variable with the string `"images/"` and the name of the image from the `locData` object you worked with in Lesson 10.

4) Choose Control > Test Movie.

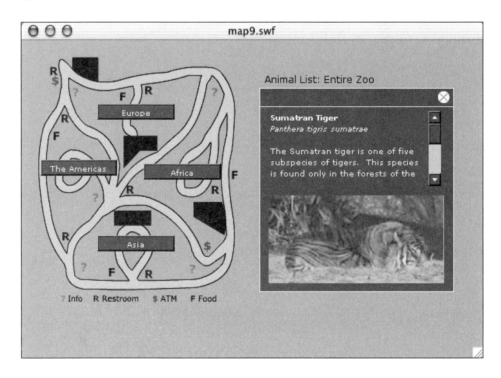

When you test the movie, click one of the animals in the list on the right side of the movie. When the Detail Clip movie clip appears, it should contain the common name, Latin name, some text about the animal, and a picture of the animal. The filename for the picture is specified in the data source that you connected to the movie in Lesson 10.

5) Choose File > Export Movie. In the Export Movie dialog box, browse to the FlashTFS folder on your hard drive, type *map.swf* in the File Name (Windows) or Save As (Macintosh) text box, and click Save.

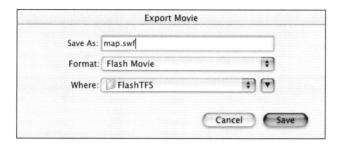

The map movie is now complete. As the movie has changed since the last time it was exported, you need to export it as map.swf once again. Make sure you export the .swf file to the FlashTFS folder, replacing the copy of map.swf that you created earlier in this lesson.

6) When the Export Flash Player dialog box opens, select the "Generate size report" option and click OK.

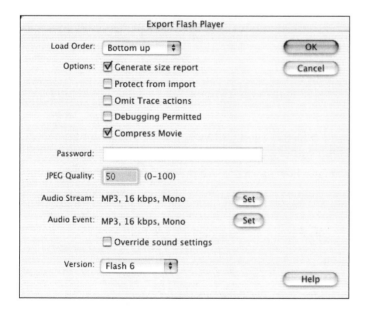

When you select the "Generate size report" option, Flash will create a text file containing information about the file size of each asset in the movie. You can use this information, in concert with the Bandwidth Profiler, to figure out which parts of your movie may need to be optimized further to decrease the file size as much as possible.

```
┌──────────────────────────────────────────────────────────┐
│  ⊖ ⊖ ⊖              📄 map.swf Report                      │
├──────────────────────────────────────────────────────────┤
│ Movie Report                                               │
│ -------------                                              │
│                                                            │
│ FrameFrame #  Frame Bytes   Total Bytes   Page            │
│ ----------    -----------   -----------   ---------        │
│   1    58366     58366      Scene 1                        │
│   2    11453     69819         2                           │
│                                                            │
│ Page              Shape Bytes   Text Bytes                 │
│ --------------     -----------   ----------                │
│ Scene 1             1170          796                      │
│                                                            │
│ Page              Symbol Bytes   Text Bytes                │
│ --------------     ------------   ----------               │
│ Symbol 19              0            31                      │
│ Symbol 18              0            31                      │
│ Symbol 17              0            31                      │
│ Symbol 16              0            31                      │
│ Visitor Info Button     0           0                      │
│ Shape Animation          0          0                      │
│ Fish Bitmap            0            0                       │
│ Frog Bitmap            0            0                       │
│ Mara Bitmap             0           0                       │
│ Lion Bitmap            0            0                       │
│ Bitmap Animation         0          0                      │
│ Logo                 0        0                             │
│ Panda                0        0                             │
│  PushButton            0           0                        │
│ FUIComponent            0           0                      │
│ Component Version         0          0                     │
│ fpb_states             0            0                       │
└──────────────────────────────────────────────────────────┘
```

The size report, which should appear in the FlashTFS folder, contains information about the movie, including the size of each frame, how large each symbol is, which fonts and characters are used (and how much file size they take up), and which sounds are used (and how much file size they add to the finished movie). You can use the size report to optimize your movie. If you notice that one symbol is very large, for example, you might want to concentrate on reducing that symbol's size.

NOTE *A movie's size report appears in the same folder as the exported movie. The name of the size report will be map.swf Size Report or something similar*

7) Save the movie as map10.fla in the FlashTFS folder.

You're done with this file for now, so you can close it.

WHAT YOU HAVE LEARNED

In this lesson, you have:

- Used the Bandwidth Profiler and Show Streaming command (pages 356–358)

- Optimized the assets in your Flash movie to reduce the file size (pages 358–367)

- Exported a Flash movie as a .swf file (pages 367–374)

- Loaded a .swf file into a Flash movie (pages 374–383)

- Loaded a JPEG image into a Flash movie (pages 383–388)

publishing a Flash web site

LESSON 12

You're almost ready to put your Macromedia Flash Web site on the Internet. First you need to add a preloader, and then you'll publish the files. A preloader will ensure that the necessary files have downloaded completely before the movie plays. You already split the whole site up into several files; your visitors won't have to download the entire site—just the files they want to view.

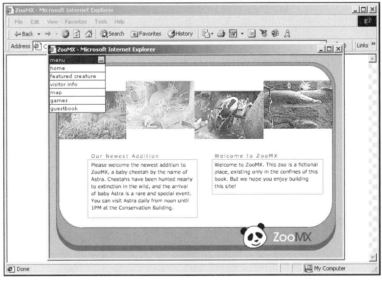

The completed ZooMX Web site.

Chrissy Rey

WHAT YOU WILL LEARN

In this lesson, you will:

- Create a preloader

- Add some programmatic movement

- Publish your movie in multiple formats

- Upload your Web site

APPROXIMATE TIME

This lesson takes approximately one hour to complete.

LESSON FILES

Media Files:

Lesson12/Assets/index.html

Lesson12/Assets/frames.html

Lesson12/Assets/blank.html

Starting Files:

Lesson12/Starting/zoo37.fla

Lesson12/Starting/top1.fla

Lesson12/Starting/guestbook9.fla

Lesson12/Starting/main1.fla

Lesson12/Starting/visitorinfo2.fla

Lesson12/Starting/map10.fla

Lesson12/Starting/feature2.fla

Completed Project:

Lesson12/Completed/top2.fla

Lesson12/Completed/guestbook10.fla

Lesson12/Completed/main2.fla

Lesson12/Completed/visitorinfo3.fla

Lesson12/Completed/map11.fla

Lesson12/Completed/feature3.fla

Lesson12/Completed/zoo40.fla

Lesson12/Completed/zoo.swf

Lesson12/Completed/top.swf

Lesson12/Completed/guestbook.swf

Lesson12/Completed/main.swf

Lesson12/Completed/visitorinfo.swf

Lesson12/Completed/map.swf

Lesson12/Completed/feature.swf

Lesson12/Completed/index.html

Lesson12/Completed/frames.html

Lesson12/Completed/blank.html

Lesson12/Completed/zoo.html

Lesson12/Completed/zoo.exe

*Lesson12/Completed/zoo Projector or
Lesson12/Completed/zoo.hqx*

CREATING A PRELOADER

After you add graphics, sound, and content to your Flash movie, the file can become rather large. Even after you optimize your movie, you might find that integral parts of the movie have frames that go above the red line in the Bandwidth Profiler. What happens if a user clicks a button to go to a particular frame, and that frame hasn't been downloaded yet? Flash will not go to frames that haven't been loaded, so you need to make sure that everything that needs to be loaded is loaded before you let Flash perform such actions. A solution to this problem is a *preloader*. A preloader is an animation that plays while the contents of the Flash movie download.

1) Add a `stop` action to frame 1 of the Actions layer in guestbook9.fla, main1.fla, visitorinfo2.fla, map10.fla, and feature2.fla. Export a .swf file for each movie to the FlashTFS folder, and save the files as guestbook10.fla, main2.fla, visitorinfo3.fla, map11.fla, and feature3.fla.

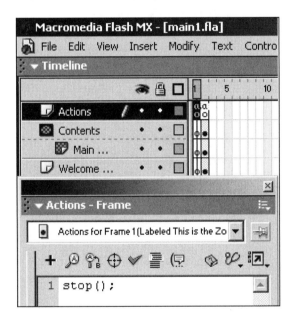

Each of the files for this step should be in the FlashTFS folder on your hard drive. If for some reason you can't locate one of the files, you can find a copy in the Lesson12/ Starting folder on the CD-ROM. Be sure to copy the file to the FlashTFS folder before you continue.

Once you've found the files, open each one and add a `stop` action to frame 1 of the Actions layer. Select frame 1 of the Actions layer in each movie, open the Actions panel, and type *stop();* in the Actions list.

392

After you add the `stop` action to frame 1 in each movie, export a .swf file for each movie. Choose File > Export Movie. In the Export Movie dialog box, browse to the FlashTFS folder. Type the appropriate name in the Save As text box and click Save. In the Export Flash Movie dialog box, leave the settings at their defaults and click OK.

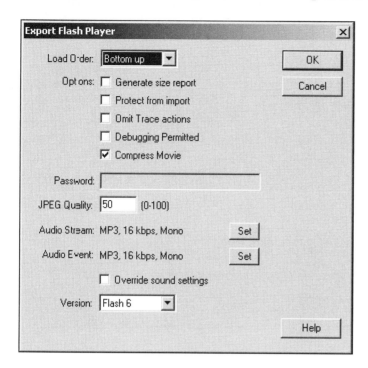

NOTE *Export the .swf files as guestbook.swf, main.swf, visitorinfo.swf, map.swf, and feature.swf. Since there are already .swf files with these names, you should choose to replace them if prompted.*

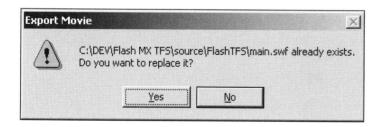

Once you've exported a movie, you should save it in the FlashTFS folder on your hard drive. Increase the number in the file's name by one when you save it, just in case you need to go back to the previous version.

2) Open zoo37.fla from the FlashTFS folder. Select frame 1 of the Actions layer, and choose Edit > Cut Frames.

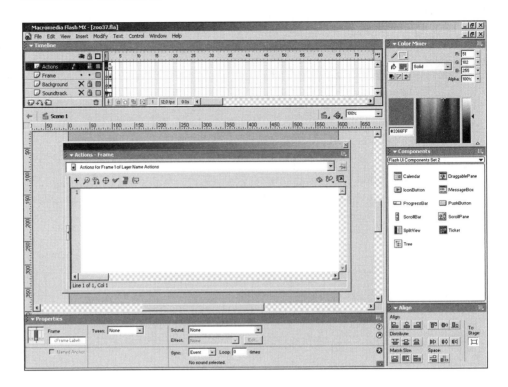

You created zoo37.fla in Lesson 11. If you can't find a copy of zoo37.fla in the FlashTFS folder on your hard drive, you can find a copy in the Lesson12/Starting folder on the CD-ROM. Open that file and save it as zoo37.fla in the FlashTFS folder on your hard drive.

NOTE *It's important that you work with zoo37.fla in the FlashTFS folder on your hard drive. If you start this lesson with zoo37.fla from the CD-ROM, you must save the file to the FlashTFS folder on your hard drive.*

3) Open top1.fla from the FlashTFS folder. Select frame 2 of the Actions layer, and choose Edit › Paste Frames. Add a `stop` action to frames 1 and 2 of the Actions layer. Set the Frame label for frame 2 to rf.

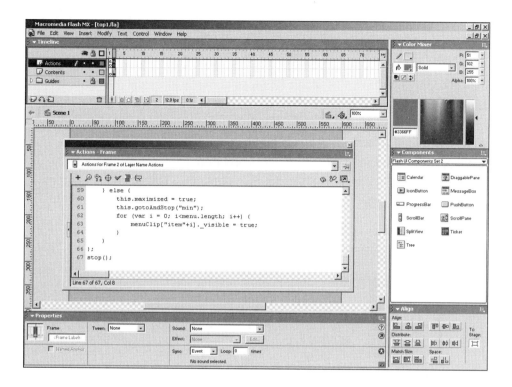

When you choose Edit > Paste Frames, the frame you cut from the zoo37.fla movie will be pasted into frame 1 of the top1.fla movie. That means that all of the ActionScript from frame 1 in zoo37.fla, which was the ActionScript that created the drop-down menu, is pasted into the top1.fla movie.

After you paste the contents of frame 1 of the Actions layer from zoo37.fla into frame 2 of the Actions layer in top1.fla, add a **stop** action at the end of the code. Then add a **stop** action to frame 1 of the Actions layer. This will keep the movie from displaying anything, since frame 1 of every layer is empty (except for ActionScript).

When you paste frame 1 of the Actions layer in zoo37.fla in frame 2 of the Actions layer in top1.fla, not only is the ActionScript pasted into that frame, but so is the frame's label. Since frame 1 of the Actions layer in zoo37.fla doesn't have a label, pasting that frame into frame 2 of the Actions layer in top1.fla will remove that frame's label. It must be labeled rf for the preloader to work, so make sure you set the Frame label to rf before you continue.

395

4) Copy the Menu Piece and Min Max Clip symbols from the zoo37.fla library to the top1.fla library. Open the Top Clip movie clip in top1.fla in symbol-editing mode, and add the following ActionScript to frame 12 of the Actions layer:

```
_level0.gotoAndStop("rf");
_level2.gotoAndStop("rf");
_parent.menuClip._visible = true;
```

You added the ActionScript to create the menu in step 3 when you pasted the contents of frame 1 of the Actions layer in zoo37.fla to frame 2 of the Actions layer in top1.fla. Now you must add the movie clips that are attached by that ActionScript. Make sure both the zoo37.fla and top1.fla libraries are open, and drag the Menu Piece and Min Max Clip symbols from the zoo37.fla library into the top1.fla library. Both movie clips will maintain their Identifier properties when they are moved from one library to the other.

NOTE *You should delete the Menu Piece and Min Max Clip movie clips from the zoo37.fla library. These movie clips are exported for ActionScript in the first frame of the movie, so they would add to the file size of the movie when you export or test zoo37.fla. You can delete an item from the library by selecting it and pressing Delete or Backspace. When the Delete dialog box opens, first verify that you are in fact deleting the correct symbols (from the zoo37.fla library, not the top1.fla library), and then click Delete.*

The ActionScript should go before the **stop** action already in frame 12 of the Actions layer in the Top Clip symbol. You should end up with the following ActionScript in frame 12 of the Actions layer after you have completed this step:

```
_level0.gotoAndStop("rf");
_level2.gotoAndStop("rf");
_parent.menuClip._visible = true;
stop();
```

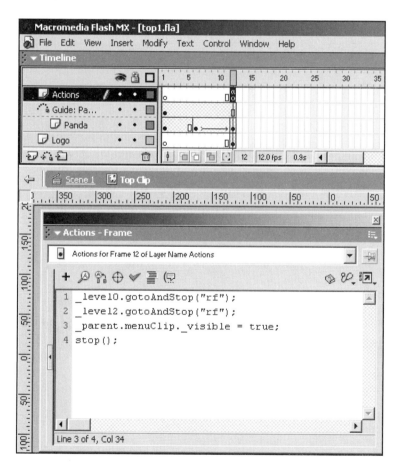

The first and second lines of code you added tell levels 0 and 2 to go to the frame labeled rf and stop playing. You set frame 2 of the main timeline for every movie in your project to rf in Lesson 11—that frame label now comes in handy. You already added ActionScript to stop every loaded movie at frame 1. Later in this exercise you'll add a `stop` action to frame 1 of the level 0 movie (zoo37.fla).

The third line of code you added sets the `_visible` property of the `menuClip` instance on the main timeline of the current movie to `true`. That means that the menu that's created by the ActionScript in frame 1 of the main movie will become visible when the Top Clip movie clip reaches frame 12.

5) Export top1.fla to the FlashTFS folder as top.swf, and save the .fla file in the FlashTFS folder as top2.fla.

| File name: | top.swf | ▼ |
| Save as type: | Flash Movie (*.swf) | ▼ |

N O T E *You should replace the copy of top.swf that you exported to the FlashTFS folder in Lesson 11.*

Make sure you export the .fla file as top.swf in the FlashTFS folder. When you choose File > Export, browse to the FlashTFS folder on your hard drive. Type *top.swf* in the Save As text box and click Save. When the Export Flash Player dialog box opens, leave the settings at their defaults and click OK. After the movie has exported, save the .fla as top2.fla in the FlashTFS folder.

Keep this file open for now, as you will modify it again later in this exercise.

6) Move frame 1 of the Soundtrack layer in zoo37.fla to frame 2. Set the Frame label for frame 2 of the Actions layer to rf. In frame 1 of the Actions layer, add the following ActionScript:

```
function preload(movies) {
  loadInterval = setInterval(checkLoaded, 10, movies);
}
loadMovieNum("main.swf", 2);
loadMovieNum("top.swf", 3);
var movies = [["_level0", "_level2", "_level3"],["_level3"]];
preload(movies);
stop();
```

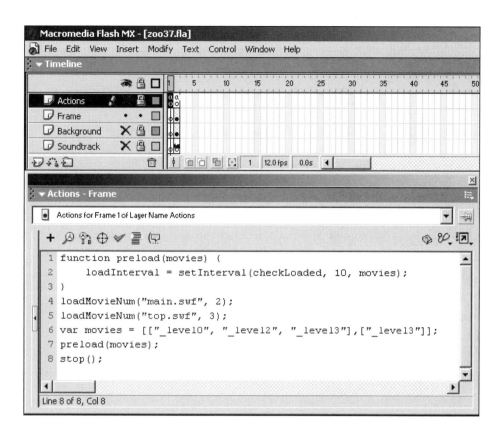

Choose Window > zoo37.fla to return to the movie—it should still be open from step 2 in this exercise.

You can move frame 1 of the Soundtrack layer to frame 2 by selecting frame 1 of the Soundtrack layer, releasing the mouse, and dragging frame 1 to frame 2. When you do this, frame 1 of the Soundtrack layer should be empty, and the sound that was in frame 1 should now be in frame 2.

After you've moved frame 1 of the Soundtrack layer to frame 2, select frame 1 of the Actions layer and add the ActionScript to the Actions panel. This ActionScript should be the only ActionScript in this frame—if there's any other ActionScript in the Actions panel, simply delete it.

The first three lines of code set up the `preload` function. This function has only one parameter (`movies`), which you'll learn more about later in this step. The ActionScript that's run when the `preload` function is called is

```
loadInterval = setInterval(checkLoaded, 10, movies);
```

This code uses the `setInterval` action, which has the following syntax:

```
setInterval(function, interval, arguments);
```

The `setInterval` action calls a function at a specified interval as the movie plays. The function called is set in the `function` parameter, while the interval in milliseconds is set by the `interval` parameter. You can pass arguments to the function, in case it requires any parameters, using the `arguments` parameter. In the ActionScript that you added, the function is `checkLoaded` and the interval is `10`. The only argument that's sent to the `checkLoaded` function is `movies`, which is the `movies` parameter that's expected by the `preload` function. So when this function is triggered, it's sort of like starting a timer to call the following code every 10 milliseconds:

```
checkLoaded(movies);
```

When the value set for the `interval` parameter is less than the movie frame, the `function` is called as close to `interval` as possible. If the function modifies the appearance of the movie, you should use the `updateAfterEvent` action, which you'll look at in the next exercise, to refresh the screen.

The next two lines of code load a couple of movies. The first movie that's loaded is main.swf, and it's loaded into level 2. Then top.swf is loaded into level 3. This code is pretty straightforward and simply uses the `loadMovieNum` action—you looked at that action in detail in Lesson 11.

Next the code creates a new multidimensional array, named movies. The movies array has two elements, each of which is a multidimensional array. The first element has three values: `"_level0"`, `"_level2"`, and `"_level3"`, each of which is a string referring to a level in the movie. The second element of the `movies` array has only a single value (`"_level3"`), though it could have more. You'll learn more about what these values mean in the next step.

The last two lines of code are pretty simple. First the code calls the `preload` function, passing it the value of the `movies` array. When you set up the `preload` function, you wrote it so that it expects a `movies` parameter—the value of the `movies` array fills in that parameter, which is then passed to the `checkLoaded` function as part of the `preload` function. The last line of code simply tells the movie to stop.

7) Now add the following ActionScript:

```
function checkLoaded(movies) {
  var total = 0;
  var done = 0;
  var pLoaded = 0;
  for (var i = 0; i<movies[0].length; i++) {
    var mc = eval(movies[0][i]);
    if (mc.getBytesTotal() != undefined) {
      total += mc.getBytesTotal();
      done += mc.getBytesLoaded();
    } else {
      total = 0;
      break;
    }
    pLoaded = Math.ceil(done/total*100);
  }
  trace(pLoaded + "% loaded");
}
```

Add this code before any other ActionScript in frame 1 of the Actions layer.

This ActionScript does the bulk of the work for the preloader. It expects a single parameter (`movies`), which it receives from the `preload` function when it calls `checkLoaded` as part of the `setInterval` action.

The first three lines of code inside the `checkLoaded` function initialize three local variables: `total`, `done`, and `pLoaded`. Each of these starts out at `0`. The `total` variable will hold the total file size that needs to be loaded. The `done` variable will hold the value of the amount of file size that has been downloaded. The `pLoaded` variable will hold the value of the percentage downloaded (`done/total*100`).

Next a `for` statement runs based on the length of the array that's the first element of the `movies` array (`movies[0]`). In step 6, you set the first value of the movies array to `["_level0", "_level2", "_level3"]`, which makes the length of `movies[0]` 3, so the `for` statement will run three times.

The first line inside the `for` statement sets up a variable that's local to the `for` statement—it exists only inside the `for` statement. The variable is named `mc`, and it has a value of the `i`th element in the `movies[0]` array, after it has had the `eval` action applied to it. The `eval` action lets you access the level set by the value from the `movies[0]` array as a path to that level.

Next, the ActionScript checks to see if the value of `mc.getBytesTotal()` is not equal to (`!=`) `undefined`. If this condition is `true`, the values of the `total` and `done` variables are modified based on the values of `mc.getBytesTotal ()` and `mc.getBytesLoaded ()`. `getBytesTotal` and `getBytesLoaded` are methods of the built-in `MovieClip` object. They get the total size and loaded size of a movie clip (or level) in bytes. If the value of `mc.getBytesTotal()` is `undefined`, which will happen if that value has not yet been set in Flash, and the condition for the `if` statement is `false`, the `else` statement is run, setting the value of `total` back to `0` and triggering the `break` action. The `break` action tells Flash to stop running the current `for` statement, so Flash will skip the rest of the `for` statement and continue on with any code that follows it.

Finally, Flash sets the value of the `pLoaded` variable to `Math.ceil (done/total*100)`. This takes the value of the `done` variable, divided by the value of the `total` variable, times `100`, and rounds it up to the closest integer. Since the variable gets a value inside the `for` statement, the `pLoaded` variable's value won't be set if the `break` action is triggered. The `pLoaded` value is then traced, along with the string `"% loaded"`.

8) Add this ActionScript to the `checkLoaded` function:

```
if (done == total && total>0) {
for (var i = 0; i<movies[1].length; i++) {
var mc = eval(movies[1][i]);
mc.gotoAndStop("rf");
}
  clearInterval(loadInterval);
}
```

Add this code following the `trace` action in the code you added in the previous step. Make sure this code is added as part of the `checkLoaded` function.

This ActionScript checks to see if the value of `done` is the same as the value of `total`, and if `total` is greater than 0. If both conditions are true, then Flash will first run a `for` statement based on the length of the second element in the `movies` array (`movies[1]`).

It will tell each target (level) in that array to go to the frame labeled rf. When you set up the `movies` array, you set the single value in the `movies[1]` array to `"_level3"`, so this code will tell the level 3 movie to go to the rf frame. The movie that's loaded into level 3 is top.swf. You added some code to the Top Clip movie clip in top.swf to tell the level 0 and level 2 movies to go to the frame labeled rf. If you hadn't done that, you could have modified the `movies[1]` array to list all the levels you wanted to play. As the `for` statement runs, it will tell the movie in each level listed in the `movies[1]` array to go to the frame labeled rf. The only problem is that the action of the `for` loop will cause all the movies to run at once—that's not the effect you want for this project, and it looks nicer if the level 3 movie (top.swf) plays first.

Finally, if both of the conditions for the `if` statement are true, the `clearInterval` action will run. This action has a single parameter: `intervalID`. The `clearInterval` action stops the action of the interval that has the name referenced by the `intervalID` parameter. In this case, the `intervalID` parameter has a value of `loadInterval`, which is the variable name you set when you triggered the `setInterval` action to call `checkLoaded`. So this line of code simply tells the `checkLoaded` function to stop running at the specified interval.

9) Add some ActionScript to preload each loaded movie in top2.fla, export the movie as top.swf, and save the file as top3.fla. Return to zoo37.fla and test the movie. Save the file as zoo38.fla in the FlashTFS folder on your hard drive.

```
29  for (var i = 0; i<menu.length; i++) {
30      menuClip.attachMovie("mpiece", "item"+i, ++cDepth);
31      menuClip["item"+i].mtext = menu[i][0];
32      menuClip["item"+i]._y = menuClip.top._height+menuClip["item
33      menuClip["item"+i].useHandCursor = false;
34      menuClip["item"+i].onRollOver = function() {
35          this.t.backgroundColor = 0xFF6600;
36          this.t.textColor = 0xFFFFFF;
37      };
38      menuClip["item"+i].onRollOut = function() {
39          this.t.backgroundColor = 0xFFFFFF;
40          this.t.textColor = 0xCC0000;
41      };
42      menuClip["item"+i].swf = menu[i][1];
43      menuClip["item"+i].onPress = function() {
44          loadMovieNum(this.swf, 2);
45          _level0.preload([["_level2"], ["_level2"]]);
46      };
47  }
```

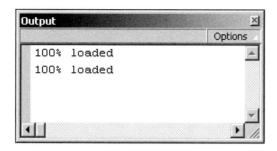

The ActionScript you need to add to preload each movie in top2.fla belongs in the onPress event given to every menu piece. It should look like the following when you've added the code:

```
menuClip["item"+i].onPress = function() {
loadMovieNum(this.swf, 2);
_level0.preload([["_level2"], ["_level2"]]);
};
```

This code goes in frame 2 of the Actions layer in top2.fla. Add it to the onPress event, which is found in the for statement that adds all of the menu pieces—the line of code you add will end up in line 45 of the ActionScript in frame 2 of the Actions layer. The line you add will call the preload function in the level 0 movie. You then need to preload whatever movie is loaded into level 2 (this.swf) and then tell the movie to go to the frame labeled rf.

When you test the movie (Control > Test Movie), the Output window should appear, displaying "100% loaded." The movies should appear as expected, but you won't get to see that the files are truly preloading, because the files are loading from your hard drive rather than over an Internet connection, so everything loads at once. In order to simulate downloading over a dial-up connection, you can choose View > Show Streaming while the Test Movie window is open, which will give you a more accurate assessment of the effectiveness of your preloader. The Output window should display the actual percentage loaded, based on the simulated download settings.

NOTE *You can change the simulated download settings using the Debug menu when the Test Movie window is open. Choose Debug and pick a download speed.*

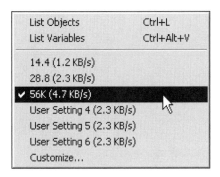

After you have tested the preloader, close the Test Movie window and save the .fla file as zoo38.fla in the FlashTFS folder on your hard drive. Keep the file open, because you're going to continue to work with it in the next exercise. You can close any other .fla files you may have open, as zoo38.fla is the only file you will work with for the rest of this book.

NOTE *If your preloader doesn't work, and the movies loaded into levels 2 and 3 never appear, check to make sure that the file you're working in has been saved to the FlashTFS folder on your hard drive, along with the .swf files that are to be loaded into the levels. If any of the files are located in a folder other than the FlashTFS folder, the preloader may not work.*

CREATING PROGRAMMATIC MOVEMENT

You can use ActionScript to create movement in Flash. Animation is simply a change in appearance over time, so now that you know how to change the appearance of movie clips in Flash, and you know how to make ActionScript run at a specified interval, this should be easy for you. In the next exercise you will add an ActionScript-generated animation, which will run while the preloader is loading all of the movies.

You should still have zoo38.fla open when you start this exercise.

1) Right-click (Windows) or Control-click (Macintosh) the Shape Animation symbol in the library, and choose Linkage. When the Linkage Properties dialog box opens, select the Export for ActionScript option and set the Identifier to plClip. Make sure the "Export in first frame" option is also selected, and click OK.

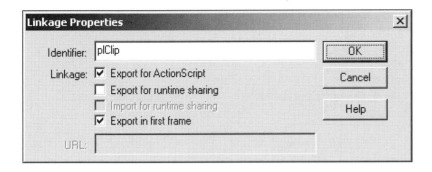

You are going to use the `attachMovie` method of the built-in `MovieClip` object to attach an instance of the Shape Animation movie clip to the stage. Before you can do that, you have to make sure that it's exported for ActionScript and has an identifier.

2) Add the following ActionScript to frame 1 of the Actions layer:

```
xSpeed = 10;
ySpeed = 5;
```

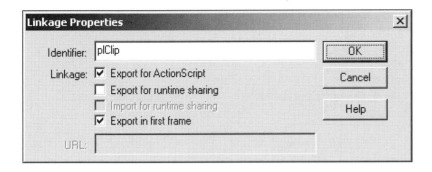

```
25  function preload(movies) {
26      loadInterval = setInterval(checkLoaded, 10, movies);
27  }
28  loadMovieNum("main.swf", 2);
29  loadMovieNum("top.swf", 3);
30  var movies = [["_level0", "_level2", "_level3"], ["_level3"]];
31  xSpeed = 10;
32  ySpeed = 5;
33  preload(movies);
34  stop();
```

This ActionScript should be added after the `movies` array is created but before the `preload` function is called. This code initializes the values of `xSpeed` and `ySpeed`, which you will use in the function you'll create in the next step.

407

3) Now add a function named `moveClip`:

```
function moveClip(obj) {
  obj._x += xSpeed;
  obj._y += ySpeed;
  if (obj._x <= 0 || obj._x >= 600) {
    xSpeed = - xSpeed;
  }
  if (obj._y <= 0 || obj._y >= 400) {
    ySpeed = -ySpeed;
  }
  updateAfterEvent();
}
```

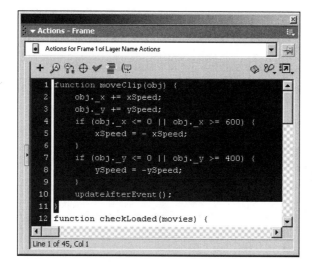

Add this function before any other ActionScript in frame 1 of the Actions layer. This might look like complicated code at first glance, but as you go through the function, line by line, you'll see that it's actually very simple.

The first line of code declares the function's name as `moveClip`. This new `moveClip` function will expect a single parameter, `obj`, from whatever movie clip, button, or frame calls it. That parameter will be used several times in the `moveClip` function, so it's important that it be included in the definition for the function.

The next two lines of code modify the *x* and *y* positions of `obj`:

```
obj._x += xSpeed;
obj._y += ySpeed;
```

Remember, **obj** is passed to the function by whatever calls it. So if, for example, you have a button call this function, and you set the **obj** parameter to **myClip**, the code will modify the *x* and *y* positions of **myClip**. The code for this example would look like this:

```
on (press) {
  moveClip(myClip);
}
```

The addition assignment operator (+=) assigns the value of the left side of the equation plus the value on the right side of the equation to the original value of the left side of the equation. It's sort of like typing **obj._x = obj._x + xSpeed**, but much shorter.

After the new values for the _x and _y properties are assigned, the code checks to see if **obj** is outside the "boundaries" of the movie. This is done with two **if** statements. The first **if** statement checks to see if **obj._x** is less than or equal to **0** (the left side of the movie) or greater than or equal to **600** (the right side of the movie). If either of these conditions is true, the **if** statement reverses the value of the **xSpeed** variable, which you initialized in step 2, effectively reversing the direction that **obj** will move the next time through the function. The second **if** statement does essentially the same thing, but in the *y* direction.

The last line of code refreshes the screen using the **updateAfterEvent** action. This code simply lets Flash update the display independent of the frame rate when the function is called using the **setInterval** action, which is just what you're going to do in the next step. So if the **interval** for the **setInterval** function is greater than the frame rate for the movie, the speed at which **obj** moves is faster than the frame rate would allow.

4) Add this ActionScript to the `preload` function:

```
this.attachMovie("plClip", "plClip", 1);
moveInterval = setInterval(moveClip, 10, plClip);
```

```
36 function preload(movies) {
37     loadInterval = setInterval(checkLoaded, 10, movies);
38     this.attachMovie("plClip", "plClip", 1);
39     moveInterval = setInterval(moveClip, 10, plClip);
40 }
41 loadMovieNum("main.swf", 2);
42 loadMovieNum("top.swf", 3);
43 var movies = [["_level0", "_level2", "_level3"], ["_level3"]
44 xSpeed = 10;
45 ySpeed = 5;
46 preload(movies);
47 stop();
```

Add this code after the code already in the `preload` function. After you add the code, the `preload` function will look like the following:

```
function preload(movies) {
  loadInterval = setInterval(checkLoaded, 10, movies);
  this.attachMovie("plClip", "plClip", 1);
  moveInterval = setInterval(moveClip, 10, plClip);
}
```

This code simply attaches an instance of the Shape Animation movie clip—you already set its Identifier to plClip. Then the `moveClip` function is called by the `setInterval` function. The interval has the name `moveInterval`, which you can use to clear the interval when you no longer want the `moveClip` function to run. The argument that's sent to the `moveClip` function is `plClip`—remember, `moveClip` expects an `obj` parameter, and in this `setInterval` action that parameter will have a value of `plClip`.

5) Add the following code to the `checkLoaded` function:

```
clearInterval(moveInterval);
plClip.removeMovieClip();
```

410

Add this code inside the `if` statement that clears the `loadInterval` interval. The finished `checkLoaded` function will look like this:

```
function checkLoaded(movies) {
  var total = 0;
  var done = 0;
  var pLoaded = 0;
  for (var i = 0; i<movies[0].length; i++) {
    var mc = eval(movies[0][i]);
    if (mc.getBytesTotal() != undefined) {
      total += mc.getBytesTotal();
      done += mc.getBytesLoaded();
    } else {
total = 0;
      break;
    }
pLoaded = Math.ceil(done/total*100);
  }
  trace(pLoaded + "% loaded");
  if (done == total && total>0) {
    for (var i = 0; i<movies[1].length; i++) {
      var mc = eval(movies[1][i]);
      mc.gotoAndStop("rf");
    }
    clearInterval(checkInterval);
    clearInterval(moveInterval);
    plClip.removeMovieClip();
  }
}
```

This code clears the `moveInterval` interval, so the `plClip` instance will stop bouncing around on the stage. Then the code removes the movie-clip instance using the `removeMovieClip` method.

NOTE *The `removeMovieClip` method can only remove movie-clip instances that have been dynamically added to the movie using `attachMovie` or `duplicateMovieClip`.*

6) Choose Control > Test Movie. Save the file as zoo39.fla in the FlashTFS folder on your hard drive.

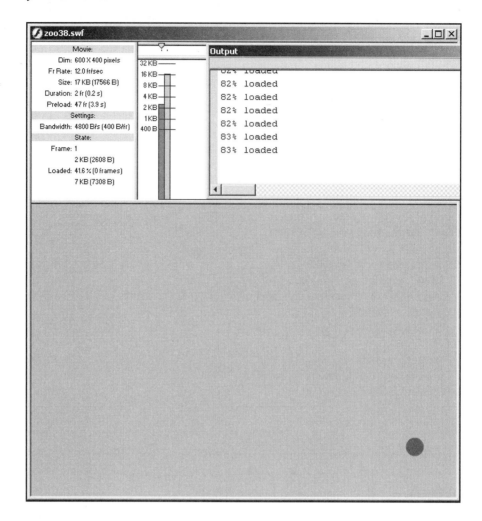

Be sure to choose View > Show Streaming, or the Output window will pop up saying "100% loaded." When you simulate streaming, the Shape Animation movie clip should appear. It will bounce around on the screen until the movies have finished preloading. It will then disappear, and top.swf, which was loaded into level 3, will start to play.

Close the Test Movie window when you're finished. Then save the movie as zoo39.fla in the FlashTFS folder on your hard drive. You're almost done! Keep the file open for now.

PUBLISHING A MOVIE

You now have a working Flash site, complete with a preloader. All you have left to do is publish the content and upload it to your Web site so that other people can view it. When you publish a Flash movie, you can create multiple formats for it, along with the HTML required to embed it for viewing on the Web.

You should have zoo39.fla from the last exercise still open.

1) Choose File > Publish Settings to open the Publish Settings dialog box.

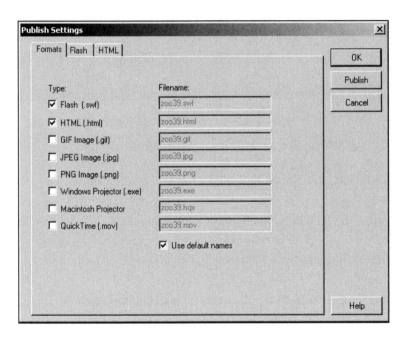

When you're ready to publish your movie, you first have to check the Publish Settings dialog box to make sure that all the settings are correct.

The Publish command (File > Publish) creates all the files you need to deliver your Flash movie. By default, the Publish command creates a .swf file containing your movie and an HTML file containing the code to embed the .swf file. After Flash creates these files for you, you must upload both of them to your Web server. Visitors then just have to view the HTML file to see the .swf file. They have to have the Flash Player installed for this file to work correctly, of course.

If you are concerned that your audience might not have the Flash Player, you can change the settings in the Publish Settings dialog box so that the Publish command also creates executable versions of the Flash movie for Windows and Macintosh computers. The executable version of the Flash movie is known as a *projector*. You can also make Flash publish a GIF image, JPEG image, PNG image, or QuickTime movie.

413

2) Under the Formats tab of the Publish Settings dialog box, select the Flash, HTML, Windows Projector, and Macintosh Projector types. Deselect the "Use default names" option.

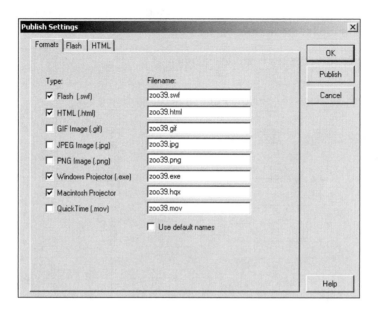

Flash will publish all of the formats selected under the Formats tab of the Publish Settings dialog box. When the "Use default names" option is deselected, you can edit the filenames for each of the formats listed.

3) Set the filenames for the Flash, HTML, Windows Projector, and Macintosh Projector types to *zoo.swf*, *zoo.html*, *zoo.exe* (Windows), and *zoo.hqx* or *zoo Projector* (Macintosh).

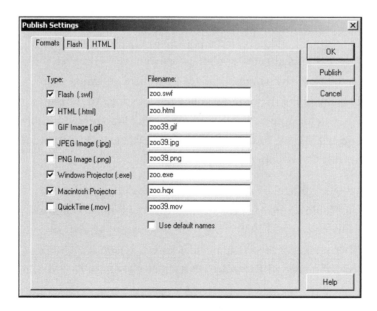

These filenames will be used when you publish the files. Since you saved zoo39.fla to the FlashTFS folder, the files will be published to that folder.

4) Select the Flash tab in the Publish Settings dialog box, and choose the "Generate size report" option. Leave the other settings at their defaults.

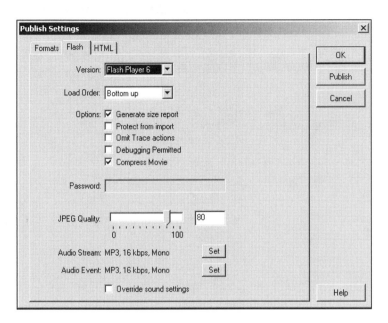

Many of the formats you can publish from Flash have settings you can modify to customize the finished file. When you publish a Flash Player movie (.swf), you have the option of generating a size report. This option, which is also available when you export a movie as .swf, creates a text file containing information about the movie.

The settings in the Load Order drop-down menu determine the order in which the layers in each individual frame load—an important setting when files are being downloaded over slow modems. Flash shows each layer as soon as it has downloaded. "Top down" loads the top layer in each frame first and then loads each frame below it in order; "Bottom up" does the opposite.

When you choose the "Protect from import" option, the published .swf file cannot be imported into Flash. This setting keeps other people from stealing your movie.

The Compress Movie option, which is selected by default, lets you compress the size of the .swf file when it's published. Files published with this option selected can only be played in Flash Player 6 or higher.

The JPEG Quality, Audio Stream, and Audio Event settings are useful if you don't specify compression settings for each individual bitmap or sound file.

You have the option of choosing Flash versions other than MX from the Version drop-down menu, but if you do, you will you lose some of the functionality of your movie. If you use anything that is Flash MX–specific and export it as an earlier version of Flash, you lose all the Flash MX–specific portions of the movie.

5) Click the HTML tab in the Publish Settings dialog box. Set the Dimensions to Percent, and uncheck the Display Menu option.

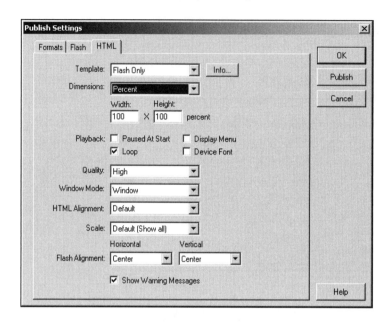

When you deselect the Display Menu option, you disable the contextual menu that appears when users Right-click (Windows) or Control-click (Macintosh) the movie while viewing it through the HTML file in the browser.

In the Template drop-down menu you specify the HTML template you want to publish. When you choose Flash Only (the default), Flash creates the HTML to embed your Flash file.

The Dimensions drop-down menu lets you specify the dimensions of the movie in percentage or pixels. If you choose Match Movie from this menu, you can't set the height and width of the movie. If you choose Pixels or Percent, you can modify the height and width settings. Since you set the Dimensions to Percent, 100 should appear in both the Height and Width settings—leave these settings at their defaults.

You should usually set the Quality drop-down menu to High, which gives appearance priority over playback. Low gives playback priority over quality, turning off anti-aliasing. Auto Low is similar to Low but improves quality if possible. (If Flash determines that the computer can handle anti-aliasing, it turns on that feature.) Auto High gives

416

playback and quality equal priority, reducing appearance first if playback problems occur; it turns off anti-aliasing if the frame rate continues to decrease. Medium produces better quality than Low. It does not anti-alias bitmaps but does apply some anti-aliasing. Best produces the best-quality appearance without considering speed; all images and bitmaps are anti-aliased.

6) Click OK to close the Publish Settings dialog box. Save the movie as zoo40.fla in the FlashTFS folder. Choose File > Publish to publish the movie.

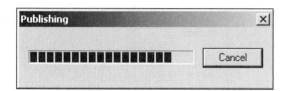

The Publishing dialog box opens, indicating the progress of the publishing operation.

7) Open the size report in the FlashTFS folder.

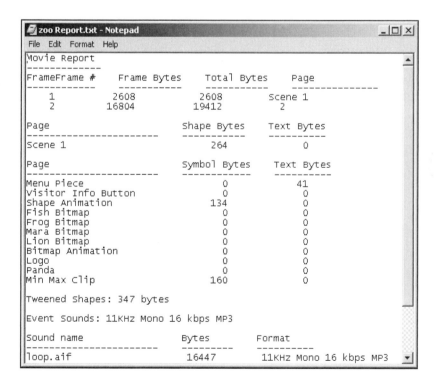

This file will be named zoo Report.txt (Windows) or zoo.swf Report (Macintosh). You can open it in your favorite text editor. This is similar to the size report you looked at in Lesson 11, only it's for a different movie.

417

8) Open zoo.html (in the FlashTFS folder) in your browser.

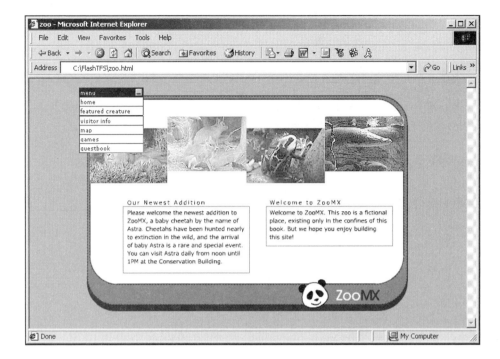

This file contains all the HTML needed to view zoo.swf in the browser properly, provided that you have the correct version of the Flash Player installed.

9) Open zoo.exe (Windows) or zoo Projector (Macintosh).

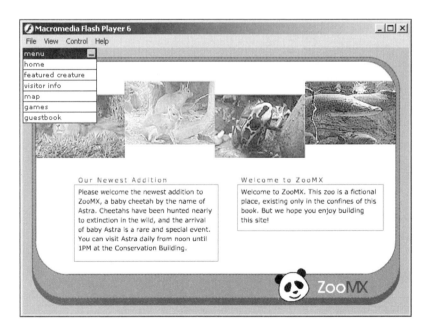

This file is a stand-alone version of your movie. Flash wrapped the .swf file in a stand-alone projector. You can send this file to other people to view without requiring them to install the Flash Player. Be sure to send the right file; you published both Windows and Macintosh projectors. Also be sure to send the loaded .swf files.

NOTE *Programs such as SWF Studio let you wrap all your .swf files for a single project into one executable file. You can learn more about this program, and others, by following the links in Appendix C.*

GETTING YOUR MOVIE ON THE WEB

Now that you have published your movie, it's time to put it on the Web. This is a simple but often misunderstood process. You have to make sure to upload all the required files to your Web server, or the Flash Web site won't work. That means that all HTML files and .swf files, including those loaded into other movies, have to be included.

In this exercise you will create an HTML file that opens the zoo.swf file in a pop-up window. Then you will figure out which files need to be uploaded. If you have access to a Web server, you will upload all of the files so you can view your Flash Web site on the Internet!

1) Copy the index.html, blank.html, and frames.html HTML files from the Lesson12/ Assets folder to the FlashTFS folder on your hard drive.

```html
<html>
    <head>
        <title>ZooMX</title>
        <script language="javascript">
<!--
        function launchWin(url, name, winW, winH) {
        var winleft = (screen.width - winW) / 2;
        var wintop = (screen.height - winH) / 2;
        features = 'width='+winW+',height='+winH+',left='+winleft+',top='+wintop;
        popup = window.open(url, name, features)
        if (parseInt(navigator.appVersion) >= 4) { popup.window.focus(); }


        }
        // -->
        </script>

    </head>
    <body bgcolor="#FFFFFF" onLoad="launchWin('frames.html','zoo','600','400');return false;">
    </body>
</html>
```

419

If you know JavaScript, you would have no problem creating an HTML file with the code necessary to open a pop-up window. The index.html file looks like this:

```html
<html>
  <head>
    <title>ZooMX</title>
    <script language="javascript">
    <!  --
      function launchWin(url, name, winW, winH) {
      var winleft = (screen.width - winW) / 2;
      var wintop = (screen.height - winH) / 2;
      features =
'width='+winW+',height='+winH+',left='+winleft+',top='+wintop;
      popup = window.open(url, name, features)
      if (parseInt(navigator.appVersion) >= 4) { popup.window.focus(); }
      }
    //  -->
    </script>
  </head>
  <body bgcolor="#FFFFFF"
onLoad="launchWin('frames.html','zoo','600','400');return false;">
  </body>
</html>
```

A copy of index.html, with all the necessary JavaScript, is included in the Lesson12/ Assets folder. Just copy the file to the FlashTFS folder on your hard drive. This file will open the frames.html file, which looks like this:

```html
<html>
<head>
<title>ZooMX</title>
</head>
<frameset FRAMEBORDER="0" BORDER="0" FRAMESPACING="0" cols="100%,*">
  <frame NAME="top" SRC="zoo.html" FRAMEBORDER="0" BORDER="0"
FRAMESPACING="0" scrolling="no" MARGINWIDTH="0" MARGINHEIGHT="0" >
  <frame NAME="bottom" SRC="blank.html" FRAMEBORDER="0" BORDER="0"
FRAMESPACING="0" scrolling="no">
  <noframes>
  </noframes>
</frameset>
</html>
```

This file opens blank.html and zoo.html in a frame set. The blank.html file is just an empty HTML file, while zoo.html has all of the HTML required to open zoo.swf in the browser, as you can see in the figure below.

2) Make sure you have all the necessary files for the ZooMX Web site in your FlashTFS folder. If you're missing any files, you can find a copy in the Lesson12/ Completed folder on the CD-ROM.

You need to make sure you have the following files in the FlashTFS folder on your hard drive: index.html, frames.html, blank.html, zoo.html, zoo.swf, main.swf, top.swf, feature.swf, visitorinfo.swf, map.swf, and guestbook.swf.

NOTE *While there's a games item listed in the menu for the Web site, you didn't make the games.swf file during the course of this book.*

If you can't find one of the files listed, be sure to copy the missing file to the FlashTFS folder from the Lesson12/Completed folder on the CD-ROM.

3) Upload index.html, frames.html, blank.html, zoo.html, zoo.swf, main.swf, top.swf, feature.swf, visitorinfo.swf, map.swf, and guestbook.swf to your Web site, and browse to index.html.

You can't just upload the HTML files and expect to see the Flash content; you have to upload the .swf files, too. The HTML file is set up so that the .swf files should be in the same directory. If you know a little HTML, you can easily change this setup.

NOTE *You do not have to upload any .fla files. Those are the editable files—the .swf files are the ones that Flash compresses for use on the Web.*

If you try to use the dynamic aspects of the map in your uploaded version, it probably won't work, because the PHP file you're trying to connect to is on another domain. Because of security measures in the Flash Player, you won't be able to connect to that file.

You're done! You have just created your Flash Web site.

WHAT YOU HAVE LEARNED

In this lesson, you have:

- Created a preloader (pages 392–406)

- Added some programmatic movement (pages 406–412)

- Published your movie in multiple formats (pages 413–419)

- Uploaded your Web site (pages 419–422)

windows shortcuts

APPENDIX A

Flash has many keyboard shortcuts, which you can use to streamline your workflow. This appendix lists the default Flash MX Windows keyboard shortcuts.

NOTE *Flash lets you modify the keyboard shortcuts to suit your needs. You can learn more about this in Lesson 1.*

FILE MENU	
Command	**Shortcut**
New	Ctrl+N
Open	Ctrl+O
Open as Library	Ctrl+Shift+O
Close	Ctrl+W
Save	Ctrl+S
Save As	Ctrl+Shift+S
Import	Ctrl+R
Export Movie	Ctrl+Alt+Shift+S
Publish Settings	Ctrl+Shift+F12
Publish Preview > Default	Ctrl+F12
Publish	Shift+F12
Print	Ctrl+P
Exit	Ctrl+Q

Command	Shortcut
Undo	Ctrl+Z
Redo	Ctrl+Y
Cut	Ctrl+X
Copy	Ctrl+C
Paste	Ctrl+V
Paste in Place	Ctrl+Shift+V
Clear	Backspace
Duplicate	Ctrl+D
Select All	Ctrl+A
Deselect All	Ctrl+Shift+A
Cut Frames	Ctrl+Alt+X
Copy Frames	Ctrl+Alt+C
Paste Frames	Ctrl+Alt+V
Clear Frames	Alt+Backspace
Select All Frames	Ctrl+Alt+A
Edit Symbols/Edit Document	Ctrl+E
Preferences	Ctrl+U

Command	Shortcut
Go to › First	Home
Go to › Previous	Page Up
Go to › Next	Page Down
Go to › Last	End
Zoom In	Ctrl+=
Zoom Out	Ctrl+-
Magnification › 100%	Ctrl+1
Magnification › Show Frame	Ctrl+2
Magnification › Show All	Ctrl+3
Outlines	Ctrl+Alt+Shift+O
Fast	Ctrl+Alt+Shift+F
Anti-alias	Ctrl+Alt+Shift+A
Anti-alias Text	Ctrl+Alt+Shift+T
Timeline	Ctrl+Alt+T
Work Area	Ctrl+Shift+W
Rulers	Ctrl+Alt+Shift+R
Grid › Show Grid	Ctrl+'
Grid › Snap to Grid	Ctrl+Shift+'
Grid › Edit Grid	Ctrl+Alt+G
Guides › Show Guides	Ctrl+;
Guides › Lock Guides	Ctrl+Alt+;
Guides › Snap to Guides	Ctrl+Shift+;
Guides › Edit Guides	Ctrl+Alt+Shift+G
Snap to Objects	Ctrl+Shift+/
Show Shape Hints	Ctrl+Alt+H
Hide Edges	Ctrl+H
Hide Panels	F4

INSERT MENU

Command	Shortcut
Convert to Symbol	F8
New Symbol	Ctrl+F8
Frame	F5
Remove Frames	Shift+F5
Keyframe*	F6
Blank Keyframe*	F7
Clear Keyframe	Shift+F6

MODIFY MENU

Command	Shortcut
Scene	Shift+F2
Document	Ctrl+J
Optimize	Ctrl+Alt+Shift+C
Shape › Add Shape Hint	Ctrl+Shift+H
Transform › Scale and Rotate	Ctrl+Alt+S
Transform › Rotate 90° (degrees) CW	Ctrl+Shift+9
Transform › Rotate 90° (degrees) CCW	Ctrl+Shift+7
Transform › Remove Transform	Ctrl+Shift+Z
Arrange › Bring to Front	Ctrl+Shift+Up
Arrange › Bring Forward	Ctrl+Up
Arrange › Send Backward	Ctrl+Down
Arrange › Send to Back	Ctrl+Shift+Down
Arrange › Lock	Ctrl+Alt+L
Arrange › Unlock All	Ctrl+Alt+Shift+L
Align › Left	Ctrl+Alt+1
Align › Center Vertical	Ctrl+Alt+2
Align › Right	Ctrl+Alt+3
Align › Top	Ctrl+Alt+4
Align › Center Horizontal	Ctrl+Alt+5
Align › Bottom	Ctrl+Alt+6
Align › Distribute Widths	Ctrl+Alt+7
Align › Distribute Heights	Ctrl+Alt+9
Align › Make Same Width	Ctrl+Alt+Shift+7
Align › Make Same Height	Ctrl+Alt+Shift+9
Align › To Stage	Ctrl+Alt+8

MODIFY MENU (cont'd.)

Command	Shortcut
Frames › Convert to Keyframe	F6
Frames › Convert to Blank Keyframe	F7
Group	Ctrl+G
Ungroup	Ctrl+Shift+G
Break Apart	Ctrl+B
Distribute to Layers	Ctrl+Shift+D

TEXT MENU

Command	Shortcut
Style › Plain	Ctrl+Shift+P
Style › Bold	Ctrl+Shift+B
Style › Italic	Ctrl+Shift+I
Align › Align Left	Ctrl+Shift+L
Align › Align Center	Ctrl+Shift+C
Align › Align Right	Ctrl+Shift+R
Align › Justify	Ctrl+Shift+J
Tracking › Increase	Ctrl+Alt+Right
Tracking › Decrease	Ctrl+Alt+Left
Tracking › Reset	Ctrl+Alt+Up

CONTROL MENU

Command	Shortcut
Play	Enter
Rewind	Ctrl+Alt+R
Step Forward	.
Step Backward	,
Test Movie	Ctrl+Enter
Debug Movie	Ctrl+Shift+Enter
Test Scene	Ctrl+Alt+Enter
Enable Simple Buttons	Ctrl+Alt+B

426

Command	Shortcut
New Window	Ctrl+Alt+N
Tools	Ctrl+F2
Timeline	Ctrl+Alt+T
Properties	Ctrl+F3
Answers	Alt+F1
Align	Ctrl+K
Color Mixer	Shift+F9
Color Swatches	Ctrl+F9
Info	Ctrl+I
Scene	Shift+F2
Transform	Ctrl+T
Actions	F9
Debugger	Shift+F4
Movie Explorer	Alt+F3
Reference	Shift+F1
Output	F2
Accessibility	Alt+F2
Components	Ctrl+F7
Component Parameters	Alt+F7
Library	Ctrl+L or F11

HELP MENU

Command	Shortcut
Using Flash	F1

DRAWING TOOLS

Command	Shortcut
Arrow	V
Subselection	A
Line	N
Lasso	L
Pen	P
Text	T
Oval	O
Rectangle	R
Pencil	Y
Brush	B
Free Transform	Q
Fill Transform	F
Ink Bottle	S
Paint Bucket	K
Eyedropper	I
Eraser	E
Hand	H
Zoom	M, Z

ACTIONS PANEL

Command	Shortcut
Normal Mode	Ctrl+Shift+N
Expert Mode	Ctrl+Shift+E
Go to Line	Ctrl+G
Find	Ctrl+F
Find Again	F3
Replace	Ctrl+H
Check Syntax	Ctrl+T
Show Code Hint	Ctrl+Spacebar
Auto Format	Ctrl+Shift+F
Import From File	Ctrl+Shift+I
Export As File	Ctrl+Shift+X
View Line Numbers	Ctrl+Shift+L

macintosh shortcuts

APPENDIX B

Flash has many keyboard shortcuts, which you can use to streamline your workflow. This appendix lists the default Flash MX Macintosh keyboard shortcuts. Some of the Flash MX menus in Mac OS X are slightly different from those in Mac OS 9. Where differences exist, they are noted.

NOTE *Flash lets you modify the keyboard shortcuts to suit your needs. You can learn more about this in Lesson 1.*

FLASH MENU (OS X)

Command	Shortcut
Hide Flash	Command+H
Quit Flash	Command+Q

FILE MENU

Command	Shortcut
New	Command+N
Open	Command+O
Open as Library	Command+Shift+O
Close	Command+W
Save	Command+S
Save As	Command+Shift+S
Import	Command+R
Export Movie	Command+Option+Shift+S
Publish Settings	Command+Shift+F12
Publish Preview > Default	Command+F12
Publish	Shift+F12
Print	Command+P
Quit (OS 9)	Command+Q

EDIT MENU

Command	Shortcut
Undo	Command+Z
Redo	Command+Y
Cut	Command+X
Copy	Command+C
Paste	Command+V
Paste in Place	Command+Shift+V
Clear	Backspace
Duplicate	Command+D
Select All	Command+A
Deselect All	Command+Shift+A
Cut Frames	Command+Option+X
Copy Frames	Command+Option+C
Paste Frames	Command+Option+V
Clear Frames	Option+Backspace
Select All Frames	Command+Option+A
Edit Symbols/Edit Document	Command+E

VIEW MENU

Command	Shortcut
Go to › First	Home
Go to › Previous	Page Up
Go to › Next	Page Down
Go to › Last	End
Zoom In	Command+=
Zoom Out	Command+-
Magnification › 100%	Command+1
Magnification › Show Frame	Command+2
Magnification › Show All	Command+3
Outlines	Command+Option+Shift+O
Fast	Command+Option+Shift+F
Anti-alias	Command+Option+Shift+A
Anti-alias Text	Command+Option+Shift+T

VIEW MENU (cont.'d.)

Command	Shortcut
Timeline	Command+Option+T
Work Area	Command+Shift+W
Rulers	Command+Option+Shift+R
Grid › Show Grid	Command+'
Grid › Snap to Grid	Command+Shift+'
Grid › Edit Grid	Command+Option+G
Guides › Show Guides	Command+;
Guides › Lock Guides	Command+Option+;
Guides › Snap to Guides	Command+Shift+;
Guides › Edit Guides	Command+Option+Shift+G
Snap to Objects	Command+Shift+/
Show Shape Hints	Command+Option+H
Hide Edges	Command+Shift+E
Hide Panels	F4

INSERT MENU

Command	Shortcut
Convert to Symbol	F8
New Symbol	Command+F8
Frame	F5
Remove Frames	Shift+F5
Clear Keyframe	Shift+F6

MODIFY MENU

Command	Shortcut
Scene	Shift+F2
Document	Command+J
Optimize	Command+Option+Shift+C
Shape > Add Shape Hint	Command+Shift+H
Transform > Scale and Rotate	Command+Option+S
Transform > Rotate 90° CW	Command+Shift+9
Transform > Rotate 90° CCW	Command+Shift+7
Transform > Remove Transform	Command+Shift+Z
Arrange > Bring to Front	Command+Shift+Up
Arrange > Bring Forward	Command+Up
Arrange > Send Backward	Command+Down
Arrange > Send to Back	Command+Shift+Down
Arrange > Lock	Command+Option+L
Arrange > Unlock All	Command+Option+Shift+L
Align > Left	Command+Option+1
Align > Center Vertical	Command+Option+2
Align > Right	Command+Option+3
Align > Top	Command+Option+4
Align > Center Horizontal	Command+Option+5
Align > Bottom	Command+Option+6
Align > Distribute Widths	Command+Option+7
Align > Distribute Heights	Command+Option+9
Align > Make Same Width	Command+Option+Shift+7
Align > Make Same Height	Command+Option+Shift+9
Align > To Stage	Command+Option+8
Frames > Convert to Keyframe	F6
Frames > Convert to Blank Keyframe	F7
Group	Command+G
Ungroup	Command+Shift+G
Break Apart	Command+B
Distribute to Layers	Command+Shift+D

TEXT MENU

Command	Shortcut
Style > Plain	Command+Shift+P
Style > Bold	Command+Shift+B
Style > Italic	Command+Shift+I
Align > Align Left	Command+Shift+L
Align > Align Center	Command+Shift+C
Align > Align Right	Command+Shift+R
Align > Justify	Command+Shift+J
Tracking > Increase	Command+Option+Right
Tracking > Decrease	Command+Option+Left
Tracking > Reset	Command+Option+Up

CONTROL MENU

Command	Shortcut
Play	Return
Rewind	Command+Option+R
Step Forward	.
Step Backward	,
Test Movie	Command+Return
Debug Movie	Command+Shift+Return
Test Scene	Command+Option+Return
Enable Simple Buttons	Command+Option+B

WINDOW MENU

Command	Shortcut
New Window	Command+Option+N
Tools	Command+F2
Timeline	Command+Option+T
Properties	Command+F3
Answers	Option+F1
Align	Command+K
Color Mixer	Shift+F9
Color Swatches	Command+F9
Info	Command+I
Scene	Shift+F2
Transform	Command+T
Actions	F9
Debugger	Shift+F4
Movie Explorer	Option+F3
Reference	Shift+F1
Output	F2
Accessibility	Option+F2
Components	Command+F7
Component Parameters	Option+F7
Library	Command+L or F11

HELP MENU

Command	Shortcut
Using Flash	F1

DRAWING TOOLS

Command	Shortcut
Arrow	V
Subselection	A
Line	N
Lasso	L
Pen	P
Text	T
Oval	O
Rectangle	R
Pencil	Y
Brush	B
Free Transform	Q
Fill Transform	F
Ink Bottle	S
Paint Bucket	K
Eyedropper	I
Eraser	E
Hand	H
Zoom	M, Z

ACTIONS PANEL

Command	Shortcut
Normal Mode	Command+Shift+N
Expert Mode	Command+Shift+E
Go to Line	Command+G
Find	Command+F
Find Again	F3
Replace	Command+H
Check Syntax	Command+T
Show Code Hint	Command+Spacebar
Auto Format	Command+Shift+F
Import From File	Command+Shift+I
Export As File	Command+Shift+X
View Line Numbers	Command+Shift+L

additional resources

Once you get started with Macromedia Flash, you will find that no matter how many times you read this book, or the manual, you are still going to have some questions. You may also find that you sometimes need additional tools to help make your Flash projects even better. And you will undoubtedly need some great new fonts and sounds to make your Flash movies look and sound their best. The resources listed in this appendix will help you find all that, and more.

Be sure to also visit the companion Web site for this book: www.flashtfs.com.

FLASH RESOURCE WEB SITES

The Internet has a number of resources that can help further your understanding of Flash. These are some sites you might find useful:

- **Flash TFS:** www.flashtfs.com
- **FlashLite:** www.flashlite.net
- **Flashmagazine:** www.flashmagazine.com
- **Macromedia Flash Support Center:** www.macromedia.com/support/flash
- **Macromedia Online Forums—Macromedia Flash:** http://webforums.macromedia.com/flash
- **moock.org:** www.moock.org/webdesign/flash
- **Robin Debreuil's OOP Tutorial:** www.debreuil.com/docs/
- **Ultrashock:** www.ultrashock.com
- **Virtual-FX.net:** www.virtual-fx.net
- **We're Here:** www.were-here.com

OPEN SOURCE AND COMPONENTS

Many members of the Flash community have been great about sharing their code with the public. These open-source Flash resources let you pick apart source files to see what makes them tick. Also listed are Web sites that provide components for Flash.

- **Macromedia Exchange for Flash:** www.macromedia.com/exchange/flash
- **PrayStation:** www.praystation.com
- **Robert Penner:** www.robertpenner.com
- **Ultrashock:** www.ultrashock.com

FLASH MAILING LISTS

If you can't find what you're looking for on one of the Flash Resource Web sites listed above, then you can always try one of these mailing lists. Some of them are very high-volume, so get ready for lots of email!

- **Chattyfig:** http://chattyfig.figleaf.com
- **Flash TFS:** www.flashtfs.com
- **Flasher:** www.chinwag.com/flasher

SOUND RESOURCES

When it's time to add sound to your Flash projects, these resources may be very useful.

- **CSS Music:** www.cssmusic.com
- **DoReMedia:** www.doremedia.com
- **killersound:** www.killersound.com
- **Sonic Foundry:** www.sonicfoundry.com

FONT RESOURCES

These Web sites have great fonts you can use in your Flash projects:

- **Astigmatic One Eye Typographic Institute:** www.astigmatic.com
- **Atomic Media:** www.atomicmedia.net
- **Chank.com:** www.chank.com
- **Fontface.com:** www.fontface.com
- **Fontalicious Fonts:** www.fontalicious.com
- **FontFreak:** www.fontfreak.com
- **Letterhead—Letterville:** www.letterhead.com
- **miniml:** www.miniml.com

MIDDLEWARE INFORMATION

You had a taste of working with middleware in Lesson 9. These Web sites will provide you with more information about the various middleware servers available.

- **Macromedia ColdFusion MX:** www.macromedia.com/software/coldfusion
- **Active Server Pages (ASP):** www.microsoft.com
- **Java Server Pages:** http://java.sun.com/products/jsp
- **PHP:** www.php.net

TOOLS

There are many tools available that make working with Flash much easier. Some of them create three-dimensional artwork for use in Flash, others create dynamically generated Flash content, and still others make working with projectors incredibly easy.

DYNAMIC FLASH TOOLS

These tools let you create dynamic Flash content. Some of them require a bit (sometimes a lot) of back-end expertise.

- **ASP Flash Turbine:** www.blue-pac.com/products/aspturbine
- **Direct Flash Turbine:** www.blue-pac.com/products/directturbine
- **JGenerator:** www.flashgap.com
- **Ming:** www.opaque.net/ming
- **PHP Flash Turbine:** www.blue-pac.com/products/phpturbine
- **Swift Generator:** www.swift-tools.com

PROJECTOR TOOLS

Flash projectors let you take your content to the desktop. These tools, which are all Windows-based, can add awesome functionality to those projectors.

- **JTools:** www.flashjester.com
- **Jugglor:** www.flashjester.com
- **SWF Studio:** www.northcode.com

SOUND-CREATION TOOLS

These tools let you create your own music, using royalty-free loops as the base elements. Many of them output to MP3, which is great for importing into Flash.

- **Acid Music:** www.sonicfoundry.com
- **Acid Pro:** www.sonicfoundry.com
- **Magix Music and Video Maker:** www.magix.com
- **Plasma:** www.cakewalk.com
- **Sound Forge:** www.sonicfoundry.com

TEXT-EFFECT TOOLS

If you'd like to add complex text effects to your Flash projects but don't want to spend lots of time actually creating them, these tools are just what you'll need. They can create very complex text animations in just minutes, and they output to .swf, which you can then import into Flash.

- **FlaX:** www.flaxfx.com
- **Swish:** www.swishzone.com
- **SWfX:** www.wildform.com

3D TOOLS

Want to add some 3D artwork to your Flash project? These tools are just what you need. You can use them to generate .swf files containing complex 3D artwork.

Amorphium Pro:

www.electricimage.com/products/amorphium/overview/amorphoverview.htm

Swift 3D: www.swift3d.com

OTHER TOOLS

These tools don't really fit in any other category, but they are still very useful!

- **Flix:** www.wildform.com
- **Screenweaver:** www.screenweaver.com
- **Toon Boom Studio:** www.toonboom.com

ActionScript quick reference

APPENDIX D

This appendix is a condensed reference for some of the ActionScript you used in this book. It is organized in alphabetical order, starting with operators. For a complete ActionScript reference, choose Help › ActionScript Dictionary from Macromedia Flash.

NAME	SYNTAX AND DESCRIPTION	EXAMPLES

--
(decrement)
	`--expression`
	`expression--`
	
	Subtracts 1 from the expression. The pre-decrement form (--expression) subtracts 1 from expression and returns the result. The post-decrement form subtracts 1 from the expression and returns the initial value of the expression.
		`--myVar;`

–
(subtraction and
negation)
	`-expression1`
	`expression1-expression2`
	
	Used for subtraction and negation. If used for negation, it reverses the sign of the expression. If used for subtraction, it finds the difference between the two numbers
		`x = 5;`
		`y = 4:`
		`trace(-x);`
		`trace(x-y);`
		
		The Output window would display –5, then 1.

!= **(inequality)**	`expression1 != expression2` Tests for inequality. If expression1 is not equal to expression2, the result is true.	`1 != 2 returns true.`
#include	`#include "filename.as"` Includes the contents of the file specified in the argument	`#include "style.as"`

Name	Syntax and Description	Examples

&&
 (logical AND)
	expression1 && expression2
	
	 Performs a Boolean (true or false) operation on both expressions. Both expression1 and expression2 must be true for the operator to return a final result of true.
		```x = 10;```
		```y = 20;```
		```if ((x == 10) && (y == 20)) {```
		``` trace ("ZooMX is great!");```
		```}```
		
		The Output window would display:
		```ZooMX is great!```

* **(multiplication)**	expression1*expression2 Multiplies two numbers.	```trace (2*4);``` The Output window would display 8.
. **(dot operator)**	object.property object.method instancename.variable instancename.child.variable Used to navigate movie-clip hierarchies to access nested movie clips, variables, or properties. The dot operator is also used to retrieve or set the properties of an object, execute a method of an object, or create a data structure.	The following identifies the color property of the animal object: ```animal.color```
/ **(division)**	expression1/expression2 Divides expression1 by expression2.	```trace (21/3);``` The Output window would display 7.

//
 /* ... */
 (comment delimiters)
	// comment here
	 /* comment here */
	
	 Inserts a comment into your code that is ignored by the ActionScript interpreter.
		```/* set value of the variable```
		```called common```
		```*/```
		```common = "Bactrian Camel";```

_alpha	instancename._alpha instancename._alpha = value; Sets or gets the alpha transparency (0 is fully transparent, 100 fully opaque).	```mPiece._alpha = 50;``` Sets the alpha property of the movie clip called mPiece to 50%.
_height	instancename._height instancename._height = value; Sets or retrieves the height of the space occupied by the movie clip.	```this._height = 200;```

437

NAME	SYNTAX AND DESCRIPTION	EXAMPLES
_level	_levelN A reference to the root movie timeline of levelN. N is an integer specifying depth level (default 0). You must load movies using the loadMovie action before targeting them using _level property.	_level2.gotoAndStop("rf");
_name	instancename._name instancename._name = value; Specifies the movie-clip instance name.	trace(this._name);
_root	_root _root.movieClip _root.method Specifies or returns a reference to the root movie timeline.	_root.mc1 _root.gotoAndStop(4);
_visible	instanceName._visible instanceName._visible = Boolean Determines whether or not the movie specified by the instanceName is visible.	mPiece._visible = false;
_width	instancename._width instancename._width = value; Sets or retrieves the width of the space occupied by the movie clip.	this._width = 300;
_x	instanceName._x instanceName._x = integer; Sets or retrieves the x-coordinate relative to the parent timeline.	mPiece._x = 10;
_y	instanceName._y instanceName._y = integer Sets or retrieves the y-coordinate relative to the parent timeline.	mPiece._y = 10;

NAME	SYNTAX AND DESCRIPTION	EXAMPLES

||
(logical OR)
	`expression1 && expression2`
	
	Performs a Boolean (true or false) operation on both expressions. The operator will return a final result of true if either `expression1` or `expression2` is true.
		```x = 10;```
		```y = 20;```
		```if ((x == 10) || (y == 10)) {```
		``` trace ("ZooMX is great!");```
		```}```
		
		The Output window would display:
		```ZooMX is great!```

" " **(string delimiter)**	`"text"` When used before and after a string, quotes indicate that the string is a literal, not a variable, numerical value, or other ActionScript element.	```obj = "image" + i;```

+
(addition)
	`expression1 + expression2`
	
	Adds numeric expressions and concatenates strings. If one expression is a string, all other expressions are converted to strings and concatenated. If both expressions are integers, the sum is an integer; if either or both expressions are floating-point numbers, the sum is a floating-point number.
		Example 1:
		```trace(1+2);```
		
		The Output window would display 3.
		
		Example 2:
		When `myVar = "lion"`, the following expression returns "Oh no! It's a lion!":
		
		```trace("Oh no! It's a " +myVar+"!");```

++
(increment)
	`++expression`
	`expression++`
	
	Adds 1 to the expression. The pre-increment form (++expression) adds 1 to the expression and returns the result. The post-increment form adds 1 to the expression and returns the initial value of the expression.
		```++myVar;```

NAME	SYNTAX AND DESCRIPTION	EXAMPLES

+=
(addition and assignment)
	expression1 += expression2
	
	Assigns expression1 the value of expression1 + expression2.
	
	x += y is equivalent to x = x+y
		Example 1:
		x = 5;
		x += 10;
		trace (x);
		
		The Output window would display 15.
		
		Example 2:
		x = "I am afraid of";
		x+=" lions!";
		trace(x);
		
		The Output window would display:
		I am afraid of lions!

‹ **(less than)**	expression1 < expression2 Compares two expressions and determines whether expression1 is less than expression2.	1 < 2 returns true.
‹= **(less than or equal to)**	expression1 <= expression2 Compares two expressions to determine if expression1 is less than or equal to expression2 in value.	4 <= 4 returns true. 5 <= 3 returns false.
= **(assignment)**	expression1 = expression2 Assigns the type of expression2 to the variable, array element, or property in expression1.	latin1 = "Pongo pygmaeus";
== **(equality)**	expression1 == expression2 Tests two expressions for equality. If expression1 is equal to expression2, the result is true.	When myVar = "lion", the following expression returns true: myVar == "lion"
› **(greater than)**	expression1 > expression2 Compares two expressions to determine if expression1 is greater in value than expression2.	300 > 900 returns false
›= **(greater than or equal to)**	expression1 >= expression2 Compares two expressions to determine if expression1 is greater than or equal to expression2.	8 >= 5 returns true 30 >= 30 returns true

NAME	SYNTAX AND DESCRIPTION	EXAMPLES
Array.length	`myArray.length;` Property of the Array object. This returns the length of the array.	`animals.length`

Array.push	`MyArray.push(value);`
	
	Adds the specified value to the end of the array.
		`animals = new Array("lion", "bear");`
		`animals.push("tiger");`
		`trace(animals);`
		
		The Output window will display:
		`lions,bears,tigers`

break	`break;`
	
	Tells the ActionScript to skip the rest of the loop it is in.
		`x = 0;`
		`while (true) {`
		`  if (x >= 100) {`
		`    break;`
		`  }`
		`  ++x;`
		`}`

delete	`delete (reference);`
	
	Deletes the object or variable specified in reference. Useful for removing no-longer-needed variables in your ActionScript.
		`x = 10;`
		`delete x;`
		`lion.teeth = "large";`
		`delete lion.teeth;`

else	`else{statement(s)}`
	
	Specifies the actions, clauses, arguments, or other conditional to run if the initial if statement returns false.
		`if (x == 2) {`
		`  startDrag("myClip");`
		`else{`
		`  stopDrag();`
		`}`

else if	`else if (expression) {`
	`  statements`
	`}`
	
	Specifies the actions, clauses, arguments, or other conditional to run if the initial if statement returns false and expression returns true.
		`if (x == 1) {`
		`  gotoAndStop("africa");`
		`} else if (x == 3) {`
		`  gotoAndStop("asia");`
		`}`

eval	`eval(expression)` Accesses variables, properties, objects, or movie clip by name.	`this._x = eval(this._droptarget)._x;`

NAME	SYNTAX AND DESCRIPTION	EXAMPLES

for

```
for (int; condition; next) {
  statement;
}
```

int: The expression to evaluate before beginning the loop sequence.

condition: An expression that evaluates to true or false. The loop will execute the commands contained in it until the condition evaluates to false.

next: An expression to evaluate after each loop, usually an assignment using ++ or --.

statement: The code that will execute when the condition is evaluated to true.

The loop evaluates the int value once, then begins a looping sequence until the condition evaluates to false.

```
for (var x = 0; x < 5; ++x) {
  trace ("ZooMX");
}
```

The output window would show:
ZooMX
ZooMX
ZooMX
ZooMX
ZooMX

function

```
function functionName (argument1, argument2){
  statement(s)
}
```

A set of defined statements that perform a certain task. You can define a function in one location and call it from a different movie. The arguments are optional.

```
function calcTax(price,tax){
  cost = price*tax + price
  return cost;
}
```

getTimer

```
getTimer();
```

Returns the number of milliseconds that have elapsed since the movie started playing.

```
time = getTimer();
```

returns a numeric value.

getURL

```
getUrl(url [,window[,variables]]);
```

Loads a document from a specific URL into a window, or passes variables to another application at a defined URL.

```
getURL("http://www.flashtfs.com",
"_blank")
```

442

NAME	SYNTAX AND DESCRIPTION	EXAMPLES
globalStyleFormat	globalStyleFormat.styleProperty Object that lets you specify the style for all components in a movie. The styleProperty property can be one of the following: arrow, background, backgroundDisabled, check, darkshadow, face, foregroundDisabled, highlight, radioDot, scrollTrack, selection, selectionDisabled, selectionUnfocused, shadow, textAlign, textBold, textColor, textDisabled, textFont, textIndent, textItalic, textLeftMargin, textRightMargin, textSelected, textSize, textUnderline. The applyChanges method applies the changes you define for the globalStyleFormat object.	globalStyleFormat.selection = 0xFF9933; globalStyleFormat.applyChanges();
gotoAndPlay	gotoAndPlay (frame); Sends the playhead to the specified frame and plays from that frame.	gotoAndPlay(1);
gotoAndStop	gotoAndStop(frame); Sends the playhead to the specified frame and stops at that frame.	gotoAndStop(1);

if	if (condition){
	  statement;
	}
	
	Evaluates the condition given. If the condition is true, Flash runs the statements that follow.
		if (done != true) {
		  this.startDrag();
		}

loadMovie	loadMovie (url [location/target, variables]]); Plays additional movies without closing the Flash Player. Use target to specify a particular movie-clip timeline.	loadMovie("movie.swf", _root.targetMC);
loadVariables	loadVariables (url [.location/target, variables]]); Reads data from an external file and sets values for variables in a movie or movie clip. Also see LoadVars.	loadVariables("myvariables.txt", _root.variableTargetMC);

NAME	SYNTAX AND DESCRIPTION	EXAMPLES
LoadVars.getBytesLoaded	`varsObject.getBytesLoaded()` Returns the number of bytes loaded by the load or sendAndLoad method.	`done = myVars.getBytesLoaded();`
LoadVars.getBytesTotal	`varsObject.getByteTotal()` Returns the total bytes for a load or sendAndLoad method.	`total = myVars.getBytesTotal();`
LoadVars.load	`varsObject.load(url);` Loads the variables from the specified URL into the varsObject object.	`myVars = new LoadVars();` `myVars.load("data.cfm");`

LoadVars.send	`varsObject.load(url, [target, method]);`
	Sends the variables to the specified URL. The target parameter specifies the frame in which any result is displayed.
		`myVars = new LoadVars();`
		`myVars.var1 = "update";`
		`myVars.send("data.cfm", _blank);`

LoadVars.sendAndLoad	`varsObject.load(url, targetObj, [method]);`
	
	Loads the variables from the specified URL into the targetObj object.
		`myVars = new LoadVars();`
		`myVars.var1 = "update";`
		`myVars.sendAndLoad("data.cfm", myVars);`

Math.abs	`Math.abs(x);` Computes the absolute value of the number specified by x.	`Math.abs(-15);`
Math.random	`Math.random();` Creates a random number between 0.0 and 1.0.	`trace (Math.random());` Outputs a random number.
MovieClip.attachMovie	`anyMovieClip.attachMovie(idname, newname, depth);` **idname:** The name of the movie in the library to attach. **newname:** A unique instance name that is going to be attached. **depth:** An integer specifying the depth level where the movie is being placed. Creates a new instance of a movie and attaches it to the movie specified by anyMovieClip.	`this.attachMovie("lion", "lion"+x, x);`

444

NAME	SYNTAX AND DESCRIPTION	EXAMPLES
MovieClip.getBytesLoaded	`anyMovieClip.getBytesLoaded()` Returns the number of bytes loaded for a movie-clip instance.	`done = myClip.getBytesLoaded();`
MovieClip.getBytesTotal	`anyMovieClip.getByteTotal()` Returns the total bytes for a movie-clip instance.	`total = myClip.getBytesTotal();`
MovieClip.gotoAndPlay	`anyMovieClip.gotoAndPlay(frame);` **frame:** The frame number or label where the playhead will be sent. Starts playing the movie at the specified frame.	`zoo.gotoAndPlay(413);` `_level2.gotoAndPlay("rf");`
MovieClip.gotoAndStop	`anyMovieClip.gotoAndStop(frame);` **frame:** The frame number or label where the playhead will be sent. Goes to the frame specified and stop.	`lion.gotoAndStop(73);` `lion.gotoAndStop("growl");`
MovieClip.loadMovie	`anyMovieClip.loadMovie(URL, variables);` **URL:** The absolute or relative URL for the SWF file to load. **variables:** Specifies the method for sending variables. GET appends the variables to the end of the URL, POST send the variables in a separate HTTP header.	`this.loadMovie("games.swf");`

MovieClip.on...	The `MovieClip` object has the following event handlers:
	
	`onData, onDragOut, onDragOver, onEnterFrame, onKeyDown, onKeyUp, onKillFocus, onLoad, onMouseDown, onMouseMove, onMouseUp, onPress, onRelease, onReleaseOutside, onRollOut, onRollOver, onSetFocus, onUnload`
	
	Each event handler is invoked when the event occurs. You can specify a function that will occur when the event handler is invoked:
	
	`anyMovieClip.onLoad = function() {`
	`  function;`
	`};`
		`anyMovieClip.onLoad = function() {`
		`  this._x = 10;`
		`};`

NAME	SYNTAX AND DESCRIPTION	EXAMPLES
MovieClip.play	`anyMovieClip.play();` Plays the movie clip.	`lion1.play();`
MovieClip.removeMovieClip	`anyMovieClip.removeMovieClip();` Removes the movie-clip instance created with the `duplicateMovie` action.	`lion1.removeMoveClip();`
MovieClip.startDrag	`anyMovieClip.startDrag(lock, left, right, top, bottom);` **lock:** Specifies whether the draggable movie clip is locked to the center of the mouse position. **left, top, right, bottom:** Values relative to the coordinates of the movie clip that constrains the drag of the clip.	`this.startDrag();`
MovieClip.stop	`anyMovieClip.stop();` Stops the movie clip that is referred to.	`lion1.stop();`
MovieClip.stopDrag	`anyMovieClip.stopDrag();` Ends a drag action started with the `startDrag` method.	`this.stopDrag();`

MovieClip.swapDepths	`anyMovieClip.swapDepths(depth):`
	`anyMovieClip.swapDepths(target);`
	
	target: The movie-clip instance that is being swapped.
	
	depth: The depth level that the movie clip is being swapped to.
	
	Swaps the depth of two movie clips.
		`lion1.swapDepths(lion2);`
		`lion1.swapDepths(100);`

MovieClip.unloadMovie	`anyMovieClip.unloadMovie();` Removes the movie clip that was loaded with the `loadMovie` or `attachMovie` method.	`lion2.unloadMovie();`

446

NAME	SYNTAX AND DESCRIPTION	EXAMPLES
new	`new constructor(arguments);` Creates a new object, calls the function identified by the constructor argument, and passes additional optional arguments in the parentheses.	`tiger = new Cat ("large", "aggressive");` `kitten = new Cat ("tiny", "playful");`

null	`null`
	
	A special keyword that can be assigned to variables. It will be returned by a function if no data was provided.
		`if (common == null) {`
		`  gotoAndStop(10);`
		`}`

on	`on (mouseEvent) {`
	`   statement;`
	`}`
	
	The mouseEvent argument can be press, release, releaseOutside, rollOver, rollOut, dragOver, dragOut, KeyPress("key").
	
	Specifies a mouse action or key press that triggers an action.
		`on (rollOver, dragOver) {`
		`  gotoAndStop(5);`
		`}`
		`on (rollOut, dragOut) {`
		`  gotoAndStop(10);`
		`}`

onClipEvent	`onClipEvent(movieEvent) {`
	`   statements;`
	`}`
	
	movieEvent: An event that executes actions that are assigned in the statements of the onClipEvent. Can have one of the following events—load, unload, enterFrame, mouseMove, mouseDown, mouseUp, keyDown, keyUp, data.
	
	Triggers actions defined in the statements for a specific instance of a movie clip.
		`onClipEvent(load) {`
		`  gotoAndPlay(14);`
		`}`

play	`play();`
	
	Move the playhead forward on the timeline.
		`if (x == 2) {`
		`  play();`
		`} else {`
		`  gotoAndPlay (45);`
		`}`

stop	`stop();`
	
	Stops the current timeline from playing.
		`if (x > 0 ) {`
		`  stop();`
		`}else {`
		`  gotoAndStop(50);`
		`}`

NAME	SYNTAX AND DESCRIPTION	EXAMPLES

this	`this`
	
	 A keyword that is used to refer to the current movie clip, the clip that contains the script.
		`//sets the x position of the`
		`//current movie clip to 300`
		`this._x = 300;`

trace	`trace (expression);` Evaluates the expression and displays the result in the Output window. Similar to the alert function in JavaScript.	`trace (x+=5);` `trace ("Hi everyone!");`

undefined	`undefined`
	
	 A keyword indicating that a variable has not yet been assigned a value.
		`if (common == undefined) {`
		`  gotoAndStop(10);`
		`}`

updateAfterEvent	`updateAfterEvent();` Updates the display after a movie-clip event has completed.	`updateAfterEvent();`

while	`while (condition) {`
	`  statements;`
	`}`
	
	 Runs a series of statements in the loop as long as the loop conditions continues to be true.
		`while (x > 5) {`
		`  trace(hammerhead);`
		`  x++;`
		`}`

448

index

451

452

458

WWW.PEACHPIT.COM

Quality How-to Computer Books

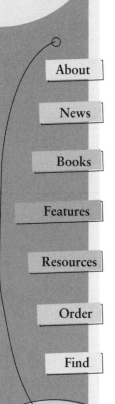

About

News

Books

Features

Resources

Order

Find

Welcome!

Visit Peachpit Press on the Web at www.peachpit.com

- Check out new feature articles each Monday: excerpts, interviews, tips, and plenty of how-tos

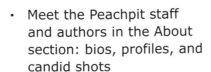

- Find any Peachpit book by title, series, author, or topic on the Books page

- See what our authors are up to on the News page: signings, chats, appearances, and more

- Meet the Peachpit staff and authors in the About section: bios, profiles, and candid shots

- Use Resources to reach our academic, sales, customer service, and tech support areas and find out how to become a Peachpit author

Peachpit.com is also the place to:

- Chat with our authors online
- Take advantage of special Web-only offers
- Get the latest info on new books